Rice in the Time of Sugar

RICE
in the Time of
SUGAR

**THE POLITICAL ECONOMY
OF FOOD IN CUBA**

Louis A. Pérez Jr.

THE UNIVERSITY OF NORTH CAROLINA PRESS | CHAPEL HILL

© 2019 The University of North Carolina Press
All rights reserved
Set in Minion by Copperline Book Services, Hillsborough, N.C.
Manufactured in the United States of America

The University of North Carolina Press has been a
member of the Green Press Initiative since 2003.

Cover illustrations: rice © iStockphoto.com/PicturePartners;
sugarcane © iStockphoto.com/oasistrek

Library of Congress Cataloging-in-Publication Data
Names: Pérez, Louis A., Jr., 1943– author.
Title: Rice in the time of sugar : the political economy
of food in Cuba / Louis A. Pérez Jr.
Description: Chapel Hill : University of North Carolina Press, [2019] |
Includes bibliographical references and index.
Identifiers: LCCN 2018051397| ISBN 9781469651415 (cloth : alk. paper) |
ISBN 9781469651422 (pbk : alk. paper) | ISBN 9781469651439 (ebook)
Subjects: LCSH: Cuba—Foreign economic relations. | Exports—Social aspects—Cuba. | Sugarcane industry—Social aspects—Cuba. | Cuba—Economic conditions—History. | Balance of trade—Cuba—History. | Food supply—Cuba—History.
Classification: LCC HC152.5 .P473 2019 | DDC 338.1/97291—dc23
LC record available at https://lccn.loc.gov/2018051397

*In memory of
Jorge R. Ibarra Cuesta (1931–2017),
esteemed colleague and
dear friend*

Contents

Acknowledgments xi

INTRODUCTION
1

CHAPTER ONE
Prosperity So Easily Obtained
27

CHAPTER TWO
Passing into Economic Darkness
61

CHAPTER THREE
An Uncertain Source of Wealth
85

CHAPTER FOUR
To Overcome Sugar
109

CHAPTER FIVE
To Tremble in Fear
135

EPILOGUE
To Return to What Was Before—
Plus ça change . . .
165

Notes 185

Index 239

Figures and Tables

FIGURES

The cover of an 1864 cookbook 2

The cover of an 1862 cookbook 11

Advertisement for a rice mill 44

Route of the Central Highway of Cuba 92

Map showing the most productive zones
of Cuban rice production 124

Advertisement for domestic rice product 128

Her majesty Norma I, Queen of Rice 131

President Fulgencio Batista visiting a rice mill, 1954 132

Advertisements for heavy rice-farming machinery 133

Advertisement for Uncle Ben's Rice 160

An advertisement proclaiming support of
the newly triumphant revolution 171

Advertisement expressing the gratitude of rice growers for the newly
announced policies in support of domestic production 173

Affirmation of the renewed commitment to the
expansion of national production 176

TABLES

1.1. Sample weekly menu, 1933 19

1.1. Quantity and value of select U.S. food imports, 1891–1894 58

1.2. Tariffs on U.S. food imports, 1893–1895 59

2.1. Cuban rice imports by country of origin
during U.S. occupation, 1899–1902 70

2.2. Cuban rice imports by country of origin, 1903–1914 73

2.3. Cuban rice imports by country of origin, 1915–1920 73

2.4. Value of Cuban food imports, 1914 and 1916 79

3.1. Cuban rice imports by country of origin, 1913 and 1920–1923 87

3.2. Proportion of total Cuban rice imports from the United States, 1919–1934 89

3.3. Cuban sugar exports to the United States, 1925–1933 93

3.4. Cuban rice imports by country of origin, 1936–1941 105

4.1. Number and production volume of Cuban sugar mills by country of ownership, 1939 and 1958 112

4.2. Cuban rice production, 1940, 1945, and 1950–1955 127

5.1. Cuban rice imports from the United States, 1949–1958 138

Acknowledgments

THIS BOOK has been in the making for nearly ten years. The writing advanced in fits and starts, intervals of progress alternating with interludes of pauses. Much had to do with composition and organization, both of which proved to be far more difficult than originally anticipated—specifically, the challenge to render into some kind of readable prose an array of complex and often arcane matters pertaining to tariffs and customs duties, taxes, assessments, quotas, and surcharges; issues related to changing shipping weights, import/export freights, and international supply chains; and the meaning of dense trade regulations and the logic of bewildering schedules of reciprocity treaties.

The fits and starts also had to do with the very quality of the research materials to which I had access, a vast mass of rich archival records and manuscript collections spanning almost 150 years. At times viewed grudgingly, perhaps also—on occasion—with some impatience, as if too much of a good thing. Research materials that seemed to have no to end . . .

The Rice Millers Association Records, the Louisiana State Rice Milling Company Records, and the Godchaux Family Papers at the Edith Garland Dupré Library at the University of Louisiana at Lafayette, spanning much of the twentieth century, make for sources that most historians can only dream about. The materials are breathtaking, not only for the expanse of the collections but for the depth of information they offer and the richness of insight they provide about close-quarter politics, lobby networks, influence peddling, about the extortions and the exactions that shaped the norms through which Cuba-U.S. relations were transacted. The collections preserve records in the form of correspondence, memoranda, internal reports, confidential trade analyses, marketing surveys, and unpublished statistical data: in sum, the stuff that allows the historian to plumb deeply into infrastructure of empire, to behold the little gears of hegemony in action—the grass roots of power—that work to set in motion the systems of domination. The records shed light on the intricacies of commodity transactions, the social dimensions of the liaisons that extended from producers to politicians to policy makers, the role of the personal and the workings of the political, the convergence and confluence of civil servants, pressure groups, and power brokers, all of whom were to a greater or lesser extent implicated in and executors of moral systems that served to justify the subjugation of the many by the few. From a distance these circumstances often assume the appearance of "forces," those abstract historical forces—opaque and obscure—that do not readily acquiesce to interrogation but, in fact, upon closer examination are revealed to be interests, self-interests to be exact, enabled by privilege and power. Nothing complicated, really: where privilege provides access to power and power replicates privilege.

These materials at the Edith Garland Dupré Library at the University of Louisiana at Lafayette constitute a formidable collection. For assistance with these archival records and manuscript collections, I am indebted to I. Bruce Turner, head of Special Collections, and his staff at the Dupré Library. I owe too a special debt to friend and colleague Tom Schoonover, who first alerted me to the existence of these marvelous records.

For the historian given to the study of Spanish colonialism during the twilight years of the Enterprise of the Indies in the nineteenth century, official government publications and the unpublished mass of record collections produced by the dense bureaucracy of colonial administration are no less spectacular—and no less daunting. The vast numbers of volumes of printed texts in the form of *anales, diarios,* and *boletines* are surpassed only by the reams of manuscripts in the form of *relatos, relaciones,* and *memorias* contained in the collections of the Correspondencia de los Capitanes Generales, the Gobierno Superior Civil, the Gobierno General, and the Consulado de Agricultura, Comercio y Junta de Fomento. So too for the archival materials of the Cuban republic. The records of the Banco Nacional de Cuba, and especially the Banco de Fomento Agrícola e Industrial de Cuba, are equally revelatory of the inner workings of politics, privilege, and power, the reach of special interests and radius of influence peddling, especially during the governments of Carlos Prío Socarrás (1948–52) and Fulgencio Batista (1952–58). These records make for vast collections indispensable for the study of the Cuban economy all through the first half of the twentieth century. For access to and assistance with these materials, I am grateful to the staff of the Archivo Nacional de Cuba, and especially to Director Martha Ferriol Marchena.

Nor could this research have been completed without consulting the rich collections in the Biblioteca Nacional José Martí, including the *periódicos, gacetas,* and *revistas,* so necessary to understand the public debates and political deliberations attending the emergence in the nineteenth century of an agriculture dedicated to export production—at the expense of almost everything else. A heartfelt appreciation to Director Eduardo Torres-Cuevas and Associate Director Nancy Machado and the members of the staff at the Biblioteca Nacional, whose uncommon courtesy and unfailing hospitality made the many hours in the Sala Cubana a time remembered with warm nostalgia.

A special expression of appreciation goes to Miguel Barnet and Nancy Morejón of the Unión de Escritores y Artistas de Cuba for the generous assistance of UNEAC all through the years this book was in the making.

A debt of gratitude is similarly owed to the archivists, librarians, and staffs of the Instituto de Literatura y Lingüística, Havana; the Manuscript Division of the Library of Congress, Washington, D.C.; the National Archives, Washington, D.C.; the Pennsylvania Historical Society, Philadelphia; the Franklin D. Roosevelt Presidential Library and Museum, Hyde Park, N.Y.; the Cuban Heritage Collection at the University of Miami, Coral Gables, Fla.; and the Rare Book and Manuscript Library, Butler Library, Columbia University, N.Y.

The Davis Library at the University of North Carolina at Chapel Hill occupies a special place among the aforementioned libraries. The reference staff and the staffs of the interlibrary loan office and the office of the Latin American and Caribbean collection are the best. Beth L. Rowe, Renée Ann Bosman, and especially Thomas J. Nixon performed recurring acts of research magic and—to remain within the metaphor—never failed to pull a rabbit out of the hat when all hope seemed lost. Magicians indeed to whom I am enormously grateful. I owe much also to Teresa Chapa and Becky Huckaby, who through expertise and experience—and no small amount of perseverance—have contributed mightily to the creation of a splendid resource-rich environment in which to conduct research on Latin America at UNC. To borrow from the undergraduate vernacular: the Latin America and Caribbean collection at Davis Library is awesome!

A project in preparation for ten years inevitably provides many occasions for discussions and opportunities for conversations with friends and colleagues —and on occasion, conversations with complete strangers—about food, often while preparing food or, best of all, in the act of dining. Ten years also provide more than ample time to circulate many drafts of chapters in various stages of completion—often more than once—among many of the same friends and colleagues, who have given unstintingly of their knowledge and wisdom, to offer critical insight, provide thoughtful commentary, and suggest bibliography references, for which I am enormously grateful. They include Cecilia Bermúdez, Maikel Fariñas Borrego, Joshua Nadel, Beatriz Riefkohl Muñiz, Eduardo Torres-Cuevas, José Viera, and Oscar Zanetti. I appreciate too the careful appraisal provided by Robert Whitney and especially by Reinaldo Funes Monzote, whose finely textured and thoughtful reading of the completed manuscript provided many helpful insights. In this regard, I owe a special debt to my colleague Peter Coclanis, whose breadth of knowledge and wisdom on almost all aspects of global rice production and commerce, past and present, must be considered unrivaled. Augusta Dell'Olmo, who provided research assistance spanning the critical years of the 1940s and early 1950s and who demonstrated time and again a complete command of the new technologies of historical research, deserves a special acknowledgment. She located information in places I did not know even existed. She has a promising career as a historian.

I appreciate too the support of the Department of History and the College of Arts and Sciences at UNC–Chapel Hill for making available a semester Research and Study Leave. The leave provided the opportunity to bring the ten-year research/writing project to a successful completion, for which I am grateful. I am appreciative too of the support extended by Elaine Maisner, executive editor at the University of North Carolina Press: a commiserating presence over the years listening to the travails of writing about rice. Julie Bush provided expert attention to the final copy editing of the manuscript. The thoughtfulness of her comments and suggestions are so very much appreciated.

So much for which I am grateful above would not have been possible without the steadfast support and generosity of spirit of Gladys Marel García and Fidel Requiejo. Ours is a friendship that extends many decades, colleague to colleague, friend to friend, family to family. It is a history that serves to bind with steadfast constancy.

No one has been subjected more to disquisitions about the production, consumption, and commerce of rice in Cuba than Deborah M. Weissman. She early shared the wonder of the capacity of a grain of rice to refract light to illuminate the workings of systems of power. Everything followed.

This book, lastly, is dedicated to the memory of Jorge Ibarra Cuesta, colleague, collaborator, and friend. For more than twenty-five years, over the course of many conversations about the Cuban past—and about the future of the Cuban past—ranging from details of colonial trade and commerce through the implications of the death of Fidel Castro, Jorge never failed to display a remarkable intuitive acuity and keen learned knowledge about what makes for a very special history. He understood well the times he studied and also the times in which he lived. He possessed fearless intellectual courage and was not reluctant to challenge the mischievous orthodoxies to which the study of the history of Cuba has often been subjected. He will be missed . . .

Louis A. Pérez Jr.
Chapel Hill, North Carolina
October 2018

INTRODUCTION

THE CLAIM OF a shared predilection for distinct foods often provides a reference point through which a people entrust themselves to a common destiny. The palate as a politics, of sorts: to imagine a discernible cuisine and a distinct cookery as antecedents from which to infer the plausibility of nation, a gastronomy possessed of a past and invoked as something akin to a patrimony—in much the same way that a people point to music, art, and literature as something uniquely of them. This is to propound the preference for a distinct assortment of foods as a matter of a temperament, shared tastes invoked as a source and means of nationality. To speak of a national cuisine, Sidney Mintz correctly suggested, "requires a population that eats that cuisine with sufficient frequency to consider themselves experts on it. They all believe, and care that they believe, that they know what it consists of, how it is made, and how it should taste."[1]

The premise of national cuisine tends to form within a proto-national environment, as a matter of implied affinities and inferred sensibilities, a people arriving to the recognition that in being alike with one another they are different from others. Self-awareness is informed with self-esteem, a people becoming alike and liking who they have become: a complex moral order expanding within an ensemble of cultural norms from which nationality obtains meaning. Awareness of a shared history has much to do with self-awareness, of course, the past discerned as a source of common antecedents from which conventions, customs, and traditions are transacted into the premise of nationality, thereupon to prescribe the cues and codes of conduct through which to perform the canons of nation.

At some point early in the nineteenth century, the proposition of a distinctive Cuban cuisine entered the creole imagination. Identified variously as *la cocina criolla*, *la comida criolla*, and *la cocina cubana*, the claim to a discernible national cuisine was itself a facet of a larger process by which the notion of nationhood assumed narrative coherence, where certain kinds of food and

NUEVO MANUAL
DEL
COCINERO CUBANO
Y
ESPAÑOL.
CON UN TRATADO ESCOJIDO
DE DULCERIA, PASTELERIA Y BOTILLERIA,
AL ESTILO DE CUBA.
INDISPENSABLE
PARA APRENDER Á COMPONER DE COMER CON LA MAYOR PERFECCION Y ECONOMIA, Y NECESARIO Á TODAS LAS CLASES DE LA SOCIEDAD, Y EN PARTICULAR Á LOS GASTRÓNOMOS, MADRES DE FAMILIA, FONDISTAS, &c.

DIVIDIDO EN TRES PARTES,
POR
J. P. LEGRAN.

HABANA.—1864.

Véndese en las papelerías La Principal, Plaza del Vapor, y la Cruz Verde, calle de Mercaderes.

The cover of an 1864 cookbook offering recipes for dishes "in the style of Cuba."

certain types of dishes and certain styles of preparation acquired the status of "*típica*"—"typical"—as if to invite the inference of a larger meaning from the presence of tradition and the practice of culinary arts.

The purport of the premise was self-evident: taste for certain dishes and preference for certain preparations to suggest culturally determined dispositions as a function of being Cuban, to corroborate the proposition of a national palate, a cuisine to enact a custom as a source of affinity. In the novel *Dos habaneras* (1880), writer Pascual de Riesgo depicts a meal as a ritual of tradition: "According to custom [*según costumbre*] . . . the lunch commenced with white rice, eggs and fried plantains [*arroz blanco, los huevos y los plátanos fritos*]."[2] This implied the presence of a recognizable assortment of foods, of course, arranged in a more or less prescribed combination and given to a specific preparation, thereupon proclaimed to be *una comida criolla*. But it also served to embody the proposition of nation. "We hold," culinary writer Blanche Z. de Baralt reflected on the meaning of *la cocina criolla*, "that the cuisine of a country is one of its psychological aspects, an accumulation of slow growth, almost a synthesis of its civilization"[3]—what Marcelo Alvarez described as "la cocina como patrimonio (in)tangible."[4]

The subject of food insinuated itself early into narratives of nationality, by way of allegory and allusion, as metaphor and metonymy, to inscribe into an essence of nationality the premise of a shared culinary taste (*sabor cubano*)—the way, Pierre Bourdieu suggests, that taste preferences serve to internalize group values—that is, as a matter of "coherent sets of preferences stemming from distinct and distinctive systems of dispositions."[5] Certainly the stew *ajiaco* achieved folkloric status as the emblematic cuisine of *lo cubano,* and perhaps more than any other dish *ajiaco* provides an exemplary instance of the capacity of a cuisine to represent "Cuban." "There is much pride in Cuba to consider *ajiaco* our favorite dish," commented Esteban Rodríguez Herrera, "designating it as the *national dish [plato nacional]*."[6] "Without doubt," pronounced the *Diccionario gastronómico cubano, ajiaco* is "the dish recognized by the vast majority [of people] as the most genuine and the most creole representation of Cuban cuisine. It epitomizes the national cuisine in the fullness of its reach."[7]

The very word *"ajiaco"* implied a means of differentiation, something autochthonous peculiar to the island. Reference to *ajiaco* as an attribute of Cuban appeared as early as the seventeenth century in the commentary of a Spanish traveler to Havana: "The food here is seasoned in such a strange way as to be at first repugnant. But Europeans eventually become accustomed to the food and forget about the food of their country and prefer the local dishes. One dish is mixture of fresh and salted meats, divided into small pieces cooked with diverse root vegetables that are spiced with a caustic pepper [*aji-ji-ji*] and to which is given color with a seed [*vi-ji-ja*] which grows abundantly. This is the principal dish, not to say the only dish, that these primitive inhabitants serve themselves."[8] "The language and technical names of the *habaneros*," commented Antonio López Matoso during a visit to the island in 1818, "are the drivel of the devil," noting in particular *"ajiaco,"* described as a "stew of beef, tasajo, plantains, yuca, and many spices."[9] One midcentury traveler to Cuba provided a detailed description of an encounter with *ajiaco*:

> It is formed by mixing a large number of articles which I will here mention, endeavoring not to forget any, to enable you to form an idea of the composition. Salt beef, smoked pork, fresh pork, especially the tail, ham, black

pudding, sausages, bacon, calf's feet, sweet potatoes, yams, sweet yuca, green bananas and pumpkin. Cabbages, peas and kidney-beans are sometimes added to the already long list of components. The whole is placed in a very large and deep dish together with the sauce in which it has been cooked, and a piece of every thing is served to each person in a plate large enough to contain them. The variety of tastes forms a savory compound.[10]

Several years later, Julia Ward Howe visited a sugar estate in Matanzas and recounted her experience with "a Cuban country-dish," something of "a stew, composed of ham, beef, mutton, potatoes, sweet potatoes, *yuca*, and yams. This is called *Ayacco*," she wrote, adding, "As is usual in such case, it is more relished by the inhabitants than by their visitors. On the present occasion, however, it was only one among many good things, which were made better by pleasant talk and were succeeded by delicious fruits and coffee."[11]

Ajiaco, "the national dish of Cuba," as pronounced by Baralt,[12] soon lent itself to an idealized embodiment of *lo cubano*, a way to represent the ethnic complexity and racial diversity that made up the Cuban people[13]—"an extraordinary reach of the metaphor of *ajiaco*," commented Graziella Pogolotti.[14] The play *Un ajiaco, o la boda de Pancha Jutía y Canuto Raspadura* (1847) by Creto Gangá deployed metaphorical tropes to address the matter of ethnic diversity, which Jill Lane indicated to be "among the first to articulate a notion of mestizaje as the foundation for a Cuban imaginary."[15] With *ajiaco*'s mixture of multiple local ingredients of tubers, cereals, fruits, vegetables, and meats, variously associated with the population of Indians, Europeans, Africans, and Asians, the stew offered an ideal metaphor for *cubanidad*.[16] Its commonly available and readily accessible ingredients served to associate *ajiaco* with the diet of families of modest means. "There is no dish more Cuban than *ajiaco*," Graciela DuBroco pronounced, "for *ajiaco* consists entirely of everything that is produced in Cuba."[17] For Josefina Ortega, the relationship between *ajiaco* and national identity was self-evident,[18] while Fernando Ortiz offered a sweeping— and enduring—pronouncement in 1940: "For us the image of the creole *ajiaco* [*ajiaco criollo*] fully symbolizes the formation of the Cuban people ... with Cuba, the island, as the pot [*la olla*] ... into which is placed ingredients of the most diverse types and origins [*de los más diversos géneros y procedencias*]." And to the point: "Cuba is an *ajiaco*."[19]

NARRATIVES OF *la comida criolla* spread into realms of the popular imagination through multiple aesthetic forms, expanding knowledge of the products, preparation, and presentation of what made for a Cuban cuisine. Food looms large in multiple literary genres. Writer José Ramón de Betancourt includes an evocative meal setting in his novel *Una feria de la caridad en 183* . . . (1858): "Mi mujer ha hecho una buena sopa de puré de frijoles negros, con casabito tostado y una *guacamole* no sólo de aguacatessino con piña. Su hermana, tiene en el horno un rico pastel de cativia y perdices; bajo las cañas bravas, atravesado en su pua y sobre una hoguera de gajos de guayabos se tuesta un tierno de lechón [y] también casabe con salsa de huevos, yuca cocido de esa que se abre y destila su pulpa, media docena de anones, conserva de guayabas [y] queso de mano."[20] Food also served as a rich repository of metaphors of romantic intent in Luis F. Domínguez's parody "A Chichita" (1867):

> Tu eres galleta, yo soy gorgojo;
> Tu eres azúcar, yo soy la sal,
> Tu eres, hermosa, la mantequilla,
> Yo soy el pan.
> Tu eres la carne, yo soy el hueso,
> Tu eres la tinta, yo soy el papel;
> Tu eres el techo de algun palacio,
> Yo el comején.
> Tu eres la gansa, yo soy el ganso,
> Tu eres manteca, yo soy arroz;
> Tu eres un plato de ropa vieja,
> Y el hambre yo.[21]

In *Cecilia Valdés* (1879), novelist Cirilo Villaverde's narrator marvels at the "variety of dishes": "Además de carne de vaca y de puerco frito, guisada y estofada, había picadillo de ternera servido en una torta de casabe mojado, pollo asado relumbrante con la manteca y los ajos, huevos fritos casi anegados en una salsa de tomates, arroz cocido, plátano maduro también frito, en luengas y melosas tajadas, y ensalada de berrios y de lechugas."[22] In the novel *El fatalista* (1866), writer Esteban Pichardo offers an evocative account of a sumptuous *almuerzo*: "Sobre un mantel blanco y limpio estaba la sopera á que seguia una gran fuente de *ajiaco* humeando y sazonado á lo *tierradentro*, con costillas de puerco, tasajo de Cayo-Romano, *plátanos movidos*, & que habia de saborearse con los limones y *ajíes* portados en dos platillos y *casabe* de Guanabacoa. Otra fuente de arroz acopado; otra de *frijoles* á la veracruzana; otra de luchugas tiernas; otra de *aporreado* y en el medio tendido el *lechón* cuya piel tostada quebraba como vidrio, además de otras golosinas y bebidas."[23] In *Recuerdos de antes de ayer* (1893), novelist Francisco Calcagno depicts a Christmas Eve banquet in Havana, where a variety of national dishes were placed on display: "Cuba was represented by un lechón, un pavo, un arroz criollo, plátanos y otros excesos."[24]

The experience of dining also appears in Martín Morúa Delgado's novel *La familia Unzúazu* (1896), with a dinner of "carne de puerco ahumada y plátanos verdes, salcochados desde el día anterior."[25] In the novel *Sofía* (1891), Morúa Delgado describes "an exquisite creole dish [*un exquisito plato criollo*]" consisting of "frijoles negros, en potaje, . . . revueltos al comerlos con el arroz cocido en blanco, seco, suelto y mantecoso."[26] Years later, Raimundo Cabrera would recall fondly "the picnic outings during colonial times [*las romerías de los tiempos coloniales*]" and especially remembered the meals: "Se llevaban las provisiones para la merienda y la comida, y algunos de los concurrentes, ya famoso por su habilidad en preparar lechones, cocer el arroz, los frijoles y asar los plátanos, actuaban de cocineros. . . . A la hora de comerse el lechón y los plátanos, asados a fuego lento, sazonados en mojo agrio, de naranja, sal y manteca, era cuando llegaba a su intensidad la alegría, algazara y jovialidad de la fiesta."[27] Carlos Loveira, perhaps among the most *criollo* of the early twentieth-century novelists, was especially fond of celebrating *la cocina criollas* as a facet of *lo cubano*. In *Los inmorales* (1919), Loveira depicts one family meal in which "figuraban una botella de vino y el clásico, sabroso y humeante, arroz con pollo."[28] In *Generales y doctores* (1920), Loveira describes a sumptuous table upon which "humeaba la dorada y bien oliente sopa de pan en los platos. Escoltada por las fuentes de arroz y de puerco, la de ensalada de lechuga ponía su alegre nota verde en el centro de la mesa," and at another point a meal of "el arroz, los frijoles y el café molida, [con] el tasajo, el bacalao, los camarones fosilizados en sal y otros miserables y exóticos alimentos." The narrator describes a table set with "la olorosa y humeante sopa, el arroz amarillo con jamón, el clásico boliche asado y la dorada fuente de tostado 'chatino,' se me despertó un apetito incontenible."[29] The Cuban national poet Nicolás Guillén was very much given to celebrate *lo cubano* through the celebration of *la cocina criolla*. It was in "Epístola" (1959), an epic ode to *la comida cubana*, that Guillén set in relief the varieties of Cuban cuisine, both in the form of social commentary and as a facet of national sensibility, to celebrate "blanco arroz y oscuro picadillo," with "chicharrón de puerco con su masa/dandole el brazo al siboney casabe," together with "gordo tasajo y cristalina yuca," and reference to "el quimbombó africano" and "guiso de camarones," acknowledging "el arroz con pollo/que es a la vez hispánico y criollo," and concluding, "Al final, buen remate a tanto diente/una taza pequeña/ de café carretero y bien caliente."[30]

A CONSENSUS developed early in the nineteenth century on the plausibility of *la cocina cubana* as a facet of nationality. It is important to emphasize that much of the cuisine that makes for *la cocina cubana* is not substantially dissimilar from the gastronomy of the Dominican Republic, Puerto Rico, Venezuela, and Colombia, among other countries.[31] What confers distinction on *la cocina cubana* has less to do with what makes *up* the cuisine than what was made *of* the cuisine—that is, the efficacy with which food served as a usable discursive framework through which to articulate aspirations to nationhood, of a people disposed to infer that a shared taste for a cuisine signified an inchoate attribute of nationality, thereupon to substantiate the logic of national sovereignty, and that in choosing "to eat and cook specific foods," Atsuko Ichijo and Ronald Ranta correctly observed, "people engage with their national identity and project who they are."[32] Anything that could contribute to the realization of an independent nation was seized upon and incorporated into an ever-expanding master narrative of *la nación integral*. Leví Marrero was most assuredly correct to suggest that the nineteenth century comprised the "years of development of a creole cuisine [*los años desarrollándose una cocina criolla*]," that is, the time during which the claim to *lo cubano* assumed discernible form.[33] "The development of *la cocina cubana*," Marta Vesa Figueras insisted, "as a facet of our national culture and our identity as a people, has been a coherent process similar to the development of other artistic expressions of Cuban society."[34] Alberto Pozo Fernández was categorical: "Cuban cuisine is the identity of our people [*identidad de nuestro pueblo*], a fundamental element of our national culture [*elemento fundamental de la cultura nacional*]"[35]—what Ana Sofía Peláez described as "a pure expression of the culture."[36] Drawn to its logical conclusion, culinary writers Cecilio Rodolfo Cortés Cruz and Sergio Eduardo Chinea Díaz argue, "cuisine is one of the earliest cultural manifestations [of a people] and should be recognized, on it own merits, as one of the fine arts [*reconocida como una de las bellas artes*]."[37]

The proposition of a shared palate as a facet of *lo cubano* assumed fully the status of received wisdom. Ramona Abella Forcada writes of "eating the Cuban way" and "eating Cuban" as intrinsic to identity as Cuban.[38] "Our food forms part of our image [*Nuestra comida forma parte de nuestra imagen*]," pronounced writer José Lezama Lima. Lezama Lima continued: "The majority of nations [*mayoría de los pueblos*] upon eating ... appear to force or exaggerate a distinction between man and Nature, but the Cuban upon eating appears to incorporate Nature."[39] Put in slightly different terms, novelist Eliseo Alberto affirmed outright, "The nation is a plate of food. I eat my country every day [*La patria es un plato de comida. Yo como mi país todos los días*]."[40]

What is especially striking about the presence of food in the calculus of Cuban was the degree to which the "value" of *la comida cubana* underwent social transformations in function of national formation. José García de Arboleya could take pride in 1859 that "the culinary arts have made great progress in Havana" and indeed celebrated *la cocina cubana* as a cuisine of distinction.[41] But it is also true that many of the dishes to be commonly identified as "national" cuisine had popular origins, with antecedents in the kitchens and from the tables of Cubans of modest means, among enslaved Africans and indentured Chinese, including *ajiaco, aporreado, picadillo, quimbombó, calalú, butifarra, calalú, tamal,* and tasajo, among others.[42] In the novel *Generales y doctores*, Carlos Loveira alludes to the "rice, beans, and coffee with tasajo, *bacalao,* and shrimp encrusted with salt and other miserable and exotic foods introduced during the dark times of slavery."[43] García de Arboleya acknowledged that "the special dishes of Cuba [*los platos especiales de Cuba*] are few, and are found almost only on the table of the poor, for the well-to-do [*la clase acomodada*] dine á la española, á la italiana, á la francesa, etc." *Ajiaco*, for example, García de Arboleya insisted, "is a cheap meal [*comida barata*], nutritious and tasteful, but never for a table of distinction."[44] Poet Juan Nápoles Fajardo (known as El Cucalambé) spurned *ajiaco* precisely for its association with the "unhappy masses" (*plebeyo infeliz*):

> I swear to God, and not to Bacchus
> That I abhor even the name of *ajiaco*
> From my childhood I have detested that meal
> That in Cuba is obligatory on every table.[45]

The evolving culinary culture of Cuba offers evidence of ongoing cultural transitions, food possessed of the capacity to transcend social barriers and traverse thresholds of class and color even as it served to bind all Cubans to common reference points, where Cubans across the island identified in common with "*platos especiales.*" The narrator in writer Pascual de Riesgo's novel *Dos habaneras* describes the meals to be served on the "table of every well-to-do family in Havana [*en las mesas de toda famila bien acomodada*]": "Un mundo de platos, que constituían siempre el almuerzo de familia, el *arrocito blanco,* la carne de puerco, el *tasagito,* la ropa-vieja (carne picada, con tomate, cebolla, manteca, etc., etc., etc.), el *platanito* frito, los huevos fritos, las costillas de carnero, las *frituritas* de sesos, todas las delicias de la cocina casera habanera, que tanto acaban por complacer á los europeos que visitan aquella tierra hermosa."[46]

Nineteenth-century cookbooks offer rich possibilities for insight into the relationship between cuisine and culture, between palate and politics, and into ways that preparation of food discharged the premise of nationality—and vice versa—and the presumption of taste as an expression of an emerging national sensibility. "The recipes of a people," pronounced José Luis Santana Guedes, "are as important and as eloquent facets of the culture of a people as literature or music, and represent a treasure that must be preserved."[47] Recipes are thus transformed into historical artifacts, written sources of the ways of cookery, to serve as a source of knowledge about the ways a people were enjoined to discharge the practice of cooking as a prescriptive national protocol and about how the conventions of an emerging literary genre lifted the possibility of culinary arts as a means through which to enact a nationality.

The significance of the nineteenth-century cookbooks lies precisely in the fact that they were not advancing a claim to *la cocina cubana*: they simply assumed its existence. Indeed, by midcentury, the idea of *un almuerzo criollo* and *una cena criolla* had taken hold: meals with specific and generally recognizable attributes.[48] Novelist Julio Rosas could propound unabashedly the existence of a cuisine that was "so creole [*tan criollo*]" as to make the claim of a national cuisine entirely plausible. In the novel *La campana de la tarde, o vivir muriendo* (1873), Rosas presents protagonist Angelina serving the time-honored *almuerzo criollo*: "*Casabe* blanco como la leche cuando sale de la ubre de la vaca, un *tasajito* que resucita los muertos, *picadillo* con arroz blanco, y un lechón tostado con hojas de guayaba y humecido con un *mojito* tan sabroso que nos vamos a chupar los dedos. Y al medio dia comeremos *ajiaco*, aporreado de vaca, *guisito* de maíz, *tamal* de *cazuela*, *majarete*, tortillas, y arroz con leche y flores de azahar."[49] Later in the novel, the table is set with a "meal intrinsically creole [*una comida esencialmente criolla*]": "Ajiaco, *plátanos* verdes asados, *plátanos* maduros fritos, tortas de *casabe*, ensalada de *guacamoles*, *montería de lechón*, tasajo ahumado, *tallullo, calalá, chicharrones, bollos de frijoles*, empanada de maíz, *mojo* crudo, *aporreado de tasajo*, arroz blanco, rosquitas de *catibía*, majerete, *buñuelos de viento*, queso de *mano* envuelto en *yagua*."[50]

Cookbooks celebrated the use of fruits and vegetables unique to Cuba to propound a claim to time-honored conventions of preparation, that is, preparations possessed of a proper lineage, a history, thereupon presumed to possess a tradition to which all were enjoined to adhere as a matter of custom—what Beatriz Calvo Peña characterized as "recipes of identity [*recetas de identidad*]."[51] They specified distinct cookware, utensils, and methods of measurement, mindful too of the ways that the "technology" of the kitchen affected the outcome of preparation. The *Manual del cocinero cubano* (1857) explained that it offered "recipes properly of the country [*propias del país*] arranged according to the national temperament per the practices and customs of this enviable land," including "the use of all the fruits of this fertile land to make desserts."[52] The cookbook by José Legrán—*Nuevo manual del cocinero cubano y español* (1857)—boasted that is was "indispensable to learn to prepare food with maximum perfection and economy and necessary for all classes of society," adding, "The text is easy to comprehend.... We write for the people [*escribimos para el pueblo*] and we speak to them in their language [*en su lenguaje le hablamos*]."[53] Legrán also included pages of illustrations of the varieties of cookware to which he referred in his recipes. Linguist Colleen Cotter makes a persuasive argument in behalf of approaching recipes through sociolinguistics—that is, to examine "how language is actually used by real people in real-world contexts," the premise being that "a recipe can be viewed as a story, a cultural narrative that can be shared and has been constructed by members of a community."[54]

The instructions inscribed into the texts of the recipes implied something of a cultural imperative, specified—and stylized—ways to prepare and arrange the ingredients that made for *una comida típica*. Recipes as text served as a means to expand knowledge of a method and contribute to a common source from which a national cuisine would develop. What previously had accumulated as folk wisdom was collected and organized into a culinary dictum and was passed from one generation to another, as a matter of memory, by word of mouth and in the example of the practice: written recipes as text—more precisely, a narrative—to implicate Cubans in a common endeavor as a shared performance, per prescribed methods. The cookbook *El cocinero de los enfermos, convalecientes y desganados* (1862) by Enrique Langarika offered a collection of recipes gathered by way of the "talent of able assistants of this Island of Cuba, for each country and each climate requires its own proper cuisine," and to the point: "Recipes are prepared for the taste of the Island of Cuba."[55]

Recipes implied a protocol of preparation within a prescriptive narrative framework, offered with the promise of making available to all—to disseminate within an inchoate community—culinary practices, cooking techniques, seasoning methods, and proper use of cooking utensils: that is, another way by which a people fashioned a recognition of themselves. Beatriz Calvo Peña examined the recipes for *ajiaco*, *ropa vieja*, and *picadillo* appearing in three cookbooks published between 1858 and 1914 and found them to be identical in the selection of ingredients and the methods of preparation. "The virtual absence of any variation in these three books on the ingredients used to prepare these dishes," concluded Calvo Peña, "confirms that already by the mid-nineteenth

EL COCINERO

DE

LOS ENFERMOS, CONVALECIENTES

Y

DESGANADOS

Arte de preparar varios caldos, atoles, sopas, jaleas, galatinas, ollas, agiacos, frituras, azados, &c. Dulces, pastas, cremas, pudines, masas, pasteles, &c.

DEDICADO A LAS MADRES DE FAMILIAS,

ARREGLADO TODO

al gusto de la Isla de Cuba.

HABANA.
IMPRENTA Y LIBRERIA LA CUBANA.
CALLE DE O-REILLY NUM. 52.
1862.

The cover of an 1862 cookbook dedicated to the "art of preparing" various dishes—"all prepared to the taste of the Island of Cuba."

century there existed the premise of a Cuban cuisine, that certain dishes were already identified as authentic and properly belonging to the Island."[56]

Cookbooks in the nineteenth century, perhaps without meaning to—or perhaps purposely meaning to—could contemplate cuisine as the embodiment of nationality, suggested in such designations as *la cocina cubana, el cocinero cubano, al estilo de Cuba, a la criolla, la cocina típica,* and *la cocina tradicional,* that is, as a way to claim a cuisine uniquely Cuban. To specify *a la criolla,* affirms the *Diccionario gastronómico cubano,* is to suggest "a manner of cooking according to the traditions of Cuban cuisine"; to refer to *la cocina tradicional* is to convey a "concept to underscore certain ways of preparation and certain dishes of a national cuisine that have transcended time across several generations and have established themselves as the prevailing tastes within that social context [*en ese entorno social*]."⁵⁷ Christine Folch argues further: "Cuban identity is constructed in and through the cookbook."⁵⁸

Recipes implied instruction as if a mode of initiation into a tradition, informed with something of a proprietary authority in discharge of *lo cubano* (as in *huevos rellenos a lo cubano, pescado asado a lo cubano, pastel de arroz a lo cubano, bacalao a la cubana, berejenas fritas a la cubana*) or *a lo criollo* (as in *frijoles negros a lo criollo, salsa verde criolla, aporreado criollo, mondongo criollo*) or *a lo habanero* (as in *sopa a la habanera, patas fritas a la habanera, embozado habanero, ropa vieja habanera*). To these must be added scores of styles of preparation claiming distinct regional variations—what the *Diccionario gastronómico cubano* identifies as "*la cocina regional*"—such as *palanqueta de Sancti-Spíritus, leche quemada al estilo de Villaclara, lechuga rellena al uso de Holguín, huevos estrellados con tomates a lo santiaguero, tortuga guisado a lo matancero, pudín de Cienfuegos,* and *frangollo al estilo Bejucal,* among many others: a "cuisine whose recipes," indicates the *Diccionario gastronómico cubano,* "are based on local ingredients and traditions and practices within a given geographic zone."⁵⁹

The choice of certain foods and not others often implied the practice of differentiation and a process of divergence, that is, one more way through which to advance the claim of a separate nationality: a cuisine essentially—and often purposefully—different from Spanish gastronomy,⁶⁰ "a cuisine as an expression of culture apart or expression of the 'non-Spanish' [*o expresión de lo 'no español'*]," commented Marta Vesa Figueras.⁶¹ Historian María Teresa Cornide Hernández correctly identified food as a defining marker of *una sensibilidad criolla,* noting that early in the nineteenth century "the *criollos* never lost an opportunity to distinguish themselves from the *peninsulares;* evidence of this was to flaunt matters of taste so simple as to drink black coffee and eat white rice and black beans, instead of chocolate, chickpeas and paella, the favorite dishes of the Spaniards."⁶² "It is said," wrote Cuban culinary authority Fernando Fornet Piña, "that around 1830, the taste of the average inhabitant of Cuba took a [distinctive] turn coinciding with the affirmation of nationality," adding, "The Cuban, that is to say, the *criollo* or the *nativo,* took pleasure in his culinary taste by identifying himself with white rice, various types of beans [*frijoles de varios tipos*] and strong coffee, and differentiated himself from the Spaniard who remained attached to his chocolate drink and imported chickpeas, and who remained bound to his traditions and rice dish known as paella . . . as the cuisine *la madre patria.*"⁶³ Alberto Pozo Fernández similarly took note of coffee as "something whose intent is implicitly a means of differentiation, with chocolate substituted among creole families with *café con leche*."[64] Coffee had indeed developed into the beverage of choice among *criollos*. "The children wake up at 7 A.M., and at that hour began to drink *café con leche*," commented the *constumbrista* writer Luis Victoriano Betancourt.[65] "Cubans drink more coffee than pure water," observes the narrator in Virginia Felicia Auber's novel *Ambarina* (1856). "You have hardly awakened, and they offer you coffee. At lunch, they give you coffee. You snack, and they present you with coffee. At dinner, they place coffee next to your sleeping cap. . . . An upset stomach? Drink coffee. To celebrate? Have coffee. In sum, coffee is an indispensable item for all the urban and rural residents of Cuba."[66] Maturin M. Ballou observed at a café on the Plaza de Isabela that Cubans "drink often, but not strong liquors, and one is surprised to hear coffee so often called for in place of wine."[67]

NOTHING PERHAPS so fully defines the character of *la cocina cubana* as much as rice. Indeed, rice accompanies almost all meals, and on almost all occasions: "Upon the completion of the wedding vows," read one news story of a wedding in Jagüey Grande in 1912, "the guests were treated to a 'buffet' and served fine desserts and exquisite liquors, as well as a tasty *lechón asado* and indispensable *arroz con pollo*."[68] The "typical *arroz con pollo*," explained Ramona Abella Forcada on another occasion, was usually reserved "for those very special occasions such as birthdays, holidays, or when the family received guests."[69]

Rice assumes many presentations: the main course, or as a side dish, or as dessert. It complements a meal even as it completes it: as the principal dish (*arroz con pollo, arroz con pescado, arroz con carne de macho*—known too as *arroz con carne de puerco*), as a side dish (*arroz blanco, arroz amarillo, arroz frito, arroz con garbanzos, croquetas de arroz, arroz con quimbombó, moros/congrí, ensalada de arroz, huevos en crema de arroz*), as soup (*sopa de arroz, sopa de arroz con leche*), as a snack (*frituras de arroz*), as dessert (*pastel de arroz, buñuelos de arroz, arroz con leche, arroz con leche de coco*). And it has many forms of preparation: *arroz salteado*, rice cooked with small portions of different vegetables and meats to which is added a coloring sauce; *arroz a la chorrera*, yellow rice cooked with excessive water; *arroz sin compadre*, rice seasoned with salt, lard, and garlic and cooked in water; *arroz con frijoles obsoletos*, rice to which beans are added after cooked.[70]

Rice occupies a very special place in the cosmology of Cuban. Rice is more than a food: it is a way of life, an obligatory presence on the Cuban table—"there is hardly a table in Cuba that does not serve rice daily," Antonio Bachiller y Morales pronounced in 1856.[71] It is perhaps impossible to contemplate *la cocina cubana* without the presence of rice—"indispensable on every table," insisted José García de Arboleya in 1859[72]—what Gonzalo de Quesada in 1896 deemed essential to all "*bona fide* Cuban dishes," pointing out, "Boiled rice is never dispensed with at any meal, and the cooking of it is understood to perfection."[73] Indeed, vernacular usage is rich with adages and aphorisms propounding the proverbial truths of the importance of rice in Cuba cuisine: the "obligatory dish of the homes of Cuban families," declared one maxim; "if there is no rice on the table it is as if one has not eaten," insisted another adage; "Cuban cuisine can never lack rice," offered another dictum.[74]

Culinary writers agreed. "Rice forms an essential part of the Cuban table," one commentator stated. "It is said that rice goes with everything, and indeed it does: its taste does not counteract the taste of meats. On the contrary it complements and enhances. It accepts all the flavors of the condiments and combines well with sauces and broths."[75] And: "As far as we are concerned, rice for us has become nearly irreplaceable on our tables [*insustituible en nuestras mesas*]."[76] Leví Marrero was categorical on the matter of rice: "The presence of rice on our table—for all social and economic classes—is an inevitable condition."[77]

The proposition of rice as a "condition" is not all hyperbole. Rice is ubiquitous. The taste for rice developed early in life; indeed, Cubans were socialized into the consumption of rice at infancy: "[It is] the first food that our children chew and savor [*el primer alimento que mastican y saborean nuestros hijos*]," pronounced Miguel Escalada in 1845.[78] Cuban infants were weaned at infancy on rice water (*agua de arroz*), setting into place a taste shaped as an early sensory experience.[79] Josefina Alvarez writes of the Cuban practice of mothers serving rice water to newborn children, "which for being a cereal has much nutritious value. It is prepared by using two tablespoons of rice for one cup of water, cooking until soft, and thereupon drained. It is a very good way to introduce cereal into the diet of an infant. It is nutritious and healthy."[80] Childhood gastronomic experiences to last a lifetime.

The culinary culture in which rice has risen to a "condition" has also fostered a keen sensibility about the nature of rice, about its texture, flavor, smell, and appearance, about the length of its grain and color and condition, about its preparation and presentation, and most of all about its requisite taste. Cubans know rice well. Most Cubans—certainly most Cubans who cook—can offer informed disquisitions on the characteristics of rice, often with the nuanced knowledge of a gourmet chef, and can hold forth with bedazzling oratorical flourishes: long-grain rice with a long slender kernel, usually three times longer than wide, that cooks light and fluffy and tends to separate during cooking; medium-grain rice with a shorter and wider kernel that cooks moistly and tenderly with a greater tendency to cling together; short-grain rice, almost a round kernel, nearly as wide as long, that cooks softly and tends to aggregate during cooking. They know which type of rice—long-grain or medium-grain or short or round—to use for what dish to obtain the best results: round-grain preferred for *paella*; long-grain best for *arroz blanco, arroz con lentajas, arroz con garbanzos, ensalada de arroz, moros y cristianos, congrí*; short-grain best for *arroz amarillo con pescado, arroz con pollo,* and *arroz con leche*.[81]

A full-fledged taxonomy has developed to classify the varieties of rice: *arroz silvestre* (wild rice produced in the Zapata swamp, used principally for animal feed); *arroz de costa* (rice produced in Varadero); *arroz canilla* (long-grain rice); *arroz de grano corto* (short round rice); *arroz de Manila* ("the poorest in size, color, taste, and preference"); *arroz de Valencia* ("of pleasant appearance, egg-shaped and round"); *arroz perla* (short-grain rice that sticks together when cooked); *arroz criollo* (rice consumed by peasant families, "delicious and preferred by some"); *arroz de la tierra* ("rice produced in the country with a color not very white [*se cultiva en el país no tiene color tan blanco*]"); *arroz de fuera* (imported rice); *arroz del Norte* (from the United States, "the best, whitest, and generally preferred" and "very much prized for its good size and immaculate whiteness").[82] Enrique Langarika's 1862 recipe for *arroz blanco criollo*, on the other hand, insisted that it was "preferable to use rice produced in Cuba, for it had a much more pronounced and delicious taste than North American rice."[83] Linguist Esteban Rodríguez Herrera similarly indicated that the "*arroz de la tierra* was always preferred by the Cuban people, notwithstanding the lack of whiteness of imported rice or the lack of polish of Valencia rice."[84]

The protocols of preparation imply something of a practiced ritual, as family tradition and time-honored recipes passed down from one generation to another, and not to be tampered with. It is a "transgression," protested María Josefa Llúria de O'Higgins, to "use long-grain rice to cook Spanish-style yellow rice dishes," adding, "To substitute long-grain rice for short-grain Valencia rice is a culinary mortal sin!"[85] For Llúria de O'Higgins, the preparation of rice was a serious matter: "Fluffy white rice is served at almost every Cuban meal, and the ability to make perfect white rice is perhaps the most indispensable skill of Cuban cooking. Cuban rice should be neither mushy nor, as the Italians say, al dente. It should be light and airy—never sticky. It is the foundation of such a large proportion of Cuban's distinctive dishes that woe to the cook who has not mastered its secrets."[86] Ramona Abella Forcada offered strict instructions about the preparation of rice:

> To cook perfectly fluffy white rice every time, always use the same proportions of water and rice *and* cook covered over a *very* low flame. Do *not* keep lifting the lid to see if it is ready; this will cause the ratio of water to rice to be disturbed by the loss of moisture each time you lift the lid. Stir the rice only when it is ready and do so with a fork to prevent mashing it up prior to serving. In general, cooking white rice with this method should take 15 to 18 minutes for 1 cup of dry rice and 20 minutes for 2 to 3 cups.[87]

Nitza Villapol, the grande dame of the Cuban kitchen, was similarly exact in the preparation of rice: "There are some important points to consider so as to guarantee that rice cooks fluffy and separate. First, the rice must be of high quality, so that it separates well. Rice should be washed only at the moment it is placed in the water to be cooked, for rice that is washed too soon absorbs moisture and will come out mushy. While cooking, rice should not be stirred, and never with a spoon. If it becomes necessary to stir, use a kitchen fork with wide prongs."[88]

Rice insinuated itself deeply into the popular imagination, in literature, and in folklore. Cubans of all classes, men and women of means and of modest origins, are often given to sentimentality on the matter of rice. "We all begin our nostalgic gastronomic recollections," Eliana Rivero suggested, "with memories of some delicious dish created by our mother or grandmother, or sometimes an aunt and her rice pudding."[89] Indeed, historian Eusebio Leal Spengler suggested that Cubans "finding themselves in other parts of the world, long for rice with nostalgia [*lo añora con nostalgia*]."[90] Eduardo Machado recalled boyhood years in exile and the realization that "I had not missed Cuba. I missed the food, for sure." Machado remembered fondly his grandmother's "smooth puree, served over bowls of flaky white rice, [that] managed to elevate a staple to a culinary treasure," and a poignant moment at the table with *arroz con pollo* soon after his arrival from Cuba: "It was the rice that did me in. I felt my whole life in every bite, resistant to the tooth, eventually yielding into creaminess. We were neither here nor there, and our dinner tasted exactly the same."[91] The exiled protagonist in Margarita Engle's novel *Skywriting* (1995) "dreamed with mountains of rice and black beans," while Pablo Medina's *Exiled Memories* (1990) evoked "the smell of food," of "families gathered round big pots fill with *moros con cristianos* [rice and black beans] and roast pork."[92] Richard Blanco remembered his grandmother wanting to "fatten me up" through "double portions of rice with *frijoles negros* at dinner, and mandatory desserts: *arroz con leche*."[93] Rice as a means through which to remain connected to another time, another place; memory of rice as a matter of binding attachment. "Now, so many miles and years from this life, in a new place called home," Virgil Suárez brooded, "rice, like potatoes, goes unnoticed when served. Often, my daughters ignore it and I won't permit it. Rice, I say to them, needs respect, needs worship, their full attention, for blessed is that which carries so many so far."[94] Arsenio Rodríguez Quintana alluded to the "Ulysses syndrome"—chronic ill effects associated with emigration—in his remembrance of Cuba:

> potaje de frijoles negros
> carne de cerdo frito
> frituras de maíz
> arroz blanco
> café solo
> ron[95]

Víctor Vega Ceballo recalled fondly the rice of Camagüey (*el arroz camagüeyano*), "something typical and very special," a dish "prepared with boned chicken and into which was added rice, with olives, raisins, and almonds. The secret was the time cooking. It's exquisite!"[96] María Josefa Lluriá de O'Higgins reminisced about her childhood in Cuba:

> When I was a child, preparing rice was a time-consuming process that began early in the day. Once the cook had put the day's broth on to simmer, she would sit down to *escoger* (choose) the rice, that is, separate the good grains from the bad. Rice in those days was not clean, nor did it come in neat packages, ready to cook. It was brought *al por mayor* (wholesale) and kept in large ceramic containers. The cook had to pick through it grain by grain, selecting only the perfect ones for cooking. Then she would wash it well but quickly, for soaked rice cooks into a mushy mess.[97]

Nicolás Guillén remembered the rice of restaurants in La Habana Vieja, and one in particular in which "our favorite meal was simple and creole [*simple y criollo*]: black beans, white rice, and eye of round roast with potatoes [*boliche con papas*]."[98]

Few were the number of foreign visitors who failed to note the ubiquity of rice. "Rice and fried plantains form . . . the staples of [Cuban] existence," one traveler observed as early as 1859.[99] "Boiled rice is never dispensed with at any meal," Samuel Hazard commented in 1871, "and the cooking of it is understood to perfection."[100] Ten years later James Steele came to understand quickly that "an absolute necessity is rice," adding, "At a Christmas-eve supper . . . the company will regard but indifferently the sliced ham, boned turkey, and cold confections, if the huge dish of boiled rice is not there to accompany them."[101] "Never is lunch prepared without the serving of white rice and beans, and at times [Cubans] serve rice over lettuce salad and atop a fried egg," observed Frank Ewert in 1919.[102] Rice made an impression on Erna Ferguson during her travels through Cuba in 1945. "I was served chicken and saffron-yellow rice," she recalled of her lunch in Bayamo. In Cienfuegos she enjoyed *lechón asado*, "served with white rice, fluffy and dry." Lunch in Pinar del Río, Ferguson wrote, "was a feast of many courses," highlighted with "a rich bean soup served with fluffy rice." Ferguson remembered Havana for its "most savory *arroz con mariscos*, rice with shell fish, and *paella*" and the sidewalk tables serving "*arroz con pollo*, and rice with black beans."[103] Thomas Barbour was enchanted by the ubiquity of rice during his travels in Cuba and offered a "prayer that the day may come when rice becomes the refined delicacy with us that it is when cooked by our neighbors, yellowed with a touch of saffron and with each well-cooked grain not too soft and coated with the most delicious film of olive oil."[104] "Ask the newly arrived visitor what food he associates in his mind with Cuba," Walter Adolphe Roberts enjoined in 1953, "and he will probably name *arroz con pollo*."[105] Laurence Crosby could only marvel at Cuban consumption of rice. "The Cubans are one of the biggest and best rice-eating people in the world," Crosby observed in 1955. "Their consumption is simply fantastic to an American mind.... They eat it every day, and twice a day. They love it. They know how to cook it very well."[106]

Entire cookbooks were devoted exclusively to the preparation of rice in its multiple forms and multifaceted varieties.[107] "There is perhaps no country in the world, other than China or India," affirmed José Triay in *Nuevo manual del cocinero criollo* (1914), "where rice has come to signify the meal par excellence, that is used to provide the principal source of nourishment."[108] Blanche Z. de Baralt agreed: "We eat almost as much of it as Orientals do, and know how to prepare it. Rice appears on creole tables, rich or poor, twice a day and largely substitutes bread, without excluding it."[109]

Rice loomed large in the daily diet. One 1933 guide to "balanced nutrition" in *La comida diaria* outlined a weekly dietary program to assist "the mother or the person charged with the nutrition of the family."[110] The recommended daily meals for lunch and dinner included servings of rice almost twice a day (see table I.1).

Cubans were indeed among the highest per capita consumers of rice in the world. In the early twentieth century, rice accounted for 11 percent of the volume of food consumed in Cuba and nearly 20 percent of the total amount of money Cubans allocated wholesale for food.[111] By the mid-twentieth century,

TABLE I.1. Sample weekly menu, 1933

Day	Lunch	Dinner
Monday	corn tamale, *ropa vieja*, roasted boniato, white rice, bread	plantain soup, stew of black beans, white rice, meat, bread, dessert
Tuesday	*quimbombó, picadillo a la criolla*, white rice, fried plantains	*sopa de chicharo, frituras de papas rellenas de carne*, black bean puree, yellow rice with ham or pork, lettuce salad, bread
Wednesday	eggs, meat and potatoes, roasted plantains, onions or carrots *a la crema*, corn flour with tomato sauce, bread	*sopa de fideos, potaje de frijoles blancos*, white rice, roast meat, bread, dessert
Thursday	Italian macaroni, meatballs, white rice, fried plantains, mixed salad	vegetable soup, *col a la crema*, pot roast, potatoes, bread, dessert
Friday	potato stew with green peas, meatballs, white rice, bread	noodle soup, *aji o papas rellenas de carne*, yellow rice with ham or pork, mixed salad, dessert
Saturday	eggs, white rice, breaded beefsteak, *yuca con mojo*, white rice, bread, dessert	plantain soup, meat croquettes, fish, white rice, kidney bean salad, bread, dessert
Sunday	fried eggs with tomato sauce, white rice, *guiso de maiz tierno con papas*, beefsteak, boniato or plantain, bread, dessert	vegetable soup, potato croquettes, yellow rice with ham, roasted meat, lettuce salad, bread, dessert

Source: Ambrosio González del Valle, *La comida diaria. Selección, proporción, distribución y usos de los alimentos de utilidad a las madres o encargadas de dirigr la alimentación de la familia* (Havana, 1933)

rice accounted for almost 25 percent of the total source of caloric intake.[112] Some 50 percent of the nutrition obtained by families in rural Cuba was derived from rice and beans.[113] The Cuban consumption of rice in the early twentieth century averaged more than 200,000 pounds daily, making up three-quarters of the total of 730 million pounds of rice imported into the Western Hemisphere during the 1940s.[114] The national per capita consumption of rice in Cuba consistently ranked among the highest non-Asian countries in the world,

115 pounds per capita in 1910, 128 pounds in 1925, 102 pounds in 1940, and 127 pounds in 1953.[115] Sociologist Lowry Nelson determined that rice consumption in rural Cuba actually exceeded 200 pounds per capita. "Rice is more important than corn and wheat combined as a food in Cuba," Nelson commented.[116] In the United States, in comparison, yearly per capita consumption of rice averaged 6 pounds during the 1940s and 1950s, while consumption of rice in Europe was led by Italy (20 pounds), Portugal (18 pounds), and Spain (12 pounds). Among the Latin American republics, Cuba was second only to Panama (150 pounds) and was followed by Brazil (66 pounds), Peru (33 pounds), Colombia (25 pounds), Ecuador (25 pounds), Chile (20 pounds), Uruguay (16 pounds), Venezuela (15 pounds), Argentina (12 pounds), and Mexico (9 pounds).[117]

RICE RESIDES in those places where the ethos of a people dwells, to register a national idiosyncrasy and a cultural disposition, to delineate a social condition, as marker of means and measure of well-being, and the way that the times—good and bad—are experienced on a daily basis. "Rice is, in a measure, the staff of life down here," Baralt pronounced.[118] A reference librarian at the Biblioteca Nacional José Martí in 2010, during a time of scarcity of rice, upon locating a folio published in 1893 that I requested titled *La cuestion del arroz en Cuba* happened to take note of the title and year of publication and scoffed: "Look at that! The rice question in 1893! And we continue to face the rice question" ("¡Mira eso: la cuestión del arroz, en 1893! Y todavía seguimos con la cuestión del arroz"). Insights into a culture are often obtained in unexpected places, in popular metaphors and common stereotypes, in the wit and whimsy of everyday banter, transmitted through colloquial usage, the way deeper truths often assume the form of folk wisdom and popular custom: all in all, the narrative devices through which a people often transact social complexities into things manageable and real. Rice looms large in colloquial usage and common slang. Consider the use of the word "*moros*" as shorthand for the popular Cuban dish *moros y cristianos*—a designation loaded with historical allusion: the black beans and white rice referring, conventional wisdom tells, to the Muslim conquest and Christian reconquest of the Iberian peninsula. It is "a racialized metonym," suggests Ann Cristina Pertierra, "that not only alludes to the racial dynamic of blacks and whites living in fairly equal proportions in Cuba, but also points to the legacy of Spanish colonialism by referring to the historical religious divide of (white Spanish) Christians and (black north African) Muslims."[119] The white rice–black bean mix obtained still another metaphorical designation in the late nineteenth century, when it was referred to as *voluntarios y bomberos*, alluding to white Spanish volunteers and black Cuban firemen. Yellow rice with no condiments other than the coloring was known as *"arroz en silencio."*[120] The familiar *piropo* "Si cocinas como caminas, me como hasta la raspa" made one point.

The vernacular of *cubanismos* is filled with colloquial allusions to rice as saws and sayings. The phrase *"arroz con mango"* is used to describe conditions in a state of confusion and chaos. *"Tener el arroz mucho macho"* conveys extreme jealousy. *"Ser algo arroz blanco con frijoles negro"* refers to something without importance. The idea of a worthless person can be conveyed through the phrase *"tener la personalidad de arroz con leche."* The phrase *"estar como el arroz blanco"* describes a person who appears to be everywhere, and *"ser como el arroz"* suggests plenty and abundance. *"Ser como el arroz Jon-Chí"* was a reference to a popular brand name of a rice known to expand greatly when cooked and hence denoted expansion and enlargement. *"Aquí quiriquí, arroz con ají"* is the children's refrain upon discovering someone up to mischief. *"Formarse un arroz con chorizo y tener que echarle garbanzos"* is used when confronting a problem requiring resolution.[121]

Rice insinuates itself into Cuban fiction, in short stories: Dora Alonso's "Arroz" and Vicente del Olmo's "Arroz a la cubana."[122] And in realms of popular music: the *contradanza* "El arroz" (ca. 1870s);[123] the *guaracha*, "Arroz con frijoles" (1882); Armando Rodríguez, "El saquito de arroz" (1907) and "Arroz con leche" (1921); Miguelito Valdés/Sonora Matancera, "Arroz con manteca" (1951); and the lyric of the Beny Moré/Pérez Prado mambo "Anabacoa" ("Arroz con picadillo, yucca / Arroz con picadillo, yuca").[124] *Arroz con leche* is also a children's song to accompany a game by the same name.[125] And rice insinuates itself into symbolic meaning and religious significance. The orishas of Cuban *santería* are known to have their favorite rice dishes: Babalú Ayé (*arroz con quimbombó*); Ogún (*congrí*); Ochosi (*arroz con pollo*); Orula (*arroz con camarones*); Oyá (*arroz con frijoles colorados*); Odúa (*arroz blanco*); Ochaoko (*arroz con vegetales*).[126]

AND YET...

For all the vaunted and indeed celebrated centrality of rice in *la cocina cubana*, it is remarkable indeed to learn that the obligatory dish of the national cuisine—"indispensable on every table"—has depended almost entirely on foreign imports. At no time since the end of the eighteenth century, and through the early twenty-first century, has Cuba attained self-sufficiency in rice production. Between 1945 and 1954, each Cuban consumed an annual average of 110 pounds, 90 pounds of which came from abroad.[127]

The anomaly, of course, has a proper history, having to do mostly with the purpose to which land was put and resources allocated, with the character of trade and commerce, with tariffs and taxes, with the interests of privilege, power, and property. And almost always it had something to do with sugar, a structural relationship of such compelling nature as to warrant a reworking of Fernando Ortiz's paradigm of *contrapunteo cubano*: it is not sugar and tobacco. It is sugar—and everything else. To confront the subject of rice in Cuba is to engage the problematic of sugar, for the history of rice is a facet of the history of sugar—if by other means.

No less anomalous has been the near absence of food production in Cuba as subject of historical scholarship. The "weight" of the historiography has long favored the study of export agriculture, principally sugar, of course, but also coffee and tobacco, that is, the history of agricultural commodities produced for foreign markets. So large does sugar production loom in the landscape of the Cuban political economy that it has been all but impossible for historians to resist the logic of the enduring "truth" that the history of Cuba is the history of sugar, implied in the adage that without sugar there is no country (*sin azúcar no hay país*).

It could hardly have been otherwise, of course. It is the received wisdom into which successive generations of historians have been socialized. Sugar early captured and has long held the historical imagination in its thrall. Sugar summons the attention of the historian to what appears to be a self-evident and self-confirming master narrative and thereupon yields a series of derivative subnarratives. It starts with sugar, from which lines of inquiry expand into multifaceted directions: to production modes and labor systems, and from there to slavery and race relations, land tenure and *latifundio*, to trade and commerce, investment, banking, and finance, much of which eventually converges into the complicated history of Cuba-U.S. relations.

These themes dominate much of the historiography of Cuba and possess several definable characteristics. The conventional—and prevailing—historiographical tradition has tended to privilege the study of international markets over local ones, to favor production over consumption, to prefer agriculture for foreign markets over agriculture for domestic markets, to favor wage labor over subsistence farming, to focus on the workplace rather than the domestic space.

Not adequately studied have been the circumstances of subsistence agriculture, the production of food, the ways agriculture met—or did not meet—the needs of the Cuban people. The subject of domestic agriculture systems from which Cubans obtained the necessities of daily life—food, simply put—has largely escaped the gaze of the historian. The basic staples of the Cuban diet— "articles of primary necessity" (*artículos de primera necesidad*)—including rice, to be sure, but also malangas, boniatos, yuca, plantains, corn, and beans, among other products, have been commonly designated, and not without significance, *frutos menores, cultivos menores, agricultura menor,* and *cultivos secundarios,* that is, "minor" products of lesser importance, as compared with sugar, tobacco, and coffee, understood presumptively as of "major" importance (*frutos mayores*).[128] The *cultivos menores* in Cuba, pronounced *Diario de la Marina* in 1922, "merely provide the sustenance of the poor . . . , products that serve to vary the menu of the poor in the interior of the island."[129] The history of the production of the basic staples of the diet of the overwhelming majority of the Cuban people, precisely those products that made up much of *la cocina cubana*, has been treated as a matter of lesser importance and in the process has overlooked the history of recurring scarcity of food.[130] In fact, hunger is a facet of the Cuban condition.

THIS BOOK SEEKS to redress the imbalance, to lift rice out of historiographical obscurity, to situate rice at the center of the very way to think about the Cuban past. To render rice as subject of historical inquiry is necessarily to raise corollary issues, for the study of rice in Cuba implies the need to interrogate the ways that global market forces insinuated themselves into the national system, thereupon to determine the patterns of everyday life of ordinary people across the island. Much has to do with sugar, of course, but with sugar not as an agriculture, exactly, but rather as a commodity hub into which the interests of transnational networks of power brokers converged; sugar as a source of prosperity, such as it was, of course, but also as a prosperity sustained at the expense of almost everything else. The plausibility of sugar depended increasingly upon access to U.S. markets, an access obtained through a Faustian bargain that could not but produce "collateral" consequences, routinely, as the cost necessary to protect sugar interests, to exchange tariff relief for Cuban sugar in U.S. markets for tariff advantage for U.S. imports in Cuban markets. The Foster-Cánovas Reciprocal Trade Agreement (1891), the Reciprocity Treaty (1903), the Reciprocity Treaty of 1934, and a score of lesser trade arrangements all through the late nineteenth century and the first half of the twentieth century served to open vast swaths of the Cuban economy to U.S. imports. Reciprocity served to privilege U.S. agricultural and manufactured imports over foreign competitors, certainly, but it also acted to arrest the development of domestic production, agricultural and nonagricultural alike.[131]

Sugar sustained Cuban good times, of course: as the principal source of foreign exchange, and the principal source of employment, and the principal source of national income. But the days of sugar good times were coming to an end by the mid-twentieth century. Cuba was emerging as a seller with fewer and fewer buyers. The Cuban share of the total world market of sugar had declined by half, from 20 percent during the 1920s to 10 percent by the 1950s. Informed observers could not but despair over the future of an economy dependent upon sugar exports in a global environment of expanding production, increasing competition, decreasing prices, and diminishing markets. All the more reason to cleave to U.S. markets, of course, but also all the more reason to contemplate new strategies of economic well-being, to diversify agriculture and to expand manufacturing, that is, to reduce dependency on sugar, as Cuban economists had advised and admonished since the nineteenth century.

The idea of diversification has a long and proper history, possessed of an incontrovertible logic. If sugar looms large in the Cuban experience, so most assuredly does the imperative of diversification, which underscores the gnawing awareness that something was not right—or better said, that something was wrong—about sugar. "We need to diversify the means of production," exhorted the Real Sociedad Económica de La Habana as early as 1849.[132] No one doubted this need.

Diversification was a complicated matter, of course. The argument for diversification seemed always to possess a commonsensical merit. But it was also an idea unable to escape the grip of the historical forces from which it derived its internal logic. Diversification—however compelling an economic project—seemed always to imply the disruption of a larger supply chain around which the export economy had formed: to displace, dislodge, or otherwise diminish the advantage of powerful interests, both Cuban and foreign. Through much of the first half of the twentieth century, the expansion of domestic food production could not be attained by any way other than at the expense of U.S. imports, and to challenge U.S. imports to Cuba was to threaten Cuban exports to the United States—sugar. An intractable Cuban dilemma indeed.

RICE OFFERS a microcosm of the complexities of the Cuban anomaly. The export economy formed around a structural dependency upon food imports, much of which originated from the United States. Commodities of vital importance and necessary consumption—*artículos de primera necesidad*—essential to the everyday diet and upon which the nutrition of tens of thousands of households across the island depended arrived on Cuban tables mostly in the form of foreign imports. All in all, an utterly incomprehensible state of affairs, of course: a people dedicated principally to agricultural production dependent upon agricultural imports. At some point in the nineteenth century, Cubans lost the capacity to feed themselves.

The history of rice in Cuba, as a matter of national production and popular consumption, as a facet of the political economy of commodity exchange, lays bare the structural tensions of the export economy. The logic of rice as the choice for diversification was self-evident indeed: a product central to a national cuisine and for which existed a national market. The expansion of rice production promised to generate employment in an environment of chronic underemployment and unemployment, and to arrest and reverse the loss of foreign exchange, and to achieve self-sufficiency in a staple vital for the Cuban diet.

Repeated efforts at diversification by way of rice production failed, even after auspicious beginnings. Supported with government subsidies and low-interest loans, and sustained with technical assistance and agricultural extension programs, the inauguration of rice programs were celebrated as model projects, designated as pilot programs to demonstrate the efficacy of agricultural diversification. The problem—for Cuba—was that import substitution implied the substitution of Cuban rice for American imports: any net gain of Cuban producers in the domestic market represented a net loss for American producers. American rice producers exercised near-complete control of Cuban markets, upon which U.S. rice interests depended for their very well-being. That the principal customer for Cuban sugar exports was also the principal supplier of Cuban rice imports meant that a threat to displace the latter would be met with a threat to reduce the former. U.S. rice producers had no better allies than Cuban sugar producers.

The chronicle of rice in Cuba is a history of a people confronting the consequences of an export economy almost 150 years in the making—and in the end failing. The forces set in motion early in the nineteenth century profoundly shaped the structural framework in which possibilities offered themselves as plausible outcomes—or not. It had to do with habit, with the capacity to imagine new paradigms and the will to execute new practices, to prevail over a combination of powerful forces summoned explicitly to defend interests deeply vested in the status quo. Change was not an easy matter, and indeed, on the matter of rice, little changed—not even after the far-reaching changes overtaking Cuba after 1959. Many decades after the triumph of the revolution, *la cocina cubana* continues to depend on imported rice.

CHAPTER ONE

Prosperity So Easily Obtained

To date, agricultural production has concentrated all its energy exclusively on two or three products, not essential to the well-being of the inhabitants [*no esenciales para la vida de los habitants*], consigning to [foreign] commerce responsibility to provide for the population all the innumerable objects indispensable for its existence.... The Island of Cuba does not even produce the most basic necessary products.—Ramón de la Sagra, *Cuba en 1860, o sea cuadro de sus adelantos en la poblacíon, la agricultura, el commercio y las rentas públicas* (1863)

All other agricultural production ... is in a state of backwardness because sugar has received most attention.—Félix Erénchun, *Anales de las isla de Cuba. Diccionardio administrative, economico, estadístico y legislative. Año de 1856* (1857)

Will the earnings of sugar and coffee always be adequate to defray the costs of our consumption? Will the increase in the costs of our consumption be sustained by the price that our products will bring?—"Consideraciones económico-políticas sobre la Isla de Cuba," *Anales de Ciencias, Agricultura, Comercio y Artes* (1827)

One of the misfortunes of prosperity so easily obtained [i.e., sugar] is that it is always accompanied with a lack of foresight.—María de las Mercedes Santa Cruz y Montalvo, *La Habana* (1844)

CUBA APPROACHED the end of the eighteenth century as something of an anomaly in the Caribbean: a self-contained economy situated at the periphery of a declining Spanish New World empire, at the margins of an expanding sugar prosperity that had transformed much of the economic demography of the West Indies but seemed to have passed Cuba by. Agriculture in Cuba tended to small-scale sugar production, some tobacco, and some ranching, interspersed with subsistence farming, mostly vegetable farms, generally adequate to meet the needs of a population of 272,000 inhabitants.[1] In comparison with other islands, Cuba had fewer sugar estates and smaller estates, modest sugar production and meager exports. Measuring 46,000 square miles in size—approximately the area of all the West Indies combined—Cuba accounted for a mere 3.2 percent of the total sugar produced in the Caribbean. The annual average sugar production in Cuba during the 1770s—10,000 tons—was surpassed by the tiny island of St. Christopher (68 square miles).[2]

Revolution in Saint-Domingue changed everything. The ensuing years of civil strife lay waste to what had been the most productive plantation colony in the Western Hemisphere. Production descended into disarray and eventually into demise. Sugar plantations passed into various states of ruination: harvests diminished, production decreased, exports declined, planters departed.

The downfall of sugar production in Saint-Domingue was a windfall for sugar producers in Cuba.[3] The law of supply and demand wrought its inexorable havoc on the world sugar markets: supplies dwindled, demand increased, prices soared—all in all, more than adequate incentive to motivate planters in Cuba to expand production.[4] It happened too that favorable market conditions coincided with the availability of new technologies, a coincidence of circumstances that enabled sugar production in Cuba to grow exponentially. The introduction of steam power increased the efficiency and capacity of sugar mills; greater efficiency in milling sugar revealed the need for greater quantities of sugar cane and inevitably the need to extend zones of cultivation and enlarge the acreage dedicated to sugar cane.[5] The introduction of the railroad enabled planters to penetrate deeper into the interior hinterland, to traverse larger expanses of land, at longer distances, at greater speed and wider zones of production: railroads to deliver capital imports of machines, equipment, and provisions; rail systems within the plantations to link larger fields to bigger mills; rail networks to connect mills to ports, many of which were themselves constructed to provide ready access to developing markets abroad, all tending to lower production costs and increased productivity in a highly competitive global environment.[6] "Thanks to the expansion of the railroads," commented the Círculo de Hacendados, "vast extensions of new lands [*grandes extensiones de terrenos nuevos*] have been planted with sugar cane and much land otherwise destined for the cultivation of food production has been converted to sugar cane fields [*cañaverales*]."[7]

The effects were stunning. By midcentury, sugar production accounted for 65 percent of all Cuban agricultural outputs.[8] The number of sugar mills almost doubled, from 529 in 1792 to 1,000 in 1827, and increased again to 1,442 in 1846 and to 2,400 mills by 1860.[9] The average per-mill output increased from 72 tons in 1830 to 120 tons in 1841 and more than doubled to 316 tons in 1860.

Production increases were no less dramatic: 17,000 tons of sugar in 1791 more than doubled to 37,000 tons in 1810 and nearly doubled again to 60,000 tons in 1823, thereafter to swell to 165,000 tons in 1836, 223,000 tons in 1850, 726,000 tons in 1870, and 976,000 tons in 1892. By midcentury the island had emerged as the single largest source of the world supply of sugar, increasing from 18 percent (223,000 tons out of a world supply of 1.2 million tons) in 1850 to 26 percent (447,000 tons out of 1.7 million tons) in 1860 to 31 percent (575,000 tons out of 1.8 million tons) in 1864.[10]

THERE WAS SOMETHING of an inexorable tenacity about the way that sugar established its grip in Cuba: it seized hold and held sway, extending its command over almost all facets of agricultural production and shaping the very logic of the economy at large. Vast expanses of land—farms, fields, and forests—were plowed under in preparation for sugar.[11] Land passed into sugar production at an accelerated pace: an estimated 1,700 acres annually in the 1790s, to 3,500 acres by the 1810s, reaching 13,000 acres by the 1840s.

The expansion of sugar signaled a shift of the balance of life from maintenance of the many toward profits for the few. Sugar overran established agricultural zones and overturned old land tenure forms, dislodging small commercial farmers and displacing subsistence farms (*fincas de cultivo*). The conversion of tobacco farms (*vegas*) in the jurisdiction of Güines in Havana province began as early as 1797, resulting in what Intendant Rafael Gómez Roubaud characterized in 1807 as the "expulsion virtually by force [*arrancando casi de por fuerza*] of the poor workers of the fields and *vegas* previously dedicated to tobacco."[12] At the other end of the island, in the region of between Manzanillo and Bayamo, Miguel Rodríguez gave account of many local farmers engaged in the production of beeswax, rice, and "all the other fruits of the country" who were "abandoning their fields and homes, expelled by the landowners [*espulsados por los dueños de los terrenos*] and suffering abuses at every step of the way."[13]

The expansion of sugar had other consequences no less baneful. The cost of almost all facets of agricultural production increased and further exacerbated the circumstances of small producers. A yoke of oxen (*yunta de bueyes*) costing 70 pesos in 1790 had risen to 120 pesos by 1807.[14] The value of land also increased. Land in the province of Havana selling between 600 and 850 pesos per *caballería* [1 *caballería* = 33.3 acres] during the 1760s–80s increased to as much as 1,700 pesos by the end of the 1790s. Land values in the province of Matanzas also increased during the early decades of the nineteenth century, from 250 pesos per *caballería* to 2,500 pesos per *caballería*. In Güines, land valued at 100 pesos per *caballería* increased to 2,000 pesos in less than fifteen years.[15]

Farmers dispersed into the interior hinterland, there to face problems of other kinds, including the absence of adequate interior roads and diminished access to local markets. The Lonja Mercantil de La Habana complained as early as 1800 about "the lack of canals, bridges, and roads to enable travel and reduce the cost of haulage and transportation.... Without the means to facilitate sales and allow for the movement of surplus agriculture, there is no commerce, no communication, no culture.... It is painful to acknowledge that as a result of this condition commerce between one part of the island with another is unknown."[16] Transportation expanded—principally railroads—to service the needs of sugar production "due to its important public value," Spanish authorities acknowledged, noting, "The majority of the railroads have been conceived not with idle speculation but principally to create the means to provide support for the development of the sugar estates, specifically to facilitate and reduce the cost of transportation from the sugar mills to the ports."[17]

Otherwise, internal transportation received little attention. Roads languished in execrable conditions, in various states of disrepair and deterioration—"mere tracks or gullies worn free of soil by the rains," observed Robert Francis Jameson during his travels in Cuba in 1820, "traversing the naked rock and partaking of all its ruggedness."[18] Without adequate roads, farmers lacked the ability to move their products to local markets. "The difficulties of communication," María de las Mercedes Santa Cruz y Montalvo observed in 1844, "the poor condition of the road, the distances between the villages and the cities, and the scarcity of population in relation to the territory all serve to deny the farmer of the means necessary to sell his crops."[19] In 1849, farmers in Pinar del Río complained of "not having the slightest way of getting corn, rice, fruits, and vegetables to market. So too with all types of timber, notwithstanding that the plains are rich with pine and the extensive mountain ranges are filled with ebony, granadillo, mahogany, cedar, and walnut."[20] The agriculture that did reach local markets often arrived in poor condition, damaged in transport, often bearing signs of spoilage occurring en route, and almost always offered at high prices. "The vegetables and roots sold here are very expensive," observes the narrator in Virginia Felicia Auber's novel *Ambarina*, "and lack good quality, largely because they are haphazardly cultivated, nor are they harvested in a timely fashion, nor does the farmer concern himself with tending to the care of the field after the initial planting."[21] Poor roads that reduced access to local markets also reduced incentives to expand production. Hardship begat hard times, with no prospects of relief and no promise of remedy. "If only Cuba had roads," José Antonio Saco lamented in 1846, "how different the fate of the farmer would be!"[22] Economist Ramón de la Sagra provided a sober assessment of the adversity that had befallen Cuban agriculture early in the nineteenth century:

> One serious obstacle [*un gravísimo obstáculo*] to the development of agriculture on the island is due to the scarcity of roads and the deplorable condition of the roads that do exist. Many landowners have ceased to cultivate rice, corn, and other fruits and vegetables on their farms because the excessive costs associated with the transit served to raise the price to such an extent as to make it impossible to sell their products profitably in the market. The transportation of commercial fruits and vegetables, whether in oxen-carts [*carretas*] or on the back of pack animals, in some regions of the island and during some seasons of the year, involve costs so exorbitant that would appear to be incredible in Europe. . . . Some fruits and vegetables of great volume but of modest value paid transportation costs higher than they were worth.[23]

The archives of the Junta de Fomento, charged with responsibility to promote economic development, are thick with protests and petitions denouncing chronic problems of inadequate roads and insufficient transportation.[24]

SMALL FARMERS PRACTICED a precarious agriculture, tending to peripheral parcels of land, engaged in marginal production to meet subsistence needs.[25] Conditions in the jurisdiction of Trinidad at midcentury had become commonplace almost everywhere sugar had expanded. "I believe it impossible for the country to make rapid progress in prosperity," *fiscal* (government attorney) Francisco Letamendi reported in 1840, "especially in regard with the population of whites, for the existing wealth is connected to the owners of the *ingenio* [sugar mill]. Having fixed the boundaries on all the land, they have created a fiefdom out of the entire jurisdiction." Letamendi warned, "Thus it can be said that there is no agriculture other than that of those estates, where only what is necessary for the owners is planted, and since they are the ones who determine what is planted they do not leave the poor with any recourse, no matter how industrious they may be. They do not rent even 3 inches [*un palmo*] of land, so that the people are left with a great need for land."[26] Twenty years later, Ramón de la Sagra traveled through the same region of Cienfuegos-Trinidad. Nothing seems to have changed. "Unfortunately," Sagra observed, "the cultivation of sugar cane has displaced almost everything else, and poor families lack the land upon which to produce crops on small farms. Likewise, the price of the local subsistence vegetables, which could be produced abundantly and with such ease, has increased markedly."[27]

Almost everywhere production for export increased, production for consumption decreased, all in plain view, and all with consequences no less plainly visible—"the abandonment of the necessary to promote the expedient [*el abandono de lo necesario por fomentar la útil*]," protested Diego José de Sedano as early as 1812.[28] Production of the staples of the Cuban diet, characterized variously as *frutos menores, cultivos menores, agricultura menor, pequeños cultivos, producciones menores*, and *agricultura de subsistencia*, deemed to be "lesser crops"—principally rice, beans, chickpeas, corn, plantains, and root vegetables (*viandas*), including yuca, ñame, boniatos, and malanga—faltered and floundered, disclosing a diminished diversity of agricultural production and signaling a declining capacity for agricultural self-sufficiency. The production of corn all but collapsed, falling from 324 million pounds in 1827 to 17 million pounds in 1846. *Viandas* declined from 733 million pounds to 520 million pounds.[29] By 1862, the combined value of all *frutos menores* represented only 22 percent of the total agricultural production.[30] The expansion of sugar, journalist José María de Andueza decried in 1841, "which constitutes the principal wealth of the country, has resulted in the spurning of other lines of agriculture which are of the greatest importance to meet the most urgent needs of the population. And with consequences: for planters to base their wealth exclusively on the colossal products of sugar and coffee, upon which without doubt they owe their prosperity, they neglect that eternal spring [*eterno primavera*] in which nature produces without need for human labor its abundant produce."[31] Economist Fermín Figuera was forthright in his denunciation of the expansion of the sugar plantation as an "ill-conceived organization of property . . . that [has] neglected the cultivation of corn, rice, and vegetables and what in general is designated as *frutos menores* and dedicated itself solely to the production of sugar."[32]

Unrest roiled among the producing classes, between producers for export, on one hand, and producers for consumption, on the other; between proponents of specialization and promoters of diversification; between defenders of small farms and advocates of large plantations. "Our [large] landowners," Gaspar Betancourt Cisneros wrote in 1838 of the great cattle haciendas of Camagüey, but not without implications for the sugar estates, "are like all monopolists [*monopolistas*], defenders of those legislative systems and customs that serve their inflated pretensions, and detractors of everything that restricts them. Thus we see in the possession of a single man two or three thousand *caballerías* of land when there are two or three thousand men without any land. We should aspire that all men be landowners, for this is most assuredly the best guarantee of social order. A society in which are found one thousand landowners lives with greater tranquility than the society with one hundred landowners and nine hundred workers."[33]

THERE WAS NOTHING complicated about these developments, of course: simple cost-benefit analysis revealed some obvious truths. Land was far too valuable and profits on export production far too high to tend to agricultural production for local consumption.[34] "Given that the tobacco farms, coffee estates, and sugar mills yield far more profits than the orchards and small farms," observed the narrator in the novel *Ambarina*, "almost everyone prefers to cultivate the former, while the latter is relegated to producers who lack sufficient capital and adequate labor."[35] Capital was drawn to high-return profits associated with export commodities, to the virtual neglect of everything else.[36]

Soaring land values also implied the need to develop production strategies in which earnings were commensurate with expenditures.[37] Landowners—large and small—could hardly gainsay the market logic of high-profit crops for foreign consumers at the expense of low-profit production for domestic consumption. Indeed, it was far more efficient (and hence practical) and far more cost-effective (and hence profitable) to rely on food imports for domestic markets rather than sacrifice sugar exports for foreign markets. "The extraordinary prosperity of sugar and coffee," the Real Sociedad Patriótica de La Habana acknowledged in 1830, "resulted in the neglect of the cultivation of some *cultivos menores*, creating a need that the foreigners hastened to fill, for the farmer exerting the same amount of work and deploying the same amount of capital in order to produce one arroba [1 arroba = 25 pounds] of sugar or of coffee, or one barrel of molasses, obtained the same earnings as cultivating six or eight arrobas of those grains. The farmer thus preferred to buy the products from foreigners rather than dedicate himself to its cultivation."[38] The Real Junta de Fomento offered a simple calculus to confirm the logic of export production: "If the North American market offered us $3,000 for rice produced on one *caballería* as it does for one *caballería* of tobacco, it would not make sense to produce the latter instead of the former. But since the value of rice is two-thirds less, it is cost effective to produce tobacco and import rice."[39] The production of foodstuffs, commented John Glanville Taylor—himself a planter—was "almost entirely neglected by the sugar planters, who, in their haste to become great sugar producers, obtain their supplies of corn and provisions from the United States and South America."[40]

SUGAR CHANGED THE WAYS Cubans thought about the world—and about themselves. These were prosperous times in Cuba, a time of vast profits and the amassing of great fortunes, not a time for indecision and certainly not a time to call into question the logic of sugar. Almost everything was subordinated to the priority of sugar production: nothing seemed to matter more or matter more immediately than sugar. The trajectory of the export economy was established early, historian Manuel Moreno Fraginals correctly noted, and to "an extraordinary extent" resulted in the "abandonment of all that did not have something to do with sugar, directly or indirectly."[41] Who could possibly lament the displacement of *frutos menores* and the decline of rice, wheat, vanilla, cotton, and "other types of necessities," bristled the *Anales de Ciencias, Agricultura, Comercio y Artes* in 1829. "In view of the vast and rapid fortunes offered by the production of and commerce in sugar, who would want to waste their time cultivating puffs of cotton?"[42]

Sugar production assumed a momentum of its own, within the self-evident truths of an inner-driven purpose sustained by expansion and more expansion: expanded cultivation and expanded production, expanded exports in function of expanding markets—Cubans "producing to provide others," observed Gaspar Betancourt Cisneros[43]—and at the expense of providing for themselves. To provide for themselves, Cubans also turned to others.

Production strategies were fixed early around the logic of an export economy, to produce for foreign markets and consume foreign products. Cuba had consigned its fate to foreign commerce, Ramón de la Sagra brooded at midcentury. "For some time now," Sagra accurately summarized the prevailing economic wisdom of the nineteenth century,

> the agriculture of the island has taken a vicious direction [*una dirección viciosa*] which, together with circumstances of commerce, has displaced from [Cuban] fields a great number of crops not only appropriate for the nature of the land and climate, but necessary for the subsistence of the inhabitants. In general, preference was given to dependency on foreign commerce for a great number of important products that could have been produced with extreme abundance in the interior of the island. To such an extent that other than the great products destined for export,

cultivation has concentrated only on some crops that were impossible to locate abroad.[44]

Ominous portents indeed. "Three-quarters of the island are under-populated and idle [*despoblados y sin cultivo*]," warned the Real Sociedad Patriótica de La Habana in 1837; "we are a new country and weak. It is necessary to strengthen it with the products of the land, which are the only sources of well-being, from which we derive all that is necessary for our existence and progress. We do not have any other type of industry. To permit the free entry of the only thing we can produce . . . would be to destroy us completely."[45]

The imperative of sugar reached deeply into almost all facets of the colonial political economy. A dense network of mutually reinforcing policies and practices—interlocking, interacting, and interdependent—was ordered and arranged to accommodate the needs of production for export, thereupon to shape the purpose to which the Cuban economy would be given. Sugar not only lay claim to the purpose of the land and the purpose of production; it also lay claim to the purpose of public policy. It could hardly have been otherwise, of course. The solvency of colonial administration was deeply implicated in the success of production for export. Revenues produced by sugar exports filled the coffers of an appreciative royal exchequer, who henceforth would act with uncommon solicitude in behalf of sugar interests. Production for export accounted for the principal source of foreign exchange and the primary source of public revenues, upon which the well-being of almost everything else depended. Sugar products accounted for 60 percent of Cuban exports earnings in 1840 (12.8 million pesos out of 21.3 million) and increased to almost 75 percent by 1860.[46] The needs of production for export served to inform the very raison d'être of public administration, thereupon to influence almost all decisions bearing on the conduct and content of foreign trade: determining schedules of taxes, tariffs, and customs duties; guiding fiscal planning; and influencing budget priorities— sometimes more, sometimes less, to be sure, depending on the circumstances, but almost always as the overriding consideration to which decisions of colonial administration were subject. "We assign a preferential attention [*una preferente atención*] to everything related to our sugar industry," affirmed the Junta General del Comercio of Havana, "which is preeminent among all that contributes to the general wealth of Cuba, and which is indisputably fundamental to all that makes for Cuban prosperity."[47]

The expansion of sugar production had one other consequence. Even as sugar displaced agriculture for domestic consumption, it also and at the same time contributed to increased demand for foodstuffs to sustain the vast labor force enslaved to produce sugar. A population of 272,000 in 1792 more than doubled to 553,000 in 1817 and almost doubled again to 1 million by 1841.[48] Almost half of the enlarged population consisted of enslaved Africans (436,500 out of 1 million), to which was added at midcentury tens of thousands of indentured Chinese contract workers, upon whose labor the solvency of the export economy—and almost everything else—depended, all of whom had to be fed. "With the massive importation of slaves," Leví Marrero wrote, "the hacendados would find ways with which to provide food, avoiding even for brief periods of time the allocation of slave labor to the cultivation of food supplies, for to take time away from the purpose for which the new plantations were organized was considered uneconomical. Thus, the practice of importing jerked beef tasajo, codfish, and rice to feed the slave labor force was established early."[49]

The need for food imports thus expanded as a corollary condition of the expansion of the export economy. Codfish imports, a staple of the slave diet, increased from 11.8 million pounds in 1844 to 13.6 million in 1845 and to 14.1 million in 1846.[50] Foreign flour imports, almost entirely North American in origin, increased from 6,700 barrels in 1846 to 43,500 barrels in 1847, with a slight decrease of imports of Spanish flour, from 128,900 barrels to 125,000 barrels.[51] "The cereals of the United States," John Thrasher wrote in his edited volume of Alexander von Humboldt's *The Island of Cuba* (1856), "have become a real necessity, under a zone where for a long time, maize, yuca, and the plantain were preferred to any other kind of food," adding,

> We find, in 1816, a million, and in 1823, three and a half million dollars in [imported] *salted meats, rice,* and *dried pulse*. During the last named year, the importation of rice (in Havana alone, and by the custom-house returns, exclusive of contraband), has been 8,075,000 pounds (in 1852, in all of the island, 20,940,925 pounds), that of salted and dried meats, the tasajo (jerked beef), so necessary for the support of the slaves, 11,625,000 pounds (in all the island, 41,750,450 pounds). This absence of the means of subsistence characterizes that part of the tropical regions where the unwise activity of the European has inverted the order of nature.[52]

Sugar production expanded within the logic of foreign commerce, of course, trade an indispensable factor of Cuban well-being. But it was more complicated. The export economy was celebrated within an emerging cultural paradigm around which the cosmology of Cuban was taking form, thereupon to corroborate a swelling sense of self-importance. Sugar had lifted Cuba into realms of modernity and into the heady swirl of the global economy, providing Cubans with entrée into the company of the most advanced capitalist nations of the world—Cubans exulted—to register a presence in transnational commercial networks. The *Revista de La Habana* was rhapsodic over the expansion of foreign trade, "which has placed Cuba in a relationship with all the nations of the World. Its ports have filled with the ships of the commercial nations of the Americas and Europe, and through them the light of civilization was diffused across the entire island."[53] Among the most influential economic thinkers of his generation—and planter— Francisco de Arango y Parreño celebrated the virtue of production for export precisely for enabling Cuba to escape the bane of a self-contained "closed" subsistence economy and to engage the market economies of the world at large. "The agricultural products known on this Island by the name of *frutos menores*," Arango y Parreño scoffed, "do not warrant the importance possessed by other products.... To some it may appear illogical that part of the rice and other foodstuffs that this city [Havana] consumes are imported from abroad.... It is commonly held to be neglect or error of our economy." But no, Arango y Parreño insisted, on the contrary; the Cuban economy possessed all attributes of progress and modernity, evidence of the Cuban presence and participation in the expanding world economy:

> The civilized man, or at least contemporary man in the Americas and Europe, subject always by custom to so many different needs, cannot either through his own work or collectively with his fellow countrymen, satisfy all of them. He must always depend on something [*depender en algo*], or better said, depend on other countries and nations.... This is in general a great truth, all the more so for people precisely like those of this Island, simple farmers [*simplemente agricultores*] who live, as a result, dependent on others for everythin g that has to do with industry and an infinite number of goods and products that in the aggregate makes for human necessities. Without question priority is given to the production of commodities other than rice and other foodstuff that we can receive from other parts because it is so cost effective.[54]

Foreign trade conferred status and standing, economist Alvaro Reynoso agreed, a way for Cuba to claim membership within the community of advanced nations of the world. "A country that produces everything it needs," Reynoso warned,

> will naturally suffer in its relations with other peoples, for not needing anything from the foreigner ... [it] will find itself in a state of isolation from the rest of the world.... From the most remote times of antiquity, the importance of commerce has been recognized as a bond among

nations which has determined the advanced cosmopolitanism of a people. Every nation should seek always to expand to the fullest its foreign relations, [and] thereby not only attain maximum benefit for its production and expand the sum total of its wealth, but also effectively contribute to the wealth of other nations.[55]

Foreign commerce was an indisputable necessity, Manuel Costales pronounced: "In a country like ours that has little or no industry, agriculture cannot be considered independent of or separate from commerce, for trade is the sure and certain means to our wealth and well-being, given that the agricultural products can neither be consumed on the island nor can they create sufficient industry to meet the needs of the people."[56]

SPANISH AUTHORITIES acquiesced to the logic of foreign trade early. The enactment of free trade regulations in 1818 opened Cuban ports to international commerce, not exactly without tariff fees and customs differentials, to be sure, but sufficiently "free" to integrate the island into an expanding network of international trade. Free trade, the *Revista de La Habana* exulted at midcentury, "has been one of those memorable achievements in the history of Cuba, second only to its discovery."[57]

Foreign commerce increased in value and expanded in volume all through the nineteenth century, from a total of $18 million in 1792, to $31 million in 1827, to $51 million in 1842, and almost doubling to $97 million in 1862. These totals included increases from $11 million in imports and $7 million in exports in 1792, to $17 million imports and $14 million exports in 1827, to $25 million in imports and $26 million in exports in 1842, to $41 million in imports and $56 million in exports in 1862.[58]

Foodstuffs made up an ever-increasing portion of Cuban imports and indeed served as strategic exchange commodities through which to transact the logic of an expanding foreign trade, thereupon to confirm the efficacy of commerce based on specialization of production. "In an underpopulated country [*un país despoblado*] like ours, that lives and prospers solely by way of foreign trade, it is necessary to take measure of production not by what we consume but by what we can offer other countries," insisted the Real Sociedad Económica de La Habana in 1849. "We would not for the time being wish to see the development in our country of any product of the type that enters our port in abundance, those products used to buy from us sugar, molasses, coffee, and tobacco. We are opposed to the cultivation of wheat to produce flour. We are opposed to our production of all the rice, lard, and corn we may need, despite the fact that these are considered products of primary necessity." The Real Sociedad continued:

> Even if we could produce these products in abundance, the high cost of protection required during the initial phases [of production] would result in the stagnation of the industries that constitute the principal sources of our wealth, thereby depriving us of the merchandise with which to engage in trade and commerce. We need many more centuries of existence as a country, we need to diversify the means of production, and we need to increase the size of the population in proportion to the size of the island before we can begin to think about supplying ourselves.[59]

The proximity of the United States made strategies of production for export and consumption of imports eminently plausible. The logic seemed incontrovertible. The United States could meet Cuban capital needs and consumer demands from a short distance in a short period of time and with lower transportation costs. Increasingly the United States absorbed the larger portion of Cuban sugar exports: 36 percent of total sugar exports in 1820 increased to 43 percent in 1850 and increased again to 60 percent by 1870.[60] Increasingly too Cuba developed dependency upon food imports from the United States. "The vast bulk of imports from the Anglo-Americans consists of rice, corn, and other foodstuffs," commented the daily *Diario de la Marina* at midcentury. "Due to its proximity, this is the nation that provides us with those products when our own production fails to meet domestic demand."[61]

Foodstuffs poured into Cuba and piled high on wharves and piers across the island, representing an expanding portion of total imports. Economist José Quintín Suzarte calculated that between 1870 and 1880, imports totaled approximately 300 million pesos, of which foodstuffs [*artículos de alimentación*] accounted for 200 million pesos.[62] The basic staples of the local diet reached Cuban tables in the form of foreign food imports: codfish (*bacalao*), flour, ham, cheese, onions, potatoes, bacon, lard, and rice from the United States; jerked beef (tasajo) from Argentina and Uruguay; beans, chickpeas, and wine from Spain.[63] Docks swarmed with workers hauling and hoisting, loading and unloading, packing and unpacking: activities, Gilbert Haven observed in 1875, conducted "ceaselessly ... the busy unloading of bales and barrels of Northern fields and mills."[64] Spaniard Manuel Fernández Juncos could hardly contain his awe at the "vast confusion on the wharves due to the presence of voluminous objects such as crates, casks, barrels, great piles of dried meat."[65] John Wurdemann walked among the crowded Havana docks in 1844 and observed the enormous quantities of shipments of foodstuffs arriving in Cuba. "After breakfast," Wurdemann recorded in his travel memoir, "I strolled along the extensive quay, to which all the vessels are moored bows on.... It was so covered with bales of merchandise, barrels and boxes of produce, heaps of not very fragrant dried beef, of cheese, garlic, hides, lard, etc., and was so crowded with negro laborers engaged in loading and unloading the vessels, custom-house officers, and merchants' clerks, that it was almost impassable." Visiting the port of Matanzas, Wurdemann noted that shipments were "chiefly confined to articles of food," with merchants engaged in a brisk trade "of rice, cheese, tasajo, or flour for sale."[66]

Few indeed were the number of foreign visitors who failed to take note of Cuban dependency on imports of foodstuffs. "The quantity of soft goods sold in Cuba...," commented Richard Madden in 1849, "in proportion to the population, far exceeds the sales made in any other country. All the flour, rice, lard, salt fish, salt beef (tassajo [sic]), oil and wine, cheese and butter, come from abroad. Those foreign commodities consumed in Cuba amount in value ... to seventy-nine dollars for each individual."[67] Visiting French writer Xavier Marmier similarly took note of Cuban "dependency upon those so-called civilized countries for its supplies of primary necessities, including rice, codfish, lard, and flour."[68] James Steele arrived at the same conclusion thirty years later: "When you sit down to a meal you are surprised that all the essentials are of foreign production."[69] The *Anales de Ciencias, Agricultura, Comercio y Artes* estimated as early as 1831 that each inhabitant of Cuba consumed annually four times as much foreign foodstuffs as the North American.[70] "No country in the world perhaps," commented the U.S. consul in Matanzas in 1880, "is so entirely dependent for the needs of its daily life on other lands as this rich fertile and tropical Island."[71]

NOTHING PERHAPS SET the anomaly of the emerging export economy in sharper relief than Cuban dependency on rice imports. By the mid-nineteenth century, domestic rice production had dwindled to a near-insignificant portion of total agricultural wealth, representing barely more than 1 percent of the total value of agricultural production (521,000 pesos out of 41 million pesos) and accounting for a mere 7 percent of the total acreage given to agricultural production.[72] A sobering realization indeed in 1858 when José Antonio Saco pronounced that rice had "ceased to figure among the principal agricultural products of Cuba."[73]

The demise of rice was not atypical of the larger decline of food production attending the expansion of sugar, of course. But rice was different. It occupied a special place on the Cuban kitchen table. Rice was deemed to be the indispensable food, the principal staple of the popular diet across the island, in almost all households, among Cubans of means and Cubans of modest origins. "Rice on this island, a product of general consumption," *Diario de la Marina* commented at midcentury, "could be said to be of greater necessity to our population than bread."[74]

No one disagreed. "There is hardly a table in Cuba that does not serve rice daily," Antonio Bachiller y Morales affirmed in 1856;[75] "indispensable on every table," insisted José García de Arboleya in 1859;[76] a staple, Jacobo de la Pezuela offered seven years later, that "has for a long time constituted one of the principal and most prevalent sources of nutrition of the population."[77] "The favorite dish of the Cubans [*el plato favorito de los cubanos*]," pronounced economist Miguel Escalada; "rice is for the Cuban what wheat is for the Spaniard and corn for the Mexican."[78] "An absolute necessity is rice," James Steele noted in 1881 during his travels to Cuba, adding, "At a Christmas-eve supper, eaten at twelve o'clock at night, the company will regard but indifferently the sliced ham, boned turkey, and cold confections, if the huge dish of boiled rice is not there to accompany them."[79]

The demise of rice production, hence, was a source of chagrin and bewilderment for many. "Rice is fundamental to all the meals in Havana," María de las Mercedes de Santa Cruz y Montalvo remarked with incredulity, "but yet we are obliged to turn to our neighbors of the North for our supplies.... Does it not appear as a deplorable condition that one needs to seek abroad a product of primary necessity, a product that Nature has so generously enabled us to produce?"[80] How utterly incomprehensible indeed: "We have said often, and we repeat," *Diario de la Marina* decried in 1845, "that the land and the climate are excellent for the cultivation of rice," and to the point:

> Hence we cannot look upon our state of dependency [on foreigners] in which we find ourselves with anything less than pained puzzlement, when in fact our fields are perhaps fully capable of supplying rice to other countries. And why is it that we cannot cultivate rice sufficient even for the needs of the population of this island? This is a question ... of primary interest to the country and should concern all who care about the prosperity of Cuba.... Land to dedicate to rice exists in abundance; there is no lack of labor; and surely our wise government would provide the needed protection and stimulation.[81]

That rice imports signified the loss of foreign exchange, moreover, served to add insult to injury, and to add too one more factor to irk Cuban sensibilities:

a wholly irrational element to an illogical condition. "Anyone who knows the suitability of the land and climate of Cuba for the planting of rice . . . ," agronomist Francisco Javier Balmaseda insisted, "[knows] that instead of being an exporter of this grain it is an importer, and that year after year it invests enormous sums of money in providing itself with a product that it should have in abundance."[82] Given the importance of "a product of primary necessity for our diet," *Diario de la Marina* protested, "it is baffling that the island pays enormous sums of money to foreign nations for rice imports, a sum that surpassed 935,950 pesos in 1843."[83] The newspaper was categorical:

> We consider the cultivation of rice to be a matter of the greatest urgency. It is a staple of the diet of the poor as well as the rich, and is without doubt one of the most widely consumed products on the island. When the fertility of this land lends itself so admirably to its production, it appears strange to us that farmers neglect to expand its production, not only to free us from the loss of foreign exchange [*tributo que pagamos al esterior*] but also because it is a matter of compelling interest to produce at home those articles of primary necessity, especially when it can be done with clear advantage over competitors. It is for that reason that we never missed an opportunity to insist on the advisability of expanding the production of rice.[84]

"There are some intelligent men in the island," Robert Jameson learned during his travels to Cuba as early as 1820, "not insensible to the advantage that would accrue from the enlarged cultivation of these necessaries of life, and the retention of above two million dollars annually that are paid for them."[85] Indeed, what made dependency on rice imports especially irksome was the widely held conviction that Cuba possessed the conditions and the capacity to produce sufficient rice to meet domestic demand—and "even produce [rice] in such quantities as to serve as an export commodity," *Diario de la Marina* insisted. How was it possible that "rice would be produced in such pitiful quantities as to require imports not only from the United States and from Spain [*la Madre Patria*], but from places as far away as Asia, rice that reaches us only after a long journey of nearly half a year"?[86] Given the "fertility and fecundity" and "the superiority of the quality of the land," agronomist José Labadía argued, Cuba was "capable of producing three times the amount of rice that is consumed in all of Cuba, and it could be a new fountain of wealth as it is for the southern part of the United States. . . . Even the most impoverished farmer with little work of planting and fertilizing can obtain a secure livelihood."[87] No country more than Cuba, insisted the Havana daily *El Siglo*, "is blessed with as favorable conditions to eradicate misery, to expand well-being, to extend education, and to ratify the kingdom of abundance [*el reinado de la abundancia*] in culture and in social refinement."[88] Economist Miguel Escalada was lucid in his analysis of the larger implications, emphasizing that "it is well known that consumption induces us to the cultivation of those articles and grains of urgent necessity [*imperiosa necesidad*], not only to develop our industry and internal and foreign commerce, but also to guarantee our subsistence and not to depend upon the foreigner for a product of such essential importance to our well-being."[89]

But the neglect of rice production was only in part an issue of markets and agriculture. Lacking too was the capital necessary to underwrite technology. It was all interrelated, of course. Farmers milled rice under primitive conditions, using inefficient methods and dependent on obsolete equipment: an archaic hand-pounding process with pestle and mortar, typically a wooden mallet within a hollowed-out log. The Real Sociedad Patriótica de La Habana lamented the "inefficient methods,"[90] a lack of machinery, *Diario de Matanzas* insisted in 1830, that required "milling to be done by hand [*a fuerza de brazos*]."[91] "They use a large wooden mortar made out of the trunk of a tree," observed one midcentury traveler to Cuba, "where the rice is put and pounded by a man with a heavy pestle, with much trouble and a slowness that is easy to imagine"[92]—what agronomist Francisco Javier Balmaseda mocked as practices "reminiscent of primitive times, or better said, exactly what is used today among the savage peoples of Pacific islands."[93] The "small farmers to whom [rice] has been relegated," commented María de las Mercedes de Santa Cruz y Montalvo at midcentury, "have been unable to secure the milling machinery necessary for the hulling of rice and have been obliged to substitute in its place manual labor, which often results in breakage of the grain, tires the worker, and adds higher cost to the product."[94]

Inefficient milling methods affected more than the quantity of domestic rice production; they also affected the quality. Backward milling practices produced rice deemed to be of inferior quality, most commonly described as "dirty" and broken. Consumption of domestic rice was associated with Cubans of modest means—rural families and the urban poor. Cuban milling methods failed to produce sufficiently unbroken white rice to satisfy consumer preferences. The Junta de Fomento decried the lack of "adequate machinery," resulting in "producers contenting themselves with imperfect conventional methods, with significant detriment to the quality of the grain."[95] "The method generally used to hull rice in a wooden mortar," complained the *Anales de Ciencias, Agricultura, Comercio y Artes* in 1831, "results in too many broken and scorched grains."[96] The inferiority of domestic rice, *Diario de la Marina* remarked ruefully, was the

Advertisement for a rice mill to improve "the imperfect way in which rice is prepared on this Island" (*Diario de la Marina*, February 25, 1868).

result of "the carelessness with which rice is hulled, the variety of rice that is produced in our fields, and the absolute lack [*la carencia absoluta*] of machinery capable of producing a grain as clean and as white as that which comes to us from abroad and which places the rice of this Island in a highly disadvantaged competitive position in our market."[97] In 1894, Faustino López in Pinar del Río purchased a modern rice mill valued at $5,000, capable of hulling almost 1,000 pounds of rice daily, said to have been "so white, so beautiful, so clean: just like the best rice imported from the United States."[98] Within eighteen months, though, the fields and farms of Pinar del Río were laid waste in the war for independence.

WITHOUT THE CAPACITY TO expand production (land), without the means to access domestic markets (transportation), without adequate milling equipment (technology)—without, in sum, the interested support of colonial administration—rice production languished and failed to develop into an agriculture of value, notwithstanding its recognized importance as a staple of "urgent necessity." "Small farmers needed more than land," historian Susan Fernández correctly noted. "They needed lower interest rates for operating capital; they needed technical assistance and transportation infrastructure that could link them to each other and to markets for processing and sales of raw materials; they needed the development of processing and packaging centers able to access investment capital to support food security."[99]

Domestic demand exceeded domestic supply, and the expanding deficit between demand and supply set in motion a circular—and fateful—sequence of cause-and-effect relationships. The inability of Cuban farmers to meet domestic demand opened the Cuban market to foreign rice imports, which competed with domestic producers. Rice imports developed into a key commodity staple of Cuban foreign commerce exchange, averaging 571,000 arrobas annually between 1826 and 1830.[100] Imports increased from 590,000 arrobas in 1835, to 649,000 arrobas in 1842, to 894,000 arrobas in 1847.[101] Domestic consumption of rice in 1827 was recorded at 1.1 million arrobas—almost twice the amount produced on the island—and was met through 520,900 arrobas of domestic production and 590,800 arrobas of foreign imports.[102]

Rice imports originated from Valencia, Manila, and Campeche, but the most highly prized and the greatest quantity of rice arrived from the United States, principally from South Carolina and Georgia, out of the ports of Charleston and Savannah. Cuban dependency on the United States for its rice imports was almost total. More than 95 percent of the total volume of imported rice in 1843 (590,000 arrobas out of a total of 619,600) and more than 80 percent of total rice imports in 1847 (720,000 arrobas out of a total of 894,000) originated from the United States.[103] U.S. rice accounted for almost 75 percent of the total value of 1852 supplies, an estimated $811,000 out of a total value of $1.1 million.[104] The total value of U.S. rice for the five-year period of 1854–58 surpassed $3.3 million.[105]

U.S. imports expanded easily into Cuba, principally through the port of Havana and the provincial ports of Matanzas, Cárdenas, Nuevitas, Cienfuegos, and Santiago de Cuba, where they were distributed into interior markets through the railroad networks that had expanded across the full breadth of the island. Railroads constructed to transport sugar exports out also served to transport rice imports in—one more way that sugar contributed to the demise of domestic foodstuff production.[106] There was indeed truth to the conventional wisdom that the price of foreign food imports was often cheaper than domestic production. "The railroads were not designed to integrate the diverse regions of the island with one another," historians Oscar Zanetti Lecuona and Alejandro García Alvarez determined, "but rather to provide each region with a convenient link to the nearest port"—and with dire consequences: "The reduction of transportation costs acted to dismantle the barriers of [higher] costs that had served to protect local artisan and agricultural production, and which were subsequently displaced from local markets by lower-priced imports. The same railroad that facilitated production for export also facilitated the consumption of imports. By increasing the profitability of sugar production and decreasing the price of food imports in the domestic market, the railroad acted to accentuate the defining characteristics of the Cuban export economy."[107]

The practice of import assumed structural form—and not without an internal logic. That imports of low-cost rice expanded to make up the deficit of domestic production could not but act further to arrest the expansion of local agriculture. "This important grain has been harvested in great quantity on many farms," observed Real Sociedad Patriótica de La Habana in 1837, "but its cultivation is slowly being abandoned day by day as a result of the abundance of low-cost rice from the United States."[108] Economist Miguel Escalada commented on "the great quantity of rice" consumed in Cuba but noted too that it "pained me to see the indifference with which this important production and commerce was viewed, for supply was entrusted almost entirely to the foreigner, with prejudice to the farmers of the country."[109] Fully one-half of total Cuban consumption depended on imports. "The participation of foreigners in the Cuban market," bemoaned *Diario de la Marina*, "has suffocated rice production in this country," adding, "Foreigners produce cheaper rice due to the high cost of production in this country. The rice from the United States is far more highly regarded in our markets and is sold at lower prices, notwithstanding the fact that the rice of this country possesses more nutritional value.... The advantages that rice from the United States holds over us in rice production are clearly manifest, advantages that are further enhanced by virtue of its proximity and its flourishing merchant marine."[110]

The expansion of rice imports provided consumers with a choice, of course, but more than a choice, it also offered the opportunity for comparison. A distinct consumer preference developed in favor of rice with specific characteristics, central to which was whole-grain white rice, features associated principally with North American rice. Foreign rice came to serve as the standard against which to judge the quality of domestic rice, a standard that Cuban producers increasingly were unable to meet. Francisco de Paula Serrano could write as early as 1837 of the "power of custom that already has us preferring foreign rice with greater pleasure."[111] Rice produced in Cuba, José García de Arboleya commented in 1859, "is less white than rice from the North and, due to a lack of machines to hull the rice[,] appears dirty and broken, for which reason its consumption is limited to rural farms and towns [*fincas y pueblos rurales*]. If such defects were to be eliminated, it is likely that domestic production would be preferred to that from abroad for it is far more fluffy and very tasteful. The island would then produce sufficient rice to meet its needs."[112] The "defect" of domestic rice, Jacobo de Pezuela complained in 1863, was that it lacked the "whiteness of the rice that comes from the Southern States of the United States," a condition that could be remedied if "the simple and inexpensive machines used to clean and mill rice that have been common for more than 50 years in Valencia, the United States, the Philippine Islands, and other lands producing rice [were] introduced into the island," adding, "This condition is the reason why the consumption of Cuban rice has not expanded among the classes of means [*la clases acomodadas*] of the cities, who naturally prefer rice from abroad. The consumption of Cuban rice continues limited to African slaves and country people [*las negradas y habitantes de los campos*]."[113] Juan Dihigo characterized *arroz de la tierra* as "less white than the rice from the North, and due to the lack of adequate milling machines cannot be offered in any way other than dirty and broken."[114] Certainly Cuba was capable of producing quality rice—"comparable to the rice from the North," one producer insisted in 1828—"but [at present] it is ruined in the hulling process as a result of manpower using the mortar, breaking the grain."[115]

The ideal of the "perfect" rice was early associated with North American imports, a preference given vernacular resonance as "*arroz del Norte*," described in *Diccionario provincial casi-razonado de vozes cubanas* (1862) as "the best, the whitest, and of popular preference."[116] The *Diccionario cubano* (1888) characterized the "*arroz del Norte*" originating from the United States and "commonly preferred by all for its whiteness and nutritional value."[117] The "*arroz del Norte*," affirmed the *Vocabulario cubano* (1921), "is the rice imported from the United States highly coveted due to its ideal size and its immaculate whiteness."[118] Economist Francisco Javier Balmaseda urged farmers to introduce American rice seeds into Cuba, to produce "what has been for some time the preferred rice among our people for being the most beautiful and of exquisite taste [*hermoso y de exquisito sabor*]."[119]

Patterns of consumption reflected an emerging cosmopolitan sensibility of an expanding urban middle class—*la clases acomodadas*—preferences often enacted as affirmation of modernity. To be part of the world at large was to avail oneself of the bounty of the global market, of course. But it also implied consumption as performance of social distance and affirmation of cultural ascendancy, that is, food as cultural capital, to affirm affinity with foreign products deemed superior to domestic production. There was often a politics to consumer preference, to be sure, a way to register a disposition: to prefer U.S. rice implied rejection of Valencia rice as an expression of an emerging national mood and a means of delineating national distinction. In sum: a repudiation of things Spanish.

DEPENDENCY UPON food imports developed into a subplot of a larger national drama, to reveal deepening social tensions in the most fundamental transactions of daily life. A brooding disquiet insinuated itself among a people perplexed by the apparent inability to feed themselves and obliged to depend on foreign imports for the essential staples of daily life. The island had been overtaken by the larger logic of market forces, leaving Cubans to ponder the illogic of an inadequate agriculture. How to make sense of the failure of agriculture to sustain a population in an agricultural economy? "No one can deny that the wealth of the country has declined," insisted the *Revista Económica* in 1880, "and not because the Island has ceased to be rich, but because its inhabitants, accustomed to follow the same paths of their forbearers [*antecesores*][,] have not wished or do not know how to pursue new sources of wealth.... To what does our neighbor the United States owe its prodigious and vast wealth? Is Cuba any less than the United States?"[120] The daily *El Siglo* repeatedly sounded the alarm of the danger of dependency on sugar exports and reliance on food imports. "No one," the newspaper warned in 1865, "can boast of greater tenacity in attacking the inherent vice of the system of extensive agriculture that currently prevails and which will lead us to scarcity of the production of vital foodstuffs."[121] And on another occasion:

> The time has arrived for our farmers [*agricultores*] and especially our plantation owners [*hacendados*] to dedicate some portion of their land to

the cultivation of wheat and other cereals no less important to our diet.
... Plant wheat and cereals to provide our workers with fresh inexpensive
bread. Do not allow yourselves to be dazzled any longer by the imaginary advantages and rarely realized benefits of sugar production. Your
immense cane fields [cañaverales] are also immense powder kegs capable
of reducing in a single instant your apparent wealth into extreme poverty.
The wind will not always blow in the same direction nor will circumstances always be as favorable as in the past. To persist with the same
system is madness.[122]

"Few countries can rival the quality of rice produced in Cuba," *Diario de la Marina* bemoaned, "and yet few are the number of producers who have given thought to the development of this industry, limiting planting to small parcels of land." It continued:

It is shameful to think that with the opportunity to produce rice on the
very sugar estates, their owners have for a long time been paying between
12 and 16 reales per arroba for the maintenance of Chinese workers when
the very Chinese, so inclined to the cultivation of rice, could easily provision the estates and at the same time provide great earnings to the owners.
No one in Cuba should consume rice not grown in the country.... May
God enlighten the intelligence of men to preserve and think of the future
without those who choose the easy way in the belief that everything can
be obtained by planting cane and making sugar.[123]

The *Revista Económica* called for the "decentralization" of Cuban wealth to improve and diversify agriculture, to expand the variety of production, to open new lands for farming, and to establish credit centers [*centros de créditos*] to provide farmers "with relief from the precarious and difficult situation in which they find themselves."[124] Benigno Gener exhorted authorities to adopt the long view of economic development, insisting that it was not in the "interest of Cuban agriculture to achieve momentarily great profits [*realizar momentáneamente grandes ganancias*], as a result of an extraordinary price for sugar, to be negated always by the need for Cuba to import articles of primary necessity from the foreigner."[125]

Across the island, in large urban centers and distant interior *municipios*, the Cuban diet consisted less of food obtained from local production than food imports from foreign producers. "The stores are well supplied with American canned meats and fruits, hams, biscuits, etc.," wrote the U.S. consul in Sagua la Grande. "In all cases American goods are preferred."[126] Agriculture for consumption had fallen upon hard times. "Nowhere else is land so poorly distributed as it is among us," writer José Calderón spoke through the narrator in his 1893 novel, *El castigo de tres granujas*. "It is the principal cause of the backwardness and the obstacles to agriculture as well as to the poverty and demoralization of the farmer.... To whom does the farmer sell or with whom does he exchange corn, rice, beans, and boniato harvested deep in the interior of the Island [*en las entrañas de la Isla*]?"[127]

The anomalies of Cuban production systems developed into the "normal" of the colonial political economy and did not readily admit redress. Duties on rice imports, critics insisted, offered one way to support domestic producers. But to increase duties on a staple consumed widely by households across the island as well as a staple of the slave diet could not but increase the cost of living and raise the cost of production. There was no gainsaying the need to promote the production of rice, the Real Sociedad Patriótica de La Habana acknowledged in 1837, "to strengthen it with the products of the land, the only sources of progress and existence, the only source of wealth. We do not have any other type of industry." However, "to restrict the importation of the commodities that the country produces or can produce [through higher tariffs] would result in the imposition of a heavy burden on consumers." Affirmed the Sociedad,

> To prohibit, for example, the importation of rice from the United States with which we cover the necessities of subsistence, or to impose higher duties on rice imports, which is tantamount to prohibit importation, for the single reason that rice is also produced and can be produced on the island in abundance ... is not fair, for the worker will be the one to bear the consequences of foreign competition. What happens to the nonagricultural population that cannot plant and harvest rice? It would have to forgo the consumption of a staple priced beyond its means, or pay a very high price.[128]

It was folly, proponents of foreign commerce insisted, to contemplate duties on rice imports. "We will not enter into the question of the efficacy of expanding the cultivation of rice to the extent of making unnecessary the importation of the rice that presently supplies the needs of us consumers," Junta de Fomento taunted in 1849. The consequences were dire: "We will for the time being put aside these questions to address the important one, which is the necessity of a people to meet their needs for themselves, when through easy means they can acquire [needed goods] from the outside and at the same time provide [to others] products far more important, more suited to the climate, and adapted to the land upon which the material well-being of the country depends."[129]

PRACTICES ASSUMED the form of patterns, and the patterns served to confirm a self-evident logic from which the purpose of trade and commerce was derived. Dependency on food imports produced tightly wrought tensions in a colonial system already riven with internal contradictions. The expansion of production for export and the demise of production for consumption had exposed Cuba to the uncertainties of foreign food supplies, subject always to circumstances over which Cuba had no control. For years, informed observers warned of the perils associated with dependency on foreign food imports. "The need to depend upon the United States for corn, rice, all kinds of legumes and vegetables, meats and fowl, even to import potatoes and lard," economist Mariano Torrente warned at midcentury, was an issue of grave concern, for "it would be a matter of transcendental negligence in those critical situations in which U.S. ports would be closed to us."[130]

The consequences of dependency on foreign imports—and particularly dependency upon the United States as a source of food supplies—were experienced during the years of the U.S. Civil War. The Union naval blockade of southern ports—especially New Orleans, Savannah, and Charleston—plunged the island into crisis.[131] Cuba experienced the Union blockade as if a belligerent party to the conflict, losing access to one of the principal sources of food supplies. Scarcities increased; so did prices. "It is undeniable that the blockade of the Southern States of the neighboring Anglo-American Union is causing and will continue to cause considerable harm to the commerce of Havana and indeed to all the inhabitants of the island," warned *Diario de la Marina*. "Every day the prices of articles of primary necessity rise higher and higher, and this combination of rising prices and scarcities of foodstuffs may well reach the point where we are threatened by hunger."[132] Lard from New Orleans selling in 1861 for 17 reales per quintal sold a year later for 22 reales per quintal (1 quintal = 100 pounds). Corn selling for 3.5 reales per arroba increased to 7 reales. The price of rice from Georgia and South Carolina increased from 12 reales per arroba to 15 reales—if available at all. In fact, rice imports from South Carolina soon collapsed: 410,000 arrobas in 1855, to 190,000 arrobas in 1861, to 2,700 arrobas in 1862, to nothing in 1864 and 1865.[133] "We all know the difficulties occasioned by the war in the United States," economist Alvaro Reynoso later wrote, "with regard to the importation of goods that had previously reached us with such regularity.... It is thus indisputable that the cost of living for a large portion of the population, as well as the cost of feeding livestock, will experience a sharp increase in prices, and even with this increased cost foodstuffs will be scarce."[134]

The loss of foreign food supplies was a future long foretold—with dread. "Today we appear to be on the verge of paying dearly for our lack of foresight," wrote Francisco J. de la Cruz from Matanzas in 1861, "for our recklessness, for our old errors":

> Today we can say that we find ourselves blockaded by the United States, given that the ports from which we imported a large part of the articles that have served as the principal source of our daily food supplies are under blockade. It is clear that it will cause far more hardship on us than on the very states under blockade. Other than tobacco, we have no significant rural industry other than sugar, and therein lies the problem. Rather than our population providing itself with products of daily necessity from our land, our farmers have neglected the production of rice, corn, potatoes, and beans . . . so that by only planting sugar cane we have entrusted the acquisition of all that we need to the foreigner, from objects of pure luxury and fantasy to those of the most indispensable nature for daily life, products that no one could do without for a single day.[135]

"The truth is," wrote the resident *New York Times* correspondent in Havana in 1861, "this Island does not produce sufficient for the consumption of four months of the year, and to the South we have, for a number of years past, looked for our necessary food."[136]

THE EXPERIENCE OF food shortage insinuated itself into the popular imagination, something of a foreboding uneasiness, an awareness of daily life as a precarious condition, with matters of social peace and political order implicated in the contingency of food. Ramón de la Sagra was among many to warn that the "consequences that result from the abandonment or inattention to the production of foodstuff" were grave, for they placed in jeopardy "the individual existence of the poor classes."[137] Cuba could not feed itself, José Quintín Suzarte warned, and he exhorted Spanish authorities to increase "the production of *frutos menores* as much as possible in order to prevent the possibility that hunger assail the working classes [*las clases proletarias*], the largest and most turbulent population."[138] Any shortage of rice threatened social peace, warned *Diario de la Marina*, for "the largest part of the population [*la parte más numerosa de la población*] would suffer greatly, for this is not a luxury item but an article indispensable to the popular diet."[139] The newspaper emphasized,

> It is well known that rice has long been considered as a food item of primary necessity among the poor classes, in the countryside as well as the cities, being preferred over all other grains. This explains the immense consumption that this article enjoys among our population, which has increased significantly in recent years as a result of the Asian immigration, for whom rice forms part of its basic subsistence. But the cultivation of rice, like that of other *frutos menores,* has been in inverse proportion to the increase in the consumption, or at best, it has remained unchanged. This explains the necessity of having to turn to foreign countries in search of the major part of the total amount of rice demanded by consumption.[140]

Increasing numbers of Cubans lived within the contradictions of the export economy, within the anomaly by which an agricultural economy had become dependent on agricultural imports. "The subsistence of our country [*la subsistencia de nuestro pueblo*] is threatened," warned the *Revista de Jurisprudencia y de Administración* in early 1861, "and if some remedy is not found, Cuba will soon present the singular spectacle of a very rich country in which there is nevertheless hunger."[141] Appeals to expand domestic food production were unheeded.[142] *Diario de la Marina* was incredulous. "Here, in this virgin country," the newspaper puzzled, "so productive and with lands so rich, with a population of so many intelligent men, and situated at one of the points of the Americas at which thousands of the ships of the most commercial nations in both hemispheres [dock], we are obliged to import a significant portion of almost every known type of agricultural product."[143] Warned *Diario de la Marina* in 1861,

> There was a time when articles of daily consumption, and especially articles of primary necessity for the provisions of the people, were produced in abundance in the country.... But today everything has disappeared. While small farms have declined the sugar mills have increased, and cane has absorbed the vital productive forces [*las fuerzas vitales*] of the country. Thus, the production of subsidiary crops, the mixed farms of poultry and agriculture ... the source of general domestic felicity in Cuba, have been abandoned for the single purpose of the planting of cane.[144]

The decline of domestic food production forged the cognizance of insecurity into something of an ethos of *lo cubano*, a people learning to adapt to and live with the circumstances of scarcity as a facet of daily life[145] — not hunger, exactly, but rather an awareness of the plausibility of hunger as a condition to which, Cubans understood, they were perforce obliged to reconcile themselves.

"Hunger is knocking at our doors," economist Marcelo Pujol y de Camps despaired, due to, among other reasons, "the loss of confidence in the future . . . and the consumption of products that we do not produce."[146] A brief news story in *El Siglo* in 1866 conveys the angst of the times:

> We have just learned that an upright head of family [*un honrado padre de familia*] in Havana has died, leaving his wife and children without bread and without the means to obtain food. We are not accustomed to seeing the poor of this country die of hunger, for if there is any part of the world where charity prevails it is without doubt the Island of Cuba. But we have learned that the family of which we speak finds itself alone, totally alone, without food. . . . The account we have of this unfortunate family is horrific and it would be a source of shame for this country if any member of this family were to die of hunger.[147]

"There is no other recourse," stated physician Marcos de J. Melero, who understood the implications of scarcity.

> It is necessary to dedicate ourselves with determination to the planting of *viandas*. . . . The increasing scarcity of these products upon which the poor among us depend makes this necessity self-evident. This scarcity is experienced not only in the population centers but in the very countryside of the entire island. The rise in price of *viandas* has reached the point that for many needy families the classic *ajiaco* dish is too expensive to prepare. . . . It is necessary for our society to dedicate itself to the cultivation of *plátanos*, boniato, ñame, maíz, yuca, malanga, *papa*, calabaza, etc., as well as vegetables.[148]

Food shortages became commonplace. "The scarcity of bread, meat, and other items necessary for our diet [*artículos necesarios para nuestra alimentación*] continues unabated," reported *El Siglo* in 1867.[149] The Cuban Academy of Medicine warned of the threat of disease in urban centers resulting from the "hunger, the misery, and the crowding into the large cities of people who previously had been able to live in the countryside but due to the lack of resources are obliged to migrate into urban centers in search of livelihood."[150] Charity hospitals in Havana complained of chronic food shortages.[151] "The scarcity of foods of daily consumption that should be produced by local farmers," wrote Francisco J. de la Cruz from Matanzas in 1860, "has us deeply concerned for the days to come." De la Cruz continued:

> Do we cultivate on this island the agricultural products we need in sufficient quantities to meet the necessities of the inhabitants? No. Here,

in this virgin and productive country, with bountiful lands . . . , we are obliged to import a considerable portion of virtually all lines of known agricultural products. . . . Thus, notwithstanding our capacity to produce these products—perhaps even to produce to export—we rely upon outsiders to provide us with adequate quantities of rice, potatoes, beans, corn, lard, salted meats, and poultry, not to improve our stock but in order to feed ourselves, to supply our markets to meet our needs. . . . Little is cultivated of everything, except for sugar. All the vital productive forces of the country, all the capital, are allocated to the production of sugar, while everything else is looked upon with an indifference that some day may prove to be disastrous for us.[152]

Midcentury food shortages in Matanzas province were attributed principally to the expansion of sugar and the attending decline of almost everything else. "With an estimated 12,000 inhabitants in the city of Matanzas and its jurisdiction," Pedro Antonio Alfonso recalled years later, "and proportionately far too few farmers available to plant cereals and vegetables to sell to the public . . . the public lacked access to adequate food supplies. On repeated occasions the municipal council [*cabildo*] was obliged to appeal to the Governor and the Captain General for authorization to permit American ships to enter the harbor and unload provisions in order to avert a calamity."[153] In 1884, residents of Vuelta Abajo petitioned the Spanish Crown—"in the most respectful form"—for "relief from the hunger and misery that has afflicted the households and to which the [residents] may soon succumb . . . as the result of grave economic errors due to the times and men who have squandered little by little the well-spring of our wealth."[154] Writer José Ramón de Betancourt used first-person experience with scarcities attending the decline of food production to inform the plot of his novel *Una feria de la caridad en 183* . . . . Cuba had plunged headlong into crisis, despairs Betancourt's protagonist, "for having totally ignored the production of *frutos menores*, like corn, rice, *viandas*, etc., in order to dedicate everything to the production of sugar and coffee, resulting in the extraordinary case that at the very time the wealth of the owners of the sugar mills and coffee estates increased, the general population was at the point of facing a crisis of survival."[155]

SUGAR PRODUCTION continued to expand all through the 1870s and 1880s but under vastly different market conditions. Cubans faced new competition, principally in the form of European beet sugar, an industry that flourished under protective government support and subsidies, which, Cubans feared, posed "the largest single threat to our principal markets."[156] By the final decades of the nineteenth century, France, Austria, and Germany had become the largest suppliers of sugar for the world market. The beet sugar share of the world market expanded from 4.4 percent in 1840 to 34 percent in 1870 and to 64 percent in 1890.[157]

Cuban producers faced daunting challenges, confronting on one hand increasing international competition and on the other diminishing world markets. By the late nineteenth century, Cuba had been displaced from almost all European markets, including much of Spain.[158] The United States was the last—and the only—important market remaining for Cuban sugar. In 1886 U.S. consul Ramon Williams in Havana provided an arresting assessment of the complex networks through which Cuba was bound to the United States:

> Practically the island is now entirely dependent upon the market of the United States, in which to sell its sugar-cane products. Also, the existence of the sugar plantations, the railroads used in transporting the products of the plantations to the shipping ports of the island, the import and export trades of Cuba based thereon, each including hundreds of minor industries, such as the agricultural and mechanical trades, store-houses, wharves and lighters, stevedores, brokers, clerks, bankers, real estate owners and shopkeepers of all kinds, and holders of the public debt, are now directly related to the market of the United States, to the extent of 94 percent for their employment, and only 6 percent to other countries, of the latter mostly Spain, simply for the reason that sugar is the principal economic basis of all those interests.[159]

All in all, circumstances that implied—Cuban producers insisted—an urgency for Spain to negotiate a reciprocal trade arrangement with the United States. Knowledge of "the dependence of Cuba upon the United States . . . ," Consul Williams concluded in his 1886 report, "now leads its inhabitants to urge upon the Madrid Government the immediate negotiation of a treaty of commerce to put the island in a more harmonious relationship with its natural market, the United States."[160] In 1890, the Chamber of Commerce of Santiago de Cuba—in defense of "the principal source of wealth of the country"—petitioned Spanish authorities to facilitate imports from the United States. Spain was superfluous to the Cuban economy, the Chamber of Commerce pronounced outright: "Spain cannot consume our production, much less provide us with [the products] we need. Spain cannot provide us what it cannot produce."[161]

The passage of the McKinley Tariff (1890) placed raw sugar on the duty-free schedule. However, Article III (Aldrich Amendment) of the new tariff law authorized the president to raise duties on the products of those countries that acted in a "reciprocally unequal and unreasonable" fashion, that is, countries that refused to extend to American imports tariff advantages commensurate with the McKinley law.[162] Within a year, Washington and Madrid negotiated the Foster-Cánovas reciprocity agreement (1891), extending to Cuban sugar privileged access to U.S. markets—"virtually the only market for what is our most important industry."[163] Planter Rafael Fernández de Castro was lucid on the subject of Foster-Cánovas: "Without the treaty our most important market would be closed to us. Without that market our principal product would have no outlet, without which no earnings would reach us. . . . Sugar is the umbilical cord that binds us to the United States and from whom the blood that sustains us originates."[164] The North American market, the Círculo de Hacendados affirmed outright, "is a matter of life and death for the sugar industry of Cuba."[165]

Foster-Cánovas served to stimulate a new round of sugar expansion, sustained principally by an infusion of North American capital. Production increased from 632,000 tons in 1890 to 817,000 tons in 1891 and again to 977,000 tons in 1892; in 1894 it surpassed the 1 million ton mark.[166] Reciprocity also allowed for increased U.S. food imports, from $53 million in 1890 to $79 million in 1893.[167] Breadstuffs, vegetables, corn, wheat flour, and corn flour saturated the Cuban market. (See table 1.1.) The increase of U.S. rice imports was stunning, from 17,500 pounds in 1891 to 2.2 million pounds in 1892.[168]

However, reciprocity was short-lived. In 1894, the enactment in the United States of the Wilson-Gorman Tariff Act imposed a new tariff of 40 percent ad valorem on sugar. Spain responded swiftly—and in kind—rescinding the tariff concessions to North American imports, raising to the maximum duties on all North American imports. "What are proving [to be] really prohibitory duties," reported the U.S. consul in Santiago de Cuba, "are imposed by the government of Spain against the importation to this island, of nearly all classes of American merchandise."[169]

The effects were jolting. Shortages increased; so did the cost of living. The total value of U.S. exports to Cuba contracted by one-third, from $79 million in 1893 to $53 million in 1895. Almost all basic foodstuffs—lard, beans, potatoes, breads, and corn—declined precipitously. U.S. flour imports into Havana during the last four months of the years 1892, 1893, and 1894 declined from 156,110 bags to 105,043 bags to 12,996 bags respectively.[170] Dwindling Cuban markets were reflected in the decline of U.S. shipping. "Under this disastrous discrimination against the United States," reported the U.S. consul in Santiago de Cuba in late 1894, "importations from our country to this island are rapidly dropping to the minimum, and already one half of the steamers . . . which have

TABLE 1.1. Quantity and value of select U.S. food imports, 1891–1894 (pounds/dollars)

	1891		1892		1893		1894	
	Quantity	Value	Quantity	Value	Quantity	Value	Quantity	Value
Beans/peas (bu)	50,466	$115,930	145,162	$282,391	183,977	$392,962	120,738	$268,265
Breads (lbs)	261,853	17,930	346,415	23,451	468,613	31,650	582,232	34,506
Corn (bu)	367,324	120,187	627,177	369,131	1,041,474	582,050	1,136,657	571,336
Hams (lbs)	2,141,208	234,458	4,766,133	529,328	5,834,286	761,082	5,272,640	668,959
Lard (lbs)	32,054,107	2,079,534	43,982,187	2,974,545	42,683,652	4,023,917	42,340,578	3,625,545
Potatoes (bu)	175,891	168,354	337,928	228,079	666,648	554,153	572,069	496,875
Wheat flour (brls)	114,447	591,886	266,175	1,826,886	618,406	2,821,557	562,248	2,473,895

Source: U.S. Treasury Department, Bureau of Statistics, *The Foreign Commerce and Navigation of the United States for the Year Ending June 30, 1894* (Washington, D.C., 1895).

TABLE 1.2. Tariffs on U.S. food imports, 1893–1895

	1893–1894	1894–1895
Corn	$.25 per 100 kilos	$3.95 per 100 kilos
Flour	1.00 per 100 kilos	4.75 per 100 kilos
Meal	.25 per 100 kilos	4.75 per 100 kilos
Wheat	.30 per 100 kilos	3.95 per 100 kilos

Source: Ramon O. Williams to Assistant Secretary of State Edwin F. Uhl, October 12, 1894, Despatches from U.S. Consuls in Havana, 1783–1906, General Records of the Department of State, Record Group 59, National Archives, Washington, D.C.

been making regular trips between the southern coast of Cuba and the United States, have been withdrawn from these waters."[171]

Cuba lost preferential access to the only market with the capacity to absorb its sugar and insulate the island from the uncertainties of world competition. The loss of markets accounting for 90 percent of Cuban exports plunged the economy into disarray—"a process of economic disintegration," reported Consul Ramon Williams in Havana in mid-1894.[172] Panic gripped the island. "Has the government stopped to reflect what would be the situation of the Island without . . . the market of the United States?" *Diario de la Marina* asked incredulously. "What future would await us?" The newspaper made the Cuban case bluntly: "The fact is that we have no other market for the sale of our products than that of the United States."[173] The daily *La Lucha* warned of "all kinds of calamities" and predicted, "Let us not mince words. . . . We are at the brink of an abyss. If matters continue in the present form, we will be part of a general collapse of all our principal economic interests."[174]

The increase of American food imports during Foster-Cánovas had delivered another blow to domestic agricultural production. Increased duties on U.S. imports meant that consumers paid higher prices for vital foodstuffs, and domestic agriculture was unable to make up the shortfall. (See table 1.2.)

"We need . . . American flour entering Cuba under reasonable conditions and Cuban sugar entering American ports under similar conditions," *La Lucha* declared in December 1894. "Our sugar has no market other than the United States."[175] In the same month, planters petitioned the Spanish parliament, warning that "the immense North American market is virtually the only market capable of consuming the sugar production of this island," without which "all Cuban industries and especially sugar would collapse."[176] Several weeks later *La Lucha* again criticized the Spanish colonial administration, complaining that "in vain . . . have been our efforts of protesting the exorbitant levies used to keep Yankee goods out of Cuba. In vain, too[,] have been our efforts against the imposition of prohibitive duties on American goods."[177]

Very bad timing indeed. The mid-1890s were years of churning political discontent. The disruption of trade added new grievances to old complaints. "The residents and commercial interests here," the U.S. consul in Santiago de Cuba reported in October 1894, "are protesting loud and strong against being thus summarily cut off from their natural commercial allies, and this action on the part of the home government adds greatly to the feeling of unrest that pervades all classes."[178] Four months later the war for independence commenced.

CHAPTER TWO

Passing into Economic Darkness

We have no cash. We cannot secure credit. We do not receive assistance, and cannot obtain needed seeds, implements, and work animals. How will we survive?—Farmer, Santa Clara province, 1901

The desires of the rice people have been for years to get into the Cuban market and though we have made efforts at Washington and elsewhere, the fact remains that except in a very small way the Cuban market has been closed to us.—*Rice Journal* (1916)

It is really disastrous for our country that we are under the necessity of importing the most important articles of consumption, such as milk, eggs, corn, rice, meat, and even beans, when with small effort, we could produce a superabundance.—Emilio Núñez, Secretary of Agriculture, 1913

Although Cuba is undoubtedly capable of producing a large proportion of her food requirements, it has been economically more desirable to import them. The cultivation of her major crop is of such long standing and it is so much easier to devote her efforts to that, importing her ordinary requirements from a near neighbor who has specialized in quantity production and distribution of such products, that she will probably continue to purchase such commodities abroad. Efforts have been made to demonstrate the desirability of diversification, but while conditions remain as they are there is little likelihood that much effort will be diverted from the easiest and more profitable source.—U.S. Department of Commerce, *Trade Information Bulletin* (1925)

The Cuban people impoverished themselves . . . as a consequence of our long ruinous wars for independence. The first—the one of ten years—cost us our great wealth [*la gran riqueza*]. The second—the one that culminated in independence—cost us nearly all our small wealth [*la pequeña riqueza*]. Our polity was proletarianized [*se proletarizó*]. Everyone passed under a [condition] of economic darkness [*la obscuridad económico*].—*El Mundo*, April 26, 1916

CUBANS EXPERIENCED the transition from colony to republic under circumstances of desolation. Only with the arrival of peace was it possible to take full measure of the devastation wrought by the war for independence (1895–98). Conditions were frightful. It had been a close and intimate war. Many tens of thousands of men, women, and children—shattered families and broken households, widows and orphans, the aged, the ill, the infirm, the maimed, and the marred—crowded into towns and cities across the island, there to expand into a swelling itinerant population of supplicants and mendicants and to confront an uncertain future, not quite certain how or where or with what to begin anew.[1] "The island of Cuba," Pedro Pablo Martín brooded through the narrator of his autobiographical novel *Adelina* (1901), "fountain of wealth and emporium of beauty, was reduced to circumstances of impoverishment and despair," continuing, "Everywhere we turned we saw nothing but misery, desolation, and ruin. . . . Scenes so horrible! Sights so painful!"[2] Where towns and villages had once stood, there remained only scattered piles of rubblestone and charred wood; what were previously landscapes of fertile fields and lush farming zones were now scenes of scorched earth and singed bush. Agriculture was in crisis in an economy predominantly agricultural—"in a state of suspended animation," commented one observer.[3] The farmlands were blighted, the pastures were barren, and the fruit trees were bare. A bleak landscape indeed, commented *Diario de la Marina*, "a truly overwhelming situation, with many—a great many—lands abandoned [*terrenos abandonados*] due to the impossibility to farm them [*la imposibilidad de cultivarlos*]."[4]

The land could no longer sustain life. "Miles and miles of country uninhabited by either the human race or domestic animal were visible to the eye on every side," reported General Fitzhugh Lee from Pinar del Río province in western Cuba in 1899, adding, "The great fertile island of Cuba in some places resembled an ash pile, in others the dreary desert."[5] And from the eastern end of the island: "There are scarcely any work animals to be found along the route," reported Major James McCleary during an official inspection of Oriente province in late 1898, "very few horses and still fewer mules and oxen, none of which can be obtained at any price.... Fields [are] abandoned and suffered to grow up in guinea grass, and the orchards which formerly covered it, are entirely gone. All the fruit trees in this section have been destroyed."[6] Of the 1.4 million acres under cultivation in 1895, only 900,000 returned to production in 1899. An estimated 100,000 small farms, 3,000 livestock ranches, 800 tobacco *vegas*, and 700 coffee *fincas* had perished during the war.[7]

Almost all the 1,000 towns and villages of Cuba emerged from the war in varying degrees of prostration. "This district," reported the mayor of San Cristobal in Pinar del Río province, "has only 5 estates and 33 small farms in existence out of 205 in antebellum days. The owners are exceedingly poor. Their need is oxen and agricultural implements."[8] "All but 3 or 4 of the 395 rural properties destroyed," cabled Mayor J. F. Fuente from Placetas in Las Villas province.[9] Mayor Julio Domínguez reported similar conditions fifty miles away in Cruces, writing in early 1899 that "no lands in this district are under cultivation, with the exception of a few very small farms surrounding the towns, devoted to the cultivation of vegetables and other products for the sustenance of their owners. Misery, hunger, sickness and general discontent prevail among the people."[10] Farmers across the island faced the prospects of extinction. "The principal and only source of wealth," reported the mayor of Bauta in Havana province, "was totally destroyed to an extent that not one single property of the 169 was saved from destruction"; fifty miles away, in Nueva Paz, the mayor wrote that "the lands of this municipality ... are abandoned. Even those which were not completely ruined are in an unproductive state."[11] Circumstances in Gibara were typical of conditions across much of eastern Cuba. "Owing to the fact that all the farms are abandoned for the lack of agricultural implements and of oxen ...," reported the mayor, "any cultivation done is by hand, producing hardly enough to cover the primary necessities of the farmer."[12] The mayor of Holguín was succinct: "Agriculture has disappeared completely."[13]

Conditions were actually worse than they appeared. The devastation of war implied more than the destruction of property. In fact, the demise of vast numbers of farms and *fincas* did not fully encompass the magnitude of the crisis in agriculture. Destroyed too were the legal papers and public documents, the deeds, the titles, the official records, the property registries: that is, the stuff by which ownership of property was corroborated. The archives of the *ayuntamientos* [town councils] and *municipios* [townships] across the island were in a state of disarray and in many instances destroyed altogether. Public buildings were reduced to rubble and their contents turned to ashes; the loss of public records, registered property titles, and deeds was often total. The municipal records of Baracoa, Banes, Las Tunas, and Jiguaní were reduced to ashes.[14] "All the records of the *ayuntamiento* disappeared during the war," reported the mayor of Jiguaní in 1900; "the district was entirely destroyed."[15] Where records were not destroyed, they were removed. Vast quantities of records in the custody of local registry offices were included among the archival materials repatriated to Spain with the evacuation of colonial authorities. Records that could not be transported were often set ablaze. "The destruction of the records of this office by Spanish troops on their evacuation of this town," reported Mayor Francisco Mastrafa of Mayarí, "prevents the recording of the number and condition of *caballerías* of land under cultivation."[16]

The loss of deeds and property titles further complicated recovery. "Cultivators do not have an exact notion of their property rights," wrote Enrique Lavedán, "nor of the extension of their property, nor of its value, nor of a way to ratify their claims."[17] Property rights were often impossible to verify; boundaries could not be confirmed and claims could not be corroborated—conditions that portended nothing good for small farmers lacking representation. "In many cases," the director of the 1899 census noted, "the area of the *fincas* were found uncertain and contradictory, and were given in many different units of measurement. The occupants were often unknown, and many portions of land were in the possession of occupants on the basis of sufferance, of necessity without defined limits."[18] Properties abandoned during the war filled with squatters after the war. Major James McCleary toured the towns of Bayamo, San Pedro, La Mula, and Cristo in late 1898 and reported coming upon newly formed communities farming the land. "None of the people who live at Cristo," McLeary noted, "claim to have title to their lands. They are mere squatters, but expect to receive the lands from the government at some time in the future."[19] General Leonard Wood reported in 1899: "During the war many of the estates in the interior were abandoned and have become overgrown. Their owners are either dead or in foreign parts or living in towns, too poor to attempt any work tending to reclaim and re-establish their estates. The result has been and is that many persons have settled on these estates ... and have remained in undisputed possession for several years. Their removal will be attended with considerable difficulty and hardship and probably with some considerable disturbance."[20]

THE TRANSITION from war to peace was administered under the auspices of a North American interregnum, nearly four years of military occupation (1899–1902) during which the principal decisions about reconstruction and revival were made by the Americans, who—as a matter of administrative fiat—acted with the presumption that economic recovery necessarily implied the need to revive export production. "The only hope for the renewal of prosperity in Cuba," pronounced the Department of State in 1899, "is first, the rehabilitation of the sugar industry; secondly, a revival of work on tobacco plantations.... These industries are the basis of prosperity of the island. It is useless to try to create new industries until the old and strong industries of the Island of Cuba are on their feet again."[21]

Policies designed to revive the export production sealed the fate of many small farmers. Banks were few in number, and fewer indeed were the number of banks disposed to lend money in an uncertain postwar environment. "It would be extremely hazardous," warned the Treasury Department, "to loan money in Cuba on any kind of collateral or property."[22] Without access to capital and without collateral for credit, farmers floundered in varying degrees of ruin, facing few prospects for immediate relief and even fewer prospects for long-term recovery.

All during the military occupation, small landowners appealed to American authorities for credit and financial aid—and almost always they were denied.[23] Municipal authorities—the *ayuntamientos*—across the island appealed to the military government for assistance but to no avail. Complained Bartolomé Falcón Paz, the mayor of Cobre: "The people of this agricultural district ... can hardly do anything due to the miserable condition in which the war left them. The bad conditions of the roads prevent the farmers from carrying their products to Santiago de Cuba where the market would buy them.... The *ayuntamiento* has requested from the Military Governor some assistance to aid the reconstruction of this district..... The small income of the *ayuntamiento* does not allow it to attend to the reconstructions of the district."[24] "No assistance has been received in this district from the Government," protested the mayor of Consolación del Sur in the province of Pinar del Río in late 1900, "not in work animals or in agricultural equipment."[25] Perfecto Lacoste, the civil secretary of agriculture, commerce, and industry, appealed to the military government for funds to aid in reconstruction. "The precarious situation in which the great majority of planters and landholders of Cuba find themselves," Lacoste pleaded, "requires that they should be helped by the State in every possible way so as to encourage the reconstruction of the Island."[26]

Again, to no avail. It is not clear that the Americans had a plan, but they certainly had a purpose—a foreign people making the life-and-death decisions over another people. The moral system of a culture of putative self-reliance insinuated itself deeply into the policy formulations with which the Americans proceeded to administer occupied Cuba. "Many requests have been made by the planters and farmers to be assisted in the way of supplying cattle, farming implements, and money; the latter to enable them to restore their houses," Governor General John Brooke reported in 1899.

> The matter has been most carefully considered and the conclusion reached that aid could not be given in this direction. The limit has been reached in other means of assistance to the verge of encouraging or inducing pauperism, and to destroy the self-respect of the people by this system of paternalism is thought to be a most dangerous implanting of a spirit alien to a free people, and which would, in carrying it out, tend to create trouble by arousing a feeling of jealousy in those who would not receive such aid.... The real solution to this question of furnishing means to those who need this kind of aid is through the medium of banks, agricultural or others; through them and through them alone, it is believed, the means now sought from the public treasury should be obtained.... This system would not destroy or impair the self-respect of the borrower; he would not be the recipient of charity, but a self-respecting citizen working out his own financial salvation by means of his own labor and brain.[27]

Brooke was adamant on the matter of aid to farmers. "I have indicated to this society," he wrote in mid-1899, "what I thought was a proper thing for it to devote itself to.... The main feature I have impressed upon it is ... to teach the people to take care of themselves."[28] General Leonard Wood agreed. "There has been considerable thoughtless talk in Cuba about making loans to aid agriculturists," Wood proclaimed near the end of the military occupation. "It is not believed that any such policy is either wise or desirable."[29]

Rather, the emphasis was on private investment. In this instance, in a capital-starved and credit-hungry environment, investments arrived principally in the form of North American capital, drawn to the promise of profits associated with the revival of the export economy. U.S. investment increased from $50 million in 1897 to $197 million in 1906. "American investors continue to place money in Cuba," reported one observer from Havana as early as 1901, "and scarcely a week passes but some new commercial enterprise, fostered in the United States for the development of the island's resources, comes to light."[30]

Almost all of which involved the revival of sugar. Hundreds of thousands of acres passed anew into sugar production, under new technologies and under new foreign ownership.[31] Aided by the infusion of North American capital, sugar quickly recovered its prewar prominence. Sugar production increased almost threefold, from 306,000 tons at the end of the war to 850,000 at the end of the military occupation.

The revival of the export economy implied a new phase of expansion and a new round of expulsion of small farmers. Without resources and without means to obtain credit, vast numbers of small farmers who survived the war succumbed to the peace.³² U.S. military attaché Matthew Hanna puzzled over the apparent demise of small farms during an official tour of Oriente province in 1903. "The increase in the number of small farms is so small," Hanna deduced, "that one is inclined to think that the instinct and taste for farming has never existed in the Cuban, or if it has that it has been lost. If left to Cuban intelligence and industry [Oriente province] will never be thoroughly developed; it will have to be done by foreigners."³³

THE COLLAPSE OF agriculture in postwar Cuba made the necessity of massive food imports a matter of urgency, of course. But imports of foodstuffs on this scale also acted to hinder the revival of domestic agriculture. Cuban farmers were entrapped in a circular loop: without access to capital, they could not revive production, and without the prospects of markets, they could not obtain capital. Nor could farmers expect protective tariffs to defend domestic agriculture from foreign imports. Cubans could not compete. "Cuban corn growers," reported one correspondent from Havana in October 1899, "request the government to enhance duty on American corn imported into this island, since that of 15 cents per bag of 100 pounds keeps prices so low that they cannot dispose of their crops without experiencing heavy losses," adding, "They accordingly ask that the duty on corn proceeding from the United States should be raised to 60 and 65 cents per bag, as a measure calculated to protect the home growth, as otherwise they are utterly unable to compete with American Western corn."³⁴

Never before were Cubans as dependent on food imports. "No one can minimize the importance for Cuba that its farmers should dedicate themselves to the cultivation of the so-called '*frutos menores*,'" exhorted the weekly *El Villareño* in 1901, "products that cost us dearly to purchase abroad, the production of which would not require the need to abandon tobacco and sugar." The editorial continued prophetically,

> Every year millions of dollars are spent in the purchase of rice, potatoes, onions, beans and many other items, products easily cultivated in Cuba. Money that is spent abroad could be easily placed in the pockets of Cuban

farmers, with the double advantage that the cultivation of these products would put us in the advantageous conditions in relation to foreign markets, which would thus be unable to impose upon us conditions without considering our interests, as is done today, obliging us to live off what they deem to give us in exchange for our only two products.... The point is that this should be studied with care, for such a strategy could serve as the basis of our true and complete independence. It should occupy the attention of all political parties and the men who are in a position to influence the destiny of the Cuban people.[35]

AND NEVER BEFORE were Cuban households as dependent on rice imports. Domestic rice production had collapsed. At the end of the nineteenth century, rice farming accounted for less than 0.5 percent of land under cultivation—approximately 4,200 acres out of a total of nearly 1 million acres. The vast portion of the land dedicated to rice—35 percent—was located in the province of Pinar del Río (1,500 acres), followed by Las Villas (885 acres), Oriente (725 acres), Camagüey (440 acres), Matanzas (415 acres), and Havana (215 acres).[36]

Rice production floundered all during the early years of the republic, unable to establish even a modest presence as an agriculture of consequence. Rice was "of little importance," commented the 1899 census—a condition later attributed to Cuban inability to produce rice: "If the country were capable of producing rice commercially," the census of 1907 concluded, "it would have done so long ago, for the necessity is obvious and great."[37] The failure to expand production, explained Estación Central Agronómica of the Ministry of Agriculture in 1905, was due to the lack of milling technology and the absence of modern plowing equipment and harvesting machinery, which could be obtained only through government support, whereupon "the Cuban farmer would recognize the profits to be made from rice and Cuba could perhaps develop into one of the principal rice-producing nations in the Americas."[38] More than a decade later, the Department of Commerce had a slightly different explanation: "The quantity of [rice] raised in the island is negligible ... and it would seem that with the enormous consumption of the cereal more should be grown.... The quality of the rice grown on the island is good, but there seems to be no particular intention on the part of anybody to go into rice growing. Some of the natives in remote districts raise small patches for their own use, but as a rule there is little planted."[39]

In fact, one of the principal obstacles to the expansion of domestic rice production was related to the massive importation of Asian rice, principally in the form of transshipments from brokers in London, Liverpool, and Hamburg.

(See table 2.1.) "From the commercial perspective," one study in 1924 of domestic rice production explained, "due to low wages [*debido a lo barato de la mano de obra*] in Asia, Cuban producers cannot compete with rice imports without tariff protection, and without which a rice industry would be impossible to establish in Cuba.... With modest tariff protection, a highly productive industry could be developed within a very short period of time and which in turn would serve to stimulate a number of subsidiary industries."⁴⁰ Of the total of 7 million quintals of rice imports into Cuba during the years of the military occupation, almost 90 percent originated from Asia transshipped through England (4.23 million quintals) and Germany (1.95 million quintals). Rice imports from the United States did not quite reach 3.5 million pounds.⁴¹ The value of rice imports expanded to meet Cuban demand and increased all through the early years of the republic, from $3 million in 1902 to $7.2 million in 1912 and increasing to $12.1 million in 1922.⁴² "Rice is in great demand in Cuba, and [is very much] a very staple food," commented the 1919 census. "Very large quantities are imported, and it is probably due to the low price of that article that greater attention has not been given to its cultivation here."⁴³

Nor could American producers compete with Asian rice. The Reciprocity Treaty of 1903 contained within its provisions a preferential tariff schedule to privilege U.S. exports, ranging from a 20 percent concession on most items to an additional 24, 30, and 40 percent on select categories. Items included in the 20 percent schedule consisted principally of exports for which the United States had already established a dominance in the Cuban market, thus making greater duty concessions superfluous. However, the higher duty concessions of 24, 30, and 40 percent were designed to wrest control of Cuban markets from European competitors. The historic advantages of many European exports in Cuba, commented the U.S. Tariff Commission, could not be offset through a mere 20 percent tariff reduction, deemed "to be totally ineffective in enabling the Americans manufacturers to share the market."⁴⁴ The vast share of the "Cuban trade which now goes to Europe will go to the United States," Leonard Wood predicted in 1902; "in other words importations from Europe will be reduced to those luxuries which we as well as Cubans purchase and must continue to purchase there. Practically everything else used in Cuba will be from the United States."⁴⁵ U.S. minister Herbert Squiers was succinct: "This market is ours for the asking."⁴⁶

Not so much with rice. The Reciprocity Treaty included rice within the 40 percent duty schedule to enhance the competitive edge over Asian imports. "I do not hesitate to say that we could not compete with Hong Kong, China, and the East in this matter," explained Louisiana congressman Samuel Robertson.

TABLE 2.1. Cuban rice imports by country of origin during U.S. occupation, 1899–1902 (quintals/dollars)

	1899		1900		1901		1902*	
	Quantity	Value	Quantity	Value	Quantity	Value	Quantity	Value
British East India	59,000	$115,361	39,000	$74,389	8,700	$18,882	N/A	N/A
Germany	345,000	721,500	471,000	930,326	604,000	1,206,939	529,500	$985,134
India	N/A	N/A	12,000	26,836	53,200	115,739	633,000	152,291
United Kingdom	1,200,000	2,316,744	1,100,000	2,164,044	985,000	1,901,583	951,000	1,844,062
United States	31,000	78,669	1,268	3,030	1,600	3,702	128	452

Source: U.S. War Department, Bureau of Insular Affairs, *Monthly Summary of Commerce of the Island of Cuba, 1899–1902* (Washington, D.C., 1899–1902).

*July 1901–May 1902

"Rice comes to Cuba from the East, for the greater part through the United Kingdom and Germany.... The quality of rice used is of the lowest quality, a grade not produced in Louisiana in any greater quantities."[47] Robertson was unambiguous: "It will be impossible for us, in Louisiana, to compete with those prices."[48] Duties on rice imports from which the United States obtained exemption promised to expand access to Cuban markets, and indeed it was to this end that the Reciprocity Treaty was directed. "It is not possible for the American rice grower to compete with the cheap labor of India or Siam," explained William Reid of the Rice Millers Association, "nor rice from the United Kingdom which is produced in the British colonies in the far East.... Therefore, the only possibility of the American rice industry taking advantage of the excellent consuming demand in Cuba depends entirely upon securing a preferential on the duty and tax in Cuba."[49]

Access to Cuban markets had developed into a matter of deepening urgency among U.S. rice producers. New lands had opened for expanded rice cultivation in Louisiana and Texas at a time when the American domestic market could no longer absorb increased production. "Production is fast overtaking consumption in the U.S.," Charles Bier, president of the Louisiana and Texas Rice Millers Association, explained to U.S. minister Herbert Squiers in Havana, "and we must seek new markets for the surplus or the industry will be profitless for all concerned."[50]

In fact, the duty discount of 40 percent provided a differential without consequence. "Even with this advantage," the U.S. Department of Commerce acknowledged, "it appears difficult for the American grain to make that headway in the markets of Cuba that growers in the United States would like see."[51] The Cuban general tariff schedule imposed a duty of $1.00 for each 100 kilograms (220 pounds) of rice imports, subsequently raised in 1904 to $1.20 per kilo, with U.S. rice paying 60 and 72 cents respectively per kilo, but this was still insufficient to offset the price advantage enjoyed by Asian products. "It is very clear," protested Charles Bier, "that unless the United States induces the Cuban republic to reconstruct the rice tariff immediately and impose a much higher duty on foreign rice imported into Cuba, it will be impossible for the American product to secure a foothold."[52] The Crowley Rice Milling Company of Louisiana solicited the assistance of the State Department to secure a duty increase in Cuba on foreign rice, from which U.S. rice would be exempt. "Even if the Cuban Congress advanced the duty on rice to $2.50 per 100 kilos (it now being only $1.20)," the chairman of Crowley explained in 1904, "it would barely let our cheapest grades of rice in without a loss, but if the duty could be raised to $3.30 per 100 kilos ... we would be able to get our medium as well as low grades (which are the principal grades used by the Cuban trade) into that market." Matters were dire: "We had an overproduction this past season, and, on account of this overproduction, prices have been depressed actually below the cost of production, and for this reason, we are asking Cuba to admit us into her market as we are compelled, at the present time, to seek outside markets to relieve the situation here."[53]

All through the early 1900s, Asian rice was selling in Havana at between 3.5 cents to 5 cents a pound, almost half of the price of U.S. rice, which fluctuated between 7 and 10 cents a pound. Texas rice grower W. P. H. McFaddin believed the difficulty of obtaining access to an "island taking more than two and one half million bags of rice per year" could be attributed to being undercut by the "coolie labor of Asia and India": "To Cuba we have a . . . preferential tariff. We have direct steamship lines plying between the United States and Cuba which name very attractive ocean freight rates. Notwithstanding all these advantages, the United States is practically barred from the rice business in Cuba. German millers can bring their rough product from the fields of India, mill it in Germany, and then ship the cleaned product to Cuba, pay a 20 per cent higher duty and yet make better prices than the American millers can make and absolutely control the business."[54] Rice was one of those products, the U.S. Tariff Commission acknowledged years later, that "did not secure in the Cuban market [a] price premium."[55] The dominance of Asian rice persisted through the mid-1910s. (See table 2.2.) "An economic error," the census of 1907 concluded, "prevents North Carolina, South Carolina, Louisiana, and other rice-producing states of the Union from taking advantage of a market so large, so near, and so natural."[56]

WORLD WAR I changed everything. The disruption of transatlantic shipping served to shift trade routes and reassign cargo transports. That the principal belligerents—England and Germany—were also the principal providers of rice to Cuba meant the disruption of almost all facets of transatlantic trade for Cuba. Rice imports from England decreased from almost 110 million pounds in 1914 to 46 million pounds in 1918. The decline of rice imports from Germany was total: from 85 million pounds in 1914 to nothing at all through the war years. (See table 2.3.)[57]

The disruption of the European rice supplies provided U.S. producers with long-coveted access to Cuban markets. Rice imports from the United States increased dramatically: from 13 million pounds in 1914 to nearly 117 million pounds in 1918 to almost 133 million pounds in 1920—an increase from 4

TABLE 2.2. Cuban rice imports by country of origin, 1903–1914 (pounds)

	1903	1906	1908	1910	1912	1914
Germany	64,229,000	65,265,000	82,466,000	103,134,000	97,414,000	84,950,000
Great Britain	76,375,000	102,520,000	86,933,000	86,400,000	83,549,000	109,018,000
India	6,737,000	22,684,000	42,716,000	51,389,000	56,703,000	63,626,000
Spain	2,178,000	2,123,000	2,943,000	3,690,000	2,038,000	3,237,000
United States	54,000	611,000	777,000	3,828,000	9,234,000	13,375,000
Total	149,573,000	193,203,000	215,835,000	248,441,000	248,938,000	274,206,000

Source: U.S. Tariff Commission, *The Effects of the Cuban Reciprocity Treaty of 1902* (Washington, D.C., 1929).

TABLE 2.3. Cuban rice imports by country of origin, 1915–1920 (pounds)

	1915	1916	1917	1918	1919	1920
Germany	12,823,000	—	—	—	—	—
Great Britain	179,587,000	180,503,000	184,105,000	46,027,000	744,000	3,750,000
India	56,650,000	59,347,000	50,570,000	80,935,000	49,638,000	48,816,000
Spain	4,857,000	4,634,000	2,551,000	172,000	—	5,460,000
United States	34,908,000	60,817,000	49,930,000	116,876,000	126,923,000	132,526,000

Source: U.S. Tariff Commission, *The Effects of the Cuban Reciprocity Treaty of 1902* (Washington, D.C., 1929).

percent of the total Cuban market in 1914 to almost 70 percent.[58] "The upshot of [the war]," the *Cuba Review* predicted as early as November 1914, "is that Cuba will have to look exclusively to the United States for her supply of rice, and her consumption of the cereal amounts to several million sacks annually."[59]

The war had one other effect: it laid waste to the European beet sugar production. French production declined by almost two-thirds, from an average annual of 900,000 tons to 332,000 tons within one year. German production, which had previously accounted for 26 percent of the world supply of beet sugar, came to a near collapse. Between 1914 and 1918, the world supply of sugar declined by half, from 8 million tons to 4 million tons.[60]

The logic of supply and demand again wrought havoc on sugar markets. Prices increased as supplies decreased: 1.9 cents per pound in 1914, up to 3.3 cents in 1915, 4.4 cents in 1916, and 4.7 cents in 1917. In 1920, the year of the "Dance of the Millions," the frenzy of sugar seized hold of commodity markets and the "price of sugar soared to unbelievable heights," Edith Pitts recalled.[61] The surge in prices was dizzying: 10 cents per pound in March, 13 cents on April 1, and 18 cents on April 15, reaching 22.5 cents per pound in May.[62] Cuban production responded—"*las vacas gordas*," these years became known—with production increasing from 2.6 million tons in 1914, to 3 million in 1916, to 4 million in 1919. "Sugar for two years has been a gold mine," Assistant Secretary of the Navy Franklin D. Roosevelt entered into his diary during a visit to Cuba in early 1917.[63]

Sugar cane was on the march again, advancing into the eastern provinces of Camagüey and Oriente. "The villages are coming under the siege of the cane fields," Carlos Martí observed traveling through Oriente province.[64] In 1899, sugar production in Oriente accounted for approximately 69,000 acres of land; by 1918, sugar had expanded onto 826,000 acres.[65] In 1902, Camagüey and Oriente accounted for 16.2 percent of total sugar production (2.7 percent and 13.5 percent respectively); in 1921, the total had increased to 55.9 percent (Camagüey 23.6 percent and Oriente 32.3 percent)[66]—an expansion, economist José Alvarez Díaz commented in understated manner, that proved to be "an obstacle to diversified agriculture in later years."[67]

Among the first lands to succumb to sugar were the old-growth forests of Oriente province. "Immense areas have been cleared for [sugar] cultivation," reported the U.S. consul in Santiago de Cuba.[68] Tens of thousands of acres of the finest hardwood forests in the New World were wantonly cleared to make way for sugar cane: by logging, by fire, by dynamite—by whatever means obtained the quickest clearing. "All the trees have been removed ruthlessly," Irene Wright described the expansion of sugar in Mayarí, "and in some cases obviously unnecessarily, till cane fields cover the country like a smooth unwrinkled blanket."[69] Years later Teresa Casuso recalled her childhood in Oriente:

> I remember, in Oriente, the great impenetrable forests that were set aflame, whole jungles that were fired and razed to the ground to make way for sugar cane. My parents were in despair for that lost wealth of beautiful, fragrant tropical wood—cedar and mahogany and mastic, and magnificent-grain pomegranate—blazing in sacrifice to the frenzy to cover the countryside with sugar cane. In the nights the sight of that flaming horizon affected me with a strange, fearful anxiety, and the aroma of

burning wood floating down from so far away was like the incense one smells inside churches.⁷⁰

Everyone seemed determined to plant sugar cane, everywhere. "If things continue like this," the daily *El Mundo* despaired in 1916, "it will become necessary to plant cane even in the patios of our homes."⁷¹

The sugar estates expanded in scope and increased in size. More and more land passed into the possession of fewer and fewer owners. Colossal corporate-owned plantations—the *central latifundio*—mostly U.S.-owned, converted vast swaths of the national territory into immense fields of sugar cane. The expansion of sugar, traveler Harry Franck commented tersely in 1920, "is swamping all other industries in the island, nay, even its scenery, beneath endless seas of cane."⁷² The concentration of property in the possession of corporate plantations bode ill, warned *El Mundo*:

> We would prefer to see in Cuba thousands of small mills rather than several dozen monster mills [*centrales-monstruos*]. They are an anathema because they are *latifundios*, because they are almost all foreign-owned corporations.... They are anathema, moreover, and repulsive, because of their tendency to absorb and devour all the small farms [*todas las fincas pequeños*] in their immediate vicinity; for their tendency to impoverish all the small farmers [*todos los pequeños agricultores*]. It would be a curse for Cuba if this property regimen were to prevail, for Cuba would then be nothing more than a colossal sugar factory owned by foreign corporations.... They insidiously appropriate all Cuban land. If this appropriation continues, the day is not far off when the entire rural population of Cuba will be proletarianized, dispossessed of land, and resulting in grave agrarian problems. We will face tremendous social convulsions, for no people will allow themselves to starve to death in their own land [*en su propia tierra*], land that has passed under the control of foreign corporations. This is not to say that the *centrales-monstruos* do not produce monstrous wealth. They do, but this wealth or most of it does not remain in the country, it is not distributed within the country. Our *centrales-monstruos* enrich the country but not its inhabitants. A country may be rich and its people poor.... These present circumstances prescribe the creation of a regimen of small mills and the development of small property owners.⁷³

Historian Ramiro Guerra y Sánchez despaired over the "decline of subsistence agriculture [*sitios de labor*]": the *latifundio* "consolidates thousands of small agriculture plots into immense agrarian units; it destroys the rural landowning and independent farming class [and] . . . is fatally and ineluctably reducing the great mass of the Cuban people to misery."[74]

Many of the problems that beset small farmers in the colony persisted into the republic. The interior road system remained in execrable condition. A long-promised road serving Santa Clara–Remedios–Yaguajay in Las Villas province languished unfinished for years. A zone of 120 square miles with a population of 45,000 inhabitants, mostly families of small farmers, had no means of delivering produce to local urban markets other than by way of packs of mule trains.[75] "The problem," *Diario de la Marina* editorialized in 1917, "is above all the absence of easy and inexpensive transportation access to reach population centers." Too much "foodstuffs [*productos alimenticios*] cannot find their way to the markets and those products that do reach the markets arrive in damaged condition."[76] Conditions in the rich agricultural districts of Baracoa, decried *Diario de Cuba* in 1918, are "today sad and miserable despite the wealth of its agriculture due to a lack of means with which to transport its products. Of what use is the fertility of the soil to the people? The people do not have any means of communication. Today all sorts of difficulties are placed in the way of transporting *frutos menores*. . . . The farmers do not have any good roads to transport their products to markets where they can be sold for profit."[77]

Nor did the extensive railway networks that developed in the early republic improve the distribution of domestic production. Exorbitant freight charges rendered the cost of internal shipment of foodstuffs beyond the reach of small farmers. "The *frutos menores*, poultry, livestock, and everything else that the country produces," *El Mundo* protested, "cannot be consumed in the large population centers due to the prohibitive fees charged by the railroads. . . . Vast quantities of beans, onions, pepper, and other products are totally lost due to the railroads."[78] The problem of *frutos menores*, insisted *Diario de la Marina*, cannot be resolved until "the farmer [*guajiro*] obtains the means to transport his merchandise to population centers with efficiency and at reasonable cost." *El Mundo* was blunt: "It does the farmer little good to bestir himself to increase production of *frutos menores* if upon completion of the harvest he faces, on one hand, prohibitively high freight fees and, on the other, impassable roads."[79]

Small farmers were being displaced, dislodged, and dispossessed faster than at any time in living memory. "The small Cuban landowner, independent and prosperous," Fernando Ortiz brooded, "the backbone of a strong rural middle class, is gradually disappearing."[80] Farmers seemed powerless to forestall their fate. "No one pays attention to the unfortunate small farmer," *Diario de Cuba* lamented, "not withstanding the fact that the high cost of [imported] provisions renders his products indispensable to the country. Who protects him?

... All the attention is bestowed on sugar cane, most of which is under the control of large foreign companies. It is not strange, hence, that the aspiration of everyone is to plant sugar cane and the dread of all is to be obliged to plant *frutos menores*."[81] Commented the *Cuba Review* as early as 1914,

> Isolated and alone ... is the sorrowful situation of the present day Cuban farmer! Rarely is there to be found a country in the world where the farmer is so left to his own resources by the government as is the Cuban "guajiro."
> ... In Cuba the government makes no effort to reach the thatched hut of the farmer who produces the wealth of the nation. They are not taken in hand and educated and told how they might improve their planting and how to double their products. They are left alone to their resources.[82]

Sociologist Lowry Nelson was succinct: "A new group of landless farm people were created."[83]

Not only did Cubans lose land sufficient to live off of, but they also lost land adequate to die on. Years later a longtime resident of Mayarí remembered the expansion of the United Fruit Company: "Those were the days when people were run off their own lands—though they had papers dating back to colonial days to show it was theirs—because corrupt officials would sell the land to La United.... You may ask yourself what a pass we had come to that eventually we had to beg La United for a tiny bit of land to have a cemetery!"[84]

THE WORLD SEEMED to have turned upside down. Land values soared. Property selling $250 per *caballería* in 1914 sold for $1,000 in 1916.[85] Rising land values made everything worse, forcing some farmers off the land and obliging others to produce crops of greater remunerative returns. Agriculture was driven by imperative of export production. "I see that the war in Europe is costing Cubans dearly," one farmer wrote to *Diario de la Marina* in October 1914. "Here in Santa Clara we are paying three pesos per arroba of rice. And one might ask: why do farmers not plant rice? Ah, learned gentlemen! We do not plant rice, or corn, or tomatoes because we do not own the land and the landowners raise the rent so high that we can pay only by planting sugar cane and tobacco."[86] Land in the district of San Antonio de los Baños rented for $500 per *caballería*, fees that could be defrayed only through revenue obtained through the production of tobacco.[87] The "earnings derived from the production of *frutos menores*," reported the mayor of Batabanó in Havana province, "are not sufficient to defray the excessive rental fees that landowners are charging tenant farmers."[88] Writer Carlos Martí observed similar conditions in Oriente, noting that "the high cost of rents of farmland do not allow us to dedicate the land to the production of *cultivos menores*. These yields will provide us with meals at the table and food for the children, but are not adequate to pay the rent for land."[89] The moral was plain. "The small Cuban population," one observer commented in 1917, "cannot produce $300 or $400 worth of sugar per capita and at the same time produce its own food."[90] Production for export expanded at the expense of production for consumption. Across the island, domestic food production faltered and floundered. "Although Cuba is plentifully endowed in both soil and climate for the production of practically all essential food commodities," commented the U.S. Department of Commerce, "its energies have been concentrated on sugar and tobacco, to the neglect of most articles of ordinary food required for the maintenance of her population, and the bulk of food requirements must be imported."[91]

Prosperity concealed the deepening fault lines coursing their way through the full breadth of production systems. Foreign exchange receipts from exports more than adequately defrayed the cost of food imports required to offset the decline of domestic production. The total value of food imports increased from $28 million in 1905, to $50 million in 1915, to $195 million in 1920, of which the U.S. share increased from $14 million (50 percent), to $29 million (58 percent), to $115 million (59 percent) respectively.[92] By the late 1910s, an estimated 75 to 80 percent of Cuban food supply originated from the United States. "We are consuming under normal conditions more than we produce," warned the Cuban Department of Agriculture, Commerce, and Labor in 1917. "We are importing many articles that we should produce. We are causing our working people to pay exorbitant duties on imported articles of sheer necessities."[93]

Not good, informed observers feared. "By planting only sugar cane and tobacco," economist Ramiro Cabrera warned, "we impoverish ourselves, simply because the production of foodstuffs has decreased. And since the cost of living has increased, we delude ourselves by thinking that our two principal products sell well, when in fact the profits are diverted to pay producers and importers from abroad. We produce four million tons of sugar, but in order to live and to eat we are obliged to spend 70 or 80 million pesos that instead of remaining in the country are carried off by the Americans. . . . We should produce great quantities of rice, which alone makes for 6 million pesos."[94] Economist Fernando Berenguer could hardly conceal his dismay. "Our imports are far too high and can be reduced substantially," he insisted in 1917, "if attention to the cultivation of other agricultural products [*el cultivo de otros frutos*] as necessary as sugar cane and tobacco was improved." Cuba had imported $1.7 million worth of beans, $1.5 million of corn, $1.2 million of potatoes, and $3.5

TABLE 2.4. Value of Cuban food imports, 1914 and 1916 (dollars)

	1914	1916	Percentage increase
Cereals	$15,394,000	$26,152,000	69.8
Fruits	722,000	1,248,000	72.8
Meat	11,269,000	18,427,000	63.5
Vegetables	5,602,000	10,362,000	84.9

Source: Henry H. Morgan to Herbert Hoover, August 4, 1917, 837.50/13, Records of the Department of State Relating to Internal Affairs of Cuba, 1910–1929, General Records of the Department of State, Record Group 59, National Archives, Washington, D.C.

million of rice in 1915, Berenguer noted. The Americans had not yet entered the European war, but it was a prospect that Berenguer contemplated with dread, for such an eventuality would inevitably require the United States to reorganize the commerce of its merchant fleet. "What would we eat? In what ships would we import rice, beans, lard, corn, potatoes, etc., that we need to eat?" Berenguer asked. He then decried the organization of the national railroad system, which was designed principally "to provide the sugar companies easy access for their exports to foreign ports.... They squeeze the life out of the people, inadequately serving our needs.... We are utterly irresponsible, or we have not adequately calculated the damage they are causing us. The present is very rosy, but if we do not correct our conduct the future that awaits us is not at all promising for the stability of the Republic." He continued,

> The solution of the problem lies in attending to the cultivation of agricultural products, for it is disgraceful that Cuba, where everything can be produced abundantly and quickly, is obliged to import all the products we consume, like corn, beans, rice, potatoes, eggs, etc., etc., from the United States and other countries, costing us millions of pesos, when all can be produced here. And let no one suggest that it is because the Cuban people do not want to work. Nothing of the kind. What we need is the Government to facilitate the means to produce ... all the aforementioned items.[95]

"One hundred twenty-four million dollars," protested an incredulous Luis Valdés-Roig in 1920, "is what Cuba sent abroad in 1917 and 1918, and which if invested in the production of *frutos menores,* would have been a new source of national wealth. How to overcome this Cuban negligence [*la incuria criolla*]?"

He asked again, "How to adjust agricultural activity efficiently toward the large-scale development of *cultivos menores*?" Valdés-Roig called for guaranteed government subsidies; low-interest loans; adjustment of railroad rates to stimulate internal trade; state-sponsored grants for seeds, fertilizers, and equipment; and obligatory state purchase of domestic food productions for the army, navy, hospitals, orphanages, and prisons.[96] A healthy diet, physician José Taboadela exhorted in 1917, should consist of locally accessible fresh vegetables and fruits, and to the point: "All Cubans should do what is within their reach to reduce as much as possible those foodstuffs of foreign origins.... This effort would not only have salutary dietary results but also limit the loss of foreign exchange to pay for foodstuffs [*la exportación de dinero en pago de efecto alimenticios*] and at the same time will stimulate and protect the production of the so-called *frutos menores* which possess far more value that our apathy acknowledges."[97] All in all, an incomprehensible state of affairs, protested Mayor Pascual Zapata of San José de los Ramos in Matanzas:

> How is it that we have to pay [to import] beans, potatoes, onions, garlic, rice, corn and other articles at such high prices when our beloved nation [*nuestra querida patria*] possesses a remarkable fertility?... Our products are of superior quality than imports. We are duty-bound to free ourselves, for to plant without rest we obtain dignity and patriotism.... If all Cubans, thinking of the future, demonstrated to Cuba the love by which we are inspired and make all the necessary sacrifice we will liberate ourselves from this foreign tutelage. Let us commit to this patriotic undertaking, to awaken the national sentiment, and we will make of our nation what it deserves to be: an emporium of wealth.[98]

THE ERA OF *las vacas gordas* ended almost as quickly as it had begun. Sugar markets collapsed at war's end. Sugar that sold for 22.5 cents per pound in May 1920 fell to 8 cents in September and to 3.8 cents in December. The boom-bust cycle took its toll. The total value of the 3.7 million ton harvest of 1920 had surpassed $1 billion; the value of the 3.9 million ton harvest of 1921 was only $292 million.

The ruin wrought by the delirium of sugar was revealed in full relief as prosperity receded. A grim reality settled over Cuba. The collapse of sugar signaled the collapse of foreign exchange receipts, which meant too that the level of food imports upon which Cubans had come to depend could not be sustained. Food imports declined; prices increased.[99] "Every day the prices of the principal provisions [*los principales víveres*] go higher and higher," protested *El Mundo* in 1915, "imposing the greatest hardship upon the poor classes of the country."[100] That production for export had so fully displaced production for consumption had rendered domestic agriculture incapable of providing adequate food supplies. "The concentration of island agriculture upon the sugar industry," reported one trade publication in 1918, "[has] caused the home production of foodstuffs to be neglected"[101]—with predictable consequences. More and more land produced less and less food. Reports of declining food production increased. "*Frutos menores* are very scarce in the province of Camagüey," *Diario de la Marina* reported tersely in 1918. Food production in agricultural districts outside Santiago de Cuba came to a near collapse.[102] Bleak prospects indeed. "When the price of sugar began to increase," *Diario de la Marina* reflected on the food crisis in 1920, "the cultivation of *frutos menores* decreased further. Now almost nothing exists."[103]

Cubans had lost the capacity to feed themselves. "We have suffered more than once the turmoil that Cuba is today experiencing as a result of sugar production," *El Mundo* editorialized. "Instead of Cuba living off sugar, we see that sugar lives off Cuba.... In very few zones have we planted sufficient *frutos menores* to provide us today with the margin of security to overcome the present crisis."[104] Writer Carlos Martí recorded his experience in Santiago de Cuba: "In Santiago, during the early hours of the evening and on a central street, a young woman in miserable condition approached me, and extending her hand explained: 'Alms, for God's sake, neither my children nor I have eaten today.' There is hunger in the city, there is hunger in the countryside.... Every day there are fewer farm plots, every day fewer *fincas*, every day fewer haciendas."[105] Years later Armando Cárdenas remembered his childhood in Bayamo:

> We were so poor there were days when we didn't eat.... Our problem was that we had no land to work and no way of making a living. Things were so bad for us that my folks migrated from place to place in search of a way to better their situation.... We kept wandering over highways and byways for almost a year to find a place to make a living.... But we had nothing. It was desperation that drove my folks on, looking for somebody to give them a piece of land.[106]

Grocery stores across the island reported recurring depletions of inventories of basic foodstuffs. Rice supplies almost disappeared from shelves of local bodegas. Bread became scarce.[107] The cost of food will "soar in price," the U.S. consul general predicted, adding, "In the matter of foodstuffs there would be absolute suffering for the reason that Cuba, in the agricultural sections, does not produce much of the quantity or the kind of foodstuffs consumed either in the cities or the country."[108]

Prices did indeed soar. The combination of scarcity and high prices plunged households into disarray. "We feel the effects of the war, even here," complained the *Cuba News* as early as 1914. "Rice, beans, lard, flour, etc., have advanced in price more than 50 per cent. It is just a case of starving if you don't pay the increase."[109] The price of rice rose by nearly 70 percent between 1916 and 1917: from $4.60 per quintal to $7.75, a difference that was reflected in the retail price increase of 3–5 cents per pound before the war to 9–12 cents in 1918.[110] "Staples of food of the laboring classes," reported the U.S. legation in 1919, "such as beans, rice, cod-fish, etc., ... have all risen in price from 200 to 400 percent since the outbreak of the world war."[111] Several years later, *Diario de la Marina* would look back upon these years and draw the obvious moral:

> We have learned with ruthless adversity of the great danger of dedicating ourselves almost exclusively to one industry.... During the days of abundance it absorbed and stifled the production of foodstuffs that could have alleviated the suffering of the country. Subsistence farms were converted into sugar estates; the plows were displaced by machetes. Sugar cane devoured the vegetables, the gardens, the legumes, the grains. The onslaught came upon us so suddenly that the country had no way of remedying the vast void created in its wake.... The economic crisis underscored the necessity to attend with urgency the cultivation of these products.[112]

Untold numbers of households in Havana succumbed to indigence. All during the late colonial period and through the years of the independence war, the capital had filled with a vast internal migration of the poor.[113] Little had changed in the early republic. Hunger persisted as a Cuban condition into the twentieth century. Disease was never far away. The medical journal *La Higiene* published a blistering indictment of conditions in Havana in 1906: "Misery reigns in our urban capital.... A great majority of the poor die of hunger or suffer from diets so inadequate that they are in a constant state of debilitation due to the lack of proper nutrition."[114] Conditions worsened during the 1910s. In early 1916, the *ayuntamiento* of Havana met in extraordinary session to address "the truly desperate problem facing our poor families created by the shortages of essential staples [*la carestia de los artículos de primera necesidad*] ... and [to] resolve this crisis of hunger confronting the poor of Havana who today live in a truly miserable state [*un estado verdaderamente miserable*]."[115] Several months later, municipal authorities inaugurated the first of a series of soup kitchens (*cocinas económicas*) in working-class neighborhoods "to meet the great scarcity [*tremenda carestía*] we are currently suffering."[116] The Department of Agriculture exhorted all Cubans to establish gardens "in which to plant vegetables in order to relieve the current scarcity of foodstuffs," affirming that "given the high cost of vegetables that prevails in the markets ... all Cubans should plant something."[117] Sugar could no longer furnish Cubans with their most basic needs. "In Cuba," commented one merchant in Santiago de Cuba, "our gold was produced by sugar and it benefited everyone, including Cubans of the most humble classes. But now we confront the absurd situation that not even with gold can foodstuffs be purchased. And one cannot eat gold."[118]

The crisis of food summoned full-scale government mobilization. The administration of Mario G. Menocal (1912–20) enjoined sugar estates across the island to expand their production of foodstuffs.[119] The Cuban House of Representatives debated a bill designed to require sugar and tobacco plantations to increase food production. "Our intention," explained Representative Estanislao Cartañá, "is not to limit the production of sugar cane and tobacco, but to require the planting of *frutos menores* in proportion to the production of *frutos mayores* and in relation to the size of the estate."[120] In 1918 the government ordered all farmers to expand production of food: "Farmers are required to plant increased crops of vegetables and grains. If the war continues, as it appears, import products will continue to decline, which means that Cuba will have to sustain itself with food produced in its own soil.... The planting of sugar cane produces only money and in these times money is not sufficient to eat. If farmers do not produce vegetables and cereals, the accumulation of money will be futile, for the moment will arrive in which there will be no food to buy."[121] The provincial governor of Havana, Celestino Balzán, ordered the mayors of the province to adopt "all measures necessary to increase the production of *frutos menores* to avoid the grave danger that the scarcity of food imports posed to the country," adding, "We cannot as a result of inexcusable inertia, punishable indifference, and criminal apathy allow our people to do without the indispensable elements of life.... We must banish the phantasm of hunger that menaces us and casts a dark shadow of misery upon Cuban homes."[122] The mayors of Havana, Batabanó, Guira de Melena, Güines, and Bejucal responded and imposed "mandatory production of *frutos menores* and other measures to alleviate the current economic crisis": "The matter of the production of *frutos menores* has ceased to be a quaint social issue of lesser or greater importance. It is now a matter of pressing urgency, a duty as necessary as military service in defense of the nation and to which the government must attend in the defense of society. And more: the obligatory production of *frutos menores*, without exaggeration, is a matter that bears on public order."[123] *El Mundo* took note of the change in official attitudes: "How times change! Before the government attended more to the interests of the 'minority' producers than to the needs of the 'majority' consumers. Now it is the reverse. The government has arrived to an understanding that great profits for producers matter less than sufficient food for consumers."[124]

In fact, the times may have changed, but attitudes did not. The crisis of food production ended in the early 1920s. Sugar markets recovered, and things went back to the way they were before. "Considerable progress has been made during the present year toward the restoration of Cuba's economic prosperity," Luis Marino Pérez, the Cuban commercial attaché in Washington, affirmed in 1923. "The notable improvement which has been brought about in a relatively short time is highly creditable to the people and government of Cuba."[125] Food imports resumed. Especially rice.

CHAPTER THREE

An Uncertain Source of Wealth

The sugar industry depends on an external market that is uncontrollable and subject to all types of fluctuations, whereas the rice industry is developed to satisfy exclusively an internal market that is stable and secure.
—*Carteles* (February 3, 1935)

The United States imports annually from Cuba better than sixty million dollars worth of sugar. The sugar and rice states of the United States are the same. If then, on one hand, we are to permit Cuban sugar to come into the United States, by the same token Cuba should grant every preferential asked on rice from the United States, as farmers of the states which produce sugar might at least offset a part of their sugar losses by increasing their rice income.
—William M. Reid [Rice Millers Association] to Franklin D. Roosevelt, 1933

We have to export at least half of our rice ... and yet when we go to Cuba to sell rice, which is the greatest rice-using nation on the continent, we find that we are met with a sales tax, which makes it almost impossible for us to sell rice in that market. Now, if preferences are going to be given in trade through this [reciprocity] arrangement with Cuba so that we will take more sugar from Cuba, do you not think that a policy ought to be worked out which would require them to do just the same thing for us, to have a reciprocity trade relationship, in reference to rice?—Representative David Glover, Arkansas, 1934

Cubans must always be mindful of the following: our economic life depends solely and exclusively upon the United States. We sell *all* our products to them. We import *almost all* the products we consume from them.—*El Mundo*, April 24, 1916 (emphasis in original)

Whatever the future of sugar may be, Cuba cannot depend solely on sugar. The guarantee of the stability of the Republic must rest on the solid basis of a national economy [*sólida base de economía nacional*]. Economic slavery leads to political slavery. Today we are not absolutely independent: our national economy practically speaking is not ours.... Sugar is an uncertain source of wealth. Nor should we continue to entrust our well-being to the single market of the United States.—José Comallonga, *La nueva economía agraria de Cuba* (1929)

THE FAR-REACHING dislocations wrought by World War I passed into a condition of permanence, which is to say, new economic arrangements around which patterns of daily life accommodated. The transformations of the material physiognomy of the island would endure deep into the twentieth century. The participation—and preponderance—of North American capital expanded into the national economy, to the point at which Cuban claims to sovereign authority were no longer plausible: in public utilities and public railways, in banking and finance, in mining and manufacture, in industry and agriculture, and especially—of course—in sugar. North American investment in Cuban sugar increased from $220 million in 1913 to $1.5 billion in 1928, enlarging too the share of sugar produced by U.S.-owned mills: from 15 percent in 1906, to 48 percent in 1920, to 75 percent in 1928.[1] The United States absorbed the better part of Cuban trade and commerce, serviced the movement of imports and exports, and managed the inner workings of transnational supply chains as if in charge of a fully integrated national market system.

This was the case with almost everything—except rice. Asian rice quickly recovered its prewar primacy in Cuban markets. By the mid-1920s, rice from India, China, Burma, Thailand, Japan, and Indo-China accounted for almost 70 percent (301,000 million pounds out of nearly 443,000 million pounds) of total imports.[2] U.S. rice had accounted for nearly 35 percent of total imports in 1918, some 117 million pounds out of a total of 342 million pounds; by 1922, the U.S. share had declined to 11 percent of the total, some 42 million pounds out of 368 million pounds.[3] (See table 3.1.)

The loss of Cuban markets resulted in vast surpluses of unsold rice.[4] Export markets were essential to sustain U.S. production. "During the period of the war," J. A. Foster, president of the Rice Millers Association, explained to the membership in 1920, "we have been operating on a sellers' market. The pendulum has now begun to swing the other way, and for the good of the industry . . . I urge you to study the foreign market and endeavor to shape your business so that it will fit into the established trade customs of foreign countries." Foster continued:

TABLE 3.1. Cuban rice imports by country of origin, 1913 and 1920–1923 (pounds)

	1913	1920	1921	1922	1923
China	N/A	179,412,000	47,977,000	37,587,000	33,039,000
Germany	106,281,000	—	6,904,000	31,579,000	35,253,000
India	61,489,000	48,816,000	81,578,000	157,627,000	244,302,000
Japan	N/A	95,348,000	9,996,000	6,751,000	3,959,000
United Kingdom	91,505,000	3,750,000	42,577,000	92,628,000	62,280,000
United States	5,734,000	132,526,000	59,122,000	41,626,000	33,198,000

Source: Leslie A. Wheeler, "The Cuban Market for American Foodstuffs," U.S. Department of Commerce, Bureau of Foreign and Domestic Commerce, *Trade Information Bulletin* 325 (1925).

I have in mind particularly the development of the Cuban market for American rice. The island of Cuba is almost exactly the same size as the State of Louisiana, but the consumption of rice is approximately one-half the consumption of the Continental United States. Havana is only forty-eight hours away from New Orleans. . . . Cuba however has been securing her rice from the Orient for 400 years. The Oriental rices do not begin to compare in quality with our American rices, but by reason of a moisture content of 12 percent to 13½ percent as against our 14 percent to 14½ percent, the Oriental rices cook up in a dryer state, which is the way the Cubans like their rice. It will take patient educational means to demonstrate the superior quality of our rices, but in the meantime the Cuban market should be intelligently studied, and we on our part should co-operate with Cuban merchants to build up an outlet for our rices, rather than adopt arbitrary rules that will cut us out entirely of this great potential market.[5]

U.S. rice producers had acquired short-lived access to Cuban markets on a scale unmatched since the nineteenth century, and with that access they acquired too a renewed appreciation of the importance of Cuba. "The export movement has come to our rescue," pronounced rice grower A. Locke Breaux in 1916.[6] "A good, strong campaign is necessary to boost American rices," insisted rice exporter Rafael Camejo, to "find out what Cuba needs and give the Cuban people what they want," adding: "American rice is just as good—and we claim it is better—than Oriental rice."[7]

American producers renewed their demands for greater access to Cuban markets, appealing to Washington to the renegotiate the terms of the 1903 Reciprocity Treaty. "Our treaty with Cuba should be revised," the *Rice Belt Journal* demanded in 1920. "This should be undertaken with a view of securing greater opportunities for American products of the soil," and to the point: "[A] 40 per cent [tariff concession] upon an article produced under American conditions of living, and conveyed to Cuba at freight rates such as prevail in the carrying trade of the Western Hemisphere, can hardly be called an adequate margin if we are to meet competition from the coolie grown rice of Asia."[8] The failure to establish a presence in Cuban markets signaled a loss of revenue, of course. But it also signified exclusion from what the Americans deemed to be a proprietary market. Indeed, the Reciprocity Treaty of 1903 was designed to integrate the Cuban economy as an extension of the American national system. Something had gone very wrong.

North American producers could not compete in Cuban markets. U.S. rice imports represented a dwindling share of total Cuban supplies, declining from nearly 40 percent in 1919 to 0.1 percent in 1934. Imports for the years 1919–20 had been the exception, due principally to the loss of Asian imports during World War I. The bumper crop of 1920 was the largest U.S. rice harvest ever produced but ill-timed, for it coincided with the contraction of postwar markets and the decline of prices.[9] American producers proceeded to flood the Cuban market with the accumulated postwar surplus—what Rice Millers Association president William Reid would later characterize as a time "when Cuba was used as a dumping ground for an after-war surplus."[10] Otherwise, U.S. rice was a nonfactor in the Cuban market. (See table 3.2.)

Cuban rice production was even less a factor. The demise of domestic rice production was itself a facet of a larger economic malaise, an economy overwhelmed by foreign capital and undermined by foreign imports. Published data of domestic rice production disappeared as a statistically significant economic activity of the early republic. The conventional wisdom posits that rice production was limited to the vegetable gardens of small farms, consumed principally by the families of the producers themselves and sold in local markets.[11] Rice as an agriculture of significance had all but vanished.

THE 1920S WERE years of transition, as a deepening national awareness of the republic having gone awry registered. The first republican-born generation had come of age, men and women eminently susceptible to the stirring of nationalist sentiments, determined to make good on ideals of national sovereignty

TABLE 3.2. Proportion of total Cuban rice imports from the United States, 1919–1934 (quintals)

Year	United States	Total	U.S. percentage of total
1919	1,269,228	3,199,328	39.7
1920	1,325,257	4,756,207	27.9
1921	591,217	2,554,897	23.1
1922	416,261	3,861,996	10.8
1923	331,978	4,429,843	7.5
1924	333,707	4,447,068	7.5
1925	325,851	4,238,488	7.7
1926	157,706	4,705,756	3.4
1927	248,925	4,295,978	5.8
1928	411,903	5,069,003	8.1
1929	181,959	4,470,874	4.1
1930	27,864	4,384,074	0.6
1931	94,315	3,371,426	2.8
1932	188,810	3,080,346	6.1
1933	57,332	2,754,101	2.1
1934	4,268	3,634,783	0.1

Source: "El mercado cubano de arroz: Fuentes de abastecimiento, precios, producción y consumo," *Cuba Económica y Financiera*, April 1956.

and self-determination. Representatives of an emerging entrepreneurial class bestirred themselves with a newfound sense of patriotic purpose in pursuit of greater ownership over and larger participation in the economy, to demand policies to defend national industry, tariffs to protect domestic markets, and government support for agricultural diversification.[12]

The Customs-Tariff Law (1927) enacted by the government of Gerardo Machado (1925–33) was both cause and consequence of a changing national mood, propounding the claim to economic self-determination in discharge of national interests. It was "the most important legislation of an economic nature enacted during the first three decades of the 20th Century," pronounced economist José Alvarez Díaz, "and may be called the first economic effort made by the Cuban government directed toward augmenting the national production with a view to the domestic market."[13] The Customs-Tariff Law claimed inspiration "within a reasonable sentiment to protect our principal industries, driven to promote the improvement of our country and its economic conditions."[14] The 1927 law committed the state to active participation in economic development, to promote national industry, to diversify domestic agriculture, to expand the capacity for self-sufficiency, and to reduce the loss of foreign exchange—what economist Jorge Pérez-López characterized as a decision by the government to intervene actively "in favor of industrialization and diversification of the economy" as a "nationalistic [attempt] to break away from the dominance of sugar."[15]

Machado was lucid on the purpose of economic policy, in critical recognition of the anomalies of the export economy. "The old colonial mold will be broken," Machado vowed in 1926, "in favor of new methods through which to expand the industrial and agricultural development of our country.... Cuba needs to diversify its production to live well and without the periodic anguish associated with recurring sugar crises that endanger the economic stability of the nation." He added,

> The State has the duty to assist all facets of individual initiative dedicated to the expansion of production.... Without economic independence there can no true political independence. We, who wish above all to preserve our political independence, obtained with the sacrifice of so many precious lives, ... must secure our economic independence in order to satisfy the greater part of our national needs. The fertility of our land allows us to guarantee an adequate and prudent production. Cuba can produce corn, rice, meat, and many more articles that today we obtain from abroad at an incredible cost of many millions of dollars.... The State will lend assistance through institutions of agricultural credit and a policy of tariffs ... to favor those productions that we presently lack. We must convince ourselves that dedicating all our efforts to one single product implies the slow but inevitable pauperization of the Republic and leads to irreparable ruin.[16]

The Customs-Tariff Law reduced duties on raw materials to stimulate expansion of domestic industrial capacities: on crude oil to encourage refining capacities; on sisal to boost rope and cordage manufacturing; on cotton to promote textiles. Tariffs on manufactured goods were raised to protect national manufacture, in some instances equivalent to more than 100 percent ad valorem, thereby rendering imports prohibitive. The production of domestic foodstuffs, including meat, milk, fruit, vegetables, and eggs, increased; imports of foreign foodstuffs declined, including tasajo, lard, potatoes, beans, coffee, corn, canned fruits, vegetable fats, and condensed milk.[17] "There has been a notable effort on the part of the Cuban Government," the U.S. Embassy reported in 1929, "to encourage the production of the so-called minor crops, notably fruit and vegetables. Coffee culture, rice culture, and the production of textile fibers have likewise been encouraged.... The new tariff, which was placed in effect in October 1927, was prepared with the idea of fostering those industries which appeared most advantageous in Cuba."[18]

Policies of diversification and self-sufficiency registered early success. Domestic production of foodstuffs increased in volume and variety. Cubans "are making successful efforts to bring about diversification of their agriculture," William Cooper, head of the U.S. Bureau of Foreign and Domestic Commerce, observed in 1930, "and are now raising a number of foodstuffs which they formerly obtained from abroad."[19] Perhaps for the first time, economic development responded to a master plan, a program in the form of a policy. "An economic psychology, new to Cuba," U.S. commercial attaché Frederick Todd reported, "is materializing, bringing changes in the entire social and economic scale and presaging the further development of national consciousness." Todd continued:

> The movement is national and grounded in national welfare.... The change is a growth, stimulated ... evolving toward a major economic readjustment dependent on the initiation and expansion of domestic industries.... [Cubans] have entered into a well-conceived plan of diversification of agriculture and the development of manufacturing industries to produce those articles which heretofore have been imported from other countries.... Even in the brief period from 1925 to 1930 great progress has been made in building up a more or less complete group of domestic industries sufficient to supply about five-sixths of the people with almost everything that they use regularly in their daily lives. Cuba is beginning to produce an astonishingly diverse lot of necessities.... [Cubans] believe that they are in the beginning of a new economic era, in which, instead of being virtually dependent on sugar and tobacco for their income[,] they will progressively expand and refine production of nearly everything they need for ordinary living, exchanging the products in domestic trade,

Route of the Central Highway of Cuba (Edwin J. Foscue,
"The Central Highway of Cuba," *Economic Geography* 9 [October 1933]).

increasing consumption and raising the standard of living through the island, steadily enlarging the volume of self-contained economic activity, and building up national prosperity along the same lines that have proven successful in the United States.[20]

The Machado government also attended to the long-overdue expansion of the road networks to stimulate internal transportation and facilitate the movement of goods and services. The completion in 1931 of the Central Highway connected the principal agricultural regions between Santiago de Cuba and Pinar del Río—"the first and most important unit of an elaborate road system designed to serve every part of the island," pronounced geographer Edwin Foscue[21]—and traversed all major provincial cities except Cienfuegos.

The Customs-Tariff Law happened also to coincide with hard times, circumstances that added urgency to the project of diversification as a means of self-sufficiency. The Depression arrived early to Cuba. The value of sugar exports declined steadily all through the late 1920s and early 1930s. In 1924, Cuba exported 8.7 million pounds of sugar, which generated $375.5 million in foreign exchange. In 1925, Cuba exported 10.8 million pounds of sugar but received only $280.3 million as a result of the declining world prices.[22] The worst was yet to come. (See table 3.3.)

The combination of decreasing export earnings at a time of increasing domestic food production acted to disrupt patterns of the transnational supply chain, consequences registered most keenly in the decline of food imports, and nowhere more striking than the decline of U.S. imports—what Charles Taussig, a member of President Franklin Roosevelt's "brain trust," characterized as a

TABLE 3.3. Cuban sugar exports to the United States, 1925–1933

Year	Volume (thousands of tons)	Price per pound (cents)
1925	3.6	2.63
1926	3.7	2.35
1927	3.2	2.88
1928	2.3	2.45
1929	3.5	1.88
1930	1.9	1.42
1931	1.7	1.26
1932	1.2	0.90
1933	0.9	1.17

Source: "Exportación de azúcar a los Estado Unidos," *Anuario Azucarero de Cuba 1959*, 33 (1959).

"catastrophic decline."[23] The Customs-Tariff Law, the U.S. Department of Commerce later acknowledged, "did weaken the [U.S.] competitive situation vis-à-vis Cuban domestic industry."[24] Between 1925 and 1929, the value of food imports from the United States decreased in every major category: in eggs, from $3.1 million to $736,000; in butter, $402,000 to $130,000; in cheese, $296,000 to $88,000; in milk, from $2.5 million to $2.3 million; in corn, $2.7 million to $767,000; in lard, $896,000 to $13,000.[25] "American exports to Cuba have been decimated in the past few years," Charles Barnes of the Department of Commerce explained in 1933, "not because the preference has been too small, but for two outstanding reasons. First, the purchasing power of the Cuban people has steadily diminished since 1924 with the falling price of sugar and second, mounting tariff and numerous taxes have made American goods too expensive."[26] The "decline of importation," Frederick Todd commented in 1930, "is due to domestic production rather than diminished consumption," observing,

> Locally raised bumper crops of yucca, malangas, plantains, potatoes, corn, eggs, and a wide range of northern varieties of vegetables are coming into the markets. The cattle and hog production has grown so that beef sells at 5 cents on the hoof. . . . Eggs are selling at 2 cents in interior cities and for less out in the country districts. . . . Shelled corn is so plentiful that it can be

bought, delivered in quantity at country stations, at $1 for 100 pounds....
The consumption of butter is rapidly expanding.... Production of milk
for distribution in bottles has greatly developed near Habana.... Cubans
can to-day feed themselves as they could not five years ago.[27]

The expansion of Cuban production in combination with the effects of the
Depression cost American producers dearly. Cuba dropped from sixth place—
surpassed only by England, Canada, Germany, France, and Japan—to sixteenth as a market for U.S. exports. The U.S. Department of Agriculture estimated that between 1928 and 1932, the loss of Cuban markets signified the withdrawal of an estimated 817,000 acres from agricultural production in the United States, contracting within five years from 1.7 million acres to 921,000 acres. Between 1926 and 1932, the total value of U.S. agricultural exports to Cuba decreased from $64 million to $9.6 million.[28] "During the past decade, and especially since 1927," U.S. ambassador Harry Guggenheim explained to the new Roosevelt State Department in 1933, "when the Cuban Government, in an effort to stimulate agricultural and industrial diversification, adopted a protective tariff policy, there have been important changes in our export trade with Cuba"—most notably, Guggenheim indicated, a loss of a substantial portion of the Cuban market. He continued, "The main reason for this decline undoubtedly is that Cuba's progress toward relative self-sufficiency has been largely at the expense of our exports to the Island. Due to increased local production, imports of a number of products formerly supplied almost entirely by the United States have been eliminated entirely ... or has been drastically curtailed."[29]

AMONG U.S. IMPORTS most "drastically curtailed" was rice. Indeed, the expansion of rice production had loomed large in Cuban plans for diversification. Between 1928 and 1930, the Machado government introduced agricultural extension programs across the island to promote production through the distribution of educational literature, offering lectures to farmers, and providing demonstrations of modern farming techniques. Shipments of new varieties of rice seeds increased. Two yearly distributions of 40,000 pounds of seeds were provided at no cost to encourage production. Programs designed to reduce costs and modernize technologies were established, principally through the allocation of modern equipment, including drills for planting, binders for harvesting, and modern threshers, which were subsequently leased or sold to local farmers through long-term low-interest loans. The government aspired to produce rice sufficient to meet as much as one-half of Cuban national demand.

Forty modern rice hulling machines were purchased by the government and distributed among municipalities across the island and thereupon sold at cost and on a deferred payment basis to local rice farmers. By the end of 1927, an estimated forty new milling centers had been established within developing rice zones.[30]

Rice production expanded. Acreage dedicated to rice increased, from 251 *caballerías* in 1929 to 1,185 *caballerias* in 1933.[31] The first available statistics of domestic rice production in the republic appeared during the Machado years. Rice production increased all through the late 1920s and early 1930s, from 91,000 quintals in 1928, to 260,000 quintals in 1932, to 306,000 quintals in 1933, to 399,000 quintals in 1935. Farms expanded across the island, principally along the southern regions of the provinces of Matanzas and Las Villas, accounting for an estimated 50 percent of national production, with important zones established in Pinar del Río and Havana, expanding into Camagüey, from Morón to Ciego de Avila, and into Oriente, between Bayamo and Manzanillo.[32] The Cuban farmer, reported commercial attaché Frederick Todd in 1930, was not only "growing enough for his family needs, but he is also producing a surplus which is responsible for the growth of a local trade. In some articles, notably corn and rice, the surplus is sufficient to aggregate a volume that is finding its way into the larger cities and towns."[33]

U.S. rice imports plummeted, in part the result of domestic production and in part the result of declining consumer purchasing power. In 1932, the Machado government introduced a consumption tax on rice of 1 cent per pound and raised the price of imported rice through the imposition of a higher duty on rice imports to $1.80 per kilo, eliminating the duty deferential enjoyed by American rice producers. The increased revenue obtained by the new decree was to be "assigned to the Department of Agriculture for use in the development of national rice production."[34] Protected by higher import costs, increasing numbers of farmers expanded the cultivation of rice for local markets. The volume of U.S. rice imports declined from 412,000 quintals in 1928 to 182,000 quintals in 1929, plummeting to 28,000 quintals in 1930 and to 4,000 quintals in 1934. The value declined respectively from $1.3 million, to $544,000, to $73,000, to $11,000.[35]

THE DEPRESSION visited calamity on American agriculture. Surpluses piled up; earnings plunged downward. A vital facet of U.S. economic recovery programs involved the revival of agricultural production through the recovery of foreign markets. Newly elected president Franklin Roosevelt was lucid on the purpose of U.S. foreign policy: "Foreign markets must be regained if America's producers are to rebuild a full and enduring domestic prosperity for our people. There is no other way if we would avoid painful economic dislocations, social readjustments, and unemployment."[36] Certainly Ambassador Guggenheim understood the importance of Cuban markets to aid U.S. economic recovery. The time had come, Guggenheim exhorted the State Department, to renegotiate the terms of the reciprocity treaty to obtain "a more favorable tariff treatment" for specific commodities, central to which was rice. "Rice would seem to offer the most promising item among Cuba's imports for tariff concessions to our exporters," Guggenheim suggested in 1933. "If American rice growers could capture fifty percent of Cuba's rice market, instead of the one and one-half percent which they obtained in 1931, our rice surplus would be readily disposed of."[37] On the matter of rice, Guggenheim was explicit. In 1931, Cuba imported 161,000 metric tons of rice valued at $7.3 million. Of this amount, the United States supplied only 4,154 metric tons valued at $101,000. "We secured only 2.6 per cent [of the total volume] in spite of a duty preferential of 40 percent," Guggenheim fretted. "The United States is reported to have an annual surplus of 2,000,000 pounds of rice . . . , and if our rice exporters could compete with shippers in the Orient we could undoubtedly secure well over half of the local rice business." Continued Guggenheim:

> As the Cuban Government is wisely trying to encourage local rice production it would probably not be feasible to secure an increase in our duty preferential on rice without a corresponding increase in the duty rate. The present duty could be increased from $1.50 per 100 kilos on cleaned rice and $1.00 on rough rice to $3.00 and $2.00 respectively and so that with our preferential raise to 50 per cent, we would have an advantage. This should be sufficient, under normal circumstances, to enable us to meet competition from the Orient successfully. At the same time it would not reduce the protection now enjoyed by local rice growers, as the duty on American rice under such an arrangement would be the same as the present rate on Oriental rice, while the duty on the latter would, of course, be substantially higher.[38]

Rice production in the United States was collapsing under the weight of mounting surpluses. Access to Cuban markets had assumed a new urgency. Within weeks of the inauguration of President Roosevelt, Rice Millers Association president William Reid appealed directly to the White House for assistance. Reid estimated rice surplus to surpass 1.8 million bags of rice annually, "which is a constant drag on the market and always a depressing influence on the entire crop." The principal rice-producing states—accounting for 80 percent of total U.S. production—bordered the Gulf of Mexico and served to place rice "right at Cuba's door." Reid drew the obvious lesson: "Notwithstanding the fact that the United States rice producing territory is closer to Cuba than any other ... the American rice industry is unable to merchandize to any extent in this market." Simply put, American producers remained unable to compete with Asian imports. "The possibility of getting into the Cuban market with United States rice," Reid pleaded, "is of very vital importance to the rice industry of this country."[39]

CUBA EARLY OCCUPIED the attention of the new Roosevelt administration. Through a series of extra-constitutional maneuvers, Machado had illegally extended his second term of office. Political opposition expanded; political violence increased. Machado's continued presence precluded the likelihood of a restoration of political stability and prevented too the likelihood of U.S. recovery of Cuban markets. On the eve of the inauguration of President Roosevelt, Philip Jessup, formerly the legal adviser at the U.S. Embassy in Havana in the early 1930s, prepared a confidential memorandum for the State Department. "Cuba has been endeavoring to get away from being practically a one-crop country," Jessup explained. "She has built up a number of industries which may or may not be suitable for permanent development. Some of these infant industries are owned or controlled by President Machado; Cuban interest in their maintenance might well therefore depend somewhat upon whether Machado remains in power.... It seems to me that a [new trade] treaty should be so designed to promote the welfare of Cuba, the sugar interests, and the interests of American exporters to Cuba."[40]

The historical scholarship on U.S.-Cuba relations has produced a rich historiography on the politico-diplomatic aspects of U.S. policy and the Cuban crisis of 1933.[41] Not as well appreciated, however, is the economic purpose to which the American policy was directed. The appointment of Assistant Secretary of State Sumner Welles as special presidential ambassador to Cuba underscored the complexity of the U.S. purpose: to restore Cuban political stability in order to negotiate a new trade agreement. "At a time when national economic recovery was the salient objective of the Government in Washington," Welles later wrote, "it was clear that the immense market for American agriculture and American industrial exports represented by Cuba should be restored to us." U.S. policy, Welles explained, sought, "first, to assist the Cuban people themselves to solve the political crisis which had developed[,] and second, to provide, by cooperation between our two Governments, a means for the rehabilitation of Cuba's national economy, and thereby likewise to reestablish, to the advantage of American agriculture and industry, the market which our own exports had previously enjoyed."[42]

Welles arrived in Havana prepared to support Machado—per the "plans which had been under consideration in Washington before my own departure"—if the "Cuban Government in turn would grant us a practical monopoly of the Cuban market for American imports." All of this was coded within thinly veiled political threats against Machado. "The present Cuban Government . . . ," Welles understood, "is well aware of the fact that it could not for long remain in power were the support of the United States to be even negatively withdrawn from it."[43] And at another point: "I told [Machado] that I did not feel that any one phase [that is, the political] of the existing Cuban problem could be dealt with separately but I thought on the contrary that the political, the economic and the financial aspects of the situation should be dealt with as parts of a whole."[44]

Welles engaged in "informal conversations" with members of the Machado administration and reported learning of "a general disposition to grant to the United States those advantages to our agricultural exports and our principal manufactures which we consider necessary"[45]—that is, to recover markets lost under the Customs-Tariff Law. "The negotiation at this time of a reciprocal trade agreement with Cuba . . . ," Welles predicted, "will not only revivify Cuba but will give us practical control of a market we have been steadily losing for the past 10 years not only for our manufactured products but for our agricultural exports as well, notably in such categories as wheat, animal fats, meat products, rice, and potatoes."[46] Welles was optimistic. "With regard to the commercial treaty," he wrote in the first week of July, "the ground work is practically completed. I expect to commence final negotiations myself about the end of the month."[47]

Welles pursued the U.S. purpose with focused deliberation, seeking to forge among competing power contenders a consensus in behalf of new trade arrangements as a condition to a political settlement, what Welles characterized as a "preliminary and tentative consideration of the basis for a reciprocal trade agreement between the United States and Cuba."[48] In a personal communication to Roosevelt, Welles was more blunt: "I am, of course, keeping the negotiation of the commercial treaty as a leverage until I know definitely where I stand on the political solution."[49]

Political events in Cuba spiraled out of control in midsummer 1933. A general strike precipitated a military coup and the ouster of Machado, with the understanding, Welles informed the White House, that "the next Government undertake the passage of much needed social and economic legislation. We will likewise regain an exceedingly important market for our exports."[50] Machado would later insist that U.S. determination to remove him from power had to do with the Customs-Tariff Law. "Our problem with the American government in 1933," he wrote, "resulted more from the efforts realized to free Cuba from American commerce than with questions of internal politics." Welles had arrived in Cuba bearing the draft of a new reciprocity treaty, Machado recounted, "one that favored the sugar producers—almost all foreigners—but at the expense of the small farmer." Machado concluded, "When we showed ourselves ill disposed to sacrifice Cuba ... Mr. Sumner Welles decided to achieve his objectives through other means."[51]

THE ROOSEVELT ADMINISTRATION moved quickly to recover Cuban markets. The enactment of the Jones-Costigan Act in May 1934 provided the legislative leverage through which to negotiate a new reciprocal trade agreement. Under Jones-Costigan, the Department of Agriculture was authorized to set annual duty-determined quotas on Cuban sugar in order, President Roosevelt explained, "to arrest the decline in Cuban sugar imports to the United States so as to increase the Cuban market for American exports of other products to Cuba"—that is, sugar would be the means with which to obtain from Cuba acquiescence to preferential tariffs on U.S. imports. The Roosevelt administration offered Cuban sugar a favorable 90-cents-per-100-pounds tariff reduction in exchange for wider access to Cuban markets for American agricultural exports. "The magnitude of this concession," Secretary of State Cordell Hull pronounced, "is a further indication of the desire of this Government to assist the Cuban people in regaining an adequate and satisfactory standard of living." But Hull also outlined the larger U.S. purpose: access to Cuban markets for American agricultural products. Explained Hull in mid-1934:

> It is to be expected that the Cuban Government, in return for this concession so vital to its national livelihood, will agree to concessions which will prove equivalent to those now being proposed by this Government. Owing to the drastic decline of Cuban imports of American products, it is essential that effective concessions be obtained for our key export commodities in exchange for our concessions to Cuba. I have no doubt that the Cuban Government appreciates this point of view and will create the desired trade advantages for our goods. Of our exports to Cuba, agricultural commodities have suffered the heaviest declines.[52]

THE NEW RECIPROCITY arrangement arrested and reversed diversification initiatives introduced under the Customs-Tariff Law, with many of the newly established projects, reported the Cuban Commission on Cuban Affairs of the Foreign Policy Association, destined to "succumb as a result of the new reciprocity treaty."[53] Between September 10 and 16, 1934, Charles Taussig exulted, "sixteen American ships brought into the port of Havana for consumption in Cuba 16,343 short tons of a wide variety of American products, including lard, meats, potatoes, [and] wheat."[54] In granting "numerous tariff reductions on items previously protected under the 1927 tariff," economist Jorge Pérez-López commented, the new reciprocity agreement represented "a step backward along the road toward industrial and agricultural diversification and political and economic independence from the United States."[55]

The United States had recovered its preponderant presence as the supplier of Cuban foodstuffs. Imports were once more the principal source of Cuban food. The value of U.S. exports fifteen months prior to the new reciprocity agreement totaled $33 million; in the fifteen months that followed the ratification of the agreement, the value increased to $71 million. "The benefit to our national economy resulting from this increased flow of trade," Secretary of State Cordell Hull affirmed, "has been widely distributed."[56]

Patterns of credit and distribution of loans again favored sugar—to the detriment of almost everything else. Between 1936 and 1947, loans to domestic rice production represented a fraction of the credit extended to sugar. In 1937, for example, sugar received $31.8 million in loans while rice received a mere $65,000, a pattern that prompted economist Henry Christopher Wallace to acknowledge "the desperate credit need of Cuban agriculturalists." Without access to bank credit, Wallace warned, farmers could obtain credit only from local store owners, produce merchants, and other commercial sources, who would also sell materials, equipment, and supplies, for which the farmer would accrue an additional debt, with interest rates of 30–40 percent not uncommon—a debt the Commission on Cuban Affairs of the Foreign Policy Association described as "ruinously high." The commission noted that "credit conditions in agriculture as a whole are primitive" and pointed to the "urgent need" for credit agencies to "offer to the honest and industrious farmer an opportunity to emerge from poverty." Among the final recommendations offered by the Foreign Policy Association was the proposal to establish "an Agricultural Bank to encourage diversification and local cooperative associations."[57] U.S. agricultural attaché Paul George Minneman reached the same conclusion in 1942. "Agricultural crops for market," Minneman reported, "are generally financed by commercial agents and by local stores or merchants, shackling the producer in such a way that he finds himself compelled to buy and sell to them at prices that are more or less unfavorable to him in direct proportion to his indigence.... This lack of sufficient credit at reasonable rates and the limited market outlets frequently prevent farmers from growing certain crops that would otherwise be profitable."[58]

THE PROMISE OF sustainable rice production faded during the 1930s. By the end of the decade, of the total 4 million acres in agricultural cultivation, some 2.3 million acres (57.5 percent of the total) were planted with sugar cane, followed by plantains with 400,000 acres (10 percent); corn with 300,000 acres (7.5 percent); coffee with 150,000 acres (3.8 percent); peanuts with 80,000 acres (2 percent); and rice with 50,000 acres (1.2 percent).[59]

Without tariff protection and lacking government support, domestic rice succumbed to Asian imports. It was impossible, economist José Cambeyro complained in 1936, for national production to expand "without significant tariff protection, for the standard of living of Asian workers and the meager day-wage they receive—the equivalent of between 2 and 5 cents daily—make it impossible for Cuban rice to compete in our own market. For that reason—from an economic point of view and from a social and patriotic perspective—it is necessary to levy maximum customs duty on Asian rice." Without protection, Cambeyro asked rhetorically, how could domestic production expand "when Cuban workers receive $1 daily and Asian workers receive between 2 and 5 cents?" He continued: "How could one expect a spontaneous production among ourselves if the Cuban rice grower struggles against a regimen like Indochina, that use[s] human resources like slaves and has in our very own country collaborators that support that system? How is it possible that Cuban rice industry in its initial phase of development can successfully confront the dumping routinely practiced by rice importers?"[60]

But if the Cubans could not compete against Asian rice, neither could the Americans. The reciprocity agreement of 1934 accorded U.S. rice imports a 50 percent reduction in Cuban tariff duties.[61] The duty preferential provided little competitive advantage, for the base price of Asian rice continued to remain competitively lower than U.S. rice. Long-grain rice was selling for $2.00 per 100 pounds, and Burmese short-grain was priced at $1.60 per 100 pounds.[62] "Such a [duty] concession was and is wholly inadequate and insufficient to accomplish anything," protested the Rice Millers Association in 1936. "We state without fear of successful contradiction that the United States Rice Industry has not enjoyed one single pound increase in rice business in Cuba because of the trade agreement.... The so-called concessions granted rice in the reciprocity trade agreement between the United States and Cuba, effective as of September 3, 1934, are merely illusory because they are so entirely inadequate that they have brought about no trade between the two countries in rice."[63]

Unable to compete with Asian imports on price, American rice producers revised their strategies, from seeking lower Cuban tariffs on U.S. rice to demanding higher Cuban tariffs on non-U.S. rice imports—that is, a policy whereby Cuba would favor U.S. imports through discriminatory tariffs on Asian rice. "It seems only reasonable," Frank Godchaux wrote to the *New York Times*, that "a provision should require Cuba to take her rice supplies from this country.... It is of vital importance to Cuba that we permit a reasonable amount of her sugar to come to this country, and our State Department is in a position to insist that in return for any concession made on sugar Cuba must buy her rice from us."[64] Rice producers despaired. "The Cuban market is the salvation of the industry. Its importance cannot be overestimated," Louisiana congressman René DeRouen pronounced outright in 1936.[65]

The leverage was sugar. Continued preferential access for Cuban sugar to U.S. markets was to be contingent on preferential access for American rice to Cuban markets, which in this instance implied the elimination of competitive rice imports. "Instead of seeking concessions for rice," William Reid exhorted members of the Rice Millers Association in 1936, "we should begin a strong propaganda campaign against importation into the United States of any commodities which are products of the soil of Cuba which compete in any way with commodities which are products of the soil of the United States. Inasmuch as practically all commodities which are imported into the United States from Cuba are agricultural commodities which compete with domestically grown agricultural commodities, this would mean practically excluding Cuban imports." Such a campaign would have little likelihood of success, Reid understood. "But," he added,

> we are firmly of the opinion that we gain much important political support by urging that if Cuban agricultural products are to be permitted entry into this Country, reciprocal concessions should be made by Cuba to such an extent as will permit the United States to sell in Cuba agricultural commodities which Cuba uses and does not produce. In other words, if we specifically name rice and seek concessions on it, we cannot expect any support except from representatives of the rice producing

areas, which are so few in number that they carry no appreciable weight in Congress. On the other hand, if we begin to spread propaganda for agricultural products, it would naturally result in securing concessions for rice, since rice is the principal agricultural commodity not produced to any extent in Cuba, but imported into the Island in large volume.... Talk of cutting the United States as a market for Cuban products should have a much greater effect in Cuba than an appeal for concessions for United States rice in that country.[66]

Congress did indeed act quickly. The American purpose was unambiguous. In 1937 a House Agriculture subcommittee debated the bill H.R. 5326, which included a recommendation to increase the Louisiana sugar quota and reduce the Cuban allotment by 128,000 tons—specifically, that "the quota of raw sugar for the continental United States be allotted in keeping with what the cane and beet areas can produce and the additional requirements be taken from those sugar-producing areas in amounts that are fair and in consideration of their national relationship."[67]

The Cubans did not fail to recognize the purport of congressional action. Within months, the Cuban government announced a new tariff schedule for rice imports. The preferential tariff to the U.S. was increased to 80 percent, reflected in a duty reduction from $1.85 per 100 pounds to 92 cents, on one hand, and on the other the duty on rice from all other countries raised from $3.70 per 100 pounds to $4.70. In addition, non-U.S. rice was subject to an additional 10-cent surcharge.[68] The Cuban government further instructed its ambassador in Washington to confer with the State Department "to determine what additional concessions Cuba could offer the United States and what points in the existing Trade Agreement which were giving rise to friction between the two Governments might well be modified in any new agreement," and to the point: "The Ambassador [Pedro Martínez Fraga]"—Assistant Secretary of State Sumner Welles reported—"said the chief concession to the United States which his Government had in mind was an increased advantage on American-grown rice."[69] In late 1938, Colonel Fulgencio Batista paid a state visit to the United States, during which he agreed to establish a duty-free quota for U.S. rice imports and committed to the reduced duty on U.S. rice outside the fixed quota allocation.[70] U.S. producers were exultant. "The Americans wanted to sell rice to Cuba and Cuba wanted a larger share of the American market for sugar," reflected rice merchant E. B. Ogden Jr. years later. "As a result of the negotiations, in 1938, the Cuban Government made certain import tariff concessions which enabled American rice to compete with that from the Far East."[71] Competition in Cuba "is not from foreign rice," the Rice Millers Association reported with some satisfaction one year later. "The competition is strictly between American Mills."[72]

Members of the Rice Millers Association congratulated themselves for success in "developing this outlet for United States rice which during the past years has been the salvation of the industry."[73] Rates would periodically fluctuate in the years to come, rising and falling in response to world conditions, but the differential tariff rate served to transform Cuba into a near-exclusive market for U.S. rice imports. "The resulting increase in the duty spread between American and Oriental rice," Albert Nufer, the U.S. commercial attaché in Havana, pronounced in 1938, "would give us the entire Cuban market for imported rice."[74] Within less six months, Nufer would report that "American millers have succeeded in capturing and maintaining a very substantial share of the Cuban rice business."[75] The Cuban market was sufficiently important to justify in 1939 the establishment of a Rice Millers Association permanent office in Havana.

American rice producers had eliminated foreign competition. American rice imports increased from 400,000 pounds in 1934 (0.1 percent of total rice imports), to 1.1 million pounds in 1937 (23 percent of the total), to 3.6 million pounds in 1941 (92 percent of total)[76]—"the largest share [the United States] has ever had of Cuba's rice trade," commented the U.S. Department of Commerce.[77] "Now that good quality United States rice is arriving in volume," reported the U.S. Embassy from Havana in 1948, "the local trade sees little prospect of other rices entering this market for some months to come."[78] (See table 3.4.)

Cuba was transformed into the single most important export market for U.S. rice. The Cuban market was "vital to the United States rice producers," Homer Brinkley, of the American Rice Growers Cooperative Association, affirmed in 1941; "the very life of the industry is almost entirely dependent on our ability to sell our surplus production to Cuba."[79] Between 1937 and 1942, total U.S. rice exports averaged annually an estimated 358 million pounds. More than 75 percent of this average—275 million pounds—was exported to Cuba. Between 1947 and 1948, total U.S. rice exports surpassed 895 million pounds, with Cuba accounting for nearly 60 percent of the total (527 million pounds).[80]

WAR CHANGED EVERYTHING, again, and changed much permanently. The dislocation of Asian production zones and the disruption of maritime trade occasioned by World War II plunged the world rice trade into disarray, with predictable consequences—scarcity of supplies, increased demands, and high

TABLE 3.4. Cuban rice imports by country of origin, 1936–1941 (pounds)

Year	United States	Thailand	India/Burma	Indochina
1936	110,000	3,570,000	49,000	22,000
1937	1,150,000	2,340,000	68,000	73,000
1938	1,990,000	1,690,000	13,000	30,000
1939	2,220,000	1,330,000	8,000	80,000
1940	2,560,000	1,290,000	18,000	24,000
1941	3,670,000	2,000	13,000	2,000

Source: Paul George Minneman, "The Agriculture of Cuba," *Foreign Agriculture Bulletin* 2 (December 1942).

prices—all more than adequate incentive for the expansion of rice production elsewhere in the world, including Cuba.[81] "High Cuban prices," reported the U.S. Department of Commerce, "indicate the substantial economic incentive which exists toward increased production."[82] The world price increased from a 1935–39 average of 74 cents per bushel to $1.70 per bushel by 1944, which meant too that rice imports that reached Cuba were also more expensive.[83]

Cuban rice production expanded during the government of Fulgencio Batista (1940–44), a project supported by the Export-Import Bank in Washington as part of a larger U.S. war effort to aid economic development in Latin America, specifically to promote agricultural diversification and increase food supplies.[84] In 1942, Cuba obtained a $25 million loan from the Export-Import Bank, funds needed, explained Cuban ambassador Aurelio Fernández Concheso, "to finance the purchase of materials, equipment and services required in the Republic of Cuba for agricultural development and diversification," specifically to expand rice production and purchase farm machinery and equipment to plant, harvest, and mill rice.[85] As a means "to aid the program for increased farm production and agricultural diversification in Cuba," the Roosevelt administration provided Cuba with an assortment of farm machinery to develop rice production, including forty tractors, forty-three disk plows, five rice binders, ten rice threshers, and fifteen rice drills.[86] "My problems in Cuba," Clarence Boonstra later recalled of his wartime service as agricultural economist in the U.S. Embassy in Havana, "were very heavily related to the supply of rice to Cuba, because they had practically no rice-growing capacity installed, and so I did a lot to get the startup of the rice industry in Cuba."[87] And indeed the rice industry in Cuba did start up during World War II, and with auspicious beginnings. By 1943, *El Mundo* could not but wax rhapsodic over Cuban achievements: "Taking into consideration the increase in rice production in Cuba during the last few years . . . it can be assumed that rice cultivation will mark a new era in the reconstruction of our agricultural economy, because total domestic production can be absorbed by the national market. In this manner, as [the pressure of] unemployment is relieved, our wealth will be distributed among a large number of farmers whose *fincas* can be used for this purpose."[88] Cuba emerged from the war years with a much-strengthened rice agriculture. Production grew in response to rising prices of rice imports.[89] Rice purchased before the war at 3 to 5 cents per pound increased in 1942 to between 10 and 13 cents per pound and a year later to between 15 and 17 cents per pound. By 1946, the price of rice had risen to 20 cents per pound.[90] All in all, powerful stimulus to expand domestic production: from 184,000 quintals in 1941, to 208,000 quintals in 1943, up to 355,000 quintals in 1944, and reaching 855,000 quintals in 1945.[91]

As matters turned out, the advantage obtained by U.S. producers through the discriminatory tariffs against Asian rice also accrued to Cuban producers. At the end of the war, rice had established itself as an important agriculture. An estimated total of 4.8 million acres were in agricultural cultivation, almost 3 percent of which—a total of 135,700 acres—was dedicated to rice production.[92]

But it is also true that North American rice interests viewed the expansion of Cuban rice warily, fearful that increased Cuban production threatened to displace American imports. By the 1940s, the Americans had come to consider Cuba as a proprietary market. It mattered little that competition originated from within Cuba rather than from Asia: competition from any source was not welcomed. Indeed, the expansion of Cuban production abetted by the U.S. government provoked indignation among rice growers and their representatives in Congress. Members of Congress demanded the State Department secure another reduction of the Cuban duty on U.S. rice as a competitive hedge against the prospects of expanded Cuban production. Congressional representatives of rice states also lobbied the Department of Agriculture against the Export-Import Bank loan for Cuban diversification. "We now get intimations from the Department of Agriculture," Warren Pierson, president of the Export-Import Bank, wrote in a "personal and confidential" letter to U.S. ambassador George Messersmith in Havana, "that Cuba is not prepared to give concessions which will protect American rice growers in the event Cuban production is stepped up substantially. . . . Our general attitude is that the Export-

Import Bank should not provide financing which will result directly or indirectly in damaging American interests."⁹³ Messersmith was incredulous. "To say that the American rice growers need protection now against eventual Cuban production," Messersmith replied—also in a "personal and confidential" communication—"is going into the future further than any of us can go into now." Messersmith defended Cuban "measures for the strengthening of her internal economy which may involve some small increase in rice production." Indeed, "every one who studies [the] Cuban economy realizes the necessity for diversification and certainly we do and the Cubans do and we cannot expect the Cubans to refrain from reasonable measures to strengthen their own economy.... I can see no reason why a reasonable amount of the twenty-five million dollar credit should not be use for diversification and in projects which will involve increased rice production." Messersmith continued:

> It would be most unfortunate for the rice growers at home to raise objections to a part of the twenty-five million dollar credit's being used for stepping up somewhat Cuban rice production. It would be an utterly unsound and unwise attitude to take in their own interests as well as our general interests. You know how true this is. There is no doubt that the rice growers are assuming as egotistic and as ill-considered [an] attitude and as unsound an attitude as any special group I have ever known of at home.... The unreasonable attitude of our rice growers at home can only have the tendency of undue stimulation of rice production here. I do wish that someone could make the rice growers understand ... what a good position they have and how they can prejudice it by a stand such as that which they are taking for which no justification can be found either economically or politically.⁹⁴

U.S. rice interests were not deterred. "We are not sure," editorialized the *Lake Charles American Press* of Louisiana in 1943, "the Federal authorities have understood ... that they may be now discouraging farmers of this area so much that next year their planting will be decreased as much or more than the amount of the Cuban increase."⁹⁵ Representative Henry Larcade from Louisiana denounced U.S. programs "to subsidize the expanding of the rice industry in [Cuba], and further with furnishing farm equipment and farm machinery for the same, in competition with our own domestic industry."⁹⁶ The congressional delegation of rice-producing states of Louisiana, Texas, and Arkansas protested to the Department of Agriculture "the plans of the Federal Government to subsidize the production of rice in Cuba at the expense of the rice industry in the United States," adding,

This is a good-neighbor policy which may be good for the "neighbor" but is manifestly unjust and unfair to the "home folks." ... In inviting Cuba to compete with [domestic rice producers] the United States Government is bringing disaster to an old and established industry and to thousands of people that depend directly or indirectly on the production, milling, and distribution of this product.... If this proposal is not abandoned we are prepared to take legislative action to protect the interests of the rice industry of the United States.[97]

Legislative action was indeed threatened with the introduction in the House of Representatives of H.R. 2226 by Representative James R. Domengeaux (Louisiana) and H.R. 2420 by Representative Henry Larcade (Louisiana), both stipulating that "no department or independent establishment in the Executive branch of Government ... shall aid by loans, subsidies, or other financial assistance, by the construction of dams or other projects, by furnishing tractors or other agricultural implements, or in any other manner, in the production of rice or the development of such production in any area outside the United States, its territories, or possessions."[98] The proposed legislation never moved out of committee but was a portent of things to come.

CHAPTER FOUR

To Overcome Sugar

The matter of rice in Cuba is, in the final analysis, nothing more than part—albeit an important part—of the great problem of the general economic development of the country.—Regino Boti, quoted in Oscar Pino Santos, "Los problemas económicos de Cuba: Protección official pide el forum arrocero," *Carteles* 37 (July 8, 1956)

Events of the past twenty years have turned Cubans' thoughts more and more in the direction of a policy of diversification and self-sufficiency. They realize the ups and downs of the United States economy, its booms and busts, spell only instability for Cuba and misery for its people, especially if they adhere to a policy of extreme reliance upon one crop.—Lowry Nelson, *Rural Cuba* (1950)

The rice industry is backed by the Cuban Government as a nationalist betterment of our economy to save exchange of currency, create employment, etc.—Publicidad Godoy y Cross, 1955

It is certain that rice represents a source of our national recovery [*recuperación nacional*].... Rice plantations would serve as a magnificent defense against monoculture and the *latifundio*. Rice could become the second Cuban harvest [*la segunda zafra cubana*] without the anxieties and difficulties associated with the sugar harvest.—*Bohemia* 27 (February 10, 1935)

Either the Republic will overcome sugar or sugar will overcome the Republic.
—José Comallonga, "La situación cubana" (1908)

THE 1950S WERE years of uncertainty. Cubans were in the throes of a crisis of faith. It was a time of confidence lost and hopes dashed, of disappointment and disillusionment: a slow descent into disarray. A brooding restlessness filled households across the island; people could see that things were not right simply by looking around but were not quite able to identify the source of their misgivings: a feeling, a fear, a foreboding.

But people in the know knew: the toll of the export economy was coming due. The days of sugar were coming to an end. Cubans were not unfamiliar with the boom-bust cycles of sugar, of course, the ups and downs, the recurring intervals of good times alternating with bad times. It was the nature of sugar, just the way things had always been.

But the 1950s were different. This was not a cycle. It had the feel of a slow descent into an abyss: production systems overtaken by internal structural disruption and overwhelmed by global market dislocations—a star-crossed alignment that bode ill for a way of life. Sugar could no longer sustain the economy. A dark and dismal future indeed, the Banco Nacional de Cuba warned: "The sugar industry is incapable of performing today or in the future the way it performed in the past."[1]

Sugar production faltered and floundered, unable to adapt to increasing competition, unable to adjust to diminishing markets, unable to arrest declining prices. In the early 1920s, Cuban exports had accounted for more than 20 percent of the world supply of sugar; by the mid-1950s, the Cuban share had dwindled to 10 percent.[2] Increasingly, world sugar markets were governed by quota-controlled practices and tariff-protected policies. Such was the case of Cuban sugar. Per the terms of the Sugar Act of 1951, the United States assigned Cuba an annual quota of 2.5 million tons, accounting for approximately half the island's total sugar exports.[3] Cuban well-being depended on a quota-fixed access to U.S. markets determined by Congress. There was no place else to go. It did little good to expand production because, simply put, there were no more markets. Cuba existed in a world, the Banco Nacional warned, that "does not offer sufficient markets to absorb all [the sugar] that the country is capable of producing today and tomorrow."[4] Sobering developments indeed.

But dwindling markets represented only one problem. No less disquieting was the declining value of sugar and the loss of foreign exchange receipts.[5] In 1952 Cuba produced 7 million tons, valued at $764 million and providing 117 days of harvest work.[6] In 1953, seeking to arrest and reverse declining world prices, Cuba voluntarily restricted production to 5 million tons, which reduced the total value of sugar exports to $461 million and shortened the length of the harvest to 84 days of work. Production was reduced again the following year, to 4.7 million tons with a diminished value of $425 million and 80 days of work. And again in 1955, to 4.4 million tons, declining in value to $390 million and reducing employment to 69 days of work.[7] Between 1952 and 1955, in sum, the value of Cuban sugar production declined by almost 50 percent.

PLANTERS UNDERSTOOD WELL the magnitude of the impending crisis. "Cuba's sugar outlook is anything but encouraging," Julio Lobo despaired in 1952. The "restriction for the forthcoming year, with the corollary of possible increase in production of other sugar areas, implies another and greater restriction for the subsequent year, and so on. Meanwhile, by reducing our crops, production costs soar, and soar to such an extent that presently many sugar mills will not cover operating costs." This chain of events, Lobo warned, "can do little else than to weaken our major industry, which is tantamount to saying that we are endangering our national economy."[8] Sugar merchant Luis Mendoza was succinct: "Instead of progressing we are retrogressing, increasing our costs out of proportion to the rising standard of living and raw materials. It is a furious race toward bankruptcy."[9]

And a sign of the times: foreigners were divesting themselves of sugar property and relinquishing ownership to the Cubans. Foreign capital was abandoning sugar. An uncertain future, the U.N. Economic Commission for Latin America (ECLA) surmised, had "removed the incentives for investment [in Cuba], which had formerly come from abroad."[10] Between 1939 and 1958, an ever-larger number of foreign-owned sugar mills—principally American, Spanish, and Canadian—were transferred to Cuban ownership. (See table 4.1.)

EVERYTHING SEEMED to be unraveling. Fewer days of work signified lower wages. "The effect of the voluntary restriction of the 1953 harvest on the Cuban economy was catastrophic," commented economist Raúl Cepero Bonilla, signifying between 1952 and 1953 a loss of wages from $412 million to $254 million.[11] The declining value of sugar exports in 1955 resulted in nearly a 12 percent reduction of salaries and wages in the sugar industry; the number of lost work days was equivalent to another 27 percent reduction in wages.[12] Between 1952 and 1954, per capita income fell by 18 percent; between 1957 and 1958, per capita income declined again, this time by nearly 10 percent, from $370 to $335.[13]

Chronic conditions of unemployment/underemployment worsened. Unemployment assumed desperate proportions. An estimated 600,000 to 800,000 men and women, approximately one-third of the total labor force, languished permanently in circumstances of unemployment and underemployment.[14]

Cubans were worse off in the 1950s than they had been in the 1920s. "The increment in net per capita income registered in the last 25 years," the ECLA reported in 1955, "and particularly during the post-war period, constitutes, in large measure, a mere return to the income levels already attained in Cuba in the past." The Cuban economy "has remained stagnant," the ECLA pronounced

TABLE 4.1. Number and production volume of Cuban sugar mills by country of ownership, 1939 and 1958

	1939			1958		
	Number of mills	Production (250 lb bags)	Percentage of total	Number of mills	Production (250 lb bags)	Percentage of total
United States	66	13,421,947	55.07	36	18,421,883	36.65
Cuba	56	5,465,023	22.42	121	31,232,031	62.13
Spain	33	3,635,748	14.92	3	475,654	0.95
Canada	10	1,175,714	4.83	—	—	—
England	4	343,903	1.41	—	—	—
Holland	3	184,622	0.76	—	—	—
France	6	145,357	0.59	1	136,292	0.27
Total	178	24,372,314	100	161	50,265,860	100

Source: "Resumen de ingenious por nacionalidad de propietarios o arrendatarios," *Anuario Azucarero de Cuba 1959* (1959).

outright, noting too that since the 1930s, Cuban economic policy had "made no marked contribution to the mitigation of the depressive effects of external factors nor to the acceleration of the country's rate of development."[15] "Virtually static" was the description of the economy offered by the International Bank for Reconstruction and Development in 1951, a "stagnant and unstable economy with a high level of insecurity," adding that "the present per capita income of about $300 is only slightly above that of the early 1920s," and to the point: "Cuba's present standard of living ... depends mainly on an industry which stopped growing many years ago." And again: "Cuba is living in—and on—the past and her present prosperity rests on foundations which can be dangerously weakened by events beyond her control."[16]

Foreign exchange receipts decreased and salaries and wages declined as the cost of foreign imports increased, from $515 million in 1950 to $649 million in 1956 to $777 million in 1958. Foreign exchange obtained through sugar exports had long served to subsidize the cost of food imports: a diminution of sugar exports could not but diminish food imports. The ratio of Cuban imports to national income ranked among the highest in the world, averaging between 21 and 30 percent between 1945 and 1949.[17] "The Cuban people," economist Antonio Riccardi warned in 1948, "and especially the popular classes, cannot live off what they earn, simply because everything becomes daily more expensive. Cuba is largely an importer country and almost everything that it needs and consumes must come from abroad for which we must pay whatever is demanded."[18]

The purchasing power (*poder adquisitivo*) of tens of thousands of families plummeted—by almost two-thirds between 1940 and 1951.[19] The increase in the cost of basic foodstuffs in Havana between 1956 and 1957 affected almost every staple of the daily diet: the price of animal products grew 4 percent; vegetable products rose by 9 percent. In some instances the increase of basic staples was dramatic: potatoes, 37 percent; black beans, 31 percent; and rice, 28 percent. In early 1958, prices rose again: potatoes, 52 percent; black beans, 88 percent; and rice, 30 percent.[20] "Cost of food has risen considerably during the month," the U.S. Embassy reported tersely in 1957, "and the scarcity of certain staple items may force the working man's expenditures for food to an even higher level."[21] Armando Cárdenas recalled these years well. "Our main problem," he explained to Oscar Lewis, "was that we didn't earn enough money to buy our food."[22]

Households across the island plunged into confusion, a time of uncertainty and insecurity, a world falling apart, collapsing in stages: a loss of days of work, a loss of wages, and loss of a standard of living; a people cutting back and doing more with less, struggling to make do and get by—and failing on both counts. Access to food diminished, diets changed. Marketing surveys in the 1950s offer insight into strategies deployed to resist the descent into indigence. Consumption of rice declined "mainly because of the decrease in purchasing power of the popular classes," Grant Advertising reported, adding, "In most homes the left over rice, which was usually thrown away, is now saved in refrigerators and consumed the next day; this is happening in the middle and higher income groups. The lower income groups are cooking less rice per day."[23] A demographic profile completed by Publicidad Alvarez Pérez suggested that rice consumption "has fundamentally been concentrated in the metropolitan and urban areas, the consumption of rice in the rural areas being of no consequence." Rice was concentrated within the urban middle classes ("consuming the greatest volume of rice") followed in order of consumption by the poor, the upper-middle class, and the wealthy. The profile concluded: "The general outlook is that the diet of the Cuban [middle-class] families will continue to be modified in detriment to rice."[24]

Mounting population pressures made everything worse. In 1922, with a population of nearly 3 million people, Cuba exported a total of 5 million tons of sugar; in 1956, with a population having doubled to 6.5 million people, Cuba still exported a total of 5 million tons of sugar.[25] Population growth was projected to increase by 200,000 inhabitants annually, a growth rate on course almost to double the population to 11 million by 1980. "Population is increasing faster than production," president of the National Bank Joaquín Martínez Sáenz acknowledged to Herbert Matthews in 1952.[26] "The sugar industry is no longer in a condition to meet the pressures of an expanding population and the yearnings to improve the standard of living," the Banco Nacional warned in 1956.[27] An estimated 40,000 men and women annually reached working age in an economy unable to generate adequate employment opportunities. Between 1955 and 1958 the economy created approximately 8,000 new jobs during a period in which an estimated 160,000 young Cubans entered the wage-labor force.[28] Leví Marrero could hardly conceal his despair: "What will be the fate of Cuba if we double our population ... without changing our economic structure?" Marrero could contemplate only one possibility: mass emigration, perhaps as many as 2.5 million Cubans, approximately one-quarter of the population, obliged to migrate to the United States.[29]

The vulnerability of the export economy was laid bare in urgent and visceral ways. Wages and salaries were in decline; the cost of living was on the rise. The public mood turned dark.[30] A restive people were dispirited and demoralized, in the throes of deepening uncertainty, in a political environment slowly descending into the abyss of civil conflagration. "Whoever lends an ear to public opinion," journalist Ernesto Ardura brooded in 1953, "can appreciate the state of uncertainty and confusion in which the Cuban people live. There is something of a sensation of shipwreck. That psychological state of desperation can be observed in all social classes: among workers, industrialists, and merchants, in the suffering middle class. The common psychological denominator of the national moment is lassitude and profound disillusionment.... There is no enthusiasm, there are no great plans with an eye to the future, for the future is a huge cloud and offers security to no one."[31] Writer José Lezama Lima despaired privately. "We are now in the chaos resulting from the disintegration, confusion, and inferiority of Cuban life of the last thirty years," he confided to his diary in 1957. "On one hand, fear, bewilderment, confusion. On the other, desperation."[32]

IT WAS NOT ONLY—and perhaps not even principally—that sugar seemed to have lost the capacity to sustain Cuban well-being. Rather, it was that sugar itself seemed to *threaten* Cuban well-being. The fate of the nation depended on an agriculture without a future. Something of common knowledge, to be sure, but it was not altogether clear what to do with that knowledge. Cubans seemed powerless to forestall the oncoming calamity, in full view, threatening the island with certain economic collapse. The fact that sugar could no longer sustain continued economic development had become apparent, but neither could it be supplanted, for however dismal the long-term prospects for sugar may have appeared, a short-term alternative did not exist. Sugar products accounted for more than 90 percent of the total exports, representing 80 percent of foreign exchange and employing a seasonal labor force of almost 500,000 agricultural and industrial workers.[33] Sugar production implied, as it always had, the subordination of everything else, and indeed as long as sugar continued to account for the substantial portion of foreign exchange—however problematical its future may have appeared—it was not altogether clear how to move beyond sugar. To contemplate the demise of sugar was to confront an economy without the capacity to reproduce its own means of production.

Resentment against sugar deepened and took hold of the public mood.[34] Rubén Ortiz-Lamadrid denounced the "yoke of vassalage" to which sugar had subjected Cuba, adding, "We have experienced years of irresponsibility sacrificing the general economic development of the country to the convenience and speculation of the sugar industry, which is now deserting us."[35] A consensus had taken hold, again: dependency on sugar was no longer tenable. "We have entered into a new phase of our republican existence," agronomist Danilo

Baeza warned in 1954. "The old rationale of a monoculture country is now a bygone possibility." Baeza continued, "The economic development of the nation should not be subject to sugar production. Those who persist in thinking along these lines are mistaken. We cannot sacrifice the ample economic opportunities offered by other lines of national production to satisfy exclusively the needs of sugar, which, notwithstanding the fact that at present it constitutes the principal source of wealth of the country, is facing today a serious crisis associated with the restriction of exports."[36] "The time of sugar prosperity ended a long time ago," pronounced Alberto León Riva. "Sugar no longer offers any possibility of expanding its payroll."[37]

The dilemma: an economy that could not continue to depend on sugar but was unable to become independent of sugar. To contemplate the reorganization of an economy given structural form around sugar implied a challenge to powerful interests—foreign and domestic—requiring a vast reallocation of resources, a reorganization of land tenure forms, and the readjustment of trade relationships, none of which would come easy. Cuba found itself ensnared in "vicious circles," the International Bank for Reconstruction and Development understood, noting that "only greater diversification can reduce Cuba's dependence on sugar but the dominance of sugar discourages diversification."[38] The bank was categorical. "Prosperity and stability cannot rest upon sugar alone.... [Sugar] is too uncertain; Cuba's economic foundations must be extended and reinforced," it warned. "Diversification is essential for Cuba's future well-being"; Cuba should "revise all existing policies ... which impede agricultural diversification."[39] The ECLA enjoined Cubans "to achieve a substantial productive increase in domestic consumption crops, to place them on a sound competitive basis with sugar and imported products." The diminution of planting and harvesting sugar, the ECLA suggested, "leave[s] room for other crops mainly for domestic consumption, such as rice, maize, and beans."[40] The implications of a "substantial reduction in income derived from sugar exports," affirmed Angel Pardo Jiménez, president of the Asociación de Colonos de Cuba, "due both to the decrease in production and the drop in price of the commodity ... [necessitates] attention to diversifying other crops for home consumption."[41] And especially for the production of food. "Cuba lives with the permanent aspiration to reduce the necessity of importing agricultural products," exhorted Juan Jacobo, adding that "the production of foodstuffs is a goal of transcendental importance. The masses require a vast abundance of agricultural food products; the country needs urgently to reduce unemployment; the economy demands an end to the flight of foreign exchange to pay for food imports."[42]

THE NECESSITY OF diversification had loomed large as a tenet in the history of Cuban economic thought. Its antecedents reached deep into the nineteenth century—indeed, to the very origins of the export economy—and diversification was itself an acknowledgment of the uncertainties attending the preponderance of sugar.[43] "The *word* diversification, if not the act," commented the International Bank for Reconstruction and Development, "has been popular in Cuba for three decades."[44] By the 1950s, the logic of diversification had acquired a new urgency as a remedy for a moribund economy. The adage of *"sin azúcar no hay país"* was turned on its head: *"solo con azúcar no hay país."*[45]

The strategy of diversification turned again to rice, as it always had. The choice of rice also possessed a proper history, of course. The arguments for rice were matters of conventional wisdom, well-rehearsed and well-received, advanced for more than 150 years. Nothing had changed except that everything was different. All the known certainties about the efficacy of rice production had assumed a new resonance in the face of the known uncertainties of sugar exports. Sugar had contributed to Cuban prosperity, Leví Marrero acknowledged, but it also had contributed to "economic backwardness which has been the source of misery and despair." Rice offered a partial remedy, Marrero insisted, but to fail to expand rice production threatened "to thwart [not only] our industry but also our agriculture designed to meet the needs of internal consumption."[46]

The logic of rice was incontrovertible. No other domestic product commanded as great a national market as rice.[47] Indeed, the premise of diversification was always the promise of self-sufficiency, to reduce dependency on food imports. Foodstuffs accounted for an expenditure of nearly $140 million annually[48]—"imports largely unnecessary and which increase with the passing of time," lamented economist Francisco Dorta-Duque. In terms of food value, 45 percent of Cuban caloric intake was derived from imported food, principally in the form of rice, beans, lard, bacon, onions, milk, butter, eggs, tomato products, garlic, and potatoes.[49] Rice accounted for fully one-third of the total value of food imports.[50]

The expansion of rice promised to arrest the loss of foreign exchange and in the long run to reduce dependency on sugar exports. How utterly implausible, the weekly *Carteles* protested in 1935, that from 1914 through 1933, Cuba imported a total of 76.4 million quintals of rice (an annual average of 3.8 million quintals) at a total cost of $302.6 million (an annual average $15 million)— "a sum that emigrated from Cuba to pay for a commodity easily produced in our soil and that would have been sufficient to liquidate the Cuban national debt."[51] It was intolerable, economist A. González de Couto protested, that Cuba had "exported" more than $93 million in eleven years to purchase a commodity "that was almost basic to our daily diet." González de Couto was at loss to explain how "efforts to improve our beleaguered national economy could fail to address an issue so basic and so simple as the matter of rice."[52] From 1902 through 1941, *El Mundo* calculated in 1943, Cuba had paid almost $400 million to purchase rice imports.[53] "Rice is very important in the Cuban diet," *El Mundo* belabored the historic truism ten years later; "it is thus detrimental to our economy that we are obliged to import a substantial portion of the rice consumed in Cuba. Our balance of trade suffers with the millions of dollars spent for rice imports. Yet the conditions of the soil, climate, and temperature found in vast zones of our country are propitious to obtain bountiful harvests of rice."[54] Leví Marrero bemoaned the "loss" of an annual average of $44 million from 1945 through 1954—more, Marrero noted, than the total earnings of tobacco and cigar exports and four times the cost of the construction of the Central Highway. In 1953, the foreign exchange loss attributed to rice imports surpassed $62 million.[55] U.S. commercial attaché H. T. Andersen provided a summary of Cuban economic thinking in 1952:

> [Rice] is one of the few industries to provide some hedge, however small, against the vulnerability of an economy dominated by one crop: sugar. It is a food crop produced in Cuba which lessens dependence on imports for food and frees money, which otherwise would be sent offshore for food, for purchases of durable and consumer goods of which the United States is the principal supplier. It is an industry which functions during the so-called "dead season" when a third of Cuban labor is normally idle, laid off from the sugar harvest which usually last only 5 months of the year. This is important in a country with a chronic over-supply of labor, taken in connection with the protection of the largest investment of Cuban growers, and moves the problem into the political as well as the economic sphere.[56]

THE IMPETUS FOR diversification obtained official endorsement under the authority of Article 280 of the 1940 constitution mandating the establishment of the Banco Nacional de Cuba "to improve the development of the economy."[57] The Banco Nacional was authorized to act as agent of the state to promote economic development through programs of public credits and subsidies to private enterprises—"to fill those vast areas of our economic map that private credit has failed to address," explained the bank.⁵⁸ As an extension of Article 280, the government of Carlos Prío Socarrás (1948–52) established the Banco de Fomento Agrícola e Industrial de Cuba (BANFAIC), charged with responsibility to promote diversification of non-sugar agriculture and sponsor programs of industrial development through long- and short-term low-interest loans, with particular attention to rice. State capital was fixed at $25 million: $15 million designated for credit and finance and $10 million set aside to subsidize development projects.⁵⁹ Long-term loans were designated to aid agricultural development, including support for permanent plantings, construction of storage facilities, expansion of irrigation networks, development of electrical power plants, acquisition of modern equipment, and development of land reclamation projects—a commitment, BANFAIC pledged, to a "policy to expand the insufficient production [of commodities] necessary for national consumption."⁶⁰ Short-term credit served to subsidize seeds, fertilizers, the cultivation and harvesting of crops, and the processing of crops.⁶¹ By 1952, BANFAIC had distributed more than 750,000 pounds of American-variety rice seeds to small farmers. In addition, BANFAIC subsidized the expansion of cooperative rural credit associations. By the mid-1950s, an estimated twelve associations extended across the island with a membership of 5,000.⁶²

The Banco Nacional also allocated additional resources to private regional banks to finance the expansion of provincial production through loans and credits to farmers and millers. Bank loans to rice production increased all through the mid-1950s, from $2.9 million in 1952, to $5.2 million in 1953, to $6.6 million in 1955, to $10.4 million through mid-1955.⁶³ Increasingly, rice producers shifted credit transactions from private brokers (*refaccionistas particulares*) to agencies affiliated with the Banco Nacional. The Molinos Arroceros Los Palacios received substantial loans from the First National Bank of Cuba. The Arrocera Mariana was a client of the Pedroso Bank, and the Arrozal Bartés was a client of Godoy Bank.⁶⁴ "To date," Manzanillo rice farmer José Ramírez León wrote to the minister of agriculture in 1950, "we rice producers have been financed by private entities who levy such high interest rates that they destroy the incentive of the small farmer [*que matan el estímulo del pequeño agricultor*]." Rice farmers in Manzanillo, Ramírez León explained, welcomed the new opportunities BANFAIC provided as the "basis through which to expand [rice production] into the internal market."⁶⁵

The expansion of rice production registered early successes during the last years of the Prío Socarrás government. Harvests increased from 850,000 quintals in 1945 to 1 million quintals in 1950 and increased again to 1.7 million quintals in 1952.⁶⁶ "The myth that the production of rice in Cuba is an artificial agriculture," exulted director-general of the Ministry of Agriculture Rodolfo Arango in 1951, "has been put to rest":

> We have demonstrated that our soils and our climate provide yields as high and indeed higher than other rice-producing nations.... As a result, extensive rice plantations have been established in Oriente province, where rice has created a source of permanent wealth.... We note with satisfaction a gain of over 40 percent in productive efficiency, in the agricultural as well as the industrial milling facets of rice. At this very moment, the installations are nearing completion in Manzanillo of a mill of such capacity and modernity that it is considered the best in its class in the Americas.⁶⁷

Indeed, production had succeeded to the point that in 1948, Cuban farmers were sufficiently optimistic to appeal for import controls to reduce rice imports.⁶⁸ "The development of the Cuban rice industry in the last decade," reported the U.S. Embassy in 1952, "little understood outside Cuba, has been little less than phenomenal":

> From an insignificant phase of the economy Cuban rice has come to play an increasingly important role, now supplying about one-fourth of Cuba's consumption requirements of this basic food.... A vigorous new industry has risen to provide buttress to Cuba's lopsided one-crop sugar economy.... They have built a flourishing industry which is a step toward putting a firmer foundation under Cuba's dangerously vulnerable one-crop economy. The growth of the rice industry has made possible the employment of several thousand workers who would otherwise be idle during the "dead season," an important consideration in a country with a major problem of over-supply of labor and over-population in relation to its resources.⁶⁹

A MILITARY COUP in March 1952 by General Fulgencio Batista toppled the Prío government and plunged Cuba into political disarray. Batista moved promptly to displace personnel in all branches of national, provincial, and municipal administration and to suspend, set aside, and modify many of the programs and policies of the Prío government. U.S. rice producers welcomed the change in Cuba, expecting that a new pro-American government in Havana would display greater solicitude toward U.S. interests. The success of Cuban rice production had caused consternation among U.S. producers. "Although the U.S. Government has not up to this writing recognized the Batista regime," John Nuber, the Rice Millers Association representative in Havana, wrote within days of the military coup, "it is expected that they will in the near future.... Batista has always been friendly to the United States, and the opportunity for securing a better deal on the new Rice Quota looms now." Nuber was optimistic. "There is now an excellent opportunity to coordinate all efforts," he predicted, "and line up the U.S. Officials in Washington to go to work immediately after the U.S. Government recognizes Batista, and have a meeting with the Cuban Officials and settle this NEW RICE QUOTA."[70] Within weeks of the coup, the U.S. Embassy made its desire "to discuss the matter of the rice quota for the year 1952–53" known to the Batista government.[71] "In the opinion of the United States Government," the State Department explained in mid-1952, "the Cuban rice-quota system has not operated satisfactorily for several years, and this Government began in 1950 to urge the Cuban Government to work out a more satisfactory arrangement for imports of rice at the low-duty rate.... This past April, after the change of government in Cuba, this Government again indicated to the Cuban Government its interest in resuming discussions regarding the rice problem."[72]

Expectations that the Batista government would reduce if not reverse the expansion of rice, however, were misplaced.[73] On the contrary, official commitment to rice continued and indeed increased.[74] It happened too that in 1952, during the Korean War, the U.S. government imposed restrictions on exports of milled rice. The 1952 rice quota assigned to Cuba was inadequate to meet domestic demand. The reduction of U.S. imports upon which Cubans depended—an estimated 80 percent of its total market needs—spread panic for fear of scarcity and high prices and exposed again Cuban vulnerability to the vicissitudes of food imports, an additional incentive to expand domestic production. "Cubans now wonder," William M. Reid of the Rice Millers Association complained to Secretary of State John Foster Dulles, "whether the United States can always be depended upon to supply Cuba's essential requirements of rice," adding, "For some time there has been agitation on the part of some groups in Cuba to increase production of rice in that country.... Considerable impetus was given to that movement by the United States['] hasty and ill-advised September [1952] act of seriously limiting exports of rice to Cuba and threatening Cuba's essential supplies of rice, thereby creating the fear of scarcity and high prices."[75] Cubans "naturally became uneasy about obtaining adequate rice supplies," Frank Godchaux, president of the Louisiana Rice Milling Company understood, "and this contributed to and increased their determination to improve their own rice production."[76]

RICE HAD CAPTURED the Cuban imagination and became something of a cause, a national project with a historic purpose in the pursuit of economic independence and self-sufficiency. Almost all Cubans could agree on the wisdom of expanded production. "Every effort that is made to diversify production," exhorted BANFAIC president Emeterio Santovenia in 1953, "is an additional guarantee that it will be possible to confront successfully the hardships caused by international competition in sugar," adding, "And in the case of rice ... it is one of the objectives with which we have entered the centennial year of the birth of Martí: to assist with the expansion of rice is to accelerate economic liberation and the social well-being of the Nation. BANFAIC aspires to assist with agricultural diversification to reduce the loss of foreign exchange and reduce to the fullest extent possible dependency on foreign supplies of the products that our people need [*los productos que necesita nuestro pueblo*]."[77] The idea that Cuba could aspire to—and attain—rice production to the level of self-sufficiency conferred on the project of rice a purpose of nationalist intent. "We have economic advantages unutilized," insisted agronomist Danilo Baeza, "land uncultivated, and men unemployed.... The cultivation of rice offers excellent possibilities for Cubans who love their *patria*."[78] The purpose of rice drew Cubans into a common cause, something akin to righteous national purpose sustained by long-deferred aspirations of self-sufficiency as a means of self-determination.

BANFAIC PROCEEDED to expand credit capacities on a scale not previously available. "We can say with pride," director-general of the Ministry of Agriculture Rodolfo Arango affirmed in 1954, "that never before has a national agricultural production other than sugar and tobacco enjoyed such a well-defined and open-ended credit resource as rice."[79]

Rice farmers were the principal beneficiaries of BANFAIC programs, receiving in 1954 $9.6 million out of a portfolio of $13.5 million. BANFAIC organized technical assistance services, agricultural extension programs, and experimental centers to develop new varieties of rice, provide diagnostic services to combat rice diseases, improve the per-acre yields, and increase the use of fertilizers.[80] Credit was extended for the purchase of agricultural machinery and milling equipment, subsidies to facilitate the acquisition of seeds, and funds to expand irrigation projects.[81] Infrastructure capacities increased to keep pace with production. A network of subsidized warehouse facilities extended across the island to accommodate larger harvests in Manzanillo, Caibarién, Bayamo, Artemisa, and Consolación del Sur.[82] New farming methods were introduced, most notably with improved soil preparation through the expanded use of chemical fertilizers and the extension of irrigation systems obtained through the use of newly acquired heavy machinery. Rice producers gained access to new technologies, including grain drills, self-propelled harvest threshers, trucks and tractors, power units for irrigation, and airplanes to assist in planting and fertilizing.[83]

The zones of rice production expanded across the island, principally in the eastern provinces of Oriente and Camagüey and in the western province of Pinar del Río, producing in 1954 some 825,000 quintals, 525,000 quintals, and 788,000 quintals respectively and accounting for 85 percent of national rice production.[84] Production in Oriente consisted of large estates of well-irrigated and highly mechanized agriculture along the contours of the Cauto valley. Traditional production zones between Manzanillo and Bayamo expanded toward Holguín. Production in Camagüey province developed on converted cattle ranches and included some of the largest rice plantations on the island, most notably a new "state-of-the-art" mechanized 33,000-acre rice farm established in 1950. Rice production flourished in Pinar del Río and expanded by way of large estates beyond the traditional area of Consolación del Sur and onto the whole of the southern plain. Seven plantations in Pinar del Río accounted for 85 percent of total provincial production. Consolación del Sur ranked third among the leading rice-producing *municipios*, accounting for an annual average of 10–15 percent of Cuban production.[85] More than half the area dedicated to the production of rice was entirely mechanized and almost all under irrigation.[86] Small rice farms expanded in the provinces of Havana, Matanzas, and Las Villas.[87] Visiting the regions of Manzanillo in Oriente and Vertientes in Camagüey in 1953, U.S. Economic Affairs officer Harold Randall reported on the "substantial extensions of areas planted to rice" and noted that "estimates placed plantings in the Manzanillo area this year at 800 *caballerías* over those of 1952. . . . The outlook for rice is very good. Expansion is brisk. Additional land is being clear and leveled for rice planting."[88]

The success of rice production was reflected in rising land values. Land in Camagüey selling in 1950 for $40 per *caballería* had soared to $300 per *caballería*

Map showing the most productive zones of Cuban rice production, from east to west: Victoria de la Tunas, Birama, Zaza, Zarzal, Manzanillo, Veguita, Bueycito, Bayamo, Chambas, Morón, west of Nuevitas, southeast of Ciego de Avila and Florida, Sagua la Grande, Jagüey Grande, Sabanillo del Encomendador, Pedro Betancourt, south of Colón, Surgidero de Batabanó, Güines and Mayabeque, Guira de Melena, zones near the lake of Ariguanabo, San Cristobal, Bahía Honda, Rio Blanco, Consolación del Sur, Viñales, San Juan y Martínez (A. González de Couto, "El arroz en nuestra economía nacional," *Carteles* 21 [November 3, 1940]).

by 1953.[89] Land values also increased in the province of Pinar del Río— "an economy presently being fundamentally transformed through the diversification of production through the frenetic expansion of rice," commented *Diario de la Marina*.[90] "Six years ago," the International Bank for Reconstruction and Development observed as early as 1950, "no rice was grown in this region. The land was idle except that some cattle were run on it. The first of this land selected for rice cultivation was purchased for $30 per *caballería*. Today, with 10,000 acres already developed and producing rice, the surrounding area of at least the same size is traded at $200 per *caballería*. This increase of nearly seven-fold in land value is due almost entirely to the rice development, and should serve as a stimulus to other landowners."[91] BANFAIC was especially pleased with developments in Pinar del Río. "During the period 1935–1939," commented BANFAIC agent Camilo Sabí in 1952, "prices of *fincas* [in Los Palacios] were very low due to low productivity of the savannah. But the increase of the cultivation of rice in Cuba during recent years and the determination that these lands were ideally suited for the cultivation of rice, an important area of rice cultivation has developed, which had contributed to the increasing present value of the *fincas* between $70 to $75 per *hectar* [1 *hectar* = 2.5 acres]."[92] "Our success with rice research and cultivation," Batista later recalled, "prompted many farmers, especially in the provinces of Oriente, Camagüey and Pinar del Río, to extend their sowing program to cover rice."[93]

The acreage of land dedicated to rice increased markedly, from 69,000 acres in 1940 to 209,000 acres in 1954.[94] The restrictions on sugar production and reduction of sugar exports facilitated the reallocation of land, equipment, and capital from sugar to rice. Emblematic of the transitions underway: increasing acreage formerly dedicated to sugar, particularly in the provinces of Las Villas and Camagüey, was converted to rice.[95]

The yields per acre increased. In 1948, Cubans produced 11.3 quintals per *hectar*, deemed low in comparison with other rice-producing countries (United States: 23.5 quintals per *hectar*; Burma: 13.6 quintals per *hectar*). By 1953, the yield of Cuban production had increased to 20 quintals per *hectar*—"which places [Cuba] in a competitive position with any other world producer," observed the ECLA. In 1940, one *caballería* produced 331 pounds of rice; in 1955, the yield had increased to 600 pounds.[96]

The number of farms dedicated to rice production expanded across the island, from 2,500 in 1951 to 6,100 in 1956.[97] Investment in rice farms and mills increased, approaching an estimated $80 million by the mid-1950s and engaging a total of 100,000 workers in the fields and mills. That the rice harvest was conducted principally between May and September offered relief to the chronic unemployment associated with the *tiempo muerto* off-season cycles between the sugar harvests.[98] The U.S. agricultural attaché commented on increased employment in eastern Cuba as early as 1952:

> In the rural areas of Oriente the new land clearings actually have become a source of work for the surplus rural population. In the large new farms in Camaguey ... which in many respects, including size, resemble the sugar centrals, almost the entire population of small hamlets have been employed, many being trained in such skilled and semi-skilled occupations as mechanic, truck driver, tractor and bull-dozer operator, combine operator, etc. While the wage scales are, in comparison to the wage scales of farm labor in the U.S., low, ... nevertheless employment at any wage scale for many of these laborers represents work they might not otherwise have had at all.[99]

BANFAIC financing was decisive to the expansion of rice, accounting for 60 percent of the 1952–53 harvest and increasing to 66 percent of 1953–54 production. An estimated 80 percent of 1954–55 production was financed through BANFAIC or affiliated banks and rural credit associations, with loans serviced upon the completion of the harvest.[100] Almost 75 percent of total production in Consolación del Sur—18,000 acres out of 24,000—was financed by the affiliate Rural Credit Association Tranquilino Sandalio de Noda.[101] "Faced with the need for a partial substitution of sugar cane, for which the export market had contracted," the ECLA reported in 1954, "the [Cuban] Government development policy has encouraged and guaranteed rice cultivation by substantial credit advances and mortgages on the harvest."[102] Increasingly, rice production consolidated into large-scale farming specialization and land concentration in the form of large capital investment. A total of sixty-three farms with an approximate size of 765 acres in 1953 had increased to ninety-three farms larger than 1,760 acres in 1955.[103] In 1955, an estimated 5 percent of all rice producers accounted for 75 percent of the area under cultivation and an even larger portion of the total production.[104]

The Batista government further extended state support to domestic rice production through the enactment of decrees and directives designed to reduce, restrict, and otherwise regulate rice imports. Through administrative fiat the government altered and adjusted import regulations to favor domestic production. The promulgation of Decree 1781 in 1953 banned rice imports containing more than 30 percent broken-grain content, with far-reaching trade implications. By the U.S. rice industry's own assessment, fully one-third of all rice exported to Cuba consisted of broken grain, and half of this amount included 50 percent or more of broken grain.[105] The prevailing conventional wisdom associated broken-grain rice with a lower quality grain, best used for brewers, rice flour, and animal feed—certainly not the quality befitting daily meals. The value of broken rice was deemed to be worth half that of whole rice.[106] Indeed, F. W. Wise, the secretary-treasurer of the Rice Millers Association, was categorical that "under no circumstances should this [broken] grain be used for table consumption."[107] In 1955 the Batista government enacted another measure, Resolution 98, to reaffirm the ban on rice with more than 30 percent broken grain and to require further that imports satisfy the U.S. Department of Agriculture certification Standard Grades 1, 2, or 3.[108] The "grading" of the quality and price of rice implied specifications based on the dimension, color, moisture, weight, uniformity, bran content, and percentage of damaged and discolored kernels, among other factors.[109]

ALL IN ALL, Cubans had achieved unprecedented success. Production increased from 180,000 quintals in 1940 to 1.7 million quintals in 1952. The 1953 harvest surpassed 1.8 million quintals, with an anticipated acreage expansion of another 20,000 acres dedicated to rice. The 1954 harvest reached 2.5 million

TABLE 4.2. Cuban rice production, 1940, 1945, and 1950–1955

Year	Harvested acreage	Production (quintals)
1940	69,000	180,000
1945	114,000	850,000
1950	135,000	1,000,000
1951	145,000	1,200,000
1952	156,000	1,700,000
1953	209,000	1,800,000
1954	N/A	2,500,000
1955	N/A	4,500,000

Sources: Instituto Nacional de Reforma Económica, "El arroz cubano ante una grave encrucijada," *Carta Pública Quincenal* 14 (March 15, 1955); "El mercado cubano de arroz: Fuentes de abastecimiento, precios, producción y consumo," *Cuba Económica y Financiera* 31 (April 1956).

quintals.[110] Cuban farmers enlarged their share of the domestic market all through the early 1950s, from 7 percent of the market in 1948 to 17 percent in 1951 to nearly 25 percent in 1952.[111] "This is a significant increase," the U.S. Embassy noted, "probably permitting a reduction in Cuban import requirements for 1952."[112] The expansion of domestic rice production, the ECLA reported two years later, "has enabled Cuba to supply a quarter of its domestic consumption and cut down rice imports, which were 70 per cent less during the first six months of 1952 than in the corresponding period of the previous year."[113] By 1955, Cuban production had grown to meet almost 60 percent of the national consumption needs.[114] "The Rice Grower and Miller in Cuba," Rice Millers Association representative in Havana John Nuber reported in 1953, "have during the past season continued to improve the methods of producing and milling. The prices they have obtained for the last season's crop were very *highly* satisfactory. This has interested more capital to be put into the rice planting business in Cuba."[115] The U.S. Department of Commerce took note: "The increase in the production of rice has been one of the most spectacular aspects of the Cuban Government's drive for agricultural diversification."[116]

The expectation that the expansion of rice would serve to arrest and reverse the loss of foreign exchange was more than fully realized. By 1955, national production saved an estimated $45 million—"money [previously] taken out of

Advertisement for domestic rice product
(*Diario de la Marina*, November 1, 1955).

national circulation to be sent abroad," noted Antonio Pérez González.[117] "If Cuba had to import, as it has in the past, the quantities of rice that it produces today," commented Senator Guillermo Aguilera, himself a large rice planter in Camagüey, "this money which today is strengthening and benefitting the Cuban economy, would be paid out to foreign markets, no doubt hurting our balance of payments."[118]

The expansion of rice served to stimulate the development of new trade networks. The mechanization of production resulted in a market for imports of a vast array of U.S. farm machinery, principally in the form of threshers, harvesters, disk plows, hulling machinery, irrigation pumps, and tractors. "The expansion of rice growing," reported the U.S. Embassy as early as 1952, "has already been felt in increased purchases of such capital goods as agricultural machinery and equipment and to some extent milling machinery."[119]

The expansion of rice also stimulated the development of corollary industries. The Cuban fertilizer industry grew. Between 1951 and 1955, the use of fertilizers on rice crops increased from 1,634 tons to a high of 33,375 tons.[120] Rice thus accounted for an expanding market for fertilizers, increasing from less than 1 percent in 1951 to 22 percent in 1954.[121] In 1957, an estimated 20,000 tons of fertilizer were used in the production of rice.[122] Additionally, new pesticide factories were established.

New rice mills sprang up across the island, almost all in possession of modern technology to process expanding domestic production.[123] By the late 1950s, more than 300 rice mills were in operation across the island, the largest of which included Molina Arrocera Los Palacios (Los Palacios, Pinar del Río), Molina de Arroz, S.A. (Florida, Camagüey), Roca y Alvarez (Manzanillo, Oriente), Arco y Campo (Manzanillo, Oriente), and Hermanos Alfonso (Vertientes, Camagüey). The larger mills were capable of producing 20 quintals of hulled rice per hour.[124] Cuban mills had sufficient capacity to complete the entire domestic rice crop in less than two months.[125] Indeed, the new mills had developed capacities beyond domestic production, which implied too the ability to process unmilled imports, after which they could market hulled rice as a finished product and reduce Cuban dependency on finished rice imports.[126] Cuban mill owners defended the expansion of industrial capabilities as "just and logical aspirations: the importation of the raw material rather than the finished product" and pointed out their goals: "That the industrial activity realized today by foreign rice mills [should] be developed in our country, that our laborers receive the wages that are paid to foreigners for work that could be done in our country, that we move away from the importation of finished products and import raw materials, and that we overcome the colonialist mentality and establish on a firm basis a prosperous Cuban industry."[127]

As the value and volume of rice production increased, so too did the network of influence of rice millers and farmers. Rice millers organized into the Asociación Nacional de Industriales Arroceros, a combination trade association and lobbying organization. Rice growers organized into the Asociación Nacional de Cosecheros de Arroz, with regional branches across the island, acquiring political influence and establishing a lobbying influence within government ministries. "The National Association of Rice Growers in Cuba," observed John Nuber in Havana, "is an important organization and have [sic] political influence. And to express it better are the Cuban Rice LOBBY but their lobbying is not done at the Congress but at the Ministers of Commerce and Agriculture Department."[128]

THE SUCCESS OF rice production gave rise to a growing optimism, a collective confidence that Cuba was on the threshold of a new economic order, at long last a step toward a remedy of the historic dysfunction of the export economy. "We are transcending one of the anomalies of our economy in vast strides," Leví Marrero pronounced in 1954. "The cultivation of rice has in a short space of time reached exceptional development, the salutary effects of which will be felt in short order as a dynamic factor in other facets of our agricultural production."[129] Everything seemed to be proceeding according to plan. "Much has been said about the necessity of diversification," exulted Leopoldo Aguilera, president of the Asociación Nacional de Cosecheros de Arroz in 1953, "and the need for Cuba to develop products unrelated to sugar in order to avoid the instabilities associated with the sugar markets.... Is there a product that better lends itself to diversification than rice, with a guaranteed market that Cuba provides?"[130]

These were heady times in Cuba. A National Rice Day (Día del Arroz) was celebrated annually on March 18–19 in the town of Yara, the principal rice region of the island, coinciding with the date of San José, the patron saint of Yara. A two-day festival (Día de la Feria del Arroz) included popular entertainment, exhibits, and shows in a county-fair ambience. A "Queen of Rice" pageant was inaugurated.[131] "Since we have long depended upon rice harvested in other lands to supply the enormous demand for this grain," *Diario de la Marina* said in commemoration of the event in Yara in 1950, "the National Rice Day acquires a high symbolic value in fulfillment of a momentous nationalist objective [*objetivo nacionalista*]: the point of departure on our way toward overcoming inadequate production in our own land."[132]

Cubans were exuberant, confident that national production would soon expand to fully meet domestic demand and end dependence on foreign imports.[133] The promise of self-sufficiency appeared within reach. In mid-1954 President Batista congratulated national rice producers "in behalf of the government and the nation for their extraordinary contribution to the economic development of Cuba and for the creation of new sources of employment."

Her majesty Norma I, Queen of Rice, coronated during the 1954 Rice Festival (Rodolfo Arango, *Guía arrocera nacional* [Havana, 1954]).

For the first time in the economic history of Cuba, Batista exulted, "it will not be necessary to import additional supplies of rice imports for the success of domestic production has more than adequately filled the national market for this important food item."[134] Cuba was committed "to follow a progressive course," Rodolfo Arango, director-general of the Ministry of Agriculture explained, "which in a few years will permit us to reach a production goal: to supply ourselves with the seven or eight million *quintales* that may represent our consumption, taking into account the logical rhythm of the increase of our population.... Rice is today, for our country, the symbol of wealth and well-being."[135] Minister of Agriculture Alfredo Jacomino was euphoric. "We continue in production favoring diversification," he pronounced in 1954, adding,

President Fulgencio Batista visiting a rice mill in the town of Florida in Camagüey province, 1954 (Rodolfo Arango, *Guía arrocera nacional* [Havana, 1955]).

We have multiplied the production of rice these past two years, a product of great demand in our domestic market, for rice is the basic food in the Cuban diet, for the poor as well as the rich. Rice is indispensable to the *menú criollo*, with such national dishes as chicken and rice, rice and beans, etc. Cuba is a rice country that is producing a great quantity of rice to meet the needs of national consumption. And for the first time there is no need to resort to imports to fill the deficit quota, something never before believed possible but today having been realized.[136]

Advertisements for heavy rice-farming machinery
(Rodolfo Arango, *Guía arrocera nacional* [Havana, 1955]).

"The success of our rice growers," *Diario de la Marina* affirmed in 1955, "demonstrates that Cuba can indeed deploy new technology and achieve diversification in our agriculture."[137] Almost everyone, it seemed, celebrated the success of rice. "The future possibilities of the rice industry," predicted Senator Guillermo Aguilera, "make us feel optimistic that one day we may be self-sufficient in the supply of this product."[138] "National production may soon meet fifty percent of consumption needs," economist Mario Greitín predicted in 1954, "and perhaps eventually even 100 percent.... If Cuba is able to produce rice at a cost and with a quality that permits it to compete with rice from the United States it will finally be able to fully conquer its internal market."[139]

Diversification had scored a notable achievement, made all the more compelling as an accomplishment of self-sufficiency via a staple of vital domestic consumption. "We will have to tell the Americans," exulted Alfredo Jacomino, "that we will no longer buy their rice but will need to purchase machinery to continue to mechanize our production."[140] The Asociación Nacional de Cosecheros de Arroz exuded similar optimism, predicting that the expansion of rice production promised to increase a more balanced Cuba-U.S. trade, for the wealth created by rice would "contribute to a higher standard of living" in certain producing areas and promote "larger consumption of other products whose natural source of importation is the United States . . . such as tractors, farm implements, radios, television sets, refrigerators, just to name a few articles that Cuba imports from the United States constantly and in increasing proportion."[141]

The Americans took note. "Most people in the rice business are quite optimistic," Harold Randall, economic affairs officer in the U.S. Embassy, reported in 1953, "some feeling that Cuba could very soon produce her entire needs of rice."[142] Juan de Zengotita, First Secretary of the U.S. Embassy, praised Cuban efforts toward self-sufficiency. "Diversification of large-scale agriculture is an obvious partial answer to the problem of seasonal unemployment in the cane industry," Zengotita reported in 1955, "and something has been accomplished along this line. The cultivation of rice, which furnishes labor opportunities complementary seasonally to those offered by cane sugar, has gone up markedly in recent years; and there is still plenty of room in the Cuban domestic market for more native rice." But Zengotita also understood there would be consequences. "For Cuba to produce its own rice means not importing rice from Louisiana," he commented.[143] And therein lay the problem.

CHAPTER FIVE

To Tremble in Fear

Sugar is not only a sword of Damocles menacing the Cuban people with perpetuation of economic slavery represented by monoculture, it is also an obstacle to the development of all other agricultural initiatives, the returns of which are almost always inferior to the sugar industry.
—Gustavo Pittaluga, *Diálogos sobre el destino* (1954)

We have never believed it desirable to mix sugar and rice, and do not believe it desirable now; however, we do believe that all reciprocal trade agreements should be precisely that, namely, reciprocal—meaning that there is a quid pro quo for every concession granted and received. The United States granted important concessions to Cuba. If such concessions are granted by the United States to Cuba without any regard whatsoever as to whether Cuba does or does not comply with its commitments, seemingly, it is self evident that Cuba may receive and never give. For this reason we are firmly of the opinion that if and when Cuba fails to conform with its commitments, the United States should withhold commitments from Cuba.
—William M. Reid, Rice Millers Association, to Senator Allen J. Ellender, 1951

We limit, some would say we severely limit, our own production of sugar from cane and beets. But when we turn to rice there is inadequate reciprocity and foot dragging by our neighbor on the southeast.... If there is not prompt progress as regards [U.S. rice exports], which I maintain is due us in reciprocity, I will recommend that we take a new and hard look at our handling of our sugar program, with particular reference to a possible decision to reduce imports from Cuba and expand our own domestic production.—Representative Theo Ashton Thompson, 1954

Some of us have worked long and hard to establish ourselves as primarily Cuban shippers.... Believe me, when I say we tremble in the fear of something happening to this very fine market.—Gordon E. Dore, President, Supreme Rice Mill, Inc., October 18, 1952

INTERNATIONAL RICE TRADE resumed after World War II principally within formal trade protocols, in conformity with quota-driven agreements and duty-protected arrangements, which were in turn integrated into the larger purpose of foreign policies and ratified through contractual trade practices and negotiated conventions. The establishment in Geneva of the General Agreement on Tariffs and Trade (GATT) in 1947, subsequently ratified through a formal rice-tariff agreement between Cuba and the United States, committed Cuba to import a minimum rice quota of 3.25 million quintals with duty set at $1.85 per 100 kilograms. Cuba could increase U.S. rice imports beyond 3.25 million quintals to fill the deficit quota (*cuota deficitaria*), that is, the differential between national production and estimates of domestic demand. Rice imports in excess of 3.25 million quintals were dutiable at $3.70 per 100 kilograms.[1]

The GATT-approved quota of 3.25 million quintals established the baseline minimum allotment accorded to U.S. rice imports. What made the Cuban market so coveted, however, was not the minimum 3.25 million quintals quota but access to the *cuota deficitaria*, the shortfall between national production and domestic demand. Prior to World War II, Cuban production had rarely filled more than 5 to 10 percent of the domestic market demand, with the difference between domestic demand and domestic production filled with foreign imports. This was the market that U.S. producers sought to capture by excluding Asian rice. In 1936, non-U.S. rice constituted 97.5 percent of total imports; in 1946, it had diminished to 12.4 percent, and by 1950, non-U.S. rice accounted for 0.1 percent of total rice imports.[2] That Cuba had agreed to all future adjustment quotas for other countries in proportion to the rice imports ten years immediately preceding the GATT agreement all but eliminated foreign rivals for Cuban markets.[3]

But American rice was not without competition. In fact, the elimination of Asian imports meant to favor American producers also served to stimulate Cuban rice. Cuban production steadily expanded to fill an ever-larger share of the domestic market, underscoring the obvious: the displacement of Asian rice would have served the U.S. interests not at all if Cuban production displaced American imports. And that was the Cuban goal: to achieve self-sufficiency, obviating the necessity of rice imports altogether. Cuban authorities, the U.S. Embassy reported in 1955, "stated quite frankly one of the main objectives of the Cuban Government was to be able to cover all its consumption needs for rice in the future, except for the basic quota of 3,250,000 quintals."[4] In 1950, domestic demand was fixed at 7.4 million quintals, of which Cuban production provided 1 million quintals and American imports supplied 6.4 million quintals, that is, a little more than 85 percent of total demand. In 1952, the expansion of Cuban rice reduced U.S. imports to 73 percent of the total (4.7 million quintals out of a total demand of 6.4 million quintals). In 1954, the U.S. share of the Cuban market declined to 60 percent (4 million quintals out of a total market of 6.7 million quintals) and declined again in 1955 to 39 percent (2.4 million quintals out of a total market of 6.1 million quintals).[5] In 1954, the Batista government promulgated Decree 1827, announcing confidently that the success of domestic production had obviated the need to import rice beyond the GATT 3.25 million quintals. Between 1950 and 1955, the value of U.S. rice imports declined from $51 million to $18.6 million, a loss of almost 63 percent.[6] The vast quantities of surplus rice in the 1954 crop, moreover, resulted in a 25 percent reduction of the acreage for the 1955 crop, accompanied with preparations for another 50 percent reduction of acreage for the following year.[7]

THESE WERE NOT developments to which North American producers were reconciled. Ill portents indeed. "One can readily see that if Cuba continues to expand the production of rice at the rate of recent years," the Rice Millers Association predicted in 1953, "it will not be many years before Cuba will be producing all the rice it needs."[8] Cuba had developed into the principal export market of U.S. rice, upon which—the Americans insisted—the very survival of the rice industry depended, accounting for nearly 85 percent of total exports to the Western Hemisphere, some 3.8 million bags out of 4.5 million bags.[9]

"It is always desirable to try and reconcile, by amicable means, differences of opinion," pronounced the Rice Millers Association in 1951, adding to warn: "However, in such cases as the instant one[,] patience is about exhausted and it may become necessary for the United States rice industry to take such measures as are available to it to persuade the U.S. Government to withdraw U.S. concessions on Cuban products unless and until Cuba in good faith makes available the full measure of concessions on rice which that country agreed to

TABLE 5.1. Cuban rice imports from the United States, 1949–1958

Year	Volume (million quintals)	Value (dollars)
1949	6.0	$51,073,478
1950	6.3	51,439,688
1951	6.4	59,180,278
1952	4.7	46,796,695
1953	5.6	58,172,707
1954	4.0	40,775,545
1955	2.4	18,608,143
1956	4.0	24,625,229
1957	4.1	38,928,741
1958	4.1	39,896,325

Source: "Las importaciones de arroz de Cuba," *Cuba Económica y Financiera* 34 (February 1959).

give in exchange for concessions granted to it by the U.S. Government on many Cuban products."[10] "I am fully aware of the fact that the Cuban government is trying to protect its own domestic rice producers," Gordon Dore, president of the Supreme Rice Mill in Louisiana, complained to the Department of Agriculture. "However, they are trying to do this at the expense of the American rice industry, who, in my opinion, have [sic] been a very good friend to the Cuban people." Dore insisted that the "Cuban market should be treated as one of our own Domestic markets and surely should be afforded the same privileges, as far as rice imports are concerned, as Puerto Rico and the Territories of Hawaii."[11] President of the Rice Millers Association William Reid warned of "the harmful effects the Cuban action is having on the U.S. rice industry and the whole U.S. economy. Cuba is our largest export market and losses which the rice industry are suffering in that market are being deeply felt."[12] Reid despaired and asked rhetorically, "Will the U.S. rice industry commit economic suicide?"

> The quantity of rice which Cuba will license for importation is governed by how much rice Cuba produces.... The Cubans [have] expanded production of rice at a rapid rate, and in the past few years Cuba has been steadily reducing imports of rice. The U.S. has lost over 30 percent of its Cuban

business in the past five years and ... there is no end in sight as to how far the Cubans can and will go in their program of expanding rice production and forcing the United States out of that market. It appears that the U.S. will suffer another huge loss in Cuba this year, as the Government of Cuba has indicated that it will limit imports of mill rice.[13]

The Americans took particular umbrage at Cuban import controls, especially Resolution 98, limiting U.S. rice to Standard Grades 1, 2, or 3. In fact, the higher grades represented only a small portion of total U.S. imports. "The masses of the Cuban population," William Reid explained to the State Department, "buy the lower priced long grain rice offered on the market. As the lower grades are lower in price, Cuban consumers choose the lower grades over the higher grade. Thus by requiring that rice imported into Cuba be of the highest grades and types, the Cuban government has placed United States rice at a tremendous disadvantage in the price-conscious Cuban market." Reid added,

> The obvious purpose of these Cuban restrictions on imported rice is to make it difficult if not impossible for the United States to sell to Cuba the basic tariff quota of 3,250,000 quintals of rice which is provided under the General Agreement on Tariffs and Trade.... Resolution No. 98 is the latest in a long list of circumventions, evasions, and outright violations of Cuba of the U.S.-Cuba Rice Agreement.... We have called each of these infractions to the attention of the State Department in protests dating back to early in 1954, but to our serious concern, no effective action against them has been taken by the Department of State in any of many instances. The situation has now reached a critical stage. The U.S. rice industry is on the verge of being totally eliminated from Cuba.[14]

American producers did not fail to recognize the prejudicial purport of Decree 1781 and Resolution 98.[15] "Such restrictive regulations as will permit only rice of U.S. grades Number 1, 2, or 3 with not more than 30 percent broken content...," George Blair of the American Rice Growers Cooperative Association warned, "will be the most serious blow to U.S. rice exports through commercial channels and particularly those from Louisiana and Texas."[16] Blair was blunt: "The restrictions can have a very decided impact on rice producers, inasmuch as the Cuban market represents a potential outlet for about 20 percent of the U.S. rice production and after 40 percent of acreage cuts in the past three years we must seek to maintain every market that we possibly can."[17] The ban on broken grain and the prohibition of lower rice grades, warned Rice Millers Association representative John Nuber in Havana, bode ill, for "if this comes to pass then we can expect anything[;] perhaps they might prevent other types of rice from coming into Cuba." Nuber understood well the issues at stake: "It is a notorious fact that if they (the Cuban Government I mean) should allow BROKENS, as well as OFF GRADES, [to] be shipped openly into Cuba it would be the funeral of the Cuban Rice Production and they know it, [and] that is why they are making so many suggestions to the Minister of Commerce so as to influence him to keep U.S.A. Rice under wraps."[18] It required no gift of prophecy, the Rice Millers Association warned, to predict the outcome of Cuban production strategies: "It is the announced intention of the Government of Cuba to foster to the fullest extent possible the increase in rice production until Cuba can supply its normal consumption requirements except for the basic United States quota of 3,250,000 quintals.... The Government of Cuba will resort to every type of device known to try and expand production of rice in that country until Cuba is self sufficient and does not require rice from any source."[19]

The regulations restricting rice imports to Grades 1, 2, and 3 and requiring a maximum of 30 percent broken kernels violated the GATT agreement, U.S. producers complained; the effect was "to shamefully evade—yes; to ruthlessly violate—contractual commitments of that country under the rice agreement," decried William Reid.[20] "We were shocked," the Rice Millers Association protested, "to learn ... that the Government of Cuba was proceeding to put into effect restrictions against imports of rice from the United States."[21]

Alleging violation of GATT had far-reaching policy implications, for a breach of a formal bilateral trade agreement served as political warrant with which to appeal to the U.S. government for assistance—to demand "some straight and strong talk from *high Washington Officials* to straighten out this matter," John Nuber insisted.[22] Rice producers had greeted the election of President Dwight Eisenhower in 1952 with expectations that the new Republican administration would act with dispatch to defend rice. "We think it is now time," rice broker E. B. Ogden wrote to the Tyrrell Rice Milling Company in Beaumont, Texas, in February 1953, "since there has been a change of government in the United States, to straighten out things of this kind." He continued: "We believe that you, as rice millers and as an American firm, could take up this matter with the new Secretaries of Commerce, State and Agriculture, in Washington, and request that export allocations and export permits be done away with on rice to Cuba, and that all Cuban import controls, such as quotas, import licenses and authorizations to Cuban consuls at ports of embarkation to visa documents, be removed. This state of affairs cannot continue if the American rice millers expect to do a satisfactory business in Cuba."[23] The failure of the previous administration to act decisively, rice producers insisted, had served to embolden the Cubans to restrict rice imports in violation of GATT protocols. Since "the U.S. has complacently accepted and condoned such action," George Blair complained, "[Cuban] interests have been encouraged to seek additional restrictions."[24] The Rice Millers Association appealed to the Department of State: "If Cuba is permitted to do this, what is to prevent Cuba from going a step further and limiting importations of rice to one class, one grade, or one variety, thereby restricting the U.S. to only a small segment of the Cuban rice market and by such administrative action eventually making it impossible for the U.S. to sell any substantial quantity of rice in Cuba[?] . . . It is quite apparent that these shameful breaches of faith by the Government of Cuba will continue and be expanded as long as the Government of the U.S. chooses to passively condone them."[25] Cuban import controls of rice imports, William Reid protested to the State Department, was designed "to make it difficult if not impossible for the United States to sell to Cuba the basic tariff quota of 3,250,000 quintals of rice which is provided under the General Agreement on Tariffs and Trade," adding,

> Resolution No. 98 is the latest in a long list of circumventions, evasions, and outright violations by Cuba of the U.S.-Cuba Rice Agreement. . . . We have called each of these infractions to the attention of the State Department in protests dating back to early 1954, but to our serious concern, no effective action against them has been taken by the Department of State in any of the many instances. The situation has now reached a critical stage. The U.S. rice industry is on the verge of being totally eliminated from Cuba. . . . We are convinced that this distressing situation could be alleviated if our Government had the will to take appropriate corrective action.[26]

But in the absence of "appropriate corrective action," the Rice Millers Association affirmed, "efforts will be made to obtain the assistance of the Senators and Congressmen from the rice producing states."[27] The elected officials from the "rice producing states" consisted of a cohort of powerful senators and representatives, all southern, all Democrats, almost all with long tenure and seniority on important congressional committees.[28] The *Rice Millers Association Newsletter* exhorted the association's membership to demand that Congress take "a firmer and more positive stand in this case than it has taken in the past. Obviously powder puff diplomacy will not work with the Cubans; it will take frank talk and firm action to bring the Cubans in compliance with the rice agreement."[29] Frank Godchaux, president of the Louisiana Rice Milling Company, wrote directly to Louisiana senator Allen Ellender, the powerful chairman of the Senate Agriculture Committee, warning that the "rice industry is now confronted with the most serious threat we have ever had to our rice trade with Cuba." And to the point: "In my opinion, our State Department should do something about it—and fast!"[30] William Reid wrote to members of both houses of Congress—with a copy to Secretary of State John Foster Dulles—explaining that the "infringement by Cuba of the Rice Agreement is serious enough in itself, but it is shocking when viewed in terms of the long list of previous flauntings by Cuba of the agreement. It is even more shocking to consider that officials of our Government who are supposed to handle such matters have permitted this problem to reach this disgraceful proportion," adding,

> It seems to me that it is time the Congress forced the State Department to develop a sounder approach to foreign problems of this country than the present costly "give-away" and "give-in" approach. Unless and until there is a change in the basic approach to foreign relations, trade agreements between this country and other countries may well be considered documents for exploitation rather than promotion of the U.S. economy, since the U.S. representatives are always ready to give something to other countries but never ready to require other countries to reciprocate, even to the extent of living up to written public agreements.[31]

Senator Ellender communicated with the State Department to register his "very strong opposition" to Cuban regulations and vowed "to continue to press the State Department for affirmative action in this matter so that our Louisiana producers will get what they are entitled to under our international agreement with the Cuban Government." However, Ellender also learned that the State Department was less than eager to defend the cause of rice. "It is my fear," he explained to the Rice Millers Association, "that our officials may be too prone to be sympathetic with the Cubans and offer to compromise, and thus give away some of the rights of American rice growers, rather than insist upon the Cubans living up to their trade agreement with us."[32] In fact, Assistant Secretary of State Thruston Morton had cautioned Senator Ellender that "now is not the time to rock the boat" but pledged to address the matter on the occasion of the renewal of the sugar agreement in 1955. "Between us," Ellender confided to Frank Godchaux in 1954, "since Cuba's economy is dependent to a large extent on sugar shipments to the United States, they would much prefer to protect the sugar growers than the rice growers," adding, "I have the assurance of the State Department that if the Cubans fail to announce the shipments of rice in accord with the agreement a strong protest will be entered by our government, and it will be called to the attention of the Cuban government that unless the Cubans carry out their agreement with respect to rice it may seriously affect the

[U.S.] sugar legislation that is now in the offing and which will be considered next year."³³

Godchaux was not mollified. "Right now is the most appropriate time possible to 'rock the boat' on the Cuban-U.S. rice and sugar programs," he chided Ellender. It had become necessary for the United States to point out "to the proper Cuban officials that they are apparently deliberately undermining the Cuban-U.S. agreement by increasing their own rice production to the elimination of their rice deficit while our Government limits our sugar production in favor of Cuban sugar," adding, "They should be told right now that the present situation calls for a new look at the whole agreement, suggesting that the same formula be used on Cuban rice imports from the U.S. and our sugar imports from Cuba. In my opinion, our State Department is being seriously outmaneuvered."³⁴

Rice producers wearied of State Department defense of Cuba. "We construe the substance of [U.S. policy]," an exasperated William Reid protested, "as indicating that the State Department made no effort to influence Cuba to comply with the rice agreement between the United States and Cuba, but rather confined its efforts to helping Cuba explain away and validate violations of the agreement."³⁵ Reid bristled at the State Department response. Writing to Representative Hale Boggs from New Orleans, Reid denounced Secretary Morton as "obsessed with a different philosophy on how to gain the friendship and respect of people" and as one who believed that "international goodwill is something that can and must be bought." Added Reid: "If the Cuban economy is in bad condition . . . , and if it is in our country's political interest that the Cuban economy be strengthened, then our Government officials should consider taking steps on a national scale to help the Cuban economy. We do not feel that the rice industry should be assigned the whole costs of performing that national service."³⁶ The Cuban intent was clear, Reid explained to a House Ways and Means subcommittee: "To put the squeeze on United States rice—to make it as difficult as possible for United States rice exporters to enter the Cuban market." He warned that the U.S. rice industry was "on the verge of being totally eliminated from Cuba." The State Department had shamefully failed to defend U.S. interests, Reid complained to Congress, and on every occasion that the rice industry had urged firm action, State Department officials resorted to "their favorite excuse—they say we might drive Cuba to communism if we force her to live up to her contractual commitments. . . . About all any country has to do today to have its way with the United States is to wave the hammer and sickle. Everybody knows it, everybody practices it, everybody laughs up their sleeve at the way the United States scampers for their favor."³⁷

William Reid appealed to attorney John Minor Wisdom of New Orleans. The future Fifth Circuit Court of Appeals judge had close personal ties to President Eisenhower, connections Reid sought to avail himself of. "Cuba is, and has been for years," explained Reid, "the United States largest and most dependable customer for rice, taking annually over 500 million pounds of milled rice, or 40 percent of total average exports of rice from the United States." Reid complained about State Department indifference to the plight of rice producers:

> The State Department considers Cuba's economy to be in bad condition, and the State Department fears that if the U.S. presses Cuba on this matter, the U.S. might provide propaganda for the Communists to expand their influence in Cuba. If the economy of Cuba is in a distressing condition, our Government should attempt to brace it through a Government aid program rather than to place the whole burden of cost on the rice industry. As to the possibility of driving Cuba to Communism, it seems to us that the State Department throws up that old bogey as an excuse for any and everything. By this reasoning we are slaves to the Communistic menace, if not to Communism itself.[38]

RICE PRODUCERS could hardly contain their indignation. The full wrath of rice was directed toward the Department of State. Reid complained to Representative Boggs about the "weak and ineffective attitude by our Government" and denounced the "total lack of willingness on the part of our Government to defend America's legitimate trade interests." The Department of State had refused to "take any forceful measures (such as retaliation against imports from Cuba) to bring rectification," Reid decried, asking rhetorically, "Has not the Cuban Government already demonstrated to our Government that it will not honor any feature of the rice agreement unless forced to do so by retaliatory measures?" Concluded Reid, "Countries which engage in that sort of shenanigans respect nothing but retaliation; they completely ignore notes and other diplomatic niceties.... Cuba will continue to violate the provisions of the rice agreement until the U.S. seriously threatens to cancel concessions granted by this country to Cuba."[39]

Rice lobbyists "worked" their contacts inside the Eisenhower administration, reaching out to and meeting with past associates and personal friends in government. Fletcher Rawls, formerly of the Foodstuffs Division of the Department of Commerce, an "insider" who moved freely within the Washington officialdom and with close ties to the rice industry, confirmed what rice producers had suspected. In fact, Fletcher reported learning from Leonard Ellis of the Department of Agriculture that the Eisenhower administration believed that Cuba was "not in violation of GATT," adding, "Ellis himself told me that in view of this attitude within our Government he felt very doubtful that any further pressure would be placed upon the Cubans." The Department of Agriculture invoked the standard cliché, Rawls grumbled, dismissing the complaints of the rice industry with "the old stock answer ... by all of the people in our Government here that Cuba is a sovereign country and consequently we cannot interfere with their domestic problems."[40] Rawls also conferred with Amelia Hood, the economic officer for Caribbean affairs at the State Department who was deeply involved with the issue of rice. Rawls was disheartened after a private conversation with Hood, with whom, he wrote, he had "a very close personal relationship": "I was not very much encouraged after talking with her," noting, "Mrs. Hood's general attitude is that the Southern rice industry should be very grateful for the business which it is getting in Cuba." Rawls summarized his conversation with Hood and other officials in the Departments of Commerce and Agriculture:

> The conclusion I reached after talking to Mrs. Hood was that our Government is very sympathetic with Cuba's problems. This is borne out by conversations which I have had not only with Mrs. Hood but also with Al Powers, of Commerce, as well as Leonard Ellis and Dexter Rivenburg in Agriculture. My feeling, as far as conversations with the two latter is concerned, is that the entire problem is being left entirely up to State.... [U.S. economic affairs attaché in Havana] Chester Davis is the person upon whom Mrs. Hood depends to do the liaison work with the Cuban Government.... Chester has been in Cuba so long that he is really inclined to think of Cuba's economic problems ahead of those of his own country.[41]

THE STATE DEPARTMENT found itself in an anomalous position. In fact, the State Department was not unsympathetic to Cuban diversification efforts. "Cuba has recognized the danger of relying on one crop, sugar, and is attempting to diversify its production," Secretary Morton explained to Representative Boggs.[42] "This is one of the reasons why it has fostered increased rice production." Morton was unambiguous in his support of Cuban rice production. "The expansion in rice production," he explained, "has been of considerable aid in keeping the Cuban economy from being further depressed," adding, "Imports into Cuba during the last three years of machinery, equipment and fertilizer in the amount of at least $25,000,000 annually for use in the preparation of new land for rice, together with the production, harvesting and milling of rice[,] played a most important part in maintaining economic stability through the country during the years when the strictest economies were being practiced by the sugar industry and those dependent upon it."[43] But larger political issues were also involved. The Eisenhower administration was loath to impose sanctions on Cuba for fear of weakening a pro-American government, wary that U.S. penalties would act to "damage the domestic political prestige of the Cuban government."[44] The stigma of illegitimacy continued to hang heavy over the Batista government. The military coup had overturned a constitutional democracy, plunging the political system into disarray. Batista had sought to legitimize his seizure of power through national elections in November 1954, in which he was elected unopposed. Yet his efforts to obtain constitutional legitimacy had failed. Political opposition increased, armed resistance expanded, and the economy remained hopelessly mired in stagnation. These were complicated times in Cuba.

The matter of rice assumed a larger meaning, one that seemed to implicate almost everything else. The State Department treaded lightly. Amelia Hood prepared a memorandum of her conversation in late 1954 with Calvin Wurslow from Senator Ellender's office:

> [Wurslow] asked what we intended to do next about the Cuban noncompliance.... I answered that we intended to have our Embassy take up the matter again with the Cuban Government and that we thought a propitious time would be immediately after the Cuban elections were over on November 1. He referred as usual to the effect which Cuban noncompliance with the rice agreement would have when consideration would be given to revision of the Sugar Act in the next session of Congress. ... He wanted to know why we could not have done more. To this I said that we and the Embassy had taken up the matter with the Cubans many times, that because of the economic recession in Cuba we had not been successful, and that consideration had to be given to the possible danger to Cuba if the recession should be deepened because of any forcing of Cuba to take more rice at a time when it was not needed. To this he remarked that we were always worrying about unemployment in Cuba and the possibility of communism there but that we should worry about unemployment and the possible spread of communism in Louisiana.[45]

In fact, officials in the U.S. Embassy in Havana continued to defend Cuban diversification strategies. "The Embassy has to marvel at the apparent lack of knowledge of the overall situation here," economic attaché Chester Davis complained to the State Department:

> The Embassy strongly feels that the rapid development of the Cuban rice industry very effectively, at least to a considerable extent, filled the gap in Cuba's economic life streams caused by the cut-back in the production of sugar ... and the continued drop in the price of sugar in the world market. The Embassy also feels [that] the partial taking up of the slack these past few years by the rice industry by (1) the saving of dollar exchange; (2) the steady employment of labor through most of the calendar year; [and] (3) the spending of approximately $25,000,000 annually over the past three years on rice machinery and fertilizer, when almost nothing in the way of capital investment or fertilizer was being spent by the sugar companies, played a great part in keeping Cuba on a comparatively even keel both economically and politically. The loss to southern rice growers in volume of rice shipped might be considered a small overall price to pay for stability here.

Davis added an afterthought: "The beneficial efforts of the expanding rice industry saved Cuba from virtual collapse in late 1952 and in 1953."[46] One month later, Davis wrote again: "Rice played a most important part in maintaining economic stability throughout the country during those years when otherwise the strictest economies were being practiced by the sugar industry and those dependent upon it as the result of the official cut-backs in production of sugar."[47]

Internal memoranda suggest that the State Department sought to calm congressional agitation over the "controversial nature of rice and sugar problems," Dulles wrote, with concern over the "sensitiveness of Congress re prerogatives on all matters affecting sugar legislation" and fearful that Congress would indeed implement retaliatory measures against Cuba.[48] The State Department assumed a conciliatory but firm position. "Efforts will continue to be made to urge the Cuban Government to announce a supplemental low-duty rice quota," Secretary Morton assured Representative Boggs—but with a caveat. "Retaliation by the United States could only worsen the economic situation in Cuba," warned Morton, "and might well have political results inimical to the best interests of the United States":

> Such action would not only hurt Cuba but would adversely affect American export and import business without improving the situation of United States exporters. . . . The great drop in [sugar] production in Cuba

between 1952 and 1954, and the drop in price of sugar has meant economic recession and distress in Cuba. There has been widespread unemployment not only in the sugar industry but in other industries that are dependent upon it. It is clear that economic distress gives communism an opportunity, which it is quick to exploit, to promote unrest and foster suspicion and hostility toward the United States. The economic situation of Cuba is therefore of great concern to the United States because of its nearness and strategic location.[49]

The matter of rice reached the highest levels of the Eisenhower administration as the State Department asserted the prerogative over foreign policy. In 1954, Dulles wrote directly to Secretary of Agriculture Ezra Benson to convey "serious concern" about efforts to impose sanctions on the Batista government, which "if adopted would seriously injure the Cuban economy, which is already suffering from severe curtailment of sugar production, greatly reduced exports and lower prices." Any proposed reduction of "Cuban participation in the U.S. sugar markets," Dulles warned, "might easily tip the scales to cause revolution in Cuba, and would certainly increase instability and promote anti-American feeling and communist activity in an area of great strategic and economic importance to the United States. The Department of State consequently opposes the proposed modification of the Sugar Act as prejudicial to our relations with the Republic of Cuba and inimical to the preservation of the important strategic and economic interest of the United States in Cuba and the entire Caribbean area."[50] Dulles communicated directly to President Eisenhower, repeating his concern that economic retaliation against Cuba "might easily tip the scales to cause revolution in Cuba and would certainly increase instability and promote anti-American feeling and communist activity."[51]

RICE INTERESTS were not deterred. Unable to obtain satisfactory policy relief from the State Department, rice producers increased demand for congressional action against Cuban sugar. The Sugar Act of 1951 was scheduled to expire on December 31, 1955, whereupon the matter of the quota would be subject to review, to be renewed or revised as a matter of the will of Congress. Lobbyist Fletcher Rawls met with Fred Rossiter of the Department of Agriculture in 1954, who—in a "completely off the record" conversation—disclosed that a Cuban delegation was arriving in Washington to commence negotiations over the sugar quota:

> Fred suggested that in his opinion when such discussions develop, by all means it would be propitious to bring up the question of Cuba's expanded

rice production; he suggested again off the record that it may be well for individuals in the South to consider some pressure with Southern representatives in Congress and make an effort to get from such representatives some public statement relating to the expansion of rice production in Cuba. In other words Fred feels there is no reason why the sugar/rice problem should not be a quid pro quo proposition.[52]

The time was propitious, wrote Gerald Doyle of the Beaumont Rice Mills, to "persuade a congressman or senator from Louisiana to use the timing of [the sugar bill] as a spring board for a statement beamed at Cuba and Louisiana which would call attention to the shortsightedness of a country that was getting 96% of our 'supplementary sugar quota' and trying to nullify a 'rice quota' equally as binding."[53] Frank Godchaux exhorted Senator Ellender to enact retaliatory measures against Cuba:

For years we have limited sugar production in this country in order to give Cuba a large quota on a favorable tariff basis. They have reciprocated by giving us a tariff preferential on rice. The catch is, however, that for a number of years they have deliberately encouraged and fostered their rice production ... and, in addition, have set up governmental regulations hampering the movement of our rice to Cuba in favor of certain large producers of rice in that country.... Sugar and rice are profitable crops in both the United States and Cuba. If the farmers in Louisiana and other rice-growing states are forced to reduce their plantings of rice for the lack of a market, they will naturally have to turn to other crops. Especially in Louisiana, cane and rice are interchangeable.... It would seem to me that a proposal should be made to have our rice shipments to Cuba on exactly the same basis as Cuba's sugar shipments to the United States.[54]

"Cuba wants the United States to continue taking a larger sugar tonnage at prices substantially above the world market," decried Cyril R. C. Laan, president of Rickert, Wessanen and Laan Rice Mills, "and likewise they expect the Rice Milling Industry to be agreeable to a reduction of milled rice exports. This cannot be the case, as reciprocal agreements should work on a give and take basis."[55] The Rice Millers Association was explicit. The United States guaranteed Cuban sugar a quota of 2.1 million tons, which implied a commensurate loss of the domestic market for U.S. sugar producers. "So that Cuba shall be able to realize that quota as a minimum," the Rice Millers Association protested, "the United States restricts the amount of sugar which may be produced in the USA," and to the point:

In other words USA gives to Cuba a sugar quota and restricts the production of sugar in the United States so that Cuba will be sure of being able to sell its quota in this country. On the other hand Cuba gives to the USA a rice quota and then proceeds to try and produce its own rice. There is no element of reciprocity in that kind of deal. The RMA feels that Cuba should take means to prevent rice production in that country making the U.S. rice quota an illusory benefit only. We have presented the facts and figures on this subject to members of the Congress with the request that they use their influence to obtain from Cuba a concession for U.S. rice comparable to the concession which Cuba has from the U.S. on sugar.[56]

The most forceful defender of rice was Louisiana senator Allen Ellender, who as chairman of the Senate Agriculture Committee would have decisive influence on the allocation of the sugar quota. Senator Ellender mounted repeated public attacks against Cuba, always with thinly veiled threats against Cuban sugar. "The United States has been very good to Cuba," Ellender insisted. "Cuba is anxious for us to purchase all the sugar she can produce, but when it comes to the purchase of rice from us, Cuba says, 'No; we want to produce our own rice.' . . . I dare say that if we treated Cuban sugar in the same manner that Cuba treats American rice, there would be very much less Cuban sugar sold in this country."[57] Ellender implored Secretary of State Dulles that "something be done by our Government to compel the Cubans to live up to their agreements or else take the consequences of non-compliance."[58] Insisting that Cuba had "once again slammed the door in the face of American rice producers," Ellender stated, "We have dealt generously with Cuba on the matter of sugar, and have accorded the Cuban sugar industry a much fairer deal than the Cuban government is willing to hand our rice people, despite the fact that we have no international agreement with Cuba concerning sugar."[59]

THE PENDING NEGOTIATIONS for the renewal of the sugar quota provided the decisive occasion of reckoning. Cuban sugar was hostage. "We have learned," reported Banco de Fomento Agrícola e Industrial de Cuba board member Antonio González López, "that the United States presumes to take advantage of the opportunity offered by the negotiations over sugar to take up with the Government of Cuba the matter of deficit rice imports, insisting to export 600,000 additional *quintales* of rice."[60]

The State Department arrived belatedly to an understanding of congressional determination to act against Cuban sugar. In mid-1954, Harvey Wellman of the Office of Middle American Affairs was informed by Senator Ellender that Congress "would make every effort to secure" passage of measures to reduce the Cuban sugar quota."[61] The reduction of Cuban access to U.S. markets, the Eisenhower administration understood, would portend calamity for Cuba. Applying a combination of moral suasion and appeals to self-interest, the State Department urged Batista to yield to U.S. rice imports as a concession necessary to defend sugar, specifically exhorting the Cubans to suspend enforcement of import regulations. On the eve of a rice convention in Washington, the State Department met with officials of the Cuban Embassy to warn, "It was pointed out that . . . there would be many American rice producers, millers and exporters attending the rice convention . . . and if rice were not allowed to be imported into Cuba, there would be considered criticism expressed at that meeting, that some of the U.S. rice people would complain to their Congressmen, and that this would be very bad at a time when bills for the revision of the Sugar Act were before Congress containing proposals for the reduction of Cuba's sugar quota."[62] The State Department acted with a newfound sense of urgency. Secretary Dulles wired Ambassador Arthur Gardner in Havana in April 1954 to "do whatever feasible and appropriate [to] encourage Cuban Government [to] eliminate rice quota. Further delay by Cuba in honoring rice agreement aggravates violation, increases hardship [of] US exporters and is likely to prejudice good will in US towards Cuba."[63] Two months later, Dulles again cabled the embassy: "Importance full compliance obligation to United States rice imports emphasized in relation [to] Cuba's position United States sugar markets. . . . Executive Branch currently resisting efforts to increase domestic sugar quota at expense [of] Cuba."[64] A State Department internal memorandum in preparation for a meeting with the Cuban chargé d'affaires in Washington underscored the urgency: "The Department and Embassy Habana have brought to the attention of Cuban officials the importance of Cuba's compliance with the rice quota agreement especially at this time. Cane sugar producers of Louisiana, where rice is also produced for the Cuban market, are pressing for amendment of the Sugar Act to increase their quota at the expense of Cuba. . . . The Executive Branch is now resisting efforts to increase domestic sugar quotas at the expense of Cuba and is defending Cuban participation in the U.S. sugar market."[65]

On the sidelines of the deepening U.S.-Cuba rice dispute were sugar interests, who early understood that the matter of GATT quotas and the *cuota deficitaria* implied more than rice. At stake was the sugar quota, upon which the very solvency of sugar and well-being of the national economy depended. As the State Department applied diplomatic pressure from the outside, sugar interests mobilized political pressure from within.

ON THE MORNING OF November 24, 1954, Cubans awoke to the ominous front-page headlines of the Havana daily *El Mundo*: "The American Senator [Ellender] will oppose the purchase of Cuban sugar." The news story continued: "Senator Allen J. Ellender said today that he will mount an offensive in Congress against the sale of Cuban sugar because Cuba has violated its commitment to the purchase of North American rice."[66] *Diario de la Marina* also dedicated front-page coverage to Ellender and included comments from the senator's press conference. Cuba had "defaulted in its commitment to uphold the agreement to purchase U.S. rice," Ellender was quoted; he vowed "to do all within my power to expand the share of domestic sugar producers at the expense of the Cuban quota," adding, "If Cuba believes that it is more important to harvest rice than to sell sugar, then my comments are of no consequences. But I am fed up and tired that Cuba receives all the participation that it seeks in our markets but does not fulfill the rice agreement with the United States."[67] Four months later, Senator Ellender introduced in the Senate and Representative Boggs in the House of Representatives a bill—the "Ellender Bill"—to expand the sugar quota assigned to mainland sugar, as well as to Hawaii, Puerto Rico, and the Virgin Islands, at the expense of Cuba.[68]

Cuban sugar interests were aghast. How utterly implausible, sugar producers protested, that Batista would endanger sugar in pursuit of a chimerical scheme of self-sufficiency in rice. The loss of American markets was unthinkable. The Ellender Bill, commented Laurence Crosby, chairman of the United States–Cuba Sugar Council and president of the Cuban-Atlantic Sugar Company, "caused great alarm and consternation throughout Cuba, whose political and economic welfare depend so largely on her sugar industry."[69]

The lines were sharply drawn. "The fact, fortunate or unfortunate," explained the Asociación Nacional de Hacendados, "[is] that there is no country in the world that can be entirely self-sufficient, much less Cuba, [a condition] that imposes sacrifices on our own creative impulses," and to the point:

> Cuba's position in this rice matter can only be, in our opinion, that of increasing our production within the limits fixed by international agreements, watching carefully for the maintenance, insofar as the United States is concerned, of the corresponding treatment, which is the only way to get them to respect what is vital to our economy. Not only is this a sensible position, but it is the only one that will continue to maintain our economic structure and give our sugar industry the permanent support

that we receive from that consuming market.... Anything that attacks this basic wealth is negative and ruinous, because "without sugar there is no country."⁷⁰

A short-sighted rice program that restricted U.S. imports to the GATT minimum, the Asociación de Colonos warned Batista, threatened to visit "grave repercussions on the sugar industry;" colonos did not hesitate to remind the government that "it was precisely the issue of rice that was one of the principal issues jeopardizing important Cuban interests during the debates surrounding the renewal of the sugar act in the United States."⁷¹ The Asociación Nacional de Proveedores e Importadores de Víveres, representing import merchants and foreign trade brokers, joined with sugar interests to warn of the consequences of government efforts at self-sufficiency in rice. "It is well known that rice," A. Valdés Rodríguez, executive director of the Asociación cautioned, "together with other products, constitutes one of the determining factors in the concessions made by the Government of the United States to Cuban sugar," continuing, "It should be noted that some of the rice-producing states are also producers of sugar, and as such are doubly affected by a policy of respecting the historic participation of Cuba in the sugar market of the United States. Inasmuch as the economy of Cuba in general, and of sugar in particular, would be [adversely] affected by a policy designed to expand the production of rice, from the standpoint of the United States, would it be advisable to pursue a program given to self-sufficiency?"⁷² Columnist Alberto León Riva exhorted Batista to exercise prudence, insisting that "the defense of Cuban participation in the sugar markets of the United States is today—more than ever before—an urgent duty and necessity to maintain the standard of living of the Cuban people," adding,

> In order to protect national economic stability Cuba should fight to preserve its historic participation in the vital sugar market of the United States to which we sell more than 50 percent of our production at a price of nearly two cents more per pound than we obtain in the world market. It is thus necessary to confront the attacks against Cuba mounted by Senator Ellender from the sugar cane– and rice-producing state of Louisiana who, under the pretext of the recent measures adopted by the Cuban government regulating the importation of rice from the United States, has sought to gain political capital in his State by urging that Congress modify the Sugar Quota Law and reduce the Cuban quota in favor of producers in Louisiana and Florida in retaliation against our country. This would represent a loss for Cuba of $10 million.... This in the end would

be prejudicial to all U.S. exports, for the effort to thwart the diversification of our production, and especially the expansion of Cuban rice production[,] would result in the loss of national revenue.[73]

The future of sugar, and hence the entire economy, producers warned, was at stake. Planter Alejandro Suero Falla returned from a visit to Washington in 1954 very much alarmed after his meeting with American officials. "On my recent trip to Washington," Suero Falla reported to Joaquín Martínez Sáenz, president of the Banco Nacional, "I found myself in an unpleasant and accusatory environment against Cuba for having breached the rice agreement with the United States." He continued:

> The study of possible revisions of the Sugar Act has begun. Given the ways the Americans do things, in careful order, they have started to discuss the nomenclature of the basic elements of the Sugar Act, that is, the [variety of] sugars and molasses. These definitions serve to expand the opportunities for alterations in terms far greater than we can imagine.... The struggle will take many forms but the most vulnerable producers will be Cuban. In the hallways of the Department of Agriculture one hears of plans to expand sugar from Puerto Rico, Louisiana, Florida, and Hawaii. ... The American Senators and Representatives will seize the slightest pretext—like rice—to attack Cuba.... I believe we should have the Department of State on our side, but it is up to us to facilitate and accommodate rice imports.[74]

Cuban officials were "very much concerned," John Nuber wrote from Havana, "inasmuch as the sugar negotiations are scheduled to come up in Congress in January 1956."[75] Nuber reported that the U.S. Embassy had met with Cuban officials to indicate "the probable impact on the U.S. Congress of this matter when the latter again will consider the sugar legislation, shortly after the turn of this year. They stress this point, I understand, although in official conversations this has to be done carefully to avoid any interpretation of being an outright threat. Apparently, however, that point is worrying the Cubans since it is known that local sugar spokesmen are bringing pressure for a moderate course by the Cuban Government in rice matters." He added a week later,

> The U.S.A. Embassy here in Havana now feels, although it has not been able so far to obtain any revocations of the restrictive measures, that it has succeeded in impressing the Cubans sufficiently so that they are not likely to impose any further restrictive measures and that they will not use the recent controls as a means to prevent sale of the low duty quota. With the

U.S. Sugar legislation coming up in Congress in early January 1956, the Embassy officials here believe that the chances are reasonably good that the Cubans may eventually revoke the recent restrictions.[76]

NORTH AMERICAN rice producers arrived at an early appreciation of the sources of Cuban vulnerabilities, recognizing sugar interests to be their "natural" allies. Sugar producers had far too much to lose in the conflict over rice. "The profusion of arguments existing in Cuba as to the national production of rice in Cuba has come to the concern of the Sugar Mills and Growers," John Nuber reported in 1953, "who are now beginning to realize that the rice production in Cuba should have its limits if they Cuba are expected to enjoyed preferential treatment by the USA on their Sugar Quotas, etc. They should be concerned as they know that the Reciprocal Trade agreement is a two way street and without SUGAR there is NO Cuba."[77]

American rice and Cuban sugar shared one goal in common: the need to access each other's markets, and as a matter of mutual interests they found more than adequate reason to collaborate. "Although nothing has been said officially on the subject," the Rice Millers Association acknowledged, "the Cuban sugar producers would be inclined to give their cooperation for a campaign in favor of American rice in Cuba, in exchange for reciprocal collaboration from the Americans to help us maintain our present position as sugar suppliers to the U.S.A."[78] U.S. rice interests actively solicited support among Cuban sugar producers in the development of mutually beneficially strategies. As early as 1951, the Americans had established communication with "certain important Cuban sugar factors," seeking to learn of their "interest to assist in developing a satisfactory understanding with officials of the Republic of Cuba with regard to the rice quota"; specifically, "the legal counsel of one of the prominent sugar companies [stated] that the Government of Cuba would establish the quota in accordance with our recommendations."[79] "The sugar growers of Cuba are reported to be as much disturbed by their government's action as your rice-growing constituents are," Frank Godchaux wrote to Ellender. "They realize that our government is in a position to retaliate by either increasing the quota of our sugar and beet growers or by removing all restrictions."[80] U.S. rice producers were certain of support from Cuban sugar interests, wrote Gerry Doyle, persuaded that "if our fair demands were laid before them 'off the record,'" their "internal assistance" would be forthcoming, adding, "This influential part of Cuba's economy is very sensitive to any threat to Cuban-American good will."[81]

RICE IMPLIED MORE than a type of agriculture, of course. Rice had a history, a past noteworthy for failure, frustration, and false starts. The rice program had developed into an endeavor bearing on national honor, something of a legacy to make good on and into which the Batista government had invested substantial moral and material resources. A foreign policy stance had been adopted in defense of the emerging rice industry. During a meeting of bilateral trade delegations in 1954 to negotiate future Cuba-U.S. commercial relations, Cuban representatives insisted that an "increase in population and the need to provide employment for the people require the development of new industrial, agricultural and commercial activities to supplement sugar production, which by itself is not sufficient to satisfy completely the needs of the Cuban people," but reassured the Americans that on the matter of rice, Cuba would "continue to develop its production of rice within the framework of its international obligations."[82]

The 1950s were years of a resurgent economic nationalism, as increasing numbers of merchants, industrialists, manufacturers, and landowners advanced claims to larger ownership of the economy, from the means of production to the means of consumption. The refrain "consume Cuban products" (*consuma productos cubanos*) had developed into something of a righteous cause. Joaquín Martínez Sáenz, president of the National Bank in the Batista government, would later recall with unabashed angst his first visit to Europe to conduct negotiations with European financial institutions, where he learned that "there existed the universal belief that we were a Republic in name only, without sovereignty and without the right to develop new markets and promote new production without the approval of the United States. In sum, we were considered a political entity dependent on the United States, without a true and independent international personality [*sin personalidad internacional real e independiente*]." Martínez Sáenz was drawn to an inescapable conclusion: "The problem of peace in Cuba could not be resolved without first remedying the displacement of the Cuban from the sources of production and work, and until the subordination of Cuba to the foreigner was ended—until we gained economic independence."[83]

A nationalist mood had insinuated itself into the purpose of rice, informed by the determination that decisions affecting vital Cuban interests should be made within Cuba, by Cubans, for Cubans. Rice production had risen fully to the level of patriotic purport, as a matter of economic self-determination in function of diversification, to be sure, but also as a requirement in fulfillment of self-sufficiency of a commodity of basic necessity. As early as 1951, Rodolfo Arango, director-general of the Ministry of Agriculture celebrated "the great patriotic sense and responsibility of rice farmers" toward the goal of self-sufficiency.[84] *Diario de la Marina* exulted in the success of Cuban rice production—and to the point, "Economic independence is a natural attribute of the sovereignty of a nation within the norms of international law. Cuba has the right to have her aspirations respected."[85] Joaquín Meyer, the representative of the Cuban Sugar Stabilization Institute in Washington, privately expressed uneasiness to the State Department over the implications of changing attitudes in Cuba. Terrance Leonhardy transcribed the meeting with Meyer, who conveyed a new mood in Cuba characterized by the "growing attitude of nationalism among conservative Cuban businessmen," adding,

> [Meyer] was seriously concerned by the expressions ... from many conservative businessmen who were now advocating that Cuba engage all type of industry, heavy and light, without any particular consideration for United States attitude. The thinking was that the United States needed Cuban sugar and that any effort to establish industries competitive to those of the United States in Cuba would result in no retaliation from us in the form of lower sugar quotas, as history has proven that we must depend on Cuba for our market. Dr. Meyer looked upon this philosophy which is gaining ground amongst conservative elements in Cuba as dangerous and that certainly in the end if such a policy was pursued it would be damaging to sugar interests. ... He was [making] an effort to work out ways and means of discouraging this type of thinking.[86]

The American campaign against Cuban rice provoked a widespread political backlash on the island at a time of mounting anti-Batista sentiment. Cuba descended slowly into political turmoil. Popular discontent was on the rise. Armed opposition was increasing. Arcane matters of grades of rice, quotas, and tariff schedules were rendered into a simple calculus having to do with national sovereignty, economic independence, and self-determination. Emilio Núñez Portuondo, the Cuban ambassador to the United Nations, insisted that Cuban regulations were consistent with the existing rice agreements, adding that "true Pan Americanism consists not only of absolute respect for our political sovereignty but also for our economic sovereignty. The Cuban government cannot be asked to cease to protect Cuban interests, such as the case of our rice production. This is exactly what the Congress of the United States has done with its domestic production of sugar, with prejudicial effects on our historic position in the U.S. market."[87] The Cubans resented the American insistence to export broken-grain and lower-grade rice. "The broken grain that was offered to the Cuban consumer," rice broker Carlos Ayala García bristled, "was rice that could not be sold in the American market at the prices fixed for the Cuban market due to domestic restriction in the United States. How dare [the Americans] criticize the measures taken by our government if the U.S. dispositions determined the broken rice must be sold at lower prevailing market prices[,] for such rice is designated as feed for poultry and livestock, which would constitute dumping in the domestic market. Yet they presume to dump cheap rice in our domestic market." Ayala García praised the Cuban restrictions, adding that the U.S. position "is nothing more than the reflection of the considerable lack of esteem that the American rice industry has had toward the development of the Cuban rice industry . . . which has contributed to the development and improvement of the standard of living."[88]

Cuban ire centered on Senator Ellender—"public enemy number one of Cuba," *Bohemia* proclaimed.[89] Senator Guillermo Aguilera, one of the largest Cuban rice producers, denounced Ellender as "an open enemy of our nation by attacking its right to progress and prosperity" whose claims were "more appropriate to an age of colonialism long ago rejected by the modern world," affirming, "Cuba is not a factory, nor are you the one who is going to teach a people with 400 years of cultural traditions how to interpret [international] agreements."[90] The Asociación Nacional de Cosecheros de Arroz denounced Ellender as "a demagogue pandering to a local electorate to which he seeks to ingratiate himself," continuing, "Cuba is asking for the same rice that is sold for public consumption in the United States. The rice that Mr. Ellender wishes to export to Cuba is rice that the United States send to the poor countries of Asia, where war and other calamities have weakened local purchasing power to such an extent to oblige the consumption of inferior commodity due to the lack of hard currency."[91]

THERE WAS SOMETHING OF AN inexorable logic—indeed, perhaps an inevitability—to the outcome of the dispute, of course. There was never any real doubt. "The fact that the United States is the principal supplier of our rice," Banco Nacional economist Julián Alienes cautioned in 1954, "and that we are among the best clients of American rice, and that they are also the principal customer of our sugar, dictates an obligatory reciprocal relationship between rice and sugar. It is likely that North American rice interests will threaten us with demands that the United States reduce the sugar quota in the North American market."[92] Sugar could not sustain Cuban economic development in the long run, informed opinion agreed, but neither could the economy survive without sugar in the short run, a survival that depended on access to U.S. markets. A threat to the latter threatened to plunge the entire economy into calamity.

Batista had no good choices. He opted for the path of least resistance: the protection of sugar. The Sugar Extension Act was enacted in May 1956. The terms of the Sugar Act did indeed reduce the Cuban quota, but it was largely a symbolic threatening gesture, the significance of which was not lost on Cuban producers. In fact, the Sugar Act also authorized import waivers to be exercised at the discretion of the secretary of agriculture in which the actual volume of Cuban sugar exports increased: from 2.5 million tons in 1955, to 2.7 millions tons in 1956, to 3.1 million ton in 1958. The sword of Damocles remained in place.

Diversification had failed, again, and again for the same reason: it had put sugar interests in jeopardy. "Cubans are often told to diversify," former ambassador Luis Machado lamented, "that they should not live off only one product. It is to that purpose to which we have dedicated ourselves for some time, and we have done everything possible to diversify. But diversification has produced problems in our relations with the United States."[93] The pursuit of rice as a way to reduce dependency on sugar over the long run and increase self-sufficiency in the short run had imperiled sugar. No one doubted the outcome of this contest. Cuba was trapped by its history.

American rice producers had prevailed. Concessions to rice imports began as early as 1954 with Cuban authorization of an additional 600,000 quintals under the auspices of the *cuota deficitaria*. A second round of rice imports was announced in 1955, another 60,000 pounds to fill the deficit quota, much of which included broken-grain rice. In mid-1957, an additional 265,000 bags—above and beyond the 3.25 million quintals GATT quota—entered Cuban markets, by which time U.S. rice imports registered their first substantial gain in years, increasing from 2.4 million quintals in 1955 to 4.1 million quintals in 1957.[94] "This indicates," U.S. commercial attaché Leonard Price reported, "that shipments of rice may be the largest this season in several years."[95] In early 1958, a presidential decree authorized an additional import quota of 500,000 quintals of milled rice from the United States, beyond the established GATT quota. Six months later, Decree No. 1865 authorized a further importation of 750,000 quintals of milled rice.[96] The value of U.S. rice imports increased from $18.6 million in 1955, to $24.6 million in 1956, to $38.9 million in 1957, reaching almost $40 million in 1958.[97]

Sugar had prevailed, at the expense of rice. The dispute produced deep fissures inside the Batista government, John Nuber reported confidentially from

Advertisement for Uncle Ben's Rice
(*Bohemia* 46 [November 7, 1954]).

Havana: "Different officials in the Cuban Government are at logger heads" over the additional rice imports.[98] A bad time to acquiesce to U.S. interests. Domestic rice production plunged into disarray. The resumption of U.S. rice imports sounded the death knell to domestic producers. BANFAIC support was no longer plausible for an agriculture that government policy had doomed. Government support for rice ended. Credit was restricted and subsidies ended. "It appears that the government," economist Raúl Cepero Bonilla bemoaned in early 1956, "accepting the counsel of the 'sugar men,' has decided to withdraw any kind of aid to the rice industry so as not to endanger the sugar quota in the United States. A decision appears to have been made to 'freeze' [*congelar*] the development of rice production and even hinder its development, if it is necessary, to please rice exporters in the United States and thereby obtain better treatment for Cuban sugar."[99] BANFAIC withdrew from rice production. "The private banks, as well as BANFAIC," the U.S. Embassy reported in mid-1955, "are pressing [rice farmers and millers] for repayment of loans. The resultant uncertainty is creating somewhat of a chaotic situation."[100] In early 1956, BANFAIC announced the suspension of all future financing of rice production. "The rice crisis began with the excessive importations in 1954," rice grower Anibal Piña decried. "It has not been resolved due to the devastating policies followed by BANFAIC: credit terms for too brief a period; high interest rates; and impenetrable bureaucratic procedures."[101] The new policy was confirmed publicly in 1956. "No further encouragement will be given to raising rice," announced Gonzalo del Cristo, head of the Agricultural Division of BANFAIC, "because the Cuban government wishes to continue buying the balance of the rice necessary for consumption from the United States in the interest of trade."[102]

The change of policy signaled the ruin of thousands of farms and mills. Rice production plunged into crisis, from which it never recovered. Production "collapsed for Cuban rice," decried farmer Pedro Pablo Echarte. "American rice has continued to enter the market at the expense of domestic producers."[103] Rice engineer Frank Senior exhorted the government to restrict imports as a way "to avoid the saturation of the market which would inevitably precipitate a collapse of prices below the cost of production, with dire consequences for the Cuban rice industry."[104] "As a result of the decision in March 1954 that was arbitrary and ill-fated for national rice interests," complained rice farmer Rafael Fanjul in early 1955, "the authorization of the importation of 600,000 *quintales* of rice undermined the national rice market of Cuba by creating a surplus that has ruined the national producers [*los productores nacionales*]."[105] A delegation of rice producers met with the editorial staff of *Diario de la Marina* to draft a "*declaración*" to protest the "inopportune and unnecessary" importation of 600,000 quintals of American rice. The arrival of new rice, the *declaración* protested, contributed to "the saturation of the national market with the result of producing a collapse in the price of rice." The future appeared uncertain: "We are unwilling to initiate preparations for a new harvest under the current economic conditions, the result of which will signal forever the loss for Cuba of the only serious effort at agricultural diversification, which presently represents an investment of $80 million in our land, the cultivation of 8,000 *caballerías* of previously unused land, providing direct employment for 2,000 peasant families, the construction of thousands of kilometers of new roads, and the saving of $30 million in foreign exchange."[106] *Diario de la Marina* rallied to support domestic production. "The limitation of imports of the necessities of national consumption is an indispensable measure to adopt," insisted *Diario de la Marina*, "for a saturated market results inevitably in a steep decline of prices and threatens to subject the Cuban rice industry to a difficult situation." The newspaper added,

> During the last three years our rice industry has provided employment for an ever-increasing number of workers who were without jobs and using to productive purpose otherwise idle capital. Producers seek legislative measures that will prevent the loss of their investment. We do not believe that to protect national wealth it is necessary to harm legitimate interests. To suppose that every legislative measure involves an attack on the national well being, or implies the breaking of international agreements to which Cuba has subscribed, is to cast aspersion unjustly on the Congress and Government of Cuba.[107]

Prices did indeed collapse. Rice selling at $9.50 per quintal prior to the expanded imports fell to $6.00 per quintal, to $5.00 in 1955, and to $3.80 by 1956.[108] "American rice imports were the beginning of the end of the Cuban rice boom," commented one rice producer.[109] These far-reaching developments were noted by the U.S. Department of Commerce in a casual passing comment on the cost of living in Cuba in 1957: "The upward trend in food prices was checked toward the end of the year primarily as a result of increased imports of rice . . . which served to compete with local products."[110]

Farmers who had financed their production at a time of high prices faced ruin, unable to meet their debt obligations. "The distribution of an additional 600,000 *quintales* . . . ," the enterprise Hermanos Alfonso warned the Banco Nacional in 1954, "will result in a far-reaching crisis for the national production of rice. . . . For the national well-being, we implore that measures be taken to avoid this most recent and unnecessary importation which threatens national producers with ruin due to the inability for meeting contracted obligations."[111] Rice farmers appealed to BANFAIC for extension of credits and deferral on loans.[112] BANFAIC refused.[113] Failures followed in rapid succession. "The market was inundated with excessive rice imports," rice planter Clemente Pérez noted. "Prices collapsed. . . . Cuban producers are at the point of ruin."[114] In Manzanillo, BANFAIC foreclosed on ten small farmers.[115] "Due to events beyond my control," protested rice farmer Ruy Gutiérrez de la Llana, "I was unable to make a payment. BANFAIC demanded for payment, and in the end, foreclosed. I lost my *finca* of 92 *caballerías* purchased by my grandfather."[116] Other producers restricted their crops. Farmer Emilio Cadenas Adam reduced his planting from sixty *caballerías* to fifteen.[117] Angel Suárez and Julio Sánchez, owners of the Arrocera Majana, on the verge of ruin, appealed to BANFAIC for relief. "We planted with imported seed," they explained, "on land cleared and prepared with dikes for irrigation, with fertilizer sprayed by airplanes, and harvested with a John Deere tractor. We have adhered to the most scientific methods and used only the seeds of the best quality. But we are failing."[118] By late 1955, reported *Diario de la Marina*, there were "many important rice farmers who are approaching bankruptcy or are on the verge of abandoning this important agricultural activity."[119] Rice grower Manuel Arca forwarded a confidential memorandum to Batista appealing for support, including subsidies to defray the cost of gasoline and oil, the enforcement of the ban on broken-grain rice imports, and a public relations campaign to promote the qualities of domestic rice over American imports "so that rice can keep on advancing or at least be stabilized in the nation['s] economy as a source of labor and saver of currency."[120] The U.S. Embassy was succinct: "All elements of the rice trade feel the Cuban Government sold them down the river."[121]

Rice growers across the island denounced expanded rice imports as unnecessary and prejudicial to the national interests, warning that additional rice supplies would doom national production.[122] They pleaded for restrictions of foreign imports at least during July, August, and September, the months when the bulk of domestic rice was harvested and distributed to local markets.[123] The Asociación Nacional de Cosecheros de Arroz of Camagüey protested increased imports of American rice from a "patriotic sense" (*sentido patriótico*), a decision that "is contrary to the policies of BANFAIC to promote the diversification of the economy."[124]

The end arrived swiftly. "Dozens of rice growers have had to abandon the production of rice, finding themselves practically ruined," wrote economist Oscar Pino Santos. "Others have reduced their planting by half or by one-third. A sense of defeatism has seized hold of many of these farmers. The boom of domestic rice production has ended." And to the point: "An objective analysis of the crisis of Cuban rice production," Pino Santos concluded in January 1957, "leads to an appreciation that there is, in certain quarters, the deliberate attempt to obstruct the production of rice or at least return it to the state in which it functioned five years ago."[125] Also in January 1957, Fidel Castro had completed his first month in the Sierra Maestra.

EPILOGUE

To Return to What Was Before—
Plus ça change . . .

If the economy cannot maintain adequate stands of living, it will be subject to great political strains. If leaders have neglected to prepare Cuba for this, they will be held to blame by the people. And, if that should happen, control may well pass into subversive but specious hands.—International Bank for Reconstruction and Development, *Report on Cuba* (1951)

Rice is Cuba's most important staple, perceived as versatile, durable and filling. In times of scarcity, if rice and beans are stockpiles, Cubans do not fear hunger.—Christiane Paponet-Cantat, "The Joy of Eating: Food and Identity in Contemporary Cuba" (2003)

Rice producers and the rice industry have paid a high price for our government's failed policy toward Cuba. First in 1960, and again in 2005, Democratic and Republican administrations alike have driven exports to one of our largest rice markets from robust levels to literally nothing.—Mike Wagner, President, Mississippi Rice Council, 2010

Cubans not only eat a lot of rice, but prefer U.S. varieties and quality. We have a tremendous marketing opportunity in Cuba, and our industry wants to make the most of it. Rice is an inoffensive product. It's not controversial. It's something [Cubans] don't grow very much of, and it's something we have a lot of. The United States consumes only half of the rice we produce, so for us, Cuba is potentially a huge market. If we were to eventually get a lion's share of the market, Cuba could return to what it was before.—Marvin Lehrer, USA Rice Federation, 2002

CUBAN ECONOMIC development had been arrested by the very sources of its prosperity. Over the course of 150 years, dependency on sugar exports was sustained through a dependency on North American markets, a cause-and-effect combination that also served to oblige Cuba to open its economy to U.S. imports. More than a half century of successive reciprocal trade arrangements—the Foster-Cánovas Reciprocal Trade Agreement of 1891, the Reciprocity Treaty of 1903, the Reciprocity Treaty of 1934, and the General Agreement on Tariffs and Trade during the 1940s and 1950s—more than adequately subjected Cuban well-being to access to a tariff-friendly, quota-driven share of U.S. sugar markets.

At the cost of almost everything else. The "reciprocity" part of the trade agreements provided scores of U.S. producers with preferential tariff entrée to Cuban markets, many of whom developed a dependency on privileged access to Cuba as vital as sugar's dependency on the United States. Patterns of trade and commerce with the United States, transacted through more than half a century of preferential tariff schedules, transformed Cuba into something of a North American proprietary market, claimed with a sense of entitlement and defended with a sense of urgency. A threat to the privileged presence of North American imports was met almost always with a threat against Cuban access to U.S. markets.

The logic of diversification had always implied the need to reduce dependency upon sugar, to promote industry and manufacturing, and to expand agriculture, specifically to develop capacities to produce for the domestic market and reduce the need for foreign imports, especially food imports. These concerns had long been the "underside" of the Cuban pursuit of self-determination and national sovereignty and very much at the center of a deepening economic nationalism. But it is also true that Cuban efforts to remedy the structural anomalies of the export economy often ran afoul of U.S. interests, with predictable consequences. The case of lard was illustrative. Nearly 95 percent of the lard consumed in Cuba arrived in the form of U.S. imports. The Cuban market accounted for more than 20 percent of total U.S. lard exports, reaching during the 1950s an annual average value of $25 million.[1] In August 1952, the Batista government extended tax waivers and tariff exemptions for the acquisition of machinery and raw materials to the newly organized Cía. Empacadora de Productos Nacionales y Extranjeros to expand Cuban manufacturing capabilities and promote economic diversification.[2] The Cía Empacadora was to operate a hydrogenation plant for animal fats and vegetable oils, projected when fully operational to provide 35 percent of Cuban consumption of animal fats.

The outcry of North American producers was immediate. "There is more at stake than the mere economic well-being of Armour and other American interests," the vice president of Armour and Company J. J. O'Connor protested to the State Department. "The consequences, involving a principal outlet for Lard of United States production, will be far-reaching and will penetrate to the grass roots of the American economy."[3] The American Meat Institute warned of the "serious and permanent damage" to U.S. interests, noting that "Cuba is America's largest export market for lard," thereupon to draw the obvious moral:

> If the Cuban government intends to persist in its discrimination against American hog and lard producers ... then we feel it would be entirely appropriate for our own government to closely examine future allocation of Cuban sugar imports into this country, particularly inasmuch as considerable quantities of sugar now are being produced in the continental United States and in Puerto Rico and Hawaii. Inasmuch as hogs are raised on millions of American farms, the Cuban market for American lard is as important to hog and lard producers as the American market is for growers of Cuban sugar and Cuban labor. It seems strange Cuba, with a sugar surplus, would discourage the importation of American products while having to depend on the American market for Cuban sugar for its economic welfare. Illustrative of the importance of the export market for American lard and hog producers, lard today is selling in the United States for about half the price of live hogs. This is having a serious effect on the price American farmers are receiving for hogs.[4]

The State Department intervened on behalf of U.S. producers. Prospects that Cuba would "obtain lard from countries other than the United States," Assistant Secretary Thomas Mann informed U.S. ambassador Willard Beaulac, implied "the potential threat of the loss of a sizeable portion of the Cuban market for Americans fats and oils. Cuba is the largest single export market of American lard." Mann warned that "a feeling may possibly develop in important and influential segments of the American economy that they have received unfair treatment, and consequently desire retaliatory actions ... with an insinuation that retaliatory action might be in connection with Cuban participation in the United States sugar market, in which Cuba enjoys a favorable position." Mann urged cancellation of the August 1952 resolution.[5] Within a year the resolution was quietly withdrawn. The Cía. Empacadora de Productos Nacionales y Extranjeros did not commence operations until 1956, without government support, and struggled to remain solvent through the end of the 1950s.[6]

Contention also attended Cuban efforts to established flour mills. All through the 1910s, Cuba had endeavored to establish domestic milling capacities. The Cuban logic was self-evident. Instead of importing flour from the United States, the Cubans would import wheat and produce flour at home. Nor would the wheat necessarily originate from the United States. Under these circumstances, Cubans could seek favorable wheat markets in Argentina and Canada. In 1949, Burrus Mills from Texas announced plans to establish a new flour mill in Havana, acquiring government support with a ten-year tax exemption, tariff waivers for imports of mill machinery, and duty relief for wheat imports, the latter especially important to allow the new mill to obtain the raw material for flour.

North American flour mills mobilized to oppose the concessions granted to Burrus. The intent, objected W. P. Bomar, president of the Bewley Mills of Texas, represented "a direct discrimination against the milling industry of this country, which represents no small investment or source of employment, as well as a substantial market for wheat producers."[7] E. W. Reed of the Flour Mills of America of Kansas City protested directly to Missouri congressman Richard Bolling:

> There is a situation directly affecting wheat production in the United States to which, it seems to me, additional attention might well be directed—this is the unusual concession extended by the Government of Cuba to encourage the construction of a flour mill in the Havana area.... Cuba has long been an extremely important market for United States flour, taking normally 2.5 million to 4 million cwts. [quintals] per year. This has been almost entirely confined to United States flour because of the favorable consideration given the products of United States agriculture or industry. ... By this move to cancel the import duty on wheat, it not only assures the immediate elimination of that market for United States flour ... but it likewise almost guarantees that the flour for Cuban consumption will be milled from other than United States wheat.... This means that the construction of this mill would remove a consuming demand for some 7 million bushels of United States wheat. Once the mill is constructed ... this market will have been permanently lost to the United States wheat producer, to the United States mills, and to United States labor.[8]

Flour mill interests were not reluctant to threaten retaliation. Given the "short-sighted" policies of the Cuban government, Bomar insisted to Secretary of State Dean Acheson, "We urge that import duties on their sugar, for which we are their principal market, be raised sufficiently to penalize their evident intent to discriminate in order to eliminate competition."[9] Reed similarly expressed his "sincere hope" that Congress "may find it possible to support a move toward such reconsideration of the entire situation with respect to sugar quotas in the light of the action by the Cuban Government."[10]

The Burrus mill—the first flour mill in Cuba—was completed in 1952 and indeed resulted in diminished imports of U.S. flour, decreasing in value from nearly $11 million in 1951 to $7.4 million in 1954.[11] Four years later, Cuban investors announced plans to construct two new flour mills, one in Cienfuegos and the other in Santiago de Cuba.[12] Panic swept over U.S. mill interests, who appealed to Congress for assistance. "If such a mill were to be built," Herman Fakler, vice president of the Millers National Federation, explained to the Senate Committee on Finance, "Cuba would no longer be a very significant market for United States Flour."[13] Fakler drew the obvious moral: "Continued access to the United States sugar market should in part, at least, be based on the continued access of United States export products to foreign suppliers of sugar interested in the United States market." Fakler exhorted the Cuban government "to reexamine its policy of restricting flour imports and not authorize the construction of another mill which would further impair the flour export trade from the United States and possibly lead to subsequent action regarding Cuban sugar."[14]

Kansas senator Frank Carlson took up the cause of wheat, addressing the Senate to "sound a note of warning for those foreign countries who are interested in the United States as a market for their products, especially agriculture, such as sugar." He continued:

> If action is taken which is directed at United States imports, particularly of basic agricultural commodities, or which hurts such trade, especially in those commodities which have had a long background of trade in the country . . . , then I believe Congress should make corresponding adjustments in United States import quotas or should adopt other measures to reduce access of such countries to the United States market. . . . If approval and special assistance shall be granted for these flour mills by the Cuban Government, United States flour exports to that country, as we have known them in the past[,] will come to an end. This will mean a permanent loss of much of the Cuban market for United States wheat as well as flour. I say there should be a limit to how far the United States will continue to grant access to its large and expanding market for a commodity, like sugar, to countries which in turn impose quota limitations and other restrictions on imports of a United States basic commodity, such as wheat flour.[15]

Within weeks, the Cuban government capitulated and refused to authorize the new mills. Carlson again took to the Senate floor:

> I appreciate very much the action which has been taken by the officials of the Cuban Government in this regard. This attitude on the part of the Cuban Government and its people further strengthens my belief in the fact that reciprocal trade is a two-way street, and can be used to the mutual advantage of two countries. . . . If more countries realize that access to the United States market also means some obligation on their part not to adopt measures which will hurt or restrict the market for United States commodities, we will have accomplished much in the way of friendly trade relations.[16]

THE TRIUMPH OF the Cuban revolution changed everything. So much was in obvious need of change, much of which had to do with the distortions of an economy 150 years in the making. To challenge the premise of the export economy implied the need to confront long-established social relationships and time-honored political networks that had assumed structural form in the service of sugar. This was an economy tightly bound within itself in which the impact of reforms, even of the most modest reach, could not but act to release powerful disruptive forces. It was not possible to modify a part without affecting the whole.

The economy was very much on the minds of the men and women who assumed positions of leadership in 1959. It could hardly have been otherwise, for much of what ailed Cuba had to do with an ailing economy. The new leaders in 1959 were well-informed, well-meaning, and well-trained, mostly liberals, many educated in the United States. They assumed power exuding self-confidence, bearing lucidity of thought and possessing clarity of purpose, understanding too the urgency of attending to an economy approaching collapse. Things had to change.

The ideal of "Cuba for Cubans" had seized hold of the popular imagination all through the 1950s. After 1959 it had expanded fully into the discursive logic of the revolution. Something had changed in Cuba, U.S. ambassador Philip Bonsal sensed in April 1959. Cubans viewed Fidel Castro's planned visit later that month to the United States as a "historical precedent," Bonsal observed, with an "attitude of confidence and assured independence," the "first time [that] a Cuban ruler has visited the United States representing a fully sovereign and equal nation, free from any domination or control."[17] During a high-level meeting at the U.S. Embassy early in 1959, Minister of the Economy Regino Boti informed the Americans "that while Cuba wanted friendly relations with the United States, from now on the [United States] would find the Cubans tougher to bargain

> # LOS ARROCEROS CUBANOS
> ## CON LA REVOLUCION
> # LIBERTADORA
>
> Los cosecheros de arroz de Sancti Spiritus expresan, jubilosos, su compenetración con todos los arroceros del país, y participan de la alegría del pueblo porque esta Revolución va a la superación agrícola de Cuba.
>
> En el umbral de esta nueva era, llamamos a todos los compañeros cosecheros para fortalecer la unión dentro de nuestra Asociación Nacional, que representa los sanos intereses de todos los arroceros cubanos.
>
> ### COSECHEROS DE ARROZ DE SANCTI SPIRITUS
>
> | | |
> |---|---|
> | Antonio Freyre | W. Knight |
> | Fermín Goicochea | Horacio Tobeña |
> | Ernesto García Rubio | A. Ponce |
> | Víctor Fernández | W. Martínez |
> | Alfredo Piedra | George Harper |
> | Rosendo Palacios | Pedro Talavera |
> | Arnaldo Martín | Aurelio Maruri |

An advertisement proclaiming support of the newly triumphant revolution (*Revolución*, January 10, 1959).

with."[18] Boti expressed the hope that "Cuba's drive for diversification could be carried out without producing some short-term conflicts of interests between American suppliers and Cuba's overall objectives of greater diversification. It well might be that Cuba will import smaller quantities of its traditional imports, such as rice and lard, but . . . in the long run Cuban imports of many other U.S. farm products, such as fresh fruit, would be substantially increased."[19]

The triumph of the revolution had released powerful nationalist sentiments, much of which served to inform the policies and inspire the purpose for which economic reforms were enacted. These were heady weeks and months for a people aroused with high hopes and great expectations, persuaded that the promise of national sovereignty and the possibility of self-determination were within reach, convinced too that the defense of Cuban interests would serve as the principal function of public policy. The Americans, Fidel Castro proclaimed early in 1959, "now know that there exists in Cuba a government disposed to defend its interests."[20] Everything was under review, and everything inevitably meant mostly relations with the United States. The economic program of the 26th of July Revolutionary Movement (MR 26/7)—"Tesis del Movimiento Revolucionario 26 de Julio"—drafted in 1958, was unambiguous. "For the pessimist the subject of economic relations with the North Americans is a taboo topic," the "Tesis" pronounced. "The danger of a reduction of the sugar quota, of decreasing from year to year, completely conditions his thinking. If Cuba aspires to produce rice, it places the quota in danger. If Cuba pursues industrialization, if Cuba seeks to produce its own foodstuffs—everything places the quota in danger."[21]

The subject of diversification was also very much on the mind of Fidel Castro. He addressed the matter of rice on the occasion of his first visit to the United States in April 1959. In conversation with Vice President Richard Nixon, Castro chided the United States for fearing "that if Cuba has land reform it will grow a little rice and the market for your rice will be reduced."[22] Six months later, he addressed the issue again in a speech at a mass rally in Havana. "I ask the people [el pueblo]," Fidel bellowed, "if they agree or disagree with us that we can produce in Cuba the rice we need instead of importing it . . . ; [that we can] produce the food we need instead of importing it, [and] thereby give employment to more than half a million Cubans who have no work." And to his point: "If we produce rice, we prejudice foreign interests; if we produce lard, we prejudice foreign interests; if we produce cotton, we prejudice foreign interests; if we reduce the electricity rate, we prejudice foreign interests; if we reduce the telephone rates, we prejudice foreign interests; if we undertake agrarian reform, we prejudice foreign interests; . . . if we organize a merchant marine, we prejudice foreign interests; if we wish to find new markets for our products, we prejudice foreign interests."[23]

No other project was as central to the pursuit of economic independence as the expansion of food production and diversification of agriculture as means of self-sufficiency. Diversification was central to the economic strategies of the revolution, and rice was central to diversification. U.S. officials did not mistake the purport of Cuban policy. "Cuba is our biggest customer in rice exports," Assistant Secretary of State Thomas Mann acknowledged to the Senate Foreign Relations Committee, "and it takes about 10 percent of our total rice crop."

Agradecimiento al Gobierno Revolucionario

La Asociación Nacional de Cosecheros de Arroz, interpretando el sentir de todos los cosecheros del país, quiere dejar constancia pública de su profundo agradecimiento hacia:

EL DR. FIDEL CASTRO RUZ, Primer Ministro del Gobierno, quien con visión clara y certera expresó desde la tribuna Ante la Prensa las medidas adecuadas para los problemas inmediatos del cultivo de arroz en Cuba.

EL DR. HUMBERTO SORI MARIN, Ministro de Agricultura, quien con el fervor y eficiencia que lo caracterizan, dando nuevas pruebas de su profunda identificación con el ideario político-económico-social del Jefe de la Revolución, Comandante Castro Ruz, ha luchado codo a codo con los cosecheros, brindándoles justiciero respaldo e inculcándoles fe para la gran empresa de la que resulta su más decidido defensor.

EL DR. REGINO BOTI, Ministro de Economía e Interino de Comercio que consciente de estar sirviendo a una causa justa, en la mañana del viernes firmó la Resolución por la que se ha modificado la número 10 del Ministerio de Comercio, abriendo con ella amplios horizontes de esperanza para los cosecheros de arroz.

EL SR. ALFREDO POLLAN GAGO, Presidente de la Administración de Estabilización del Arroz, quien en todo momento, con solidaridad y eficacia absolutas, ha estado plenamente identificado con los cosecheros de toda la República en sus legítimas aspiraciones de disponer de la cosecha actual e incrementar los cultivos futuros con garantías suficientes y sobre base conocida y firme.

ASOCIACION NACIONAL DE COSECHEROS DE ARROZ

Advertisement expressing the gratitude of rice growers for the newly announced policies in support of domestic production (*Revolución*, March 3, 1959).

Mann continued: "One of the policies of the predecessor to this government, and also Castro, is to make Cuba self-dependent on rice so that they won't have to import any more rice. Just as soon as they are able to grow enough rice to take care of their own consumption, I believe that we have to expect that they will cease to be our biggest customer and probably will cease to be even anywhere near the most significant."[24]

Cuban rice producers had welcomed the triumph of the revolution. The new policies did not disappoint. Cuba moved immediately to modernize rice production, what Regino Boti characterized as a "process of organizing the rice industry in such a way as to take full advantage of the best modern technology."[25] This implied a commitment to acquire modern harvesters and construct new silos, expand fertilization programs, and improve milling techniques—all given to avoiding "by all means possible," explained the government, "any possible increase in price of this important foodstuff."[26] In March 1959, the government enacted new revenue policies and imposed additional import regulations designed to subsidize the cost of modernization of production and protect domestic producers. The promulgation of Decree 647 in March 1959 imposed a "contribution" of $2.00 for each quintal of imported rice to create a fund "for the acquisition of agricultural machinery."[27] The enactment of Decree 695 in the same month imposed an additional $2.75 tax on U.S. rice imports.[28]

The resumption of government support for domestic rice provoked a new round of protests in the United States. American producers—"bitterly opposed to [the] imposition of tax by Cuba," the Rice Millers Association decried—denounced Cuban revenue measures, insisting that the failure to impose similar charges on Cuban production violated the GATT agreement.[29] "The taxes imposed by the decrees enumerated are fantastic in measure," William Reid complained to Senator Ellender; "they are a contravention of the agreement between the USA and Cuba, and are ulterior in motive, which is to make it economically impossible for the U.S. to sell rice to Cuba."[30] Reid forwarded his protest directly to Secretary of State John Foster Dulles, demanding that "the Government of the United States make it perfectly clear to the Government of the Republic of Cuba that this country will not stand for further violation by Cuba of the GATT agreement."[31] The consequences would ruin the U.S. rice industry, the Americans warned. "The entire Southern rice industry has been developed to feed the Cuban people the kind of rice they prefer," Claude Miller, president of Comet Rice Mills, insisted, adding,

> Some Southern mills and many, many Southern rice growers depend upon Cuba practically solely as the outlet for their rice. Without Cuba, these farmers and the employees of these rice mills could lose their lifetime investments.... The loss of the Cuban market would be such a crippling blow to the Southern rice milling industry that a large number of mills would have no choice but to go out of business. Millions more would be added to the millions of dollars now invested in idle rice farming, milling and drying facilities.... In other words, the jobs of literally thousands of people in, and directly associated with, the rice industry are dependent

upon milled rice sales to Cuba. In addition, at least one-half of the rice going to Cuba is transported in ships of United States registry. The United States shipping industry badly needs the tonnage that is created by sales of rice to Cuba.[32]

THE EXPANSION OF rice was one facet of a far more ambitious economic program, one the Cubans pursued with resolve if not always with resources. The logic of import substitution as a means of self-sufficiency was central to the agrarian reform of May 1959. "Among the great objectives of the Law of Agrarian Reform," explained *Cuba Económica y Financiera* in mid-1959, "is the age-old aspiration to develop to the maximum the production of agriculture and foodstuffs in Cuba, not only with the view to produce an abundance of products at reasonable costs but also with the intent of avoiding the vast volume of imports that absorbs every year an estimated $150 million which depletes our reserves of gold and dollars."[33] One of the most urgent economic matters, economist Franciso Dorta-Duque insisted in 1959, was the need to develop the capacity for self-sufficiency to obviate the need for food imports. Rice alone represented the "escape" of $20 to $30 million annually.[34] "We import annually, mostly from the United States," Dorta-Duque indicated, "more than $130 million, which is to say, that we return one-fifth of the dollars produced by our exports to purchase foodstuffs which, for the most part, we can produce domestically and no doubt at lower prices." And to the point: "Land held in concentration of a few hands impedes the flexibility of production, and hence obstructs agricultural diversification. The result is the bane of having to import a large variety of foodstuffs that we could cultivate on our own soil, [and] thereby retain the great quantity of dollars [*gran número de divisas*] that could otherwise be invested in the industrial development of the nation."[35]

Economic reforms transported Cuba deeply into those previously forbidden zones of challenging the premise of the propriety of North American privilege in Cuba. The U.S. response was swift and sweeping. The Americans reacted as they said they always would: cutting the sugar quota first by 700,000 tons in mid-1960 and ending it altogether by the end of the year. In early 1961, the United States suspended diplomatic relations. Denied U.S. markets, Cubans were also deprived of the foreign exchange with which to purchase the food imports upon which they had long depended.[36] This too was part of the plan. U.S. economic sanctions were designed to precipitate the collapse of the Castro government by way of economic disarray, to induce hardship as a condition of daily life, as a means through which to promote popular discontent: to "exert a

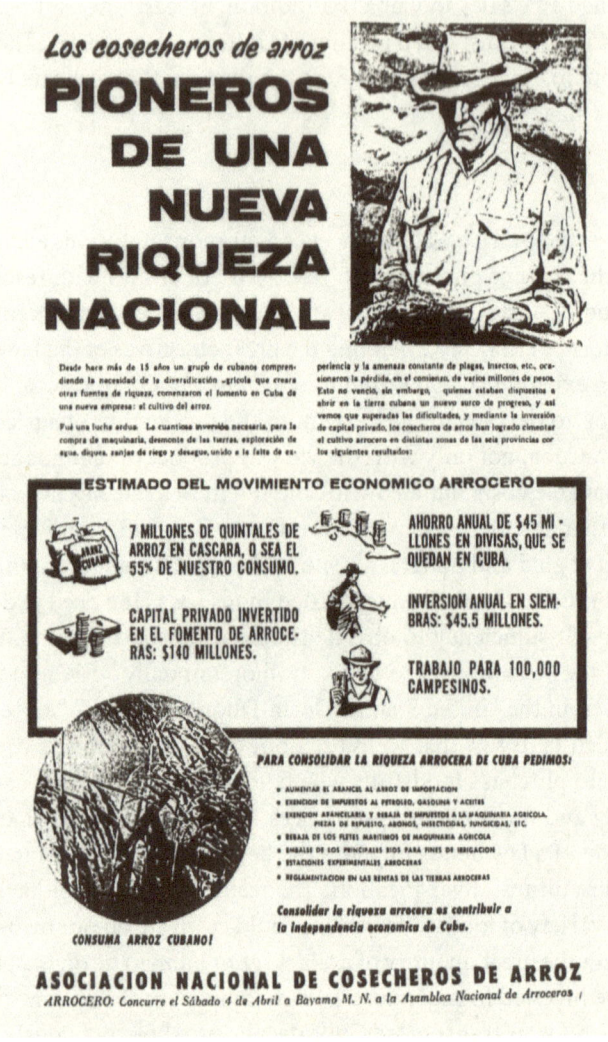

Affirmation of the renewed commitment to the expansion of national production (*Revolución*, March 24, 1959).

serious pressure on the Cuban economy and contribute to the growing dissatisfaction and unrest in the country," Assistant Secretary of State Thomas Mann explained.[37] The leverage was food, to politicize hunger with the expectation that driven by despair and motivated by want the Cuban people would rise up to overturn the Castro government. The United States sought to use "economic pressures . . . in order to engender more public discomfort and discontent," noted Assistant Secretary Roy R. Rubottom, in the form of "a relentless, firm pressure, [and] a steady turning of the screw."³⁸ The "only foreseeable means of alienating internal support," Deputy Assistant Secretary of State Lester Mallory concluded in 1960, "is through disenchantment and disaffection based on economic dissatisfaction and hardship." Mallory recommended that "every possible means should be undertaken promptly to weaken the economic life of Cuba, . . . [to deny] money and supplies to Cuba, to decrease monetary and real wages, to bring about hunger, desperation and [the] overthrow of government."³⁹ President Dwight Eisenhower was succinct: "If they (the Cuban people) are hungry, they will throw Castro out."⁴⁰

U.S. rice imports declined steadily and eventually ended altogether. Cuba diversified less its agriculture than the sources of its agricultural imports. Domestic rice demands were met with increased imports from the United Arab Republic, China, Vietnam, Thailand, and Ecuador.⁴¹

AS FOR THE FATE OF the U.S. rice industry after the loss of Cuban markets: after years of warning of the calamity certain to befall rice production without Cuba—indeed, the principal reason the United States opposed the expansion of Cuban rice—the loss of Cuban markets appears to have adversely affected the Americans not at all. "The loss of the Cuban market proved to be a nuisance," wrote Henry Dethloff, the historian of the U.S. rice industry, "not the economic catastrophe it could have been."⁴² As early as October 1960, William Reid could report with satisfaction that "the loss of the Cuba market has not been of any great economic catastrophe[,] for markets in Asia and Europe will take all of the rice that our government will permit us to market."⁴³ By 1961, U.S. rice exports found expanded markets in West Germany, India, Pakistan, and Africa.⁴⁴ "There has been a phenomenal increase in cash sales of U.S. rice during the decades [of the 1960s]," exulted the Department of Agriculture ten years later. "From 301,000 tons in 1960–61, they rose to 1,131,000 in 1967–68—almost four times the amount of U.S. rice exported for dollars in 1960–61."⁴⁵

A moral most assuredly resides somewhere in these developments. The determination with which the Americans opposed Cuban production in defense of a market that was readily replaced within eighteen months had caused widespread hardship on Cuban producers and consumers alike. It did not have to be so, it turns out. Perhaps Cuban markets were just more convenient, the habit of an easy commerce resulting from the lack of motivation to contemplate alternatives or pursue new markets, thereby denying the Cubans the opportunity for diversification and self-sufficiency. But perhaps too it is simply the nature of imperialism, the defense of convenience and the protection of easy advantage intrinsic to the prerogative of power, special interests exercising privileged access to the levers of policy. The enactment of U.S. Public Law 480 ("Agricultural Trade Development and Assistance Act") in 1954—"it is hereby declared to be the policy of Congress . . . to make maximum efficient use of surplus agricultural commodities in furtherance of the foreign policy of the United States"[46]—was amended in 1959 through Title IV, to be known as "Food for Peace." The amended law authorized the U.S. government to offer low-interest loans to foreign countries to purchase U.S. agricultural surpluses, central to which was rice.[47] In 1959, under the auspices of Food for Peace, as access to Cuban markets began to diminish, U.S. rice exports actually increased, including an agreement to provide India with 22 million bags of rice over a four-year period.

The intransigence with which the Americans defended their proprietary claim to Cuban rice markets had far-reaching political consequences. The United States had compromised Batista's ability to defend national interests and weakened his ability to govern. Not without some irony, the American determination to undermine Cuban rice production also contributed to undermining the Batista government. Confronting the U.S. threat to reduce the sugar quota, Batista faced no good choices. Forced to yield to sugar, he ended support of rice and precipitated the collapse of an industry that he had done so much to summon into existence, abandoning thousands of growers and millers and consigning many more tens of thousands of workers to an uncertain future.

The rice project had developed in an environment of expanding economic nationalism, a mood noteworthy for its aspirations of economic self-determination and self-sufficiency, of Cuba for Cubans, and all at a time when the producing classes—merchants, industrialists, manufacturers, and landowners—were eminently susceptible to the appeal of economic nationalism. That Cuba capitulated to U.S. pressure in the defense of sugar, with catastrophic consequences to an emerging national industry, reverberated across the island: economic dislocations occurring at a singularly inopportune political moment. At a time of rising economic nationalism, this was folly; at a time of increasing political opposition and expanding armed resistance, it was fatal. Rice growers and millers across the island turned against the Batista government and cast their lot with the expanding armed opposition, mostly the MR 26/7 led by Fidel Castro. That the most important rice zones were located in Oriente province, moreover, served to deepen discontent in the principal region of the anti-Batista insurgency. The Matos family—father and three sons—operating a $1 million rice plantation in Manzanillo faced ruin as a result of the collapse of domestic rice markets. Huber Matos subsequently enrolled in the rebel army, rising to the rank of comandante in Column 9 "Antonio Guiteras."[48]

THE CUBAN PURSUIT of self-sufficiency in rice continued to be an elusive project. The Agrarian Reform and the subsequent nationalization of property were accompanied by a slow downward spiral of production. Rice production increased from 283 million tons in 1959 to 307 million tons in 1960 but declined almost immediately thereafter: 213 tons in 1961, 207 tons in 1962, 204 tons in 1963, 124 tons in 1964, 50 tons in 1965. Production rose gradually in subsequent years but never recovered to prerevolutionary levels.[49] The official explanation was reminiscent of justifications offered in the nineteenth century. "Production of rice declined," the Cuban Communist Party indicated, "due to the decision to reduce cultivation as a result of favorable opportunities to acquire rice from abroad, the priority given to the production of other agricultural products, and the inability to rely on quality seeds that had previously originated from the United States."[50] Manuel de Jesús Andérez Velázquez, vice president of the Cuban Academy of Sciences, made the same point in slightly different terms. "It still costs Cuba more to grow its own rice than to import it," he explained to Medea Benjamin. [51] Fidel Castro was explicit, invoking the rationale that had justified the export economy at its very origins in the nineteenth century. "We ran tests on corn, rice, coffee, and other crops," he explained to Fred Ward in 1977, "and found we could get $400 a hectare from them. Sugar brings us $7,000 a hectare. So we will continue to sell sugar and to buy other things we need on the world market."[52]

The demise of rice production was symptomatic of the general decline in stock of food inventories. "There are no eggs, no tomatoes that were always plentiful," John Nuber wrote from Havana as early as October 1960. "U.S. can goods are about exhausted and high in price and ... many articles Cuba is accustomed to buying are not available."[53] Food shortages served to set in place the signal distributive mechanism of the Cuban revolution: *la libreta*. The rationing of basic foodstuffs was introduced in March 1962, including beans, poultry, eggs, fish, milk, potatoes, and especially rice.[54] The monthly consumption of rice in 1958 averaged approximately 10.2 pounds per capita. With the inauguration of rationing in 1962, rice allotments were reduced in 1963 to 6 pounds monthly, reduced again in 1969 to 3–4 pounds, and fixed in 1980 at 5 pounds.[55] "Our rice ration never lasts the month through," Alberto Barrera Lordi complained to Oscar Lewis in 1977. "Today nobody gets enough rice. When I think where the Revolution is leading us, a thing like that confuses me. Before the Revolution, everybody, rich and poor, had plenty of rice. A small family never consumed less than a couple of pounds a day, so you can imagine how much a large family used.... This is really terribly hard on us because rice is the basis of the Cuban diet. And where did all the rice go?"[56]

The 10-million-ton sugar harvest of 1970 plunged Cuban agriculture deeper into crisis. Sugar again subordinated everything else. With its massive mobilization of labor and far-reaching reallocation of resources to sugar production—to the virtual neglect of almost everything else, including investments, transportation, fertilizers, and of course land—the 10-million-ton crop had catastrophic consequences in food production.[57] "The costs to the rest of the economy," Medea Benjamin correctly commented, "were staggering."[58]

But the worst was yet to come. The collapse of the Soviet Union and the loss of Soviet-bloc subsidies resulted in the near collapse of food supplies. Everything was different after 1991. Food production declined by 50 percent. Milk production decreased by half, and beef production fell by two-thirds. Poultry declined by nearly 80 percent; the number of pigs declined by almost 70 percent. Production of powdered milk decreased by 90 percent.

Not for the first tine, Cuba could not feed itself. All through the 1990s—the worst years of the "Special Period"—hunger was experienced on a daily basis among many tens of thousands of households across the island.[59] The crisis resulted in "sharp decreased in food imports," wrote Cuban nutritionists, and "commonly consumed foods disappeared from the market."[60] The Cuban diet was reduced to fewer than 2,000 calories a day—the same level as Haiti's.[61] The iconic Cuban dish *ajiaco*, whose origins were long associated with Cubans of modest means—"found almost only on the table of the poor," José García de Arboleya had written in 1859[62]—was beyond the reach of most Cubans. Simply put, most of the ingredients for *ajiaco* were unavailable. Alex Fleites's short story "Ajiaco" recounts the travails associated with gathering the ingredients: "a fucking pain in the ass [*tremenda jodedera*] to obtain the vegetables; two hours on line to get a potato; to endure 45 minutes of inane conversation to purchase one plantain; a long walk in the heat of the August sun to buy calabaza.... And still so much more to gather: two tablespoons of meat for *picadillo extendido* with soy. A garlic clove. A sprout of cilantro. Boniato, corn, malanga."[63] A quest that obliged the protagonist to roam the full length of Nuevo Vedado in search of the simple fixings for *ajiaco*.

It was no longer about sugar—well, perhaps not exactly: it continued to be all about sugar, of course, in a historic sense. Sugar had laid waste to agriculture and eventually prepared the groundwork for its own demise. Cuba as the "sugar bowl of the world" was no more: in 2005, Cuba was obliged to import sugar.

Cuba again failed to attain self-sufficiency in rice. Cuban agriculture could meet the dietary requirements of only half the population.[64] By the early 2000s, Cuban rice production had collapsed. National consumption reached approximately 600,000 tons annually, 90 percent of which—540,000 tons—reached Cuban tables principally by way of imports from China and Vietnam.[65] From time to time, all through the early 2000s, newspapers celebrated successful rice harvests. Always too little, too late.[66]

Limited trade with the United States resumed in 2000. The enactment of the U.S. Trade Sanctions Reform and Export Enhancement Act authorized limited cash-only agricultural exports to Cuba. By 2015, the United States had exported a total of $5 billion worth of agricultural products, principally wheat, corn, poultry, soybeans, and rice.[67] The first shipment of U.S. rice imports arrived in Cuba in 2002—from Louisiana.

Cuba remained dependent upon food imports. "Cuba is expected to continue to rely heavily on agricultural imports," predicted the U.S. Department of Agriculture. "Cuban agricultural production is stagnant, with a production shortfall covered by nearly $1.9 billion in agricultural imports in FY 2014."[68] The expansion of tourism after 2014 added new pressures on food supplies. Food imports included corn from Argentina, Brazil, and the United States; wheat from the European Union and Canada; dairy products from the European Union and New Zealand; poultry from the United States, Brazil, and Canada; and rice from China, Vietnam, Brazil, and the United States. Some 80 percent of the food consumed in Cuba was in the form of imports.[69] "The historical subordination to imported food," economist Guillermo Jiménez summarized the Cuban condition after the Special Period, "which increased during the revolutionary period, became even more intense."[70] By 2008, the matter of Cuban food production had risen fully to the level of national security concerns due to the "escape" of foreign exchange required to purchase foreign foodstuffs. "High food imports are putting Cuban economic reforms at risk because of the drain they pose on foreign exchange resources," commented one observer in 2011.[71]

The failures of Cuban agriculture provided U.S. rice farmers with the possibility of new markets—vital to the well-being of the U.S. rice industry, American producers insisted, again. A visit to Havana of a USA Rice Federation delegation in 2001 provided an opportunity to express the industry's eagerness to reenter the Cuban market. "We need as many customers as we can get," delegate John King from Arkansas insisted. "American agriculture is in a crisis. Re-establishing exports to Cuba would certainly help our situation." He added, "We need to get the politicians to dump all the restrictions on Cuba so that the American farmer can get out of this depression and come back to life."[72] Between 2001 and 2005, Cuba contracted to purchase 320,000 tons of rice, an estimated total value of $81 million. "This established Cuba as our fastest growing market," Mike Wagner, president of the Mississippi Rice Council, explained to the House Agriculture Committee, "and one of the top five customers for long-grain rice."[73] Randy Haynie, president of Haynie and Associates, a Louisiana lobbying firm, pleaded for a resumption of trade, recalling that "Cuba was Louisiana's number one trading partner for many years during the first half of the twentieth century. This win-win relationship all ended with the introduction of the embargo in 1959." Haynie denounced a U.S. foreign policy that followed "the whims of a self serving Miami-based political engine," suggesting too that it was "grossly unfair" that Louisiana "should have to bear the brunt of a failed policy that has more to do with retribution than meeting practical American policy goals."[74]

Rice interests had indeed acquired a substantial stake in ending the embargo. In the early 2000s, the value of U.S. rice imports to Cuba increased from $6.2 million in 2002 to $39.5 million in 2006. "Rice farmers have spent decades trying to explain to Congress that the embargo is a huge loss for our sector," wrote Dow Brantley, chairman of USA/Arkansas Rice in 2016. "It is why we have been at the forefront of the push to lift the embargo since the 1990s. . . . If we are successful in lifting the outdated and harmful trade embargo, we can ensure that an island of more than 11 million people can enjoy the same rice that grew in my backyard and in thousands of backyards across our state."[75] In 2016, Cuba purchased 20 tons of rice from Missouri, a trade deal that created high expectations among Missouri producers. "Rice is a relatively high-value crop," explained Mike Martin of the Martin Rice Company of Missouri, "and we believe once the Cuban market opens up, Missouri farmers will plant and grow more rice to take advantage of this opportunity."[76] Rice from the United States was certainly competitive—for all the historic reasons: lower costs of transportation, ease of storage, and proximity of U.S. ports. Indeed, one senior Cuban official acknowledged, "the proximity of U.S. gulf ports saved freight on warehousing storage costs which gave U.S. exporters the equivalent of up to 20 percent price advantage."[77] All historic arguments possessed no less compelling logic in the twenty-first century than they had in the nineteenth. "Transit time [from the United States] is a matter of days," insisted one U.S. trade publication in 2017, "not weeks as is the case with Vietnam, which currently supplies much of Cuba's rice imports.... Not only does the proximity of U.S. ports to Cuba keep transport time (and cost) low, the U.S. is able to ship goods to multiple Cuban ports on smaller ships, while competitors depend on larger ships that can only dock at its largest ports. This is helpful because Cuba's internal distribution systems are limited."[78] In 2006, U.S. rice represented almost 80 percent of total rice imports to Cuba (158 million tons out of 199 million tons).[79] In a matter of a decade, under circumstances of a punitive economic embargo, Cuba emerged as the fourth largest market for U.S. rice exports.[80] In 2016, the Congressional Research Service ranked Cuba as "the largest foreign market for U.S. long-grain rice."[81] It requires little gift of prophecy ...

Notes

INTRODUCTION

1. Sidney W. Mintz, *Tasting Food, Tasting Freedom: Excursions into Eating, Power and the Past* (Boston, 1996), 96.
2. Pascual de Riesgo, *Dos habaneras* (Madrid, 1880), 65.
3. Blanche Z. de Baralt, *Cuban Cookery: Gastronomic Secrets of the Tropics, with an Appendix on Cuba Drinks* (Havana, 1931), 8.
4. Marcelo Alvarez, "La cocina como patrimonio (in)tangible," in *La cocina como patrimonio (in)tangible*, ed. Víctor Mariani (Buenos Aires, 2002), 11–25.
5. Pierre Bourdieu, *Distinction: A Social Critique of the Judgement of Taste*, trans. Richard Nice, 2nd ed. (London, 2010), 258. See also Jeffrey M. Pilcher, "The Embodied Imagination in Recent Writing on Food History," *American Historical Review* 121 (June 2016): 862–64.
6. Esteban Rodríguez Herrera, *Léxico mayor de Cuba*, 2 vols. (Havana, 1958–59), 1:58. Emphasis in original. Alberto Pozo Fernández similarly proclaims *ajiaco* as "our national dish" (*nuestro plato nacional*). See Alberto Pozo Fernández, *Cocina: Identidad y cultura* (Havana, 2012), 7.
7. Fernando Fornet Piña, *Diccionario gastronómico cubano* (Havana, 2007), 5.
8. "Documentos inéditos," in José Joaquín García, *Protocolo de antigüedades, literatura, agricultura, industria, comercio, etc.*, 2 vols. (Havana, 1845), 1:220.
9. Antonio López Matoso, *Viaje de Perico Ligero al País de Los Moros: A Critical Edition of Antonio López Matoso's Unpublished Diary, 1816–1820*, ed. James C. Tatum (New Orleans, 1972), 58.
10. Demoticus Philalethes, *Yankee Travels through the Island of Cuba; or, the Men and Government, the Laws and Customs of Cuba as Seen by American Eyes* (New York, 1856), 205.
11. Julia Ward Howe, *A Trip to Cuba* (Boston, 1860), 169.
12. Baralt, *Cuban Cookery*, 23.
13. See Gina Picart, "Historia de la cocina en la Siempre Fiel isla de Cuba," *Cómo nació la cocina cubana* (blog), January 19, 2008, http://ginapicart.wordpress.com/2008/01/19/como-nacio-la-cocina-cubana/; Shannon Lee Dawdy, "*La comida mambisa*: Food, Farming, and Cuban Identity, 1839–1999," *New West Indian Guide* 76 (2002): 47–80; and Christine Folch, "Fine Dining: Race in Prerevolution Cuban Cookbooks," *Latin American Research Review* 43 (2008): 205–23.
14. Graziella Pogolotti, "Los componentes del ajiaco," in *El rasguño en la piedra* (Havana, 2011), 58. For the various ethnic sources of Cuban cuisine, see Niurka Núñez González and Estrella González Noriega, "Antecedentes etnohistóricos de la alimentación tradicional en Cuba," *Revista Cubana de Alimentación y Nutrición* 13 (1999): 145–50.

15. Creto Gangá [pseud. of Bartolomé José Crespo Borbón], *Un ajiaco, o la boda de Pancha Jutía y Canuto Raspadura* (Havana, 1847); Jill Lane, *Blackface Cuba, 1840–1895* (Philadelphia, 2005), 38.

16. Ingredients in the *ajiaco* stew vary but typically include some combination of the following: yuca, malanga, yam, sweet potato, plantain, corn, tomato, chayote, green pepper, squash, garlic, onion, pork, and beef. See Dolores Alfonso y Rodriguez, *La cocina y el hogar*, 4th ed. (Havana, 1943), 139–40. A variety of regional versions of *ajiaco* are prepared across the island: *ajiaco a la camgüeyana, ajiaco bayamés, ajiaco caimanero, ajiaco del monte, ajiaco cardenense, ajiaco de tierra-adentro, ajiaco campestre,* and *ajiaco marinero,* among others. See José E. Triay, *Nuevo manual del cocinero criollo* (Havana, 1914), 79–81.

17. Quoted in José B. Fernández, *Los abuelos: Historia oral cubana* (Miami, 1987), 71.

18. Josefina Ortega, "El ajiaco y la identidad nacional," *La Jiribilla* 11 (October 27–November 2, 2012), http://epoca2.lajiribilla.cu/2012/n599_10/599_20.html. See also Christiane Paponet-Cantat, "The Joy of Eating: Food and Identity in Contemporary Cuba" *Caribbean Quarterly* 49 (2003): 20–21.

19. Fernando Ortiz, "Los factores humanos de la cubanidad," *Revista Bimestre Cubana* 45 (First Semester 1940): 167–68. "Somos ajiaco," proclaimed Astrid Barnet. See Astrid Barnet, "Somos ajiaco y constante cocedura," Radio Rebedle, December 17, 2009, http://www.radiorebelde.cu/noticias/habaneras/habaneras-171209.html.

20. José Ramón de Betancourt, *Una feria de la caridad en 183 . . . Cuento camagüeyano* (1858; Barcelona, 1885), 90–91.

21. Luis F. Domínguez, "A Chichita," *El Siglo*, September 13, 1867, 3.

22. Cirilo Villaverde, *Cecilia Valdés; o, La loma del angel. Novela de costumbres cubanas* (Havana, 1879), 79. For an expansive treatment of the prominence of food in the novel *Cecilia Valdés*, see Rita De Maeseneer, "La comida en *Cecilia Valdés*," University of Gent, Academic Year 2007–2008, http://lib.ugent.be/fulltxt/RUG01/001/414/639/RUG01-001414639_2010_0001_AC.pdf.

23. Esteban Pichardo y Tapia, *El fatalista. Novela cubana* (Havana, 1866), 181. Emphasis in original.

24. Francisco Calcagno, *Recuerdos de antes de ayer* (Havana, 1893), 14.

25. Martín Morúa Delgado, *La familia Unzúazu* (1896; Havana, 1975), 257.

26. Martín Morúa Delgado, *Sofía* (Havana, 1891), 136.

27. Raimundo Cabrera, *Sacando hilas* (Havana, 1922), 68.

28. Carlos Loveira, *Los inmorales* (Havana, 1919), 71.

29. Carlos Loveira, *Generales y doctores* (Havana, 1920), 46, 121.

30. Nicolás Guillén, "Epístola," in *La paloma de vuelo popular* (Buenos Aires, 1959), 91–94.

31. See, for example, Juan B. Nina, *El origen de la cocina dominicana: Historia y recetas típicas dominicanas* (Santo Domingo, 1999); Cruz Miguel Ortíz Cuadra, *Eating Puerto Rico: A History of Food, Culture, and Identity* (Chapel Hill, 2013); Lolita Llamozas de Lleras Condazzi, *Ayer y hoy en mis recetas venezolanas* (Caracas, 1973); and Patricia McCausland-Gallo, *The Secrets of Colombian Cooking* (New York, 2012).

32. Atsuko Ichijo and Ronald Ranta, *Food, National Identity and Nationalism: From Everyday to Global Politics* (New York, 2016), 25.

33. Leví Marrero, *Cuba: Economía y sociedad*, 15 vols. (Madrid, 1972–88), 14:224.
34. Marta Vesa Figueras, "La comida cubana," in *Conquista y comida: Consecuencias del encuentro de dos mundos*, ed. Janet Long (Mexico City, 2003), 83.
35. Pozo Fernández, *Cocina*, 61.
36. Ana Sofía Peláez, "Introduction," in *The Cuban Table: A Celebration of Food, Flavors, and History*, by Ana Sofía Peláez and Ellen Silverman (New York, 2014), 5.
37. Cecilio Rodolfo Cortés Cruz and Sergio Eduardo Chinea Díaz, *La cocina en Cienfuegos* (Santiago de Cuba, 2015), 10.
38. Ramona V. Abella Forcada, *From Cuba with Love: Recipes and Memories* (New York, 2003), 10.
39. José Lezama Lima, *Oppiano Licario* (Mexico City, 1977), 74.
40. "Entrevista: Eliseo Alberto—'Yo como mi país todos los días,'" *El País* (Madrid), June 14, 2008, http://elpais.com/diario/2008/06/14/cultura/1213394404_850215.html.
41. José García de Arboleya, *Manual de la Isla de Cuba. Compendio de su historia, geografía, estadística y administración*, 2nd ed. (Havana, 1859), 264.
42. See Renée Méndez Capote, "Recetas antiguas de la cocina cubana," *Actas del folklore* 1 (October–December 1961): 3–5.
43. Loveira, *Generales y doctores*, 28.
44. García de Arboleya, *Manual de la Isla de Cuba*, 264.
45. Juan Nápoles Fajardo (El Cucalambé), "Adios al ajiaco," December 2, 1855, in *Colección de poesías inéditas del popular vate cubano* (Gibara, 1886), 93–96.
46. Riesgo, *Dos habaneras*, 65. Emphasis in original.
47. José Luis Santana Guedes, "Prólogo," in *Cocina criolla cubana*, by Laura Gil Recio and Bartolo Cárdenas Alpízar (Santiago de Cuba, 1993), 5. Santana Guedes was vice president of the Asociación Culinaria de la República de Cuba and presided over a national initiative to recover and preserve historic recipes of Cuba.
48. See García de Arboleya, *Manual de la Isla de Cuba*, 265; and Philalethes, *Yankee Travels through the Island of Cuba*, 204.
49. Julio Rosas, *La campana de la tarde, o vivir muriendo* (Havana, 1873), 41. Italicized items in original.
50. Julio Rosas, 108. Italicized items in original.
51. Beatriz Calvo Peña, "Cocina criolla: Recetas de identidad en la Cuba independentista," *Catauro* 12 (2005): 76–84.
52. Eugenio de Coloma y Garcés, *Manual del cocinero cubano* (Havana, 1857), i.
53. José P. Legrán, *Nuevo manual del cocinero cubano y español, con un tratado escojido de dulcería, pastelería y botellería, al estilo de Cuba: Indispensable para aprender a componer de comer con la mayor perfección y economía, y necesario a todas las clases de la sociedad y en particular a los gastrónomos, madres de familia, fondistas &c* (Havana, 1857), 4.
54. Colleen Cotter, "Claiming a Piece of the Pie: How the Language of the Recipe Defines a Community," in *Recipes for Reading: Community Cookbooks, Stories, Histories*, ed. Anne L. Bower (Amherst, 1997), 52–54.
55. Enrique Langarika, *El cocinero de los enfermos, convalecientes y desganados. Arreglado todo al gusto de la Isla de Cuba* (Havana, 1862), vii.
56. Calvo Peña, "Cocina criolla," 77–78. The three books were: Juan Cabrisas, *Nuevo*

manual de la cocinera catalana y cubana (Havana, 1858); Langarika, *El cocinero de los enfermos*; and Triay, *Nuevo manual del cocinero criollo*.

57. Fornet Piña, *Diccionario gastronómico cubano*, 6, 43.

58. Folch, "Fine Dining," 206.

59. Fornet Piña, *Diccionario gastronómico cubano*, 43.

60. Langarika, *El cocinero de los enfermos*; Legrán, *Nuevo manual del cocinero cubano y español*; Cabrisas, *Nuevo manual de la cocinera catalana y cubana*.

61. Vesa Figueras, "La comida cubana," 83.

62. María Teresa Cornide Hernández, *De La Havana [sic] de siglos y de familia* (Havana, 2003), 316. George Augustus Sala took note upon arriving at Havana, "Only yesterday we had been content with an early morning cup of coffee; but chocolate is the sole recognised Spanish desayuno, or breakfast." See George Augustus Sala, *Under the Sun: Essays Mainly Written in Hot Countries* (London, 1872), 53. Carlos Belot suggested in 1828 that the Spanish predilection for chocolate originated early in the sixteenth century in Mexico, adapted from the Indigenous people. See Carlos Belot, *Observaciones sobre los males que se esperimentan en esta Isla de Cuba* (New York, 1828), 197.

63. Fernando Fornet Piña, *Recetas con arroz* (Havana, 2005), 51–52.

64. Pozo Fernández, *Cocina*, 50.

65. Luis Victoriano Betancourt, "Gente ordinaria," in *Artículos de costumbres y poesías* (Guanabacoa, 1867), 93.

66. Virginia Felicia Auber, *Ambarina: Novela doméstica cubana*, 2nd ed. (Havana, 1915), 95.

67. Maturin M. Ballou, *Due South, or Cuba Past and Present* (Boston, 1888), 151. Fornet Piña's *Diccionario gastronómico cubano* lists fifty different varieties of coffee, including *café a la criolla*, *café a lo cubano*, *café americano*, *café a la italiana*, *café ruso*, *café antillano*, *café con leche*, *café cortado*, *café tropical*, and *café royal*, among many others (27–29).

68. *El Mundo*, March 4, 1912, 8.

69. Abella Forcada, *From Cuba with Love*, 10.

70. Aurora M. Camacho Barreiro, *Del español de Cuba: Apuntes lexicológicos* (Havana, 1994), 19–20. For a comprehensive guide to rice recipes, see Fornet Piña, *Recetas con arroz*.

71. Antonio Bachiller y Morales, *Prontuario de agricultura general para el uso de los labradores i hacendados de la Isla de Cuba* (Havana, 1856), 127.

72. García de Arboleya, *Manual de la Isla de Cuba*, 264.

73. Gonzalo de Quesada and Henry Davenport Northrop, *The War in Cuba, Being a Full Account of Her Great Struggle for Freedom Containing a Complete Record of Spanish Tyranny and Oppression* (n.p., 1896), 503–4.

74. See Kwang Su [pseud.], *Desde me observatorio: Colección de artículos* (Havana, 1929), 17. "Rice is nearly indispensable [*casi imprescindible*]," pronounced historian Eusebio Leal Spengler, "without which a Cuban considers that he has not eaten." See Eusebio Leal Spengler, "Prólogo," in *Sabor cubano*, ed. Adriana Sánchez-Mejorada and Patricia Belatti (Mexico City, 2015), 11.

75. "El arroz en la cocina cubana," Guije.com, February 26, 2006, http://www.guije.com/cocina/arroz.

76. "El cultivo del arroz en Cuba y el insuperable arroz marca 'Tigress,'" *Bohemia* 31 (January 1, 1939): 40.
77. Leví Marrero, "El arroz: Anomalía y promesa," *El Mundo*, February 23, 1954, A-6. The conventional wisdom suggests that the Cuban predilection for rice has its origins with the large numbers of Spaniards who arrived in Cuba from Andalusia, introducing a preference for Arabic cooking in which rice was prominent. See Guillermo Jiménez, "Food: Colonial Period," in *Cuba*, ed. Alan West Durán et al., 2 vols. (Detroit, 2012), 1:343–46.
78. Miguel Escalada, "Cultivo y beneficio de cereales indígenas," *Diario de la Marina*, December 11, 1845, 2.
79. See "El agua como alimento," *El Museo. Semanario Ilustrado de Literatura, Artes, Ciencias y Conocimientos Generales* 1 (April 15, 1883): 158–59.
80. Josefina Alvarez, *All about Cuban Cooking* (Los Angeles, 1991), 52.
81. Some of these specifications are emphasized in Fornet Piña, *Recetas con arroz*.
82. José Miguel Macías, *Diccionario cubano: Etimológico, crítico, razonado y comprensivo* (Vera Cruz, 1888), 97; Juan M. Dihigo, *Léxico cubano: Contribución al estudio de las voces que lo forman*, 2 vols. (Havana, 1928), 1:347–50; Constantino Suárez, *Vocabulario cubano*, 14th ed. (Havana, 1921), 17; Esteban Pichardo y Tapia, *Diccionario provincial casi-razonado de vozes cubanas*, 3rd ed. (Havana, 1862), 15–16; Rodríguez Herrera, *Léxico mayor de Cuba*, 1:121–23; Fornet Piña, *Diccionario gastronómico cubano*, 13–14. See also Manuel Gómez de la Maza, *Distribución de los géneros fanerogámicos cubanos, según el sistema sexual de Linneo* (Havana, 1895), 17.
83. Langarika, *El cocinero de los enfermos*, 83.
84. Rodríguez Herrera, *Léxico mayor de Cuba*, 1:121; C. Suárez, *Vocabulario cubano*, 36.
85. María Josefa Llúria de O'Higgins, *A Taste of Old Cuba* (New York, 1994), 123.
86. Llúria de O'Higgins, 145–46.
87. Abella Forcada, *From Cuba with Love*, 160.
88. Nitza Villapol, *Cocina criolla* (Mexico, n.d.), 116.
89. Eliana Rivero, "In Search of the PBP (Perfect Bread Pudding)," *Cuban Counter Points*, March 2017, https://cubacounterpoints.com/archives/5146.
90. Leal Spengler, "Prólogo," 11.
91. Eduardo Machado and Michael Domitrovich, *Tastes Like Cuba: An Exile's Hunger for Home* (New York, 2007), 6, 83, 120. On Eduardo Machado, see Nieves Pascual Soler, "At the Postnational Table: Food, Fantasy, and Fetichism in *Tastes Like Cuba* by Eduardo Machado," *Latin American Research Review* 52 (2017): 110–23.
92. Margarita Engle, *Skywriting: A Novel of Cuba* (New York, 1995), 82; Pablo Medina, *Exiled Memories: A Cuban Childhood* (Austin, 1990), 95.
93. Richard Blanco, *The Prince of Los Cocuyos: A Miami Childhood* (New York, 2014), 151.
94. Virgil Suárez, "Arroz," in *ReMembering Cuba: Legacy of a Diaspora*, ed. Andrea O'Reilly Herrera (Austin, 2001), 193.
95. Arsenio Rodríguez Quintana, *Síndrome de Ulises* (Barcelona, 2004), 15.
96. Quoted in J. Fernández, *Los abuelos*, 70.
97. Llúria de O'Higgins, *Taste of Old Cuba*, 123.
98. Nicolás Guillen, *Páginas vueltas: Memorias* (Havana, 1982), 191.

99. "A Trip to Cuba," *Atlantic Monthly*, October 1859, 457.
100. Samuel Hazard, *Cuba with Pen and Pencil* (Hartford, Conn., 1871), 537.
101. James W. Steele, *Cuban Sketches* (New York, 1881), 191.
102. Frank C. Ewart, *Cuba y las costumbres cubanas* (Boston, 1919), 6.
103. Erna Ferguson, *Cuba* (New York, 1946), 44, 85, 104, 284–85.
104. Thomas Barbour, *A Naturalist in Cuba* (Boston, 1945), 36.
105. Walter Adolphe Roberts, *Havana: Portrait of a City* (New York, 1953), 250.
106. U.S. Congress, House of Representatives, *Hearings before the Committee on Agriculture: Amendments to Sugar Act of 1948: Hearings before the Committee on Agriculture*, 84th Cong., 1st Sess. (Washington, D.C., 1955), 436.
107. See Adriana Loredo [Rosa Hilda Zell], *Arroz con mango* (Havana, 1952); Fernando Fornet Piña, *Con arroz: Cremas, ensaladas, sopas frituras, tortillas, arroces compuestos* (Havana, 2005); Gloria Rossi, *La cocina del arroz* (Barcelona, 1989); Iván Linares Méndez, *Arroz, el insustituible* (Havana, 2011); and Jorge Argueta, *Arroz con leche: Un poema para cocinar* (Toronto, 2010).
108. Triay, *Nuevo manual del cocinero criollo*, 127.
109. Baralt, *Cuban Cookery*, 12.
110. Ambrosio González del Valle, *La comida diaria. Selección, proporción, distribución y usos de los alimentos de utilidad a las madres o encargadas de dirigr la alimentación de la familia* (Havana, 1933), 1–15.
111. H. T. Andersen, "Annual Economic Review—Cuba," April 15, 1952, 837.00/4–552, Confidential U.S. State Department Central Files, Cuba, Internal Affairs and Foreign Affairs, 1950–1954, General Records of the Department of State, Record Group 59, National Archives, Washington, D.C. (hereafter cited as State Department Central Files: 1950–1954/RG 59).
112. Myrtle H. Neblett, *Tablas de composición de los alimentos de mayor consumo en Cuba* (Havana, 1946), 54; Norman Jollifee et al., "Nutrition Status Survey of the Sixth Grade School Population of Cuba," *Journal of Nutrition* 64 (1958): 365; Margarita Rodríguez Cervantes, "La alimentación en Cuba: Aspectos socioeconómicos," *Publicaciones de Centro de Estudios Demográficos* 45 (June 1982): 3–4.
113. Francisco Dorta-Duque, *Justificando una reforma agraria. Estudio analítico-descriptivo de las estructuras agrarias en Cuba* (Madrid, 1959), 44.
114. Cuba, Oficina del Censo, *Censo de la República de Cuba 1907* (Washington, D.C., 1908), 32; John Norman Efferson, *The Production and Marketing of Rice* (New Orleans, 1952), 341.
115. Instituto Nacional de Reforma Económica, "El arroz cubano ante una grave encrucijada," *Carta Pública Quincenal* 14 (March 15, 1956): 1; "El mercado cubano de arroz: Fuentes de abastecimiento, precios, producción y consumo," *Cuba Económica y Financiera* 31 (April 1956): 22–26. It is possible that the per capita consumption was in fact higher, as high as 150 pounds a person, if waste as a result of preparing too much rice and rice discarded as burned or sticking to the side of pots were factored into the calculus. See *New York Times*, December 14, 1953, 52.
116. Lowry Nelson, *Rural Cuba* (Minneapolis, 1950), 208.
117. Paul George Minneman, "The Agriculture of Cuba," *Foreign Agriculture Bulletin* 2 (December 1942): 97; Efferson, *Production and Marketing of Rice*, 43.

118. Baralt, *Cuban Cookery*, 12.

119. Ann Cristina Pertierra, "The More Things Change, the More They Stay the Same: Rice and Beans in Modern Cuba," in *Rice and Beans: A Unique Dish in a Hundred Places*, ed. Richard Wilk and Livia Barbosa (London, 2012), 40.

120. Loredo [Rosa Hilda Zell], *Arroz con mango*, 87.

121. See Pichardo y Tapia, *Diccionario provincial casi-razonado de vozes cubanas*, 14; José Sánchez-Boudy, *Diccionario mayor de cubanismos* (Miami, 1999); José Sánchez-Boudy, *Diccionario de cubanismos más usuales: Como habla el cubano*, 6 vols. (Miami, 1978–89).

122. Dora Alonso, "Arroz," *Verde Olivo* 1 (August 14, 1960): 91–93; Vicente del Olmo, "Arroz a la cubana," *Diario de la Marina*, September 4, 1922, 10, 13.

123. The author acknowledges with appreciation Emilio Cueto for bring this *contradanza* to his attention.

124. *Guarachas cubanas. Curiosa recopilación desde las más antiguas hasta las más modernas*, 2nd ed. (Havana, 1882), 81; Allena Luce, *Canciones populares* (Boston, 1921), 132.

125. Marta Esquenazi Pérez, "Acerca de las rondas infantiles tradicionales," *Perfiles de la Cultura Cubana* 6 (November 2010–June 2011), http://www.perfiles.cult.cu/article; Cárdenas Molina et al., *Diccionaio del español de Cuba* (Madrid, 2000), 43.

126. Natalia Bolívar Arostegui and Carmen González Díaz de Villegas, *Mitos y leyendas de la comida afrocubana* (Ponce, Puerto Rico, 2000), 37–86. See also Lázaro Zamora Jo, *Comidas para orishas: Quince recetas afrocubanas* (Havana, 1996); and Fernando Ortiz, "La cocina afrocubana," *Revista Bimestre Cubana* 18 (1923): 409–20.

127. Marrero, "El arroz: Anomalía y promesa," A-6. Geographer Gerardo Canet indicated that of the 100 pounds per capita, 85 pounds originated from abroad. See Gerardo Canet, *Atlas de Cuba* (Cambridge, 1949), 53.

128. In the mid-twentieth century, the International Bank for Reconstruction and Development was critical of the use of the term *frutos menores*: "To persist in calling everything except sugar '*frutos menores*' has a psychological effect which does not help to encourage diversification." See International Bank for Reconstruction and Development, *Report on Cuba* (Baltimore, 1951), 169. See also Ramiro Guerra y Sanchez et al., *Historia de la nacion cubana*, 10 vols. (Havana, 1952), 4:159, 161.

129. "Reformas necesarias: Cultivos menores," *Diario de la Marina*, July 15, 1922, 10.

130. To this list of themes subject to the slight of the historian's hand should be added poultry and livestock, including cattle, horses, and pigs.

131. For a comprehensive examination of the impact of reciprocity on Cuban economic development, see Oscar Zanetti Lecuona, *Los cuativos de la reciprocidad* (Havana, 1989). As early as 1902, Cuban minister in Washington Gonzalo de Quesada privately expressed his fears to the U.S. State Department that reciprocity would in "some cases kill Cuban industries." Gonzalo de Quesada, "Memorandum," November 18, 1902, Despatches from the United States Ministers in Cuba, 1902–1906, General Records of the Department of State, Record Group 59, National Archives, Washington, D.C. See also Gonzalo de Quesada to Secretary of State, October 22, 1902, File C-705/237, Records of the Bureau of Insular Affairs, Record Group 350, National Archives.

132. "Notas de la redacción sobre la precedente carta," *Memorias de la Real Sociedad Económica de La Habana*, 2nd series, 7 (April 1849): 171.

CHAPTER ONE

1. Ramón de la Sagra, *Historia económico-política y estadística de la Isla de Cuba ó sea de sus progresos en la población, la agricultura, el comercio y las rentas* (Havana, 1831), 4.

2. See tables xv–xx in Lowell Joseph Ragatz, ed., *Statistics for the Study of British Economic History, 1763–1833* (London, 1928), n.p. For pre-1800 sugar production in Cuba, see Mercedes García Rodríguez, *Entre haciendas y plantaciones: Orígenes de la manufactura azucarera en La Habana* (Havana, 2007); Manuel Moreno Fraginals, *El ingenio: Complejo ecónomico social cubano del azúcar*, 3 vols. (Havana, 1978); and Leví Marrero, *Cuba: Economía y sociedad*, 15 vols. (Río Piedras, Puerto Rico, 1972–92), especially vols. 7, 9, 10.

3. The number of coffee estates (*cafetales*) also increased, from 2 in 1774 to 586 in 1804, to 1,315 in 1806, and to 2,067 in 1827. Between 1792 and 1804, Cuban coffee exports increased more than sevenfold, from 7,101 *arrobas* (1 *arroba* = 25 lbs.) to 50,000 *arrobas*, doubling thereafter every several years. Between the years 1825 and 1830 and 1836 and1840, production increased annually from an average 2 million *arrobas* to 3.4 million *arrobas*. However, by the mid-1840s, a combination of devastating hurricanes and competition from Brazil contributed to the collapse of Cuban coffee, with most estates passing into sugar production. See "Ingenios y cafetales," 1832–1833, 1834–1835, Fondo Miscelánea de Expedientes, Legajo 3772, Núm. Añ, Archivo Nacional de Cuba, Havana, Cuba (hereafter cited as ANC); Jacobo de la Pezuela, *Diccionario geográfico, estadístico, histórico de la Isla de Cuba*, 4 vols. (Madrid, 1863–66), 1:225; Francisco Pérez de la Riva, *El café: Historia de su cultivo y explotación en Cuba* (Havana, 1945); and Doria González Fernández, "Acerca del mercado cafetalero cubano durante la primera mitad del siglo XIX," *Revista de la Biblioteca Nacional "José Martí,"* 3rd series, 31 (May–August 1989): 151–59.

4. Within the decade of the 1790s, the price of sugar rose from four *reales* per pound to twenty-eight to thirty *reales* per pound. See Heinrich Friedländer, *Historia económica de Cuba* (Havana, 1944), 112.

5. By midcentury, an estimated 70 percent of all mills—some 950 mills out of a total of 1,365, as identified by Carlos Rebello in 1860—had converted to steam power and accounted for 90 percent of Cuban sugar production. See Carlos Rebello, *Estados relativos a la producción azucarera de la Isla de Cuba: Formados competentemente y con autorización de la Intendencia de Ejército y Hacienda* (Havana, 1860), 82, 107–8.

6. See "Importancia de los ferrocarriles en la Isla de Cuba," *Memorias de la Real Sociedad Económica de La Habana*, 2nd ser., 6 (February 1849): 402–15.

7. "Pobreza real de Cuba," *Revista de Agricultura. Organo Oficial del Círculo de Hacendados y Agricultores de la Isla de Cuba* 14 (August 1894): 364.

8. Félix Goizueta-Mimó, *Azúcar amargo cubano: Monocultivo y dependencia económica* (Madrid, 1972), 7, 9. Together with coffee and tobacco, sugar accounted for 85 percent of the total value of agricultural output.

9. The total number of sugar mills at midcentury is an unsettled matter. Jacobo de la Pezuela and José García de Arboleya estimated the total number of mills to be 1,442 in 1846. Félix Erénchun offered the number of mills to be 1,560. Carlos Rebello

identified a total of 1,365 mills in 1860, while Ramon de la Sagra counted 1,934 mills in the same year. The Centro de Estadísticas identified the existence of 1,531 mills in 1862. See Pezuela, *Diccionario geográfico, estadístico, histórico de la Isla de Cuba*, 1:59; José García de Arboleya, *Manual de la Isla de Cuba. Compendio de su historia, geografía, estadística y administración*, 2nd ed. (Havana, 1859), 137; Félix Erenchun, *Anales de la isla de Cuba* (Havana, 1857), 266; Rebello, *Estados relativos a la producción azucarera de la Isla de Cuba*, 108; Ramón de la Sagra, *Cuba en 1860, o sea cuadro de sus adelantos en la población, la agricultura, el comercio y las rentas públicas*, 2nd ed. (Paris, 1863), 105; and Cuba, Centro de Estadística, *Noticias estadísticas de la Isla de Cuba, en 1862* (Havana, 1864), n.p.

10. Among the most informative studies of the expansion of sugar in nineteenth-century Cuba include Moreno Fraginals, *El ingenio*; Roland T. Ely, *Cuando reinaba su majestad el azúcar* (Buenos Aires, 1963); Ramiro Guerra y Sánchez, *Azúcar y población en las Antillas*, 3rd ed. (1927; Havana, 1944); Laird W. Bergad, *Cuban Rural Society in the Nineteenth Century: The Social and Economic History of Monoculture in Matanzas* (Princeton, 1990); Fe Iglesias García, *Del ingenio al central* (San Juan, Puerto Rico, 1998); Alberto Perret Ballester, *El azúcar en Matanzas y sus dueños en La Habana: Apuntes e iconografía* (Havana, 2007); and Zoila Lapique Becali and Orlando Segundo Arias, *Cienfuegos: Trapiches, ingenios y centrales* (Havana, 2011). The "preconditions" for Cuban success after 1791 had been set in motion earlier in the eighteenth century as a result of the British occupation of Havana and the impact of the Bourbon reforms. For a general survey of these developments, see Ramiro Guerra y Sánchez, *Manual de la historia de Cuba*, 5th ed. (Havana, 1973), 130–98; and Fernando Portuondo, *Historia de Cuba*, 6th ed. (Havana, 1965), 201–23.

11. See Reinaldo Funes Monzote, *De los bosques a los cañaverales: Una historia ambiental de Cuba 1491–1926* (Havana, 2008). In the eastern jurisdictions of the island, where sugar expanded more slowly, mixed agricultural farms and diverse land tenure forms persisted into the twentieth century. See "Estado especificado de las fincas y establecimientos rurales y de industria, agrícola existentes en los diversos partidos que comprenden la jurisdicción de esta Capital [Santiago de Cuba]," May 28, 1838, Fondo Gobierno Superior Civil, Legajo 775, Núm. 26700, ANC; Jurisdicción de Las Tunas, "Padrón general de fincas rústicas," 1866, Fondo de la Miscelánea, Legajo 30, Núm. K, ANC; "Relación detallada de los nombres de fincas, sus dueños y caballerías de tierra de la Jurisdicción de Bayamo," 1866, Fondo Gobierno General, Legajo 265, Núm. 13517, ANC; Jurisdicción de Guantánamo, "Padrón de fincas rústicas," 1868, Fondo de la Miscelánea, Legajo 1565, Núm. AB, ANC; Jurisdicción de Baracoa, "Resumen estadístico de la población, riqueza urbana, agrícola e industrial, comercio y rentas del expresado año 1861," Fondo Gobierno General, Legajo 403, Núm. 19148, ANC; and Ayuntamiento de Holguín, "Padrón general de fincas," 1860, Fondo Gobierno General, Legal 562, Núm. 27533, ANC.

12. Rafael Gómez Roubaud to Miguel Cayetano Soler, May 3, 1807, in Francisco de Arango y Parreño, *Obras del Excmo. Señor D. Francisco de Arango y Parreño*, 2 vols. (Havana, 1888), 2:396. Historian Manuel Moreno Fraginals indicated that the "poor peasants [*campesinos pobres*] [of Güines] were violently dislodged from their *vegas*." See Moreno Fraginals, *El ingenio*, 1:142.

13. Miguel Rodríguez, "Historia geográfica: Civil y política del Manzanillo y sus litorales," 1830, in *Memorias de la Sociedad Patrótica de La Habana*, 13 (1841): 107.

14. Diego José de Sedano, *Dos preguntas que el Capitán General de la Isla de Cuba, como Presidente de la Junta Económica de aquel Consulado, hizo A. Don Diego José de Sedano* (London, 1812), 5. By midcentury, with the expansion of railroads and the introduction of steam-powered mills, the need for oxen—and hence the price of oxen—diminished significantly, often by as much as one half. See Antonio Bachiller y Morales, "Memoria sobre el número y valor de los ganados de la isla, obstáculos que se oponen á su producto, y medios de fomentar su consumo y el de nuestras pesquerías," *Memorias de la Sociedad Económica de La Habana*, 2nd ser., 1 (1846): 347.

15. Moreno Fraginals, *El ingenio*, 1:62; García Rodríguez, *Entre haciendas y plantaciones*, 87–88; Bergad, *Cuban Rural Society in the Nineteenth Century*, 46–48; Ramiro Guerra y Sánchez et al., *Historia de la nación cubana*, 10 vols. (Havana, 1952), 3:159–60.

16. "Agricultura: Estado de nuestros caminos," *Lonja Mercantil de La Habana* 3 (September 26, 1800): 19–20.

17. Cuba, Gobierno y Capitanía General, *Memoria sobre el progreso de las obras públicas en la Isla de Cuba, desde 1º de enero de 1859 a fin de junio de 1865 presentada al Excmo. Sr. Gobernador General de la misma por la subdirección del ramo* (Havana, 1866), 77.

18. Robert Francis Jameson, *Letters from the Havana, during the Year 1820, Containing an Account of the Present State of the Island of Cuba* (London, 1821), 106–7.

19. María de las Mercedes Santa Cruz y Montalvo (Condesa de Merlin), *La Habana*, trans. Amalia E. Bacardí (1844; Madrid, 1981), 257–58.

20. "Vuelta de Bajo—Ferrocarril," *Diario de la Marina*, September 2, 1849, 2.

21. Virginia Felicia Auber, *Ambarina: Novela doméstica cubana*, 2nd ed. (Havana, 1915), 95. "The laborious and costly means of internal communication in Cuba, increase the cost of her products in her ports, notwithstanding the short distance between the northern and southern shore," Alexander von Humboldt observed. See Alexander von Humboldt, *The Island of Cuba*, trans. John Sidney Thrasher (New York, 1856), 315–16.

22. José Antonio Saco, "Carta de un cubano a un amigo suyo," December 12, 1846, in *Obras de Don José Antonio Saco. Compiladas por primera vez y publicadas en dos tomos*, 2 vols. (New York, 1853), 1:255.

23. Ramón de la Sagra, "Historia económico-política y estadística de la Isla de Cuba," *Anales de Ciencias, Agricultura, Comercio y Artes* 4 (October 1831): 320; Sagra, *Historia económico-política y estadística de la Isla de Cuba*, 85; Ramón de la Sagra, *Historia física, política y natural de la Isla de Cuba*, 12 vols. (Paris, 1845–53), 1:244.

24. See the following in Fondo Real Consulado de Agricultura, Industria y Comercio y Junta de Fomento de la Isla de Cuba, ANC: "Expediente sobre composición de los malos pasos de caminos de la Habana a Güines," 1798, Legajo 115, Núm. 4852; "Expediente promovido por D. Juan Jesús Gómez para que se le componga el camino frente de sus estancias entre el puente de Pastrana y Luyanó," 1801, Legajo 116, Núm. 4869; "Expediente formado en virtud de oficio del Diputado de Matanzas encareciendo la necesidad de componer los caminos de aquella jurisdicción," 1828, Legajo 117, Núm. 4960; "Expediente relativo a las solicitudes de la Justicia y Ayuntamiento de Guanabacoa para que se verifique la composición de las calles de aquella villa, puentes deteriorados

y malos caminos de su jurisdicción," 1809, Legajo 116, Núm. 4891. Protests were often forwarded directly to the office of the Captain General. See "Expediente de varios hacendados, labradores, y carreteros . . . sobre el mal estado de los caminos," 1825, Fondo Gobierno Superior Civil, Legajo 682, Núm. 2222, ANC; "Papeles sueltos referentes al mal estado en que se encuentran los puntos del Camino Real de Bahía Honda," 1858–1859, Fondo de Gobierno General, Legajo 36, Núm. 2456, ANC; Diputación Provincial, Pinar del Río, to Gobernador Capitán General, October 19, 1882, Fondo de Gobierno General, Legajo 368, Núm. 17627, ANC. For a sweeping indictment of internal transportation at midcentury Cuba see José Antonio Saco, "Memoria sobre caminos en la Isla de Cuba," 1830, in *Colección de papeles científicos, históricos, políticos y de otros ramos sobre la Isla de Cuba*, 3 vols. (Havana, 1858–59), 1:58–122; and Ramón de Arozarena y Pedro Bauduy, *Informe presentado a la Junta de Gobierno del Real Consulado de la Siempre Fiel Isla de Cuba* (Havana, 1828).

25. García de Arboleya, *Manual de la Isla de Cuba*, 144–45.

26. Francisco Letamendi to Domingo del Monte, May 12, 1840, in Academia de la Historia de Cuba, *Centón epistolario de Domingo del Monte*, ed. Domingo Figarola-Caneda, Joaquín Llaverías y Martínez, and Manuel Mesa Rodríguez, 7 vols. (Havana, 1923–57), 4:147.

27. Ramón de la Sagra, *Historia física, económico-política, intelectual y moral de la Isla de Cuba* (Paris, 1861), 62. See also "Relaciones que corresponden al padrón de fincas rústicas de la jurisdicción de Trinidad," 1864, Fondo Miscelánea de Expedientes, Legajo 1164, Núm. L, ANC; and "Padrón de fincas rústicas menores de Trinidad," 1881–1882, Fondo Gobierno General, Legajo 413, Núm. 19573, ANC.

28. Sedano, *Dos preguntas que el Capitán General de la Isla de Cuba*, 19.

29. Cuba, Capitanía General, *Cuadro estadístico de la Siempre Fiel Isla de Cuba, correspondiente al año 1827* (Havana, 1829), n.p.; Cuba, Capitanía General, *Cuadro estadístico de la Siempre Fiel Isla de Cuba, correspondiente al año de 1846* (Havana, 1847), 42, 153.

30. Marrero, *Cuba: Economía y sociedad*, 10:101.

31. José María de Andueza, *Isla de Cuba, pintoresca, histórica, política, literaria, mercantil é industrial: recuerdos, apuntes, impresiones de dos épocas* (Madrid, 1841), 117.

32. Fermín Figuera, *Estudios sobre la Isla de Cuba: La cuestión social* (Madrid, 1866), 71. "Corn, *viandas*, rice, cheese, butter and other minor productions [*producciones menores*] so important to our rural economy," exhorted José de Frías, "should not remain ignored." See José de Frías, "Informe," *Memorias de la Sociedad Económica de La Habana* 18 (1841): 306.

33. Gaspar Betancourt Cisneros, "Trabajo: Sus obstáculos," *Gaceta de Puerto Príncipe*, June 20, 1838, reprinted in Gaspar Betancourt Cisneros, *Escenas cotidianas* (Havana, 1950), 157–58.

34. Moreno Fraginals noted that many agriculturists abandoned subsistence farming to seek wage-labor opportunities in the expanding sugar economy, while others converted their farmlands into cane fields. See Moreno Fraginals, *El ingenio*, 1:96.

35. Auber, *Ambarina*, 96.

36. Friedländer, *Historia económica de Cuba*, 303–4.

37. See García Rodríguez, *Entre haciendas y plantaciones*, 87–88; Bergad, *Cuban*

Rural Society in the Nineteenth Century, 46–48; Moreno Fraginals, *El ingenio*, 3:43–45; and Guerra y Sánchez, *Historia de la nación cubana*, 3:159–160.

38. "Llave del nuevo mundo, antemural de las Indias Occidentales," in Real Sociedad Patriótica de La Habana, *Memorias de la Sección de Historia de la Real Sociedad Patriótica de La Habana* (Havana, 1837), 3:292.

39. "Agricultura," *Memorias de la Real Junta de Fomento y de la Real Sociedad Económica* 1 (1832–36): 344.

40. John Glanville Taylor, *The United States and Cuba: Eight Years of Change and Travel* (London, 1851), 209–10. See also Francisco Frías y Jacott, *Colección de escritos sobre agricultura* (Paris, 1860), 257.

41. Moreno Fraginals, *El ingenio*, 1:96.

42. "Ojeada económica sobre la Isla de Cuba," *Anales de Ciencias, Agricultura, Comercio y Artes* 3 (October 1829): 97.

43. Gaspar Betancourt Cisneros, "Escenas cotidianas," *Gaceta de Puerto Principe*, June 20, 1838, reprinted in Cisneros, *Escenas cotidianas*, 32.

44. Sagra, *Cuba en 1860*, 179.

45. "Agricultura: Medios de mejorar la condición de un país," *Memorias de la Real Sociedad Patriótica de La Habana* 3 (1837): 285.

46. Cuba, Intendencia General de Hacienda, *Cuadro analítico del comercio, navegación y rentas de la Isla de Cuba en el año 1840* (Havana, 1841), 7.

47. "Manifiesto al País," *Boletín de la Junta General del Comercio de La Habana* 6 (August 31, 1886): 123.

48. Sagra, *Historia económico-política y estadística de la Isla de Cuba*, 5; Cuba, *Cuba, resumen del censo de población de la Isla de Cuba á fin del año de 1841* (Havana, 1842).

49. Marrero, *Cuba: Economía y sociedad*, 14:222.

50. Cuba, Capitanía General, *Cuadro estadístico de la Siempre Fiel Isla de Cuba, correspondiente al año de 1846*, appendix, 26; "Commerce and Resources of Cuba," *Merchants' Magazine* 21 (July 1849): 34.

51. *El Faro Industrial de La Habana*, January 6, 1848, 1.

52. John Sidney Thrasher translated and updated the Alexander von Humboldt original 1825–26 edition, adding updated and new information. See von Humboldt, *Island of Cuba*, 305–6. Emphasis in original.

53. "Influencia de la mujer en sociedad cubana," *Revista de La Habana* 4 (1855): 146.

54. Francisco de Arango y Parreño, "Expediente instruido por el Consulado de La Habana sobre los medios que convenga proponer para sacar la agricultura y el comercio de esta Isla del apuro en que se hallan," November 29, 1808, in *Boletín Oficial de la Hacienda de la Isla de Cuba* 1 (January 10, 1881): 486–87. Reprinted in Arango y Parreño, *Obras del Excmo. Señor D. Francisco de Arango y Parreño*, 2:17–64. For a splendid collection of essays assessing the importance of Arango y Parreño, see María Dolores González-Ripoli and Izaskun Alvarez Cuartero, eds., *Francisco Arango y la invención de la Cuba azucarera* (Salamanca, 2009).

55. Alvaro Reynoso, *Estudios progresivos sobre varias materias científicas, agrícolas e industriales* (Havana, 1861), 345.

56. Manuel Costales, "Jurisprudencia mercantil," *Siempreviva* 1 (1838): 297–98.

57. "Comercio libre," *Revista de La Habana* 2 (September 1853–March 1854): 233.

58. José R. Alvarez Díaz et al., *A Study on Cuba* (Coral Gables, 1965), 128.

59. "Notas de la redacción sobre la precedente carta," in Real Sociedad Económica de La Habana *Memorias de la Real Sociedad Económica de La Habana*, 2nd ser., 7 (April 1849): 171.

60. Susan Schroeder, *Cuba: A Handbook of Historical Statistics* (Boston, 1982), 413.

61. *Diario de la Marina*, July 31, 1845, 2. Midcentury patterns of trade and commerce can be discerned in "Expediente formado a virtud de oficio del Excelentísimo Señor Superintendente General de Hacienda acompañado de un ejemplar de la balanza general de comercio de esta Isla correspondiente al año anterior," 1844, Fondo Real Consulado de Agricultura, Industria y Comercio y Junta de Fomento de la Isla de Cuba, Legajo 76, Núm. 2980, ANC; and "Expediente balanza general del comercio de esta Isla en 1848, 1849–1850," Fondo Real Consulado de Agricultura, Industria y Comercio y Junta de Fomento de la Isla de Cuba, Legajo 76, Núm. 2996, ANC.

62. José Quintín Suzarte, *Estudios sobre la cuestión económica de la Isla de Cuba* (Havana, 1881), 30.

63. See *Mercantile Weekly Report* (Havana), 1846–55.

64. Gilbert Haven, *Our Next-Door Neighbor: A Winter in Mexico* (New York, 1875), 22.

65. Manuel Fernández Juncos, *Habana y Nueva-York: Estudios de viaje* (San Juan, Puerto Rico, 1886), 14.

66. John G. Wurdemann, *Notes on Cuba, Containing an Account of Its Discovery and Early History* (Boston, 1844), 24, 114–15.

67. Richard R. Madden, *The Island of Cuba: Its Resources, Progress, and Prospects* (London, 1849), 62.

68. Xavier Marmier, *Cartas de América*, 2 vols. (Mexico City, 1851), 2:79.

69. James W. Steele, *Cuban Sketches* (New York, 1881), 191.

70. Ramón de la Sagra, "Historia económico-política y estadística de la Isla de Cuba," *Anales de Ciencias, Agricultura, Comercio y Artes* 4 (November 1831): 355. See also Sagra, *Historia económico-política y estadística de la Isla de Cuba*, 212.

71. George W. Roosevelt to John Hay, December 31, 1880, Despatches from U.S. Consuls in Matanzas, 1820–1899, General Records of the Department of State, Record Group 59, National Archives, Washington D.C.

72. Sagra, *Historia económico-política y estadística de la Isla de Cuba*, 125; Cuba, Centro de Estadística, *Noticias estadísticas de la Isla de Cuba*, n.p.; Goizueta-Mimó, *Azúcar amargo cubano*, 7, 9.

73. José Antonio Saco, "Culpable abandono de Sagra en el cumplimiento de las obligaciones que contrajo con el Consulado y la Sociedad Patriótica de la Habana. Escritura de compromiso," *Colección de papeles científicos, históricos, políticos y de otros ramos sobre la Isla de Cuba*, 1:324.

74. "Agricultura—arroz," *Diario de la Marina*, March 2, 1845, 2–3.

75. Antonio Bachiller y Morales, *Prontuario de agricultura general para el uso de los labradores i hacendados de la Isla de Cuba* (Havana, 1856), 127. "There is hardly a single table in Cuba, among the rich and poor, that does not include rice daily in all the meals," pronounced economist Eugenio de Coloma y Garcés. See Eugenio de Coloma y Garcés, *Catecismo de agricultura cubana: Que contiene todos los conocimientos*

necesarios que debe tener un labrador para el cultivo del campo y lograr buenas cosechas y arreglado en lecciones para la enseñanza en las escuelas de las poblaciones rurales de la isla de Cuba (Havana, 1863), 39–40.

76. García de Arboleya, *Manual de la Isla de Cuba*, 264.

77. Pezuela, *Diccionario geográfico, estadístico, histórico de la Isla de Cuba*, 1:59–60.

78. Miguel Escalada, "Cultivo y beneficio de cereales indígenas," *Diario de la Marina*, December 11, 1845, 2.

79. Steele, *Cuban Sketches*, 191.

80. Santa Cruz y Montalvo (Condesa de Merlin), *La Habana*, 250–51.

81. "Agricultura—arroz," 2.

82. Francisco Javier Balmaseda, *Tesoro del agricultor cubano. Manuales para el cultivo delas principales plantas propias del clima de la Isla de Cuba*, 2 vols. (Havana, 1890–96), 1:294.

83. "Agricultura—arroz," 2.

84. "Cultivo del arroz," *Diario de la Marina*, December 24, 1848, 2.

85. Jameson, *Letters from the Havana*, 73–74.

86. *Diario de la Marina*, September 9, 1848, 2.

87. José Labadía, "Descripción topográfica de la Isla de Pinos," *Anales de las Reales Junta de Fomento y Sociedad Económica de La Habana* 1 (July–December 1849): 201–2.

88. *El Siglo*, October 18, 1866, 2.

89. Miguel Escalada, "Resultado del ensayo de beneficiar arroz del país en Matanzas," *Diario de la Marina*, November 23, 1845, 2.

90. "Arroz," *Memorias de la Real Sociedad Patriótica de La Habana* 3 (1837): 106–8.

91. *Diario de Matanzas*, March 11, 1830, 1.

92. Demoticus Philalethes, *Yankee Travels through the Island of Cuba; or, the Men and Government, the Laws and Customs of Cuba as Seen by American Eyes* (New York, 1856), 25.

93. Balmaseda, *Tesoro del agricultor cubano*, 1:294.

94. Santa Cruz y Montalvo (Condesa de Merlin), *La Habana*, 250–51. The matter of milling technology continued to bedevil Cuban producers into the early twentieth century. Cuba could greatly increase its production of rice, Francisco Figueras insisted in 1907, but the lack of adequate milling machinery "has created such impediments as to enable only small scale production in zones distant from population centers." See Francisco Figueras, *Cuba y su evolución colonial* (Havana, 1907), 57.

95. "Máquina para descascarar y limpiar el arroz y café," *Anales de las Reales Junta de Fomento y Sociedad Económica de La Habana* 1 (July–December 1849): 208–9.

96. "Molino para descascarar arroz, usado en Valencia," *Anales de Ciencias, Agricultura, Comercio y Artes* 4 (March 1831): 92.

97. "Agricultura—arroz," 3.

98. Francisco Javier Balmaseda, *Cultivo del arroz. Medios fáciles de surtir la Isla de ese artículo de primera necesidad* (Havana, 1903), 13.

99. Susan J. Fernández, *Encumbered Cuba: Capital Markets and Revolution, 1878–1895* (Gainesville, 2002), 65–66.

100. Sagra, *Historia económico-política y estadística de la Isla de Cuba*, 28.

101. Cuba, Administración General de Rentas Marítimas, *Balanza general del com-*

ercio de la Isla de Cuba en el año de 1835 (Havana, 1836); Cuba, Intendencia General de Hacienda, *Cuadro analítico del comercio, navegación y rentas de la isla de Cuba en el año de 1840* (Havana, 1841); Cuba, Administración General de Rentas Marítimas, *Balanza general del comercio de la Isla de Cuba en el año de 1843* (Havana, 1844); Cuba, Administración General de Rentas Marítimas, *Balanza general del comercio de la Isla de Cuba en el año de 1847* (Havana, 1848).

102. Cuba, Capitanía General, *Cuadro estadístico de la Siempre Fiel Isla de Cuba, correspondiente al año de 1827* (Havana, 1829), n.p.

103. "Expediente balanza general del comercio de esta Isla en 1848, 1849–1851," Fondo Real Consulado de Agricultura, Industria y Comercio y Junta de Fomento de la Isla de Cuba, Legajo 76, Núm. 2996, ANC; Cuba, Administración General de Rentas Marítimas, *Balanza general del comercio de la Isla de Cuba en el año de 1847*, 16.

104. von Humboldt, *Island of Cuba*, 302.

105. U.S. Congress, Senate, *Report of the Secretary of the Treasury in Answer to a Resolution of the Senate, Calling for Statistics of Trade with Cuba for the Last Five Years*, 35th Cong., 2nd Sess., Ex. Doc. No. 45 (Washington, D.C., 1859), 11–17.

106. Oscar Zanetti Lecuona and Alejandro García Alvarez, *Caminos para el azúcar* (Havana, 1987), 27–46; Duvon C. Corbitt, "El primer ferrocarril construido en Cuba," *Revista Cubana* 12 (April–June 1938): 179–95; Gert J. Oostindie, "La burguesía cubana y sus caminos de hierro, 1830–1868," *Boletín de Estudios Latinoamericanos y del Caribe* 37 (December 1984): 99–115.

107. Zanetti Lecuona and García Alvarez, *Caminos para el azúcar*, 109.

108. "Arroz," 106.

109. Escalada, "Resultado del ensayo de beneficiar arroz del país en Matanzas," 2.

110. "Agricultura—arroz," 3.

111. Francisco de Paula Serrano, *Agricultura cubana, o tratado sobe los ramos principales de la industria rural* (Havana, 1837), 78.

112. García de Arboleya, *Manual de la Isla de Cuba*, 154.

113. Pezuela, *Diccionario geográfico, estadístico, histórico de la Isla de Cuba*, 1:60.

114. Juan M. Dihigo, *Léxico cubano: Contribución al estudio de las voces que lo forman*, 2 vols. (Havana, 1928), 1:348.

115. "Partido de Guara," *Anales de Ciencias, Agricultura, Comercio y Artes* 2 (June 1828): 373.

116. Esteban Pichardo y Tapia, *Diccionario provincial casi-razonado de vozes cubanas*, 3rd ed. (Havana, 1862), 15.

117. José Miguel Macías, *Diccionario cubano: Etimológico, crítico, razonado y comprensivo* (Vera Cruz, 1888), 97.

118. Constantino Suárez, *Vocabulario cubano*, 14th ed. (Havana, 1921), 36.

119. Balmaseda, *Cultivo del arroz*, 7.

120. "Necesidades de Cuba," *Revista Económica* 3 (April 1880): 333–34.

121. *El Siglo*, August 2, 1865, 2.

122. "Correspondencia de 'El Siglo,'" *El Siglo*, March 19, 1865, 2.

123. "Correo de la Isla," *Diario de la Marina*, June 8, 1861, 2.

124. "Necesidades de Cuba," 333–34.

125. Benigno Gener, *Memoria sobre los medios que exije el mejoramiente de la*

agricultura (Havana, 1857), 19. See also Juan Bautista Sagarra, *Breves nociones de agricultura, industria y comercio* (Santiago de Cuba, 1864).

126. Daniel M. Mullen to John Davis, September 25, 1884, Despatches from U.S. Consuls in Sagua la Grande, 1878–1900, General Records of the Department of State, Record Group 59, National Archives.

127. José Calderón, *El castigo de tres granujas. Novela histórica* (Havana, 1893), 81–82.

128. "Llave del nuevo mundo, antemural de las Indias Occidentales," *Memorias de la Real Sociedad Patriótica de La Habana* 3 (1837): 285. Rice producers in Valencia similarly exhorted high tariffs on American rice, without which, warned Adolfo Llanos, U.S. rice "would enjoy a privilege and foster the development of the milled rice industry in the United States, without any benefits to national interests [*los intereses patrios*]." See Adolfo Llanos, *La cuestión del arroz en Cuba* (Madrid, 1893), 24. See also "Real Orden remitiendo informes de la Sociedad de Amigos del País de Valencia, pidiendo que el arroz que se importe en esta Isla pague iguales derechos que en la Peninsula," July 29, 1844, Fondo Real Consulado de Agricultura, Industria y Comercio y Junta de Fomento de la Isla de Cuba, Legajo 170, Núm. 55, ANC.

129. "Máquina para descascarar y limpiar el arroz y café," 208.

130. Mariano Torrente, *Bosquejo económico político de la Isla de Cuba* (Madrid, 1852), 150.

131. Henry C. Dethloff, *A History of the American Rice Industry, 1685–1985* (College Station, Tex., 1988), 56. At about the same time, the French intervention in Mexico and the ensuing war disrupted rice imports from Campeche.

132. *Diario de la Marina*, May 15, 1861, 2.

133. "Cuba—Production and Trade," *Merchants' Magazine and Commercial Review* 40 (May 1, 1865): 398.

134. Alvaro Reynoso, *Apuntes acerca de varios cultivos cubanos* (Madrid, 1867), 372.

135. *Diario de la Marina*, May 19, 1861, 2.

136. *New York Times*, September 15, 1861, 8.

137. Sagra, *Cuba en 1860*, 179.

138. Quintín Suzarte, *Estudios sobre la cuestión económica de la Isla de Cuba*, 44.

139. *Diario de la Marina*, May 12, 1861, 2.

140. *Diario de la Marina*, June 25, 1861, 2.

141. *Revista de Jurisprudencia y de Administración* 6 (1861): 154.

142. See Antonio Berbegal y Celestino, *Proyecto de escuela de agricultura para la isla de Cuba* (Havana, 1884); and Francisco Astudillo, *Agricultura moderna adoptada para la enseñanza en la isla de Cuba* (Havana, 1885).

143. Francisco de la Cruz, "Correspondencia de la isla," *Diario de la Marina*, August 3, 1860, 2. See also "Necesidades de Cuba," 333–34.

144. "De nuestro corresponsal," *Diario de la Marina*, May 19, 1861, 2.

145. Hurricanes, for example, wrought havoc on agriculture and repeatedly threatened the island with famine. No few than 100 hurricanes struck the island between the end of the 1790s and the 1890s. Hurricanes in 1796, 1825, and 1837, and especially three hurricanes of unprecedented destructive force in 1842, 1844, and 1846, followed by three in 1856, 1859 and 1879, lay waste to Cuban agriculture. Farmers lost reserves of seeds and seedling beds, maturing crops, and tools and equipment; entire herds of livestock

perished, as did work animals and stocks of domestic animals. Fields of subsistence crops, fruits, vegetables, and *viandas* were washed away. Citrus crops, mango trees, and avocado trees were stripped of their fruit. Many were uprooted and others so badly damaged that it would be years before they recovered their fruit-bearing capacity. "The planted fields of rice, corn, yuca, plantains—everything has perished," reported *El Faro Industrial de La Habana* on conditions in Pinar del Río in 1844. "In a single moment [farmers] have witnessed the destruction of the work of an entire year and now face a future of unbearable want and misery," *Diario de la Marina* described conditions in Matanzas after a hurricane in 1856, "presenting farmers with a future of unimaginable scarcity and misery." Only massive importations of emergency food supplies from the United States in the aftermath of hurricanes prevented mass starvation. However, recurring food shipments on this scale—and with some frequency—served further to expand food imports and deepen dependency on foreign supplies. See *El Faro Industrial de La Habana*, October 12, 1844, 3; *Diario de la Marina*, September 4, 1856, 2; and Leopoldo O'Donnell, "Manifestando haber dado cuenta oportunamente del huracán y que adoptó las medidas convenientes para el posible alivio de los males," December 31, 1846, Fondo Real Cédulas y Ordenes, Legajo 156, Núm. 403, ANC.

146. Marcelo Pujol y de Camps, *Apuntes para el presente y porvenir de Cuba. Nociones sobre las corrientes políticas de la época en relación con nuestros asuntos antillanos* (Havana, 1885), 4–5, 121.

147. *El Siglo*, January 11, 1866, 4.

148. Marcos de J. Melero, "Urgencia de atender a los cultivos menores," *Diario de la Marina*, February 27, 1875, 2. This was one of two articles advocating diversification of agriculture. See Marcos de J. Melero, "Urgencia de atender a los cultivos menores," *Diario de la Marina*, March 13, 1875, 2.

149. "Correspondence particular de 'El Siglo,'" *El Siglo*, December 17, 1867, 3.

150. "Informe sobre la fiebre tifoidea," *Anales de la Real Academia de Ciencias Médicas, Físicas y Naturales de La Habana. Revista Científica* 18 (1881): 127.

151. "Correspondencia de 'El Siglo,'" 2.

152. Cruz, "Correspondencia de la isla," 2.

153. Pedro Antonio Alfonso, *Memorias de un matancero. Apuntes para la historia de la Isla de Cuba, con relación a la ciudad de San Carlos y San Severino de Matanzas* (Matanzas, 1854), 223; Ismael Sarmiento Ramírez, *Cuba entre la opulencia y la pobreza: Población, economía y cultura material en los primeros 68 años del siglo XIX* (Madrid, 2004), 146–47. See also "Estado de las fincas existentes en la juridicción de Matanzas," 1856, Fondo Gobierno General, Legajo 185, Núm. 10398, ANC; and "Padrón de los sitios de labor y estancias de la jurisdicción de Matanzas," 1866, Fondo Gobierno General, Legajo 265, Núm. 13516, ANC.

154. "Notable documento," *Boletín de la Junta General del Comercio* 4 (December 31, 1884): 8–9.

155. José Ramón de Betancourt, *Una feria de la caridad en 183 . . . Cuento camagüeyano* (1858; Barcelona, 1885), 79. Betancourt served as a chronicler to his times. The 1858 edition does not include this passage. The 1885 edition, identified as the 3rd edition and described as "notably expanded," incorporates into the narrative commentary of developments that Betancourt had experienced between 1858 and 1885.

156. Luis Engel, "Cuba—sus males y sus remedios," *Revista de Agricultura. Organo Oficial del Círculo de Hacendados y Agricultores de la Isla de Cuba* 2 (1880): 301.

157. Truman A. Palmer, "Beet Sugar: A Brief History of Its Origin and Development," U.S. Congress, Senate, 57th Cong., 2nd Sess., Senate Document No. 204 (Washington, D.C., 1903), 6.

158. Even Spain was not immune to the lure of beet sugar profits. In 1882 two beet sugar factories commenced operations in Granada and Córdoba; two more opened ten years later in Zaragoza and Aranjuez. Spanish beet production increased from 35,000 tons in 1883 to 400,000 tons in 1895. See Hugh Thomas, *Cuba: The Pursuit of Freedom* (New York, 1971), 272. As early as January 1862, *Diario de la Marina* expressed a deepening concern over the declining consumption of Cuban sugar in Spain. See *Diario de la Marina*, January 10, 1862, 2.

159. Ramon O. Williams to James D. Porter, December 28, 1886, Despatches from U.S. Consuls in Havana, 1783–1906, General Records of the Department of State, Record Group 59, National Archives (hereafter cited as Despatches/U.S. Consuls Havana.)

160. Williams to Porter, December 28, 1886, Despatches/U.S. Consuls Havana.

161. *Memoria de la Cámara Oficial de Comercio de Santiago de Cuba sobre las medidas económicas que demandan las necesidades de esta isla: Acordada en sesión extraordinaria de 5 de noviembre de 1890* (Santiago de Cuba, 1890), 4–7.

162. Planters across the island petitioned Spain to conclude a reciprocity agreement with the United States as an arrangement necessary for the survival of the sugar industry. See *Información promovida por el Círculo de Hacendados y Agricultores sobre la tributación a la industria azucarera* (Havana, 1891). Spanish authorities, on the other hand, were wary of reciprocity with the United States: "Could there really be reciprocity between a country of 70 million inhabitants and one that does not have more than a million and a half?" Governor General Camilo García de Polavieja scoffed. See Camilo García de Polavieja to Francisco Silvela, November 10, 1891, in Camilo García de Polavieja, *Relación documentada de mi política en Cuba. Lo que ví, lo que hice, lo que anuncié* (Madrid, 1898), 133.

163. "El convenio con los E.U.," *Revista de Agricultura. Organo Oficial del Círculo de Hacendados y Agricultores de la Isla de Cuba* 11 (August 9, 1891): 377. To save "Cuba from an imminent cataclysm," exhorted planter Luis Estévez Romero. See Luis Estévez Romero, *Desde el Zanjón hasta Baire*, 2 vols. (1899; Havana, 1975), 2:111.

164. "El meeting económico: El Sr. Fernández de Castro," *Revista de Agricultura. Organo Oficial del Círculo de Hacendados y Agricultores de la Isla de Cuba* 12 (March 20, 1892): 139.

165. "Réplica de la Junta Directiva del Círculo de Hacendados y Agricultores," *Revista de Agricultura. Organo Oficial del Círculo de Hacendados y Agricultores de la Isla de Cuba* 11 (March 1891): 154.

166. "Commercial Relations with Respect to Cuba and Puerto Rico," July 31 1891, in *Treaties and Other International Agreements of the United States of America, 1776–1949*, ed. Charles I. Bevans, 13 vols. (Washington, D.C., 1968–76), 11:581–594; U.S. War Department, Bureau of Insular Affairs, *Monthly Summary of Commerce of the Island of Cuba, July 1901* (Washington, D.C., 1901), 10–11.

167. U.S. War Department, Division of Customs and Bureau of Insular Affairs,

Monthly Summary of Commerce of Cuba, with Comparative Tables of Imports and Exports, by Articles and Countries: July and August, 1899 (Washington, D.C., 1900), 28.

168. U.S. Treasury Department, Bureau of Statistics, *The Foreign Commerce and Navigation of the United States for the Year Ending . . .* [1891 and 1892] (Washington, D.C., 1892–93).

169. Pulaski F. Hyatt to Secretary of State, October 12, 1894, Despatches from U.S. Consuls in Santiago de Cuba, 1799–1906, General Records of the Department of State, Record Group 59, National Archives (hereafter cited as Despatches/U.S. Consuls Santiago de Cuba).

170. U.S. Treasury Department, Bureau of Statistics, *The Foreign Commerce and Navigation of the United States for the Year Ending June 30, 1896* (Washington, D.C., 1897), 984–85; Ramon O. Williams to Assistant Secretary of State Edwin F. Uhl, October 12, 1894, Despatches/U.S. Consuls Havana. See also Alan Dye, *Cuban Sugar in the Age of Mass Production: Technology and the Economics of the Sugar Central, 1899–1929* (Stanford, 1998), 48–51.

171. Pulaski F. Hyatt to Assistant Secretary of State Edwin F. Uhl, October 12, 1894, Despatches/U.S. Consuls Santiago de Cuba.

172. Ramon O. Williams to Assistant Secretary of State Edwin F. Uhl, May 10, 1894, Despatches/U.S. Consuls Havana.

173. *Diario de la Marina*, March 13, 1894, 2, and December 19, 1894, 2.

174. *La Lucha*, March 30, 1894, 2, and March 31, 1894, 2.

175. *La Lucha*, December 19, 1894, 2.

176. "La exposición a las Cortes del Círculo de Hacendados," *Revista de Agricultura. Organo Oficial del Círculo de Hacendados y Agricultores de la Isla de Cuba* 14 (December 23, 1894): 618.

177. *La Lucha*, January 3, 1895, 2.

178. Pulaksi F. Hyatt to Department of State, October 12, 1894, Despatches/U.S. Consuls Santiago de Cuba.

CHAPTER TWO

1. See María Poumier, "La vida cotidiana en las ciudades cubanas en 1898," *Universidad de La Habana* 196–197 (February–March 1972): 170–209.

2. Pedro Pablo Martín, *Adelina o, la huérfana de La Habana: Novela histórica basada en hechos ocurridos durante la guerra civil de Cuba del año 1895 al 98* (Havana, 1901), 151–52.

3. Major James H. McCleary, "Report of Tour Inspection," December 19, 1898, File 1487, Records of the United States Overseas Operations and Commands, 1898–1942, Record Group 395, National Archives, Washington, D.C.

4. "Malestar é indisciplina," *Diario de la Marina*, July 28, 1901, 2.

5. Fitzhugh Lee, "Special Report of Brigadier General Fitzhugh Lee, U.S.V., Commanding Department of Province of Havana and Pinar del Rio," September 19, 1899, in John R. Brooke, *Civil Report of Major-General John R. Brooke, U.S. Army, Military Governor, Island of Cuba* (Washington, D.C., 1900), 432.

6. McCleary, "Report of Tour Inspection."

7. See U.S. War Department, Office of Director of Census, *Informe sobre el censo de Cuba, 1899* (Washington, D.C., 1900), 45–45, 561, 563–64. See also Felipe Pazos, "La economía cubana en el siglo XIX," *Revista Bimestre Cubana* 47 (January–February 1941): 105–6; Jorge Quintana, "Lo que costó a Cuba la guerra de 1895," *Bohemia* 52 (September 11, 1960): 4–6, 107–8; José R. Alvarez Díaz et al., *A Study on Cuba* (Coral Gables, 1965), 96–97; and Richard J. Hinton, "Cuban Reconstruction," *North American Review* 164 (January 1899): 92–102.

8. "Recapitulation of the Statistical and Fiscal Condition of the Province of Pinar del Rio for the Six Months Ending June 30, 1899," in Brooke, *Civil Report of Major-General John R. Brooke*, 155.

9. J. F. Fuente, "Informe," July 20, 1900, File 1900/3678, Military Government of Cuba Records, Record Group 140, National Archives (hereafter cited as MGC/RG 140).

10. Julio Domínguez, "Informe," November 20, 1900, File 1900/3589, MGC/RG 140.

11. "Recapitulation of the Statistical and Fiscal Condition of the Municipalities of the Province of Havana for the Six Months Ending June 30, 1899," in Brooke, *Civil Report of Major-General John R. Brooke*, 150; Morales, "Informe," August 29, 1900, File 1900/3589, MGC/RG 140.

12. Manuel Hidalgo, "Informe," November 15, 1900, File 1900/3589, MGC/RG 140.

13. Francisco Fernández, "Observaciones por el alcalde," June 30, 1900, File 1900/3589, MGC/RG140.

14. Demetrio Castillo, "Civil Government of the Province of Santiago de Cuba," June 30, 1900, File 1900/3562, MGC/RG 140.

15. José Rodríguez, "Informe," November 22, 1900, File 1900/3589, MGC/RG 140. See also "Expediente formado con relaciones por los Jueces de Primera Instancia del Territorio relativos a los libros del Registro Civil de sus respectivos partidos, que hayan desaparecidos con motivo de la guerra," 1906, Fondo de la Audiencia de Santiago de Cuba, Legajo 61, Núm. 2, ANC.

16. Francisco Mastrafa, "Informe," July 18, 1900, File 1900/3589, MGC/RG 140.

17. Enrique Lavedán, "Los ladrones de la tierra de Oriente," *Gráfico* 3 (February 7, 1914): 10.

18. U.S. War Department, Office of Director of Census, *Informe sobre el censo de Cuba, 1899*, 553.

19. McCleary, "Report of Tour Inspection."

20. Leonard Wood to Adjutant General, October 31, 1899, File 1899/2594, MGC/RG 140. For proceedings against squatters, see "Rollo de la causa seguida por el delito de 'Usurpación de Terrenos' contra Pedro Paisán y Juliana Bosch," March 6, 1915, Fondo de la Audiencia de Santiago de Cuba, Legajo 2, Núm. 13, ANC; "Causa seguida por el delito de 'estafa,' contra Juan de la Rosa Teruel," November 25, 1916, Fondo de la Audiencia de Santiago de Cuba, Legajo 45, Num. 3, ANC; "Causa seguida por el delito de 'ocupación de terreno,' contra Federico Almeida," July 3, 1917, Fondo de la Audiencia de Santiago de Cuba, Legajo 4, Num. 4, ANC.

21. Department of State, Bureau of Foreign Commerce, *Commercial Relations of the United States with Foreign Countries during the Year 1898* (Washington, D.C., 1899), 110. "Everything that can be done in Cuba to assist the producers of sugar and tobacco has been done," military governor Leonard Wood insisted late in the U.S. military

occupation. See Leonard Wood to Elihu Root, October 18, 1901, Letters Sent, File 4754, MGC/RG 140.

22. John A. Porter to Lyman J. Gage, November 15, 1898, in U.S. Treasury Department, *Report on the Commercial and Industrial Condition of the Island of Cuba* (Washington, D.C., 1900), 9. See also Ambrosio de Zayas y Moreno, "Memoria sobre la creación de un 'Banco Nacional Hipotecario' para la reconstrucción y fomento de las riquezas agrícolas y pecuarias en la República de Cuba," March 1898, Fondo Archivo Máximo Gómez, Legajo 18, Núm. 6, ANC.

23. See, for example, Comerciantes y Propietarios, "Petition to Leonard Wood," January 25, 1900, File 1900/1124, MGC/RG 140; and Comerciantes y Propietarios, "Petition to Leonard Wood," February 19, 1900, File 1900/1376, MGC/RG 140.

24. Bartolomé Falcón Paz, "Informe," September 20, 1900, File 1900/3589, MGC/RG 140.

25. Antonio Ferrer, "Informe," November 15, 1900, File 1900/3589, MGC/RG 140.

26. Perfecto Lacoste to Governor General Leonard Wood, June 12, 1900, File 1900/3259, MCG/RG 140.

27. Brooke, *Civil Report of Major-General John R. Brooke*, 13.

28. John R. Brooke to Adjutant General H. C. Corbin, May 24, 1899, John R. Brooke Papers, Pennsylvania Historical Society, Philadelphia. Adjutant General Corbin responded peremptorily: "The time has come for them to no longer expect bountiful gratuities from Government sources." See H. C. Corbin to John R. Brooke, June 7, 1899, Brooke Papers. In a subsequent letter, Corbin indicated that President William McKinley "feels that we have reached the limits of giving and that the time has arrived when the Cuban people must seize the opportunity to go to work." See H. C. Corbin to John R. Brooke, June 8, 1899, Brooke Papers.

29. Leonard Wood, "Report of Brigadier General Leonard Wood," July 5, 1902, U.S. War Department, *Civil Report of Brigadier General Leonard Wood, Military Governor of Cuba, for the Period of January 1 to May 20, 1902*, 6 vols. (Washington, D.C., 1902), 1:13.

30. U.S. Congress, House of Representatives, *Reciprocity with Cuba: Hearings before the Committee on Ways and Means*, 57th Cong., 1st Sess., House Document No. 535 (Washington, D.C., 1902), 280. See "Las inversiones extranjeras en Cuba: Periódo 1900–1930," *Revista del Banco Nacional de Cuba* 2 (September 1956): 279–88.

31. See Zona Fiscal de Manzanillo, "Relación de las fincas que han adquirido en compra losno residentes en la Isla de Cuba desde la fecha de la ocupación militar americana," March 25, 1902, File LMC-1902/31, MCG/RG 140.

32. Scores of disputed land titles and contested land seizures were litigated in Cuban courts. See "Rollo de apelación del juicio de deslinde de la finca rústica hoy agrupada, marcada antes con los nombres de 'Baracaldo,' 'Mogote,' 'San Nicolás,' 'Laja Colorada' y 'San Benigono,' solicitado por Gerardo Vega," January 3, 1901, Fondo de la Audiencia de Santiago de Cuba, Legajo 20, Núm. 9, ANC; "Rollo de la causa seguida por el delito de 'Usurpación de Terrenos' de Diego Yedra," April 5, 1902, Fondo de la Audiencia de Santiago de Cuba, Legajo 12, Núm. 7, ANC; and "Rollo del recurso en el incidente promovido por la Cuba Land Sindicate en el juicio de deslinde de la finca 'El Canal,'" May 25, 1908, Fondo de la Audiencia de Santigo de Cuba, Legajo 29, Núm. 20, ANC.

33. Matthew Hanna to Herbert G. Squiers, February 12, 1903, Despatches from U.S.

Ministers to Cuba, 1902–1906, General Records of the Department of State, Record Group 59, National Archives (hereafter cited as Despatches: 1902–1906/RG 59).

34. U.S. Congress, House of Representatives, *Reciprocity with Cuba*, 280.

35. "Los frutos menores," *El Villareño* 2 (August, 25, 1901): 2.

36. U.S. War Department, Office of Director of Census, *Informe sobre el censo de Cuba, 1899*, 558–59, 564. The acreage of cultivation of rice was surpassed by sugar, 48.9 percent; boniatos, 11.3 percent; tobacco, 9.3 percent; bananas, 8.6 percent; corn, 7.5 percent; malangas, 3.6 percent; yuca, 3.3 percent; coffee, 1.6 percent; coconuts, 1.4 percent; and cacao, 1.4 percent. The notation on the lack of importance of rice was taken from the English-language version of the 1899 census. The Spanish-language edition made no mention of rice. See U.S. War Department, *Report on the Census of Cuba 1899* (Washington, D.C., 1899), 551.

37. U.S. War Department, *Report on the Census of Cuba 1899* (Washington, D.C., 1899), 551; Cuba, Oficina del Censo, *Censo de la República de Cuba 1907* (Washington, D.C., 1908), 32.

38. "Trabajos especiales realizados en cada cultivo," *Primer Informe Anual de la Estación Central Agronómica de Cuba* 1 (April 1904–June 1905): 69–70.

39. Garrard Harris, "Cuba's Trade in Foreign Rice," *Cuba Review* 14 (February 1916): 42. See also "El arroz criollo," *La Lucha*, April 3, 1921, 8.

40. "Memorandum sobre la industria de la elaboración de arroz en Cuba," June 20, 1924, Fondo Donativos y Remisiones, Legajo 400, Núm. 16, ANC. Among the subsidiary industries contemplated were mills, jute industry for packing, and fertilizers.

41. U.S. War Department, Bureau of Insular Affairs, *Monthly Summary of Commerce of the Island of Cuba, May 1902* (Washington, D.C., 1903), 1115.

42. "El mercado cubano de arroz: Fuentes de abastecimiento, precios, producción y consumo," *Cuba Económica y Financiera*, April 1956, 22–26.

43. Cuba, *Census of the Republic of Cuba, 1919* (Havana, 1919), 64–65.

44. U.S. Tariff Commission, *The Effects of the Cuban Reciprocity Treaty of 1903* (Washington, D.C., 1929), 2.

45. Leonard Wood to Elihu Root, January 6, 1902, File 75, Letters Sent, MCG/RG 140.

46. Herbert G. Squiers to John Hay, March 24, 1903, Despatches: 1902–1906/RG 59.

47. *Congressional Record*, appendix, 1902 (Washington, D.C., 1902), 195–96.

48. U.S. Congress, House of Representatives, *Reciprocity with Cuba*, 45.

49. William R. Reid to Franklin D. Roosevelt, March 22, 1933, Series D, Rice Millers Association Records, 1906–1966, the Rice Archives, Edith Garland Dupré Library, Special Collections and Archives, University of Louisiana at Lafayette (hereafter cited as Series D, RMAR).

50. Charles J. Bier to Herbert G. Squiers, March 23, 1904, Despatches: 1902–1906/RG 59. "Persistent efforts," reported the British minister in Havana in 1905, "have been made during the past year by the rice growers of Louisiana and Texas to persuade the Cuban Government to increase the import duty on rice, so that the preference accorded them by the reciprocity treaty may become large enough to enable them to undersell the Indian products." See Department of Commerce, Bureau of Manufacturers, *Commercial Relations of the United States with Foreign Countries during the Year 1905* (Washington, D.C., 1905), 47.

51. Garrard Harris, *The West Indies as an Export Field*, Department of Commerce, Bureau of Foreign and Domestic Commerce, Special Agents Series, No. 141 (Washington, D.C., 1917), 68.

52. "Cuban Rice Tariff: American Growers' President for a Much Larger Duty," *La Lucha*, December 20, 1902, 5. This article appeared in the English-language supplement of *La Lucha*.

53. Chairman, Crowley Rice Milling Company, to Herbert G. Squiers, April 21, 1904, Despatches: 1902–1906/RG 59.

54. W. P. H. McFaddin to Representative O. W. Underwood, January 15, 1913, in U.S. Congress, House of Representatives, *Tariff Schedules: Hearings before the Committee on Ways and Means: Volume III. Schedules D, E, F, G, and H*, 62nd Cong., 3rd Sess. (Washington, D.C., 1913), 2702.

55. U.S. Tariff Commission, *Effects of the Cuban Reciprocity Treaty of 1902*, 14.

56. Cuba, Oficina del Censo, *Censo de la República de Cuba 1907*, 32. For a history of U.S. rice trade, see Caroline G. Gries, *Foreign Trade of the United States, Annual, 1790–1930: Rice and Rice Products*, U.S. Department of Agriculture, Bureau of Agricultural Economics, Foreign Agricultural Service, Report F. S. 53 (Washington, D.C., 1931).

57. The ensuing deficits of rice were partially offset by way of shipments directly from Asia to Cuba through the Panama Canal, or Asian rice transported to California, thereupon transshipped to Cuba also by way of the Panama Canal. Periodically, Asian rice shipped to Seattle was transported to New Orleans by the Union Pacific Railroad and then transshipped to Cuba. See "Havana Correspondence," *Cuba Review* 15 (August 1917): 11; Harold J. FitzGerald, "Easy Come, Easy Go: The Rise and Fall of the Pacific Coast Sugar and Rice Speculators," *Sunset: The Pacific Monthly* 46 (March 1921): 26–27, 64–65, 94–96; "First Rice Train to Cross Continent," *Rice Journal* 19 (October 1916): 20.

58. U.S. Tariff Commission, *Effects of the Cuban Reciprocity Treaty of 1902*, 254–55; Cuba, Secretaria de Hacienda, Sección de Estadística, *Comercio Exterior . . .* (Havana, 1914–24).

59. "Louisiana Rice in Demand," *Cuba Review* 12 (November 1914): 22.

60. H. C. Prinsen Geerligs, "The World's Sugar Industry and the War," *Sugar* 18 (January 1916): 5–6.

61. Edith P. Pitts, *Cuba: From the Republic to Castro* (New York, 1976), 78.

62. Alvarez Díaz, *Study on Cuba*, 233–50; Antonio Santamaría García, *Sin azúcar no hay país. La industria azucarera y la economía cubana (1919–1939)* (Seville, 2001), 55–60.

63. Franklin D. Roosevelt, "F.D.R. Longhand: 1917—January 21–25: Diary of Trip to Cuba," Franklin D. Roosevelt Papers, Franklin D. Roosevelt Presidential Library and Museum, Hyde Park, New York.

64. Carlos Martí, *El país de la riqueza* (Madrid, 1918), 36.

65. U.S. War Department, Office of Director of Census, *Informe sobre el censo de Cuba, 1899*, 571–72; Leví Marrero, *Geografía de Cuba* (Havana, 1951), 682. See also Juan Jerez Villarreal, *Oriente (biografía de una provincia)* (Havana, 1960), 307.

66. "Proporción de la producción azucarera de cada provincia en las zafras de Cuba (1902–1952)," *Anuario Azucarero de Cuba 1952: Censo de la industria azucarera de Cuba y manual estadístico nacional e internacional* (Havana, 1952), 95.

67. Alvarez Díaz, *Study on Cuba*, 235.

68. Ross E. Holday, "Annual Report on the Industrial and Commercial Conditions of the Consular District of Santiago de Cuba," July 9, 1914, File 600/1914, Consulate Santiago de Cuba, Records of the Foreign Service Posts of the Department of State, Record Group 84, National Archives.

69. Irene Wright, *Cuba* (New York, 1910), 481.

70. Teresa Casuso, *Cuba and Castro*, trans. Elmer Grossberg (New York, 1961), 9.

71. "La política: Asuntos de Cuba," *El Mundo*, April 30, 1916, 2.

72. Harry A. Franck, *Roaming through the West Indies* (New York, 1920), 70.

73. "Asuntos de Cuba," *El Mundo*, April 17, 1916, 2. This description is not substantially dissimilar to one made earlier by the U.S. minister in Cuba in 1910: "As a matter of fact, the resultant benefit to Cuba of a good [sugar] crop is actually very slight. Machinery and supplies are purchased abroad, and much of the money paid out for labor goes abroad as well, as many of the laborers come from Jamaica and other islands and Spain, and leave, taking their savings with them, as soon as the 'zafra' is over. The profits, too, go either to the United States or are spent by Cuban plantation owners in Europe. The result is that when the crop is over there are many idle persons left in the country districts with practically no means of support." See John B. Jackson to Secretary of State, April 26, 1910, 837.00/377, Records of the Department of State Relating to Internal Affairs of Cuba, 1910–1929, General Records of the Department of State, Record Group 59, National Archives (hereafter cited as Internal Affairs of Cuba: 1910–1929/RG 59). On the subject of the *central latifundio*, see "Los grandes centrales," *Bohemia* 14 (June 10, 1923): 13–15, 17–24; Walfredo Rodríguez Blanca, "República cubana con territorios extranjeros," *Carteles* 14 (September 1, 1929): 12, 54; Walfredo Rodríguez Blanca, "Aquí hace falta un pueblo," *Carteles* 14 (December 29, 1929): 12, 69; and Ariel James, *Banes: Imperialismo y nación en una plantación azucarera* (Havana, 1976).

74. Ramiro Guerra y Sánchez, *Azúcar y población en las Antillas*, 3rd ed. (1927; Havana, 1944), 100–101, 111.

75. "La carretera de Remedios a Yaguajay," *La Lucha*, May 26, 1910, 9.

76. "No perdamos tiempo," *Diario de la Marina*, March 31, 1917, 2; "Por qué la vida es cara," *Diario de la Marina*, February 16, 1917, 2; "El transporte de los frutos menores," *Diario de la Marina*, May 10, 1917, 1.

77. "Caña y nada más," *Diario de Cuba*, February 11, 1918, 2.

78. "El problema de las tarifas ferroviarias," *El Mundo*, February 11, 1918, 9; "Medidas para disminuir el precio de los víveres que entregan por tierra: Rebaja de las tarifas de ferrocarriles," *El Mundo*, July 1, 1921, 13.

79. "El fomento de los cultivos menores," *Diario de la Marina*, July 13, 1921, 4. "La fórmula honrada," *El Mundo*, July 20, 1922, 2.

80. Fernando Ortiz, *Cuban Counterpoint: Tobacco and Sugar*, trans. Harriet de Onis (New York, 1970), 53.

81. "Caña y nada más," 2.

82. "Condition of the Cuban Farmer," *Cuba Review* 12 (January 1914): 24. Small farmers mobilized and organized demonstrations to protest the loss of land. See *La Lucha*, January 12, 1916, 1, and April 16, 1916, 1, 2. Many cases were litigated in the Audiencia of Santiago de Cuba; see "Rollo del recurso de apelación establecido por Joaquín Romeu

en el juicio de deslinde de la Hacienda 'Guanaybas,'" February 26, 1915, Fondo de la Audiencia de Santiago de Cuba, Legajo 21, Núm. 16, ANC.

83. Lowry Nelson, *Rural Cuba* (Minneapolis, 1950), 97.

84. Quoted in Jose Iglesias, *In the Fist of the Revolution* (New York, 1968), 41–42.

85. *Facts about Sugar* 3 (August 19, 1916): 101; Carlos Martí, *Films cubanos: Oriente y Occidente* (Barcelona, 1915), 250.

86. Carlos Tovar, "Opinión de un guajiro de Villaclara," *Diario de la Marina*, October 19, 1914, 6.

87. "Propaganda para la siembra de frutos menores en la Estación Agronómica," *Diario de la Marina*, June 15, 1921, 13.

88. "Solucionando el conflicto del carbon," *Diario de la Marina*, November 24, 1917, 11.

89. Martí, *El país de la riqueza*, 36. See also Gustavo Gutiérrez, *El desarrollo económico de Cuba* (Havana, 1952), 24.

90. *New York Times*, December 23, 1917, 7. See also Luis Marino Pérez, "La actual situación económica de Cuba," *Reforma Social* 6 (March 1916): 521–31.

91. M. J. Meehan, "Caribbean Markets for American Goods: Cuba," U.S. Department of Commerce, Bureau of Foreign and Domestic Commerce, *Trade Information Bulletin* 346 (May 1925): 1.

92. U.S. Tariff Commission, *Effects of the Cuban Reciprocity Treaty of 1902*, 235; Cuba, *Census of the Republic of Cuba, 1919*, 234. See also Henry M. Wolcott, "Cuba," *Cuba Review* 14 (August 1916): 27–37.

93. H. A. Van Hermann, "The High Cost of Living: Some Causes and Consequences," in Republic of Cuba, Secretary of Agriculture, Commerce, and Labor, *Agriculture: A Monthly Review Dedicated to Agricultural Extension, Animal Industry and Rural Progress* (Havana, 1917), 35. See also "El abaratamiento de los víveres," *Diario de la Marina*, April 28, 1917, 2.

94. Ramiro Cabrera, *¡A sitio Herrera!* (Havana, 1922), 75–76.

95. Fernando Berenguer, *Ensayo de economía política y social: La riqueza de Cuba* (Havana, 1917), 58, 61, 98.

96. Luis Valdés-Roig, *El comercio exterior de Cuba y la guerra mundial* (Havana, 1920), 35–37.

97. José A. Taboadela, "La reducción de la ración alimenticia bajo el aspecto higiénico," *Sanidad y Beneficincia: Boletín Oficial de la Secretaría* 18 (November 1917): 472.

98. "De San José de los Ramos: La crisis económica," *El Mundo*, July 8, 1921, 11.

99. "El costo de la subsistencia," *Diario de la Marina*, February 13, 1917, 2.

100. "Política interior," *El Mundo*, May 15, 1915, 2.

101. "Food Supply Problem in Cuba Causing Anxiety," *Facts about Sugar* 6 (January 12, 1918): 22.

102. "Información mercantil," *Diario de la Marina*, February 18, 1918, 12; "Del campo," *La Lucha*, April 7, 1918, 2.

103. "Asuntos del día," *Diario de la Marina*, February 19, 1920, 1. Similar circumstances had overtaken the *vegueros* of Pinar del Río. World War I had disrupted transatlantic commerce and resulted in the cancellation of European orders of tobacco products. Almost all the large Havana cigar factories closed. Having dedicated production almost entirely to tobacco, *vegueros* experienced all at once the loss of export markets,

diminished capacity to produce foodstuffs, and increased food prices. "The tobacco growers have never experienced a more disastrous year than this," reported the U.S. consul general as early as 1914. "The condition of the majority of the tobacco planters in Cuba, and of the tobacco industry in general, could not be much worse, and when to it is added the higher prices of foodstuffs ... it cannot but mean a very bad state of affairs." Reported *Diario de la Marina*: "The crisis this region is presently experiencing become more acute daily, exacerbated by the high prices of the basic necessities [*los artículos de primera necesidad*]." See James L. Rodgers, "Present Effect of European War on Business in Habana and upon Cuban Industries," August 4, 1914, 837.50/9, Internal Affairs of Cuba: 1910–1929/RG 59; and "De San Juan y Martínez," *Diario de la Marina*, November 5, 1914, 8.

104. "La fórmula honrada," 2.

105. Martí, *Films cubanos*, 75–76. See also Félix R. Garayta, "Descripción de las tierras de Cuba: Provincia de Oriente," 2 vols., unpublished manuscript, 1930, Biblioteca del Archivo Nacional de Cuba, Havana.

106. Oscar Lewis, Ruth M. Lewis, and Susan M. Rigdon, eds., *Neighbors: Living the Revolution; An Oral History of Contemporary Cuba* (Urbana, 1978), 156–60.

107. "La prensa," *Diario de la Marina*, June 14, 1917, 4.

108. James L. Rodgers to Secretary of State, April 3, 1919, 837.50/11, Internal Affairs of Cuba: 1910–1929/RG 59.

109. "Drought Continues at Paso Real," *Cuba News*, September 5, 1914, 8.

110. "Food Supply Problem in Cuba Causing Anxiety," 22; "Artículos de primera necesidad," *Diario de la Marina*, November 6, 1917, 7; "Los precios del arroz," *Diario de la Marina*, January 19, 1918, 9; "La harina llegada en el vapor 'Heredia,'" *Diario de la Marina*, January 20, 1918, 1, 10. See also Van Hermann, "High Cost of Living," 34–38.

111. Rutherford Bingham, "Economic Situation in Cuba," April 26, 1919, 837.50/26, Internal Affairs of Cuba: 1910–1929/RG 59.

112. "El fomento de los cultivos menores," *Diario de la Marina*, July 13, 1921, 4.

113. See Guadalupe García, *Beyond the Walled City: Colonial Exclusion in Havana* (Berkeley, 2016).

114. "¿Hay miseria en La Habana?" *La Higiene* 11 (February 10, 1906): 77–78. See also M. Morejón, "El hambre y la miseria," *El Pilareño* 19 (May 29, 1904): 4.

115. "La carestía de la vida ante el municipio habanero," *El Mundo*, March 11, 1916, 1. See also "El ayuntamiento trató ayer el problema de las subsistencias," *El Mundo*, October 18, 1917, 11; and "Se constituyó la Junta Municipal de Defensa," *El Mundo*, November 1, 1917, 3.

116. "Arrojo al vertedero de víveres en pésimo estado," *El Mundo*, May 2, 1916, 1.

117. "Desea usted tener una buena suerte," *El Mundo*, July 10, 1917, 6. See also Marino Pérez, "La actual situación económica de Cuba," 521–31.

118. "Del ambiente nacional," *Diario de la Marina*, August 11, 1919, 6.

119. See "Los cultivos menores: Los hacendados y agricultores responden a las excitaciones de la Secretaría de Agricultura," *Diario de la Marina*, April 24, 1917, 1.

120. "Cámara de Representantes: Declaraciones del Sr. Estanilao Cartañá sobre el problema de actualidad," *Diario de la Marina*, April 28, 1917, 1.

121. "El problema de las subsistencias," *El Mundo*, April 26, 1918, 2; "Observaciones que hace el comercio al Consejo de Defensa," *Diario de la Marina*, April 26, 1918, 1.

122. "Frutos menores deben sembrar," *El Mundo*, February 23, 1918, 1.
123. "La siembra obligatoria de frutos menores," *El Mundo*, January 13, 1918, 20.
124. "Si queremos no habrá hambre en Cuba," *El Mundo*, November 17, 1917, 2.
125. Luis Marino Pérez, "A Review of Cuban Economic Conditions," November 30, 1923, 837.50/32, Internal Affairs of Cuba: 1910–1929/RG 59.

CHAPTER THREE

1. Robert F. Smith, *The United States and Cuba: Business and Diplomacy, 1917–1960* (New Haven, 1960), 29.
2. Leslie A. Wheeler, "The Cuban Market for American Foodstuffs," U.S. Department of Commerce, Bureau of Foreign and Domestic Commerce, *Trade Information Bulletin* 325 (1925): 3; V. D. Wickizer, *Rice in the Western Hemisphere: Wartime Developments and Postwar Problems* (Stanford, 1945), 37.
3. Cuba, Secretaria de Hacienda, Sección de Estadística, *Comercio exterior. Primer semestre del año 1918 y año fiscal de 1917 a 1918* (Havana, 1919), 269; Cuba, Secretaria de Hacienda, Sección de Estadística, *Comercio exterior. Años naturales 1921 y 1922* (Havana, 1923), 164.
4. Christopher M. Lee, "Organization for Survival: The Rice Industry and Protective Tariffs, 1921–1929," *Louisiana History: The Journal of the Louisiana Historical Association* 35 (Autumn 1994): 433.
5. J. A. Foster to Members, Rice Millers Association, May 17, 1920, Series D, RMAR. For an account of the early history of the Rice Millers Association, see F. B. Wise, "Past Year One of Industry for Rice Millers Association," *Bulls'-Eye* 2 (January 1922): 16–18, 37–41; and Christopher M. Lee, "The American Rice Industry's Organization for a Domestic Market: The Associated Rice Millers of America," *Louisiana History: The Journal of the Louisiana Historical Association* 37 (Spring 1996): 187–99.
6. A. Locke Breaux, "The Rice Export Situation," *Rice Journal* 19 (March 1916): 43.
7. Rafael W. Camejo, "Cuba and Porto Rico Market Conditions as Seen by Nicolas Hernandez & Company," *Rice Journal* 24 (February 1921): 41.
8. *Rice Belt Journal*, September 4, 1920, 6.
9. Lee, "Organization for Survival," 433.
10. William M. Reid to John R. Nuber, April 5, 1955, Series D, RMAR.
11. See "El mercado cubano de arroz: Fuentes de abastecimiento, precios, producción y consumo," *Cuba Económica y Financiera*, April 1956, 22.
12. Among the most articulate exponents of an emerging economic nationalism included the Asociación de Comerciantes de La Habana, Comité de los Cien, Asociación Nacional de Industriales de Cuba, Federación Nacional de Detallistas, Federación Nacional de Corporaciones Económicas de Cuba, and Federación Provincial de Entidades Económicas de Oriente.
13. José R. Alvarez Díaz et al., *A Study on Cuba* (Coral Gables, 1965), 222. Much of the intellectual framework for the Customs-Tariff law is found in José Comallonga, *La nueva economía agraria de Cuba* (Havana, 1929).
14. *Gaceta Oficial de la República de Cuba*, Edición Extraordinaria No. 12, October 20, 1927.
15. Jorge F. Pérez-López, "An Index of Cuban Industrial Output, 1930–58," in *Quantative*

Latin American Studies: Methods and Findings, ed. James W. Wilkie and Kenneth Rudd (Los Angeles, 1977), 40.

16. Gerardo Machado, "Discurso del General Gerardo Machado en Oriente," June 1926, Box No. 6, Folder No. 1: Speeches 1925–1929, Gerardo Machado y Morales Papers, Cuban Heritage Collection, University of Miami, Fla. For a sympathetic account of the policies of the Machado government, see Fritz Berggren, "Machado: An Historical Reinterpretation" (Ph.D. diss., University of Miami, 2001).

17. Alberto Arredondo, "Características y objetivos del industrialismo cubano," unpublished ms., n.d., Alberto Arredondo Papers, Cuban Heritage Collection, University of Miami.

18. Commercial Attaché, "Memorandum," April 12, 1929, 837.51/1342, Internal Affairs of Cuba: 1910–1929/RG 59.

19. William M. Cooper, "Foreword," in U.S. Department of Commerce, Bureau of Foreign and Domestic Commerce, *Trade Information Bulletin* 725 (1930): 2.

20. Frederick Todd, "Cuban Readjustment to Current Economic Forces," in U.S. Department of Commerce, Bureau of Foreign and Domestic Commerce, *Trade Information Bulletin* 725 (1930): 3–4.

21. Edwin J. Foscue, "The Central Highway of Cuba," *Economic Geography* 9 (October 1933): 406. Machado's plans to develop a network of secondary roads were not realized during his administration.

22. Arnaldo Silva León, *Cuba y el mercado internacional azucarero* (Havana, 1975), 1–89; Oscar Zanetti Lecuona, *Economía azucarera cubana. Estudios históricos* (Havana, 2009), 35–106; Todd, "Cuban Readjustment to Current Economic Forces," 3.

23. Charles William Taussig, "Cuba—and Reciprocal Trade Agreements," in National Foreign Trade Council, *Official Report of the Twenty-First National Foreign Trade Convention* (New York, 1934), 554.

24. U.S. Department of Commerce, *Investment in Cuba: Basic Information for United States Businessmen* (Washington, D.C., 1956), 137.

25. Todd, "Cuban Readjustment to Current Economic Forces," 364–67. See also Wheeler, *The Cuban Market for American Foodstuffs*.

26. Charles M. Barnes, "Memorandum: Some Suggestions with Reference to the Pending Negotiations for the Revision of the Cuban Reciprocity Treaty," September 12, 1933, 611.3731/466, Diplomatic Post Records: 1930–1945/RG 59.

27. Todd, "Cuban Readjustment to Current Economic Forces," 7, 13.

28. J. R. McKey, "United States Trade with Latin America in 1923," in U.S. Department of Commerce, Bureau of Foreign and Domestic Commerce, *Trade Information Bulletin* 224 (1924): 40–41; Taussig, "Cuba—and Reciprocal Trade Agreements," 554; "Statement of A. J. S. Weaver, Chief Sugar and Rice Division, Agricultural Adjustment Administration," U.S. Congress, House of Representatives, *Hearings before the Committee on Agriculture: Include Sugar Beets and Sugarcane as Basic Commodities*, 73rd Cong., 2nd Sess. (Washington, D.C., 1934), 5, 12; "Statement of Dr. Mordecai Ezekiel, Economic Advisor to the Secretary, Department of Agriculture," U.S. Congress, House of Representatives, *Hearings before the Committee on Agriculture: Include Sugar Beets and Sugarcane as Basic Commodities*, 73rd Cong., 2nd Sess. (Washington, D.C., 1934), 69.

29. Harry F. Guggenheim, "Changes in Reciprocity Treaty Which Would Probably

Benefit the United States Export Trade with Cuba," March 30, 1933, 611.3731/390, Diplomatic Post Records: 1930–1945/RG 59.

30. José Comallonga, "El arroz y su economía," Carteles 17 (May 17, 1931): 16; A. González de Couto, "El arroz en nuestra economía nacional," Carteles 21 (November 3, 1940): 42; Rafael Manso, "El cultivo del arroz y la economía nacional," Carteles 23 (March 3, 1935): 36, 54, 58; Paul George Minneman, "The Agriculture of Cuba," Foreign Agriculture Bulletin 2 (December 1942): 98–100; Cyril L. Thiel, "Rice Production in Cuba," April 30, 1940, Confidential U.S. Diplomatic Post Records: Cuba 1930–1940, Records of Foreign Service Posts of the Department of State, Record Group 84, National Archives (hereafter cited as Diplomatic Post Records: 1930–1940/RG 84).

31. Thiel, "Rice Production in Cuba."

32. "El mercado cubano de arroz," 22–24; Germán Wolter del Río, Aportaciones para una política económica cubana (Havana, 1937), 196; Miguel A. Fleites y Pérez, Política económica cubana (Havana, 1946), 14–15.

33. Todd, "Cuban Readjustment to Current Economic Forces," 5.

34. Gaceta Oficial de la República de Cuba, August 12, 1932, 12235.

35. "El mercado cubano de arroz," 22–26.

36. Franklin D. Roosevelt, Public Papers of the Presidents: Franklin D. Roosevelt, 13 vols. (New York, 1938–50), 5:463.

37. Harry F. Guggenheim to Secretary of State, March 30, 1933, 611.3731/390, Diplomatic Post Records: 1930–1945/RG 59.

38. Guggenheim, "Changes in Reciprocity Treaty Which Would Probably Benefit the United States Export Trade with Cuba."

39. William M. Reid to Franklin D. Roosevelt, March 22, 1933, Series D, RMAR. See also "Statement of William M. Reid, President, Rice Millers Association, New Orleans, La.," U.S. Congress, House of Representatives, Hearings before a Subcommittee of the Committee on War and Means: Administration and Operation of Customs and Tariff Laws and the Trade Agreements Programs, 84th Cong., 2nd Sess., Pt. 2 (Washington, D.C., 1956), 891.

40. Philip Jessup, "Confidential Memorandum on the Cuban Situation," n.d. [1933], Philip Jessup Papers, Manuscript Division, Library of Congress, Washington, D.C.

41. See Luis E. Aguilar, Cuba 1933: Prologue to Revolution (Ithaca, 1972); Irwin F. Gellman, Roosevelt and Batista: Good Neighbor Diplomacy in Cuba, 1933–1945 (Albuquerque, 1973); Jules R. Benjamin, The United States and Cuba: Hegemony and Dependent Development, 1880–1934 (Pittsburgh, 1977); Lionel Soto, La revolución del 1933, 3 vols. (Havana, 1985); Lionel Soto, La revolución precursora de 1933 (Havana, 1995); José Hernández, Cuba and the United States: Intervention and Militarism, 1868–1933 (Austin, 1993); Justo Carrillo, Cuba 1933: Students, Yankees, and Soldiers, trans. Mario Llerena (Boulder, 1994).

42. Sumner Welles, Two Years of the "Good Neighbor" Policy (Washington, D.C., 1935), 5–6.

43. Sumner Welles to Cordell Hull, May 13, 1933, Foreign Relations of the United States: 1933, 5 vols. (Washington, D.C., 1950–52), 5:289 (hereafter cited as FRUS: 1933).

44. Sumner Welles to Cordell Hull, June 2, 1933, 837.00/3530, Diplomatic Post Records: 1930–1945/RG 59.

45. Sumner Welles to Cordell Hull, May 25, 1933, FRUS: 1933, 293.

46. Sumner Welles to Cordell Hull, May 13, 1933, *FRUS: 1933*, 290.

47. Sumner Welles to William Phillips, July 8, 1933, *FRUS: 1933*, 319.

48. Sumner Welles to Cordell Hull, May 13, 1933, 837.00/3514, Diplomatic Post Records: 1930–1945/RG 59.

49. Sumner Welles to Franklin D. Roosevelt, July 17, 1933, 837.00/3579½, Diplomatic Post Records: 1930–1945/RG 59. The prospects of expanded access to the U.S. market for Cuban sugar, the State Department believed, was "a plum"—in Cordell Hull's words—"which will not be granted until the Cuban Government has taken positive and satisfactory steps." See Cordell Hull, "Memorandum for the President," May 27, 1933, Official File 159-A, Cuba, Miscellaneous 1933, Roosevelt Papers, Franklin D. Roosevelt Presidential Library and Museum. Cuban ambassador Oscar Cintas in Washington lodged a protest to the State Department that Welles was "dictating a policy to President Machado" and using the demand for a new trade agreement as a means "to bring pressure to bear on President Machado to carry out Mr. Welles' wishes." William Phillips, "Memorandum by the Acting Secretary of State," August 2, 1933, 837.00/3638, Diplomatic Post Records: 1930–1945/RG 59. The Phillips memorandum is a summary of the conversation between Phillips and Cintas.

50. Sumner Welles to Franklin Roosevelt, July 19, 1933, *FRUS: 1933*, 325.

51. Gerardo Machado, *Ocho años de lucha* (Miami, 1982), 58, 74–75; Gerardo Machado to Franklin Roosevelt, September 5, 1933, Official File 159, Cuba, 1933–1934, Roosevelt Papers; Gerardo Machado to Franklin Roosevelt, April 11, 1934, Series 1: Correspondence, 1929–1940, Sub-series A: Machado y Morales Papers, Cuban Heritage Collection, University of Miami, Coral Gables, Fla. The removal of Machado did not remove all obstacles to the negotiation of a new reciprocity agreement. A reformist government under Ramón Grau San Martín delayed plans to conclude a new agreement. "Our own commercial and exports interests in Cuba," Welles wrote in September 1933, "cannot be revived under this government." See Sumner Welles to Secretary of State Cordell Hull, September 17, 1933, 837.00/3908, Diplomatic Post Records: 1930–1945: RG 59.

52. Cordell Hull to Jefferson Caffrey, July 26, 1934, *Foreign Relations of the United States: 1934*, 5 vols. (Washington, D.C., 1951–52), 5:144.

53. Commission on Cuban Affairs, *Problems of the New Cuba* (New York, 1935), 50. See also Machado, *Ocho años de lucha*, 57–58.

54. Taussig, "Cuba—and Reciprocal Trade Agreements," 556.

55. Pérez-López, "Index of Cuban Industrial Output," 40.

56. Cordell Hull, "Statement," in U.S. Congress, House of Representatives, *Sugar: Hearings before a Special Subcommittee of the Committee on Agriculture . . . on H.R. 5326*, 75th Cong., 1st Sess. (Washington, D.C., 1937), 367–68.

57. Henry Christopher Wallace, *Monetary Problems of an Export Economy: The Cuban Experience, 1914–1947* (Cambridge, Mass., 1950), 173–77; Armando Novas González, "Crédito agrícola y desarrollo productivo antes de 1959," *Inter-Press Service en Cuba*, July 27, 2011, http://www.ipscuba.net/archivo/credito-agricola-y-desarrollo-productivo-antes-de-1959/; Commission on Cuban Affairs, *Problems of the New Cuba*, 343, 494.

58. Paul George Minneman, "Cuban Agriculture," *Foreign Agriculture Bulletin* 6 (February 1942): 53–54.

59. Minneman, 50.

60. José Cambeyro, "En defensa de la industria arrocera," *Carteles* 26 (April 19, 1936): 5. See also González de Couto, "El arroz en nuestra economía nacional," 43; Comallonga, "El arroz y su economía," 16, 68; and "El problema arrocero," *Bohemia* 27 (February 10, 1935): 35.

61. "Agreement and Exchange of Notes between the United States of America and Cuba Respecting Reciprocal Trade," August 24, 1934, in *U.S. Statutes at Large of the United States of America from January 1935 to June 1936* (Washington, D.C., 1936).

62. E. B. Ogden Jr., "Louisiana Rice and Cuban Sugar among Markets Dried Up by Marxist Takeover," *Acadian Profile* 2 (1974): 22.

63. Rice Millers Association, *Information Bulletin*, No. 103 (December 4, 1936): 4, Series D, RMAR.

64. Frank A. Godchaux to Editor, *New York Times*, December 24, 1938, 14.

65. *Congressional Record*, House of Representatives, June 16, 1936, 9596.

66. William M. Reid to Members, Rice Millers Association, October 5, 1936, Series D, RMAR.

67. U.S. Congress, House of Representatives, *Sugar: Hearings before a Special Subcommittee of the Committee on Agriculture . . . on H.R. 5326*, 75th Cong., 1st Sess. (Washington, D.C., 1937), 225; *Wall Street Journal*, April 23, 1937, 1–2.

68. *Rice Millers Association Newsletter*, No. 1057 (August 9, 1937): 1–2; *New York Times*, August 16, 1937, 30; Jacinto Torras, "El arroz: De 10 a 15 millones de pesos que cada año deben dar trabajo a más de 50,000 campesinos cubanos," August 4, 1942, republished in Jacinto Torras, *Obras escogidas*, 3 vols. (Havana, 1984–86), 1:500–501.

69. Sumner Welles, "Memorandum of Conversation by the Under-Secretary of State," October 1, 1938, *Foreign Relations of the United States: 1938*, 5 vols. (Washington, D.C., 1955–56), 5:472.

70. *New York Times*, November 30, 1938, 1.

71. Ogden, "Louisiana Rice and Cuban Sugar among Markets Dried Up by Marxist Takeover," 22. See also *New York Times*, March 31, 1937, 2.

72. *Rice Millers Association Newsletter*, No. 1122 (August 30, 1938): 1.

73. William M. Reid to Members, Rice Millers Association, July 18, 1938, Series D, RMAR.

74. Albert F. Nufer, "Supplementary Trade Agreement—Concessions on American Rice," December 16, 1938, Confidential U.S. Diplomatic Post Records, Cuba, 1930–1945, Diplomatic Post Records: 1930–1945/RG 84.

75. Albert F. Nufer to Willard L. Beaulac, June 1, 1939, Diplomatic Post Records: 1930–1945/RG 84.

76. "Importance of Rice in the Cuban Economy," *Cuba Económica y Financiera*, April 1956, 22–26; Instituto Nacional de Reforma Económica, "El arroz: Su comercio nacional e internacional," *Carta Pública Quincenal* 39 (April 15, 1957): 4.

77. "Rice Production and Trade: Cuba," *Foreign Commerce Weekly* 31 (June 28, 1948): 24; "El mercado cubano de arroz," 22.

78. H. S. Tewell to Secretary of State, September 30, 1948, 837.50/9–4050, Confidential U.S. State Department Central Files, Cuba, Internal Affairs and Foreign Affairs, 1945–1949, General Records of the Department of State, Record Group 59, National Archives (hereafter cited as State Department Central Files: 1945–1949/RG 59).

79. "Rice Industry Is Seeking Increased Cuba Preferential," *Kerrville Times* [Tex.], September 18, 1941, 10.

80. *Rice Millers Association Newsletter*, No. 1590 (September 27, 1948): 2, Series D, RMAR.

81. Henry C. Dethloff, *A History of the American Rice Industry, 1685-1985* (College Station, Tex., 1988), 158.

82. "Rice Production and Consumption: Cuba," Department of Commerce, *Foreign Commerce Weekly* 17 (October 7, 1944): 36.

83. Clarence A. Boonstra, "Rice in a War Market," Department of Agriculture, Bureau of Agricultural Economics, *Agricultural Situation* 26 (July 1942): 15–18; Wickizer, *Rice in the Western Hemisphere*, 25–30.

84. William H. Becker and William M. McClenahan Jr., *The Market, the State, and the Export-Import Bank of the United States, 1934–2000* (New York, 2003), 50–59; Michale R. Adamson, "'Must We Overlook All Impairment of Our Interests?' Debating the Foreign Aid Role of the Import-Export Bank, 1934–41," *Diplomatic History* 29 (September 2005): 621–22.

85. Aurelio Fernández Concheso to Sumner Welles, May 5, 1941, *Foreign Relations of the United States: 1941*, 7 vols. (Washington, D.C., 1959–62), 7:354; *New York Times*, April 9, 1942, 9.

86. Ellis O. Briggs to Secretary of State, June 29, 1943, *Foreign Relations of the United States: 1943*, 6 vols. (Washington, D.C., 1963–65), 6:230.

87. The Association for Diplomatic Studies and Training, Foreign Affairs Oral History Project, Agriculture Series, "Ambassador Clarence A. Boonstra," interview date January 13, 2006, Lauinger Library, Georgetown University, Washington, D.C., http://www.adst.org/OH%20TOCs/Boonstra,%20Clarence%20A.toc.pdf.

88. "Cooperarán los EE. UU. para elevar al 90% nuestra producción de arroz," *El Mundo*, January 17, 1943, 14.

89. Boonstra, "Rice in a War Market," 16–18; Gustavo Gutiérrez, *El desarrollo económico de Cuba* (Havana, 1952), 206; Torras, "El arroz," 1:499–502.

90. Gutiérrez, *El desarrollo económico de Cuba*, 206; "Rice Production and Consumption: Cuba," 36. See also confidential report commissioned by the Rice Millers Association, "Report on Rice in Cuba," December 1955, Series D, RMAR.

91. "El mercado cubano de arroz," 22; Instituto Nacional de Reforma Económica, "El arroz: Su comercio nacional e internacional," 5–7; Antonio Pérez González, "Nacimiento, desarrollo y agonía de la industria arrocera cubana," *Diario de la Marina*, October 19, 1955, 7-B.

92. Cuba, Ministerio de Agricultura, *Memoria del censos agrícola nacional 1946* (Havana, 1951), 71, 186–88; Congreso Nacional de Ingeniería Agronómica y Azucarera, *Lineamientos generales para una política agracia nacional; ponencia y mociones aprobadas en el II Congreso Nacional de Ingeniería Agronómica y Azucarera* (Havana, 1946), 98–99.

93. Warren Pierson to George S. Messersmith, November 7, 1941, Diplomatic Post Records: 1930–1945/RG 84.

94. George S. Messersmith to Warren Pierson, November 12, 1941, Diplomatic Post Records: 1930–1945/RG 84.

95. *Lake Charles American Press*, October 15, 1943, reprinted in *Appendix to the Congressional Record*, October 18, 1943, A4359.
96. *Appendix to the Congressional Record*, October 18, 1943, A4358.
97. Senator Hattie W. Caraway et al. to L. A. Wheeler, Director, Office of Foreign Agricultural Relations, Department of Agriculture, March 16, 1943, in *Appendix to Congressional Record*, March 19, 1943, A1307–A1308.
98. House of Representatives, H.R. 2226, March 17, 1943, 78th Cong., 1st Sess.; House of Representatives, H.R. 2420, April 7, 1943, 78th Cong., 1st Sess.

CHAPTER FOUR

1. Banco Nacional de Cuba, "Temas sobre cuestiones económicas generales: El desarrollo económico de Cuba," *Revista* 3 (March 1956): 280.
2. Susan Schroeder, *Cuba: A Handbook of Historical Statistics* (Boston, 1982), 261–62; "Restricciones azucareras en Cuba," *Anuario Azucarero de Cuba* 23 (1959): 106; United Nations, Economic Commission for Latin America, *Economic Survey of Latin America 1953* (New York, 1954), 167.
3. "Exportación de azúcar a los Estados Unidos," *Anuario Azucarero de Cuba 1959: Censo de la industria azucarera de Cuba y manual estadístico nacional e internacional* (Havana, 1959), 97. See also Arnaldo Silva León, *Cuba y el mercado internacional azucarero* (Havana, 1975), 91–143; and Oscar Zanetti Lecuona, *Economía azucarera cubana. Estudios históricos* (Havana, 2009), 154–217.
4. Banco Nacional de Cuba, "Temas sobre cuestiones económicas generales," 273.
5. B. R. Mitchell, ed., *International Historical Statistics: The Americas, 1750–2000*, 5th ed. (New York, 2003), 194; José R. Alvarez Díaz et al., *A Study on Cuba* (Coral Gables, 1965), 481.
6. An estimated 205,000 tons of sugar cane remained standing and unharvested during the *zafra* of 1952—and with little likelihood that production prospects would improve any time soon. See Angel Pardo Jiménez, "Nuestra economía agrícola y el porvenir azucarero," *Anuario Azucarero de Cuba 1952: Censo de la industria azucarera de Cuba y manual estadístico nacional e internacional* (Havana, 1952), 27. See also Zanetti Lecuona, *Economía azucarera cubana*, 218–46.
7. Schroeder, *Cuba*, 259–62; Alvarez Díaz et al., *Study on Cuba*, 478, 480.
8. Julio Lobo, "Desacertada política azucarera," *Anuario Azucarero de Cuba 1952: Censo de la industria azucarera de Cuba y manual estadístico nacional e internacional* (Havana, 1952), 31–32.
9. Luis G. Mendoza, "El futuro está en nuestras manos," *Anuario Azucarero de Cuba Censo de la industria azucarera de Cuba y manual estadístico nacional e internacional* 15 (1951): 30. See also Banco Nacional de Cuba, *La economía cubana en 1956–1957* (Havana, 1958), 52–55.
10. United Nations, Economic Commission for Latin America, "Some Aspects of the Recent Evolution of Cuba's Economy," *Economic Review of Latin America* (New York, 1955), 49. U.S. direct investment in Cuban agriculture decreased from $575 million in 1929 to $285 million in 1956. See Philip C. Newman, *Cuba before Castro: An Economic Appraisal* (Ridgewood, N.J., 1965), 54.

11. Raúl Cepero Bonilla, "Política azucarera (1952–1958)," in *Escritos históricos* (Havana, 1989), 246.

12. International Bank for Reconstruction and Development, *Report on Cuba* (Baltimore, 1951), 6–8; Oscar Pino Santos, "El nivel de vida del pueblo cubano es hoy peor que a principios de la República," *Carteles* 26 (November 6, 1955): 46–49, 111.

13. International Bank for Reconstruction and Development, *Report on Cuba*, 6–8; U.S. Department of Commerce, *Investment in Cuba: Basic Information for United States Businessmen* (Washington, D.C., 1956), 7; Pino Santos, "El nivel de vida del pueblo cubano es hoy peor que a principios de la República," 46–49, 111.

14. Cuba, Tribunal Superior Electoral, *Censos de población, viviendas y electoral* (Havana, 1953), 176; Carlos M. Castañeda, "¡665,000 cubanos sin trabajo!," *Bohemia* 50 (February 16, 1958): supp. 16–17.

15. United Nations, Economic Commission for Latin America, "Some Aspects of the Recent Evolution of Cuba's Economy," 48.

16. International Bank for Reconstruction and Development, *Report on Cuba*, 6–8, 54.

17. International Bank for Reconstruction and Development, 726.

18. Antonio Riccardi, "¿Por qué encarece más cada día el costo de la vida en Cuba?," *Carteles* 29 (August 1, 1948): 46.

19. "El costo de vida," *Mujeres Cubanas* 1 (April–May 1951): 1. See also Antonio Iraizoz, "La vida en 1937," *El Mundo*, November 25, 1951, A-6.

20. Leonard H. Price, "Wholesale Price Index, Second Quarter of 1957," August 7, 1957, 837.01/8-757, Confidential U.S. State Department Central Files, Cuba, Internal Affairs and Foreign Affairs, 1955–1959, General Records of the Department of State, Record Group 59, National Archives (hereafter cited as State Department Central Files: 1955–1959/RG 59); E. A. Gilmore Jr., "Wholesale Price Index, First Quarter of 1958," July 14, 1958, 837.01/7-1458, State Department Central Files: 1955–1959/RG 59.

21. R. M. Connell to Department of State, March 30, 1951, 837.00/3-3051, State Department Central Files: 1950–1954/RG 59; Leonard H. Price, "Wholesale Price Index, Second Quarter of 1957," August 7, 1957, 837.01/8-757, State Department Central Files: 1950–1954/RG 59; Gilmore, "Wholesale Price Index, First Quarter of 1958." See also Oscar Pino Santos, "El alza del costo de la vida," *Carteles* 38 (April 14, 1957): 38–40.

22. Oscar Lewis, Ruth M. Lewis, and Susan Rigdon, eds., *Neighbors: Living the Revolution; An Oral History of Contemporary Cuba* (Urbana, 1978), 173.

23. Aurelio Maruri to William M. Reid, December 5, 1955, Series D, RMAR; "Motives and Results of the Rice Survey," September 1955, Series D, RMAR.

24. Rafael Eskert to William M. Reid, December 9, 1955, Series D, RMAR.

25. Schroeder, *Cuba*, 413; "Exportación de azúcar a los Estados Unidos," *Anuario Azucarero de Cuba* 23 (1959): 97; Pino Santos, "El nivel de vida del pueblo cubano es hoy peor que a principios de la República," 111–12.

26. Joaquín Martínez Sáenz, President, Banco Nacional, in conversation with Herbert Matthews, August 14, 1952, Herbert L. Matthews Papers, Rare Book and Manuscript Library, Butler Library, Columbia University, N.Y.

27. Banco Nacional de Cuba, "Temas sobre cuestiones económicas generales," 273, 277. The "situation of Cuba in the face of rising population," Ambassador Philip Bonsal

recalled learning from officials in the National Bank in 1955, "and more or less stagnant living standards was truly desperate." See Philip W. Bonsal, *Cuba, Castro, and the United States* (Pittsburgh, 1971), 271.

28. Rubén Ortiz-Lamadrid, "Sin trabajo no hay país," *El Mundo*, May 18, 1954, A-6; Luis Rolando Cabrera, "Está aumentando día y día la desocupación en el país," *El Mundo*, March 28, 1954, A-12.

29. Leví Marrero, "Cuba: 11 millión dentro de 25 años," *El Mundo*, November 14, 1956, A-6. Journalist Agustín Tamargo described in 1957 "lines of young Cubans in front of the American Embassy, youth without a future and without hope." Agustín Tamargo, "¿Por que lucha actualmente el pueblo de Cuba?," *Bohemia* 49 (July 28, 1957): 64–65. The number of Cubans admitted to the United States as lawful permanent residents increased from 1,893 in 1951, to 5,527 in 1954, to 14,953 in 1956. See "La emigración cubana a Estados Unidos," *Cuba: Economía y Financiera* 34 (August 1959): 14.

30. Pino Santos, "El nivel de vida del pueblo cubano es hoy peor que a principios de la República," 46–49, 111.

31. Ernesto Ardura, "Raíces de la crisis cubana," *El Mundo*, January 11, 1953, A-6.

32. José Lezama Lima, *Diarios*, ed. Ciro Bianchi Ross (Mexico City, 1994), 107–8.

33. Francisco Dorta-Duque, *Justificando una reforma agraria. Estudio analítico-descriptivo de las estructuras agrarias en Cuba* (Madrid, 1959), 12.

34. Ramiro Guerra y Sánchez, "Hostilidad contra el azúcar," *Diario de la Marina*, April 22, 1954, 6-B.

35. Ortiz-Lamadrid, "Sin trabajo no hay país," A-6. There is ample evidence that sugar interests discerned the changing public mood and responded in the defense of sugar. "There appear to be many Cubans," countered Aurelio Portuondo, vice president of the Asociación Nacional de Hacendados de Cuba, "who have forgotten or ignore that Cuba is a tropical country with the highest standard of living in the world. . . . With its sugar economy it is the most prosperous country in Latin America after Argentina. . . . Sugar is not and never has been an obstacle to progress in Cuba. On the contrary it has promoted and facilitated progress . . . and has provided the principal source of foreign exchange required to maintain the standard of civilized life of which we boast." See Aurelio Portuondo Jr., "Hablan los hacendados: Función social y nacional de industria azucarera," *Diario de la Marina*, January 27, 1953, 22.

36. Danilo Baeza, "Diversificación agrícola: Un pueblo en torno al arroz," *Bohemia* 46 (June 13, 1954): 22.

37. Alberto León Riva, "Coyuntura económica y desempleo," *El Mundo*, March 30, 1954, A-10.

38. International Bank for Reconstruction and Development, *Report on Cuba*, 7.

39. International Bank for Reconstruction and Development, 191, 810.

40. United Nations, Economic Commission for Latin America, *Economic Survey of Latin America 1953*, 166.

41. Pardo Jiménez, "Nuestra economía agrícola y el porvenir azucarero," 27–28.

42. Juan Jacobo, "Tabletas comprometidas," *Cuba Económica y Financiera* 32 (September 1957): 47.

43. See Leida Fernández Prieto, *Cuba agrícola: Mito y tradición, 1878–1920* (Madrid, 2005), 55–69.

44. International Bank for Reconstruction and Development, *Report on Cuba*, 94. Emphasis in original.

45. See Joaquín Martínez Sáenz, *Por la independencia económica de Cuba: Mi gestión en el Banco Nacional* (Havana, 1959), 130.

46. Leví Marrero, "¿A qué precio el azúcar?," *El Mundo*, November 30, 1954, A-6. See also Antonio Hernández Travieso, "El miserere del azúcar," *El Mundo*, December 4, 1954, A-6.

47. For a comprehensive rationale for rice as the product of choice for diversification, see Asociación de Cosecheros de Arroz, "En defensa de la producción nacional de arroz," *Diario de la Marina*, February 15, 1953, 36.

48. U.S. Department of Commerce, *Investment in Cuba*, 140. See also "La importación de alimentos de Estados Unidos," *Cuba Económica y Financiera* 35 (May 1960): 20.

49. H. T. Andersen, "Annual Economic Review—Cuba," April 15, 1952, 837.00/4-552, State Department Central Files: 1950–1954/RG 59; Dorta-Duque, *Justificando una reforma agraria*, 16.

50. ; Kathryn H. Wylie, Constance H. Farnworth, and Mary S. Coyner, "Cuba as a Market for United States Agricultural Products," in U.S. Department of Agriculture, Foreign Agricultural Service, *Foreign Agriculture Report* 81 (1954): 1.

51. Rafael Manso, "El cultivo del arroz y la economía nacional," *Carteles* 23 (March 3, 1935): 36, 55. In the course of the Republic's existence, *Carteles* calculated, "Cuba has consumed 153 million *quintales* of rice imported from abroad, for which it has had to pay the astronomical sum of $476 million." See "Sugerencias viables," *Carteles* 23 (February 3, 1935): 21.

52. A. González de Couto, "El arroz en nuestra economía nacional," *Carteles* 21 (November 3, 1940): 42. See also José Cambeyro, "En defensa de la industria arrocera," *Carteles* 26 (April 19, 1936): 5; and Miguel A. Fleites y Pérez, *Política económica cubana* (Havana, 1946), 14–15.

53. "Cooperarán los EE. UU. para elevar al 90% nuestra producción de arroz," *El Mundo*, January 17, 1943, 1.

54. "Regadío de los arrozales," *El Mundo*, November 14, 1953, A-6.

55. Leví Marrero, "El arroz: Anomalía y promesa," *El Mundo*, February 23, 1954, A-6; Mario Greitín, "¿Que sucede con el arroz?," *Carteles* 35 (April 11, 1954): 98.

56. Andersen, "Annual Economic Review—Cuba," April 15, 1952.

57. "Constitución de la República de Cuba, 1940," http://www.cubanet.org/htdocs/ref/dis/40_print.htm.

58. Banco de Fomento Agrícola e Industrial de Cuba, *Memoria 1954–1955* (Havana, 1955), 13. See also Juan Valdés Paz, "La cuestión agraria en la Constitución de 1940," in *Restrospección crítica de la Asamblea Constituyente de 1940*, ed. Ana Suárez Díaz (Havana, 2011), 205–15.

59. Carlos Du-Quesne y de Zaldo, *El desarrollo económico y el BANFAIC* (Havana, 1955), 37; Banco de Fomento Agrícola e Industrial de Cuba, *Memoria 1954–1955*, 15–24.

60. Banco de Fomento Agrícola e Industrial de Cuba, *Memoria 1954–1955*, 16. For details of BANFAIC-funded projects, see the following loan applications: Rolando Fernández Cruz to Gerente, Asociación de Crédito Rural "La Trocha," July 5, 1955, Casto Ferragut to Gerente Agrícola, BANFAIC, May 12, 1955, and June 25, 1955, and

W. Braun to Luciano Sánchez, February 8, 1956, all in "Expediente que trata otras cosas sobre préstamos y reglamentos de la cooperativa de arroz de la Asociación de Crédito Rural 'La Trocha,'" 1955–1957, Fondo Banco Nacional de Cuba, Banco de Fomento Agrícola e Industrial de Cuba, Legajo 856, Núm. 3, ANC.

61. See Armando Nova González, " El crédito agrícola y su desempeño en el fomento y desarrollo de la producción agrícola antes de 1959," n.d., http://www.nodo50.org/cubasigloXXI/economia/nova2_300410.pdf. See also U.S. Department of Agriculture, *Agricultural Policies of Foreign Governments: Including Trade Policies Affecting Agriculture* (Washington, D.C., 1957), 52–55.

62. These included La Asociación de Crédito Rural "Alvaro Reynoso" (Güira de Melena); La Asociación de Crédito Rural "Ricardo H. Beattie Brooks" (Manzanillo); La Asociación de Crédito Rural "General Serafín Sánchez" (Cabaiguán); La Asociación de Crédito Rural "Gaspar Betancourt Cisneros" (Camagüey); La Asociación de Crédito Rural "José Martí" (Santo Domingo/Cifuentes); La Asociación de Crédito Rural "Tranquilino Sandalio de Noda" (Artemisa); La Asociación de Crédito Rural "Calixto García" (San Antonio de las Vegas); La Asociación de Crédito Rural "José Comallonga" (Managua); La Asociación de Crédito Rural "Pesquero Felipe Poey" (Havana); La Asociación de Crédito Rural "La Trocha" (Ciego de Avila); La Asociación de Crédito Rural "Dos Ríos" (Jiguaní); and La Asociación de Crédito Rural "Manuel Lazo" (Guane). See Banco de Fomento Agrícola e Industrial de Cuba, *Memoria 1954–1955*, 38–45. For details of Rural Credit Association's charter, see "Asociación de Crédito Rural 'La Trocha,' afiliado BANFAIC: Ciego de Avila, Morón y Jatibonico: Reglamento de la Sección Cooperativa Arrocera," July 1955, "Expediente que trata otras cosas sobre préstamos y reglamentos de la cooperativa de arroz de la Asociación de Crédito Rural 'La Trocha,'" 1955–1957, Fondo Banco Nacional de Cuba, Banco de Fomento Agrícola e Industrial de Cuba, Legajo 856, Núm. 3, ANC.

63. Instituto Nacional de Reforma Económica, "El arroz cubano ante una grave encrucijada," *Carta Pública Quincenal* 14 (March 15, 1955): 11–12.

64. Guillermo Jiménez, *Las empresas de Cuba 1958* (Havana, 2004), 45–46.

65. José Ramírez León, President, Asociación Nacional de Cosecheros de Arroz, Manzanillo, to Carlos Hevia, Minister of Agriculture, July 24, 1950, in "Expediente que contiene correspondencia relativa entre otros asuntos al informe técnico-económico sobre la expansión de arroz," Fondo Banco Nacional de Cuba, Banco de Fomento Agrícola e Industrial de Cuba, Caja 735, Núm. 8, ANC.

66. "El mercado cubano de arroz: Fuentes de abastecimiento, precios, producción y consumo," *Cuba Económica y Financiera*, April 1956, 22–26.

67. "Cuba produjo en esta cosecha 2 millones de quintales de arroz," *Diario de la Marina*, January 7, 1951, 3.

68. H. S. Tewell to Secretary of State, May 14, 1948, 837.61317/5–1448, State Department Central Files: 1945–1949/RG 59; H. S. Tewell to Secretary of State, August 30, 1948, 837.50/8–3048, State Department Central Files: 1945–1949/RG 59.

69. Guy L. Bush, Agricultural Attaché, "Basic Cuban Rice Industry," February 1, 1952, 837.2317/2–152, State Department Central Files: 1950–1954/RG 59.

70. John R. Nuber to William M. Reid, March 20, 1952, Series D, RMAR. Emphasis in original.

71. Jack K. McFall [Assistant Secretary] to Senator Allen Ellender, June 5, 1952, Godchaux Family Papers/Louisiana State Rice Milling Company Records, the Rice Archives, Edith Garland Dupré Library, Special Collections and Archives, University of Louisiana at Lafayette (hereafter cited as Godchaux Family Papers).

72. Ben H. Brown Jr. [Acting Assistant Secretary of State] to Senator Allen Ellender, July 16, 1952, Godchaux Family Papers.

73. For a comprehensive overview of economic policies under the Batista government, see Michael Patrick McGuigan, "Fulgencio Batista's Economic Policies, 1952–1958" (Ph.D. diss., University of Miami, 2012).

74. For expressions of renewed commitment to rice production, see Joaquín Martínez Sáenz, President, Banco Nacional de Cuba, to Julián Aliones, December 24, 1952, and Emeterio S. Santovenia, President, BANFAIC, to Joaquín Martínez Sáenz, President, Banco Nacional de Cuba, June 30, 1952, both in "Expediente que contiene correspondencia relativa entre otros asuntos al informe técnico-económico sobre la expansión de arroz," Fondo Banco Nacional de Cuba, Banco de Fomento Agrícola e Industrial de Cuba, Caja 735, Núm. 8, ANC.

75. William M. Reid to John Foster Dulles, February 23, 1953, Series D, RMAR.

76. Frank Godchaux to Loring K. Macy, June 3, 1953, Godchaux Family Papers.

77. "Otorga préstamos el BANFAIC a los productores del arroz," *Diario de la Marina*, January 28, 1953, 3. For the funding of early rice projects under Batista, see Banco de Fomento Agrícola e Industrial de Cuba, "Préstamos aprobados para la producción de arroz desde julio 1/52 a junio 30/53," in "Expediente que contiene correspondencia relativa entre otros asuntos al informe técnico-económico sobre la expansión de arroz," Fondo Banco Nacional de Cuba, Banco de Fomento Agrícola e Industrial de Cuba, Caja 735, Núm. 8, ANC.

78. Baeza, "Diversificación agrícola," 22–23.

79. Rodolfo Arango, "El problema del arroz en Cuba," *Rotary. Revista Mensual. Organo del Club Rotario de La Habana* 22 (August 1954): 58.

80. Frank Senior, "¿Cuáles son sus puntos de vista sobre la producción arrocera cubana?," *Diario de la Marina*, October 16, 1955, 1-D.

81. See the following in Fondo Banco Nacional de Cuba, Banco de Fomento Agrícola e Industrial de Cuba, ANC: "Expediente que contiene solicitudes de préstamos presentados al BANFAIC," 1952–1954, Caja 701, Núm. 1; "Expediente que trata sobre el movimiento de solicitudes de préstamos de la región oriental," 1956–1957, Legajo 861, Núm. 15; "Expediente que trata sobre el movimiento de solicitudes de préstamos de la región central," 1957–1958, Legajo 861, Núm. 9,; "Expediente que contiene estadísticas de las solicitudes de préstamos de la región occidential," 1956–1957, Legajo 861, Núm. 12.

82. Banco de Fomento Agrícola e Industrial de Cuba, *Memoria 1954–1955*, 36–37.

83. See Oscar Duyos Durruty, Vice-President, "Construcción molino arrocero—ACR 'La Trocha,'" September 11, 1956, "Expediente que trata otras cosas sobre préstamos y reglamentos de la cooperativa de arroz de la Asociación de Crédito Rural 'La Trocha,'" 1955–1957, Fondo Banco Nacional de Cuba, Banco de Fomento Agrícola e Industrial de Cuba, Legajo 856, Núm. 3, ANC.

84. The principal zones included Manzanillo, Campechuela, and Bayamo in Oriente; Florida, Camagüey, Ciego de Avila, San Cruz, and Morón in Camagüey; and Con-

solación del Sur, San Cristobal, and San Luis in Pinar del Río. See "Economía agraria en general: Producción arrocera," Junta Nacional de Economía, *Boletín Informativo* 3 (September–October 1954): 600; and Arango, "El problema del arroz en Cuba," 56.

85. For a thorough analysis of the development of rice production in Consolación del Sur, see María Beatriz Masó Fernández, "Rice Production in Consolación del Sur, Cuba" (M.A. thesis, Clark University, 1964). On the expansion of rice zones in Pinar del Río, see "Solicitud de crédito efectuada por arrocera Santa Isbel, S.A., a través de la Asociación de Crédito Rural 'Tranquilino Sandalio de Noda,' filial de BANFAIC," 1952–1958, Fondo Banco Nacional de Cuba, Banco de Fomento Agrícola e Industrial de Cuba, Legajo 1037, Núm. 3, ANC.

86. "Importancia del arroz en la economía cubana," *Cuba Económica y Financiera* 32 (June 1957): 33.

87. "Mecanizan siembre a arroz," *Diario de la Marina*, June 30, 1954, 20. For a case study of the founding of the Cía. Arrocera "La Sabana" in 1953 in Consolación del Sur, see "Solicitud de crédito efectuada por arrocera 'La Sabana," S.A., a través de la Asociación de Crédito Rural 'Tranquilino Sandalio de Noda,'" 1953; "Anexo: Informes adicionales," Fondo Banco Nacional de Cuba, Banco de Fomento Agrícola e Industrial de Cuba, Caja 1044, Núm. 44, ANC; and Bush, "Basic Cuban Rice Industry." Among the most prominent rice mills and plantations included Molino Arrocero Cajigas (Bayamo), Molinos Arroceros Los Palacios, Molina Arrocero de Caibarién, Arrocera Guanahacabibes, Arrocera Majagu, Arrocera Mariana, Arrocera Oriental, Arrocera Suprema Oriente, and Arrozal Bartés. See Jiménez, *Las empresas de Cuba 1958*, 45–46, 453–54, 504; and personal communication from Carlos Alzugaray to author, May 12, 2018.

88. Harold M. Randall to Department of State, April 2, 1953, 837.0/4–253, State Department Central Files: 1950–1954/RG 59.

89. "Miles de caballerías de tierrias baldías producen hoy millones en arroz y empleo a gran número de trabajdores," *Diario de la Marina*, November 7, 1953, 22.

90. "Otorga préstamos el BANFAIC a los productores del arroz," 3. On land values in Pinar del Río, see "Solicitud de crédito efectuada por arrocera Santa Isbel, S.A., a través de la Asociación de Crédito Rural 'Tranquilino Sandalio de Noda,' filial de BANFAIC."

91. International Bank for Reconstruction and Development, *Report on Cuba*, 854.

92. Camilo Sabí, "Informe final," September 9, 1952, Fondo Banco Nacional de Cuba, Banco de Fomento Agrícola e Industrial de Cuba, Legajo 1037, No. 3, ANC.

93. Fulgencio Batista, *The Growth and Decline of the Cuban Republic*, trans. Blas M. Rocafort (New York, 1964), 168.

94. Lowry Nelson, *Cuba: The Measure of a Revolution* (Minneapolis, 1972), 54. See also Guy L. Bush, Agricultural Attaché, "Cuban Rice Situation," 1955, 837.23127/3–955, State Department Central Files: 1955–1959/RG 59; Cuba, Ministerio de Agricultura, *Memoria del censo agrícola nacional* (Havana, 1946), 186–87; Rodolfo Arango, *Guía arrocera nacional* (Havana, 1954), 21–22; and Instituto Nacional de Reforma Económica, "El arroz cubano ante una grave encrucijada," 3.

95. Julián Alienes, Departamento de Investigaciones Económicas, Banco Nacional de Cuba, "Expansión de la producción arrocera," September 8, 1954, in "Expediente que contiene correspondencia relativa entre otros asuntos al informe técnico-económico sobre la expansión de arroz," Fondo Banco Nacional de Cuba, Banco de Fomento

Agrícola e Industrial de Cuba, Caja 735, Núm. 8, ANC; Alvarez Díaz, *Study on Cuba*, 536–37.

96. This information was contained in a confidential report commissioned by the Rice Millers Association, "Report on Rice in Cuba," December 1955, Series D, RMAR.

97. Instituto Nacional de Reforma Económica, "El arroz cubano ante una grave encrucijada," 1; Oscar Fonts y Acosta, "¿Que medida propone para evitar el colapso del cultivo del arroz?," *Diario de la Marina*, October 16, 1955, 1-D; Leonard H. Price to Department of State, October 12, 1956, 737.00 (W)/10–1256, State Department Central Files: 1955–1959/RG 59.

98. Antonio Pérez González, "Nacimiento, desarrollo y agonía de la industria arrocera cubana," *Diario de la Marina*, October 19, 1955, 7-B; Leopoldo Aguilera, President, and Mario Fuentes Aguilera, Secretary [Asociación Nacional de Cosecheros de Arroz], "En defensa de la producción nacional de arroz," *Diario de la Marina*, February 15, 1953, 36.

99. Bush, "Basic Cuban Rice Industry."

100. Chester E. Davis, "Cuban Rice Situation," August 13, 1954, 837.2317/8–1354, State Department Central Files: 1950–1954/RG 59; "Otorga préstamos el BANFAIC a los productores del arroz," 3; Banco de Fomento Agrícola e Industrial de Cuba, *Memoria 1954–1955*, 35–37; United Nations, Economic Commission for Latin America, *Economic Survey of Latin America 1954* (New York, 1955), 83–84, 162–63. For a representative example of credit arrangements, see Industria Arrocera de Mayabeque, "Informe en relación con el préstamo solicitado," April 13, 1955, in "Expediente relativo a la solicitud de préstamo formulado al BANFAIC por la Cía. Industrial Arrocera Mayabeque, S.A.," 1953–1955, Fondo Banco Nacional de Cuba, Banco de Fomento Agrícola e Industrial de Cuba, Caja 735, Núm. 13, ANC; Pérez González, "Nacimiento, desarrollo y agonía de la industria arrocera cubana," 7-B; and R. Nueva Veliz, "Logrado pleno éxito en ensayo arrocero," *El Mundo*, November 28, 1954, C-2.

101. Masó Fernández, "Rice Production in Consolación del Sur, Cuba," 27.

102. United Nations, Economic Commission for Latin America, *Economic Survey of Latin America 1954*, 83.

103. This information was contained in a confidential report commissioned by the Rice Millers Association, "Report on Rice in Cuba," December 1955, Series D, RMAR. See also *New York Times*, January 6, 1954, 69.

104. United Nations, Economic Commission for Latin America, *Economic Survey of Latin America 1953*, 168; Dudley Seers et al., *Cuba: The Economic and Social Revolution* (Chapel Hill, 1964), 76; Nueva Veliz, "Logrado pleno éxito en ensayo arrocero," C-2.

105. J. P. Gaines [Rice Millers Association] to John Foster Dulles and Ezra T. Benson, September 1, 1953, Series D, RMAR.

106. James J. Spadaro, Jack Matthews, and James I. Wadsworth, "Milling," in *Rice: Production and Utilization*, ed. Bor S. Luh (Westport, Conn., 1980), 361.

107. Quoted in Christopher M. Lee, "Organization for Survival: The Rice Industry and Protective Tariffs, 1921–1929," *Louisiana History: The Journal of the Louisiana Historical Association* 35 (Autumn 1994): 433–54.

108. "Regula el gobierno las clases y calidad del arroz importado," *Diario de la Marina*, June 28, 1955, 1-A, 18-A; "Explicó el Ministro de Comercio distribución de cuotas de arroz," *Diario de la Marina*, June 29, 1955, B-7, B-20.

109. See B. D. Webb, "Rice Quality and Grades," in *Rice: Production and Utilization*, ed. Bor S. Luh (Westport, Conn., 1980), 544–61; Dexter Rivenburg, "Analysis of Selected Varieties and Grades of Rice Moving in World Trade," in U.S. Department of Agriculture, Foreign Agricultural Service, *Marketing Research Report*, No. 460 (Washington, D.C., 1961); A. J. H. Latham, *Rice: The Primary Commodity* (London, 1998), 20–26; U.S. Department of Agriculture, *United States Standards for Rice* (Washington, D.C., 2009); and John Norman Efferson, *The Production and Marketing of Rice* (New Orleans, 1952), 106–7.

110. "El mercado cubano de arroz," 22–26. See also James J. Huckaby, "The Rice Industry and Cuba" (M.A. thesis, University of Southwestern Louisiana [University of Louisiana at Lafayette], 1969), 78.

111. Leonard H. Price to Department of State, October 12, 1956, 737.00 (W)/10-1256, State Department Central Files: 1955–1959/RG 59. See also Julián Alienes, Departamento de Investigaciones Económicas, Banco Nacional de Cuba, "Expansión de la producción arrocera," September 8, 1954, in "Expediente que contiene correspondencia relativa entre otros asuntos al informe técnico-económico sobre la expansión de arroz," Fondo Banco Nacional de Cuba, Banco de Fomento Agrícola e Industrial de Cuba, Caja 735, Núm. 8, ANC.

112. H. T. Andersen, "Annual Economic Review—Cuba," April 15, 1952, 837.00/4-552, State Department Central Files: 1950–1954/RG 59.

113. United Nations, Economic Commission for Latin America, *Economic Survey of Latin America 1951–1952* (New York, 1954), 155–56; United Nations, Economic Commission for Latin America, *Economic Survey of Latin America 1953*, 167.

114. The precise data for 1955 rice production is not altogether clear. *Cuba Económica y Financiera* in January 1957 indicates increases from 164,000 metric tons in 1954–53, to 172,000 metric tones in 1954–55, to 173,000 metric tons in 1955–56. In the October 1957 issue of *Cuba Económica y Financiera*, the production of rice for 1955 is given at 215,000 metric tons and at 250,000 metric tons for 1956. Alvarez Díaz suggested production for 1956 at 665.6 million pounds, accounting for 55.5 percent of total consumption needs. See "Cuba: Producción agrícola," *Cuba Económica y Financiera* 32 (January 1957): 29; "El comercio arrocero en Cuba," *Cuba Económica y Financiera* 32 (October 1957): 26; and Alvarez Díaz, *Study on Cuba*, 536–37.

115. John R. Nuber to William M. Reid, September 14, 1953, Series D, RMAR. Emphasis in original.

116. U.S. Department of Commerce, *Investment in Cuba*, 42.

117. Pérez González, "Nacimiento, desarrollo y agonía de la industria arrocera cubana," 7-B; Fonts y Acosta, "¿Qué medida propone para evitar el colapso del cultivo del arroz?" 1-D.

118. John H. Bradley, "The Cuban Rice Industry: An Interview with Senator Guillermo B. Aguilera," *Havana Post Magazine*, April 14, 1957, 4. See also Pérez González, "Nacimiento, desarrollo y agonía de la industria arrocera cubana," 7-B; and Miguel Penabad Fraga, "Tenemos que conquistar los millones de pesos que compramos en arroz," *Diario de la Marina*, February 19, 1953, 22, 23.

119. Bush, "Basic Cuban Rice Industry." Two years later economic attaché Chester Davis reported on "imports from the U.S. during the last three years of machinery, equipment and fertilizer in the amount of at least $25,000,000 for use in the preparation

of new land for rice, the production, harvesting and the milling of rice." See Chester E. Davis to Department of State, August 13, 1954, 837.2317/8-1354, State Department Central File: 1950–1954/RG 59.

120. "Insumo aparente, producción e importación de fertilizantes y abono químicos en Cuba," *Revista del Banco Nacional de Cuba* 5 (November–December 1959): 1229–34; Mario Arizi, "¿Cómo ha influido el cultivo del arroz en la industria de abonos?" *Diario de la Marina*, October 16, 1955, 1-D; United Nations, *Economic Survey of Latin America 1957* (New York, 1959), 194.

121. U.S. Department of Commerce, *Investment in Cuba*, 93.

122. Nelson, *Cuba*, 54–55.

123. See Industria Arrocera de Mayabeque, "Informe en relación con el préstamo solicitado," April 13, 1955, in "Expediente relativo a la solicitud de préstamo formulada al BANFAIC por la Cía. Industrial Arrocera Mayabeque, S.A."

124. Miguel A. Monzón, "La economía arrocera," *Cuba Económica y Financiera* 33 (February 1958): 17; Jiménez, *Las empresas de Cuba 1958*, 453–54. By the mid-1950s, a total of $10 million had been invested in rice mills.

125. "Cuban Rice Consumption Reported Higher," *Rice Millers Association Newsletter*, No. 5 (September 5, 1955): 3, Series D, RMAR.

126. The Cuban demand for enhanced milling capacities had its antecedents in the 1920s, in response to the food crisis occasioned by World War I. See "Memorandum sobre la industria de la elaboración de arroz en Cuba," June 20, 1924, Fondo Donativo y Remisiones, Legajo 400, Núm. 16, ANC. Other proposed projects related to expanding the milling of rice in Cuba are found in the file "Varios informes y datos estadísticos de la operación de convertir el paddy arroz limpio, listo para el consumo," Fondo Donativos y Remisiones, Legajo 400, No. 16, ANC.

127. César Masó, "La verdad sobre las importaciones de arroz en cáscara," *Bohemia* 50 (July 20, 1958): 86–88.

128. John R. Nuber to William M. Reid, March 12, 1951, Series D, RMAR. Emphasis in original. See John R. Nuber, "Cuban Situation," n.d., Series D, RMAR.

129. Marrero, "El arroz: Anomalía y promesa," A-6.

130. Aguilera and Fuentes Aguilera, "En defensa de la producción nacional de arroz," 36. See also "Importancia del arroz en la economía cubana," 33.

131. Arango, *Guía arrocera nacional*, 312–14.

132. "La feria del arroz," *Diario de la Marina*, March 19, 1950, 34.

133. E. B. Ogden Jr. to William M. Reid, May 28, 1954, Series D, RMAR.

134. "No se declará este año cuota de déficit en materia arrocera," *Diario de la Marina*, June 24, 1954, A-1.

135. "Habló el Ing. Arango en el club Rotrario del problema del arroz," *Diario de la Marina*, April 23, 1953, 23. See also "Necesidad de incrementar la producción de arroz," *Diario de la Marina*, February 20, 1953, 4-A.

136. "Trataron del gran incremento de la producción arrocero en Cuba," *Diario de la Marina*, June 25, 1954, 16-A.

137. "¿A qué se debió el auge del arroz en Cuba y cuáles son las dificultades presentes?," *Diario de la Marina*, October 16, 1955, 1-D

138. Bradley, "Cuban Rice Industry," 4. For an account of the rise of the Aguilera rice

plantations, see "Miles de caballerías de tierrias baldías producen hoy millones en arroz y empleo a gran número de trabajdores," 22.

139. Greitín, "¿Que sucede con el arroz?," 98.

140. "Trataron del gran incremento de la producción arrocero en Cuba," 16-A.

141. Aguilera and Fuentes Aguilera, "En defensa de la producción nacional de arroz," 36.

142. Harold M. Randall, "Observations on Eastern and Central Cuba," April 2, 1953, 837.004-253, State Department Central Files: 1950-1954/RG 59.

143. Juan de Zengotita to Department of State, June 15, 1955, 837.06/6-1555, State Department Central Files: 1955-1959/RG 59.

CHAPTER FIVE

1. "Cuba ante el GATT," Junta Nacional de Economía, *Boletín Informativo* 3 (November-December 1954): 641-44.

2. "El mercado cubano de arroz: Fuentes de abastecimiento, precios, producción y consumo," *Cuba Económica y Financiera*, April 1956, 22-26; United Nations, Economic Commission for Latin America, *Economic Survey of Latin America 1953* (New York, 1954), 167.

3. For the complete text of the agreement, see "U.S., Cuba Reach Agreement on Rice Tariff Quotas," *Department of State Bulletin* 29 (July 20, 1953): 82-84. For a discussion of the implications of GATT, see James J. Huckaby, "The Rice Industry and Cuba" (M.A. thesis, University of Southwestern Louisiana [University of Louisiana at Lafayette], 1969), 70-97. GATT was slightly modified in 1953.

4. Chester E. Davis to the State Department, February 18, 1955, 837.2317/2-1855, State Department Central Files: 1955-1959/RG 59.

5. "El mercado cubano de arroz," 22-26.

6. "El mercado cubano de arroz," 22-26; José R. Alvarez Díaz et al., *A Study on Cuba* (Coral Gables, 1965), 536-37.

7. See John Robert Moore, *Grist for the Mill: An Entrepreneurial History of Louisiana State Rice Milling Company, 1911-1965, River Brand Rice Milling Company, 1946-1965, and Riviana Foods, 1965-1999* (Lafayette, La., 2000), 158-67.

8. *Rice Millers Association Newsletter*, No. 1763 (May 22, 1953), Series D, RMAR.

9. "U.S. Rice Exports Show Uptrend," Department of Commerce, *Foreign Commerce Weekly* 51 (May 3, 1954): 21.

10. *Rice Millers Association Newsletter*, No. 1682 (May 12, 1951), Series D, RMAR.

11. Gordon E. Dore to Fred Entermille, October 18, 1952, Series D, RMAR. Rice broker E. B. Ogden advanced a similar argument: "Cuba should be treated exactly like Canada, Puerto Rico, Hawaiian Islands and the domestic market. It is the nearest thing to a domestic market that an export market can be unless encumbered by Government export restrictions." See E. B. Ogden Jr., "Memorandum in Regard to Allocations and Controls of Rice to Cuba," September 12, 1952, 837.2317/10-352, State Department Central File: 1950-1954/RG 59.

12. William M. Reid to Hale Boogs, October 5, 1954, Series D, RMAR.

13. William M. Reid, "Will the U.S. Rice Industry Commit Economic Suicide?," *Rice*

Millers Association Newsletter, No. 1840 (February 25, 1955), William R. Reid Papers, the Rice Archives, Edith Garland Dupré Library, Special Collections and Archives, University of Louisiana at Lafayette.

14. William M. Reid to John Foster Dulles, July 11, 1956, Series D, RMAR.

15. Clarence A. Boonstra to John R. Nuber, May 8, 1956, Series D, RMAR.

16. George B. Blair [American Rice Growers Cooperative Association] to Senator Allen J. Ellender, July 6, 1956, Series D, RMAR.

17. George B. Blair [American Rice Growers Cooperative Association] to Allen J. Ellender, August 17, 1956, Series D, RMAR.

18. John R. Nuber to William M. Reid, June 21, 1956, Series D, RMAR.

19. "The Rice Situation in Cuba," *Rice Millers Association Newsletter*, No. 1844 (March 25, 1955): 1–2, Reid Papers.

20. "Statement of William M. Reid, President, Rice Millers Association, New Orleans, La.," U.S. Congress, House of Representatives, *Hearings before a Subcommittee of the Committee on War and Means: Administration and Operation of Customs and Tariff Laws and the Trade Agreements Programs*, 84th Cong., 2nd Sess., Pt. 2 (Washington, D.C., 1956), 892–94.

21. Rice Millers Association, "Violations by Cuba of the General Agreement on Tariffs and Trade with Regard to Importations of Rice from the United States," n.d., Series D, RMAR.

22. John Nuber to William M. Reid, June 30, 1955, Series D, RMAR. Emphasis in original.

23. E. B. Ogden Jr. to Tyrrell Rice Milling Company, Beaumont, Texas, February 13, 1953, Series D, RMAR.

24. George B. Blair [American Rice Growers Cooperative Association] to Allen J. Ellender, July 6, 1956, Series D, RMAR.

25. William M. Reid to John Foster Dulles and Ezra Taft Benson, July 7, 1955, and July 8, 1955, Series D, RMAR. Resolution 98 in 1956 prompted U.S. ambassador Arthur Gardner to protest orally to the Cuban Ministry of Foreign Relations. See Arthur Gardner to Department of State, July 18, 1956, 737.00 (W)/7–1856, State Department Central Files: 1955–1959/RG 59; and Vinton Chaplin to Department of State, August 5, 1956, 737.00 (W)/18–856, State Department Central Files: 1955–1959/RG 59. Rice producers similarly protested to the congressional delegations of rice producing states. See J. E. Broussard [Beaumont Rice Mills] to Lyndon B. Johnson, July 13, 1955, Series D, RMAR.

26. William M. Reid to John Foster Dulles, July 11, 1956, Series D, RMAR.

27. "Cuban Rice Imports Restrictions," *Rice Millers Association Newsletter*, No. 1853 (June 30, 1955): 2, Reid Papers.

28. These included Senators Allen J. Ellender (chair, Senate Agriculture Committee); J. William Fulbright (Senate Foreign Relations Committee); Tom Connally (Senate Foreign Relations Committee); John McClellan (chair, Senate Appropriations Committee); Russell Long (Senate Finance Committee); Lyndon Johnson (Senate majority leader); James Eastland (chair, Senate Judiciary Committee); John Stennis (Senate Armed Services Committee); and Price Daniel (Senate Judiciary Committee). House members included E. C. Gathings (Agriculture Committee); Wilbur Mills (Ways and Means Committee); W. F. Norell (Appropriations Committee); F. Edward Hébert (Armed

Services Committee); Edwin E. Willis (Judiciary Committee); Albert Thomas (Appropriations Committee); Jack Brooks (Armed Services Committee); Brooks Hays, T. Ashton Thompson (Agriculture Committee); Jamie Whitten (Appropriations Committee); and Hale Boggs (Ways and Means Committee).

29. "U.S. Government Protests Cuban Restrictions on Cuba," *Rice Millers Association Newsletter*, No. 1881 (July 16, 1956): 1, Reid Papers.

30. Frank Godchaux to Allen J. Ellender, June 28, 1954, Godchaux Family Papers.

31. The Reid letter, dated July 11, 1956—the same date as the letter to Dulles—was addressed to the eight senators from Louisiana, Mississippi, Arkansas, and Texas, as well as all the House members representing southern rice-producing districts.

32. Allen J. Ellender to Rice Millers Association, July 11, 1956, Series D, RMAR. Senator Long also agreed to join Ellender to urge the State Department to protest Cuban restrictions. See Russell Long to William M. Reid, July 12, 1956, Series D, RMAR.

33. Allen J. Ellender to Frank A. Godchaux, June 30, 1954, Godchaux Family Papers.

34. Frank A. Godchaux to Allen J. Ellender, July 5, 1954, Godchaux Family Papers.

35. William M. Reid to Allen Ellender, December 6, 1954, Series D, RMAR. (The same letter was sent to all the senators from Arkansas, Louisiana, Mississippi, and Texas, and to each House member representing rice-producing districts.)

36. William M. Reid to Hale Boggs, October 5, 1954, Series D, RMAR.

37. "Statement of William M. Reid, President, Rice Millers Association, New Orleans, La.," 892–94.

38. William M. Reid to John Minor Wisdom, November 2, 1954, Series D, RMAR.

39. William M. Reid to Hale Boggs, August 25, 1954, Series D, RMAR.

40. Fletcher H. Rawls to William M. Reid, November 23, 1954, Series D, RMAR.

41. Fletcher H. Rawls to J. P. Gaines [Rice Millers Association], August 12, 1955, Series D, RMAR.

42. Thruston B. Morton to Hale Boggs, September 20, 1954, Series D, RMAR.

43. Thruston B. Morton to Allen J. Ellender, August 27, 1954, Series D, RMAR.

44. Memorandum by Harvey R. Wellman, Office of Middle American Affairs, to Deputy Assistant Secretary of State of Inter-American Affairs Robert F. Woodward, July 26, 1954, in Department of State, *Foreign Relations of the United States, 1952–1954: The American Republics* (Washington, D.C., 1983), 4:913.

45. Amelia Hood, "Memorandum of Conversation: Cuba's Partial Non-compliance with Low-Duty Provisions of Rice Agreement," October 14, 1954, 837.2317/9–2854, State Department Central Files: 1950–1954/RG 59.

46. Chester E. Davis to Department of State, July 23, 1954, 837.2317/7–2354, State Department Central Files: 1950–1954/RG 59.

47. Chester E. Davis to Department of State, August 13, 1954, 837.2317/8–1354, State Department Central Files: 1950–1954/RG 59.

48. John Foster Dulles to Arthur Gardner, January 10, 1955, 837.2317/1–1055, State Department Central Files: 1955–1959/RG 59.

49. Thruston B. Morton to Hale Boggs, September 20, 1954, Series D, RMAR.

50. John Foster Dulles to Ezra Taft Benson, June 4, 1954, in Department of State, *Foreign Relations of the United States, 1952–1954*, 4:900–902.

51. John Foster Dulles, "Memorandum by the Secretary of State to the President,"

June 7, 1954, in Department of State, *Foreign Relations of the United States, 1952–1954*, 4:902.

52. Fletcher H. Rawls to William M. Reid, June 1, 1954, Series D, RMAR. The propriety of this conversation was very much on Rawls's mind, and he urged Reid "to keep this communication out of your files."

53. Gerald Doyle to J. P. Gaines [Rice Millers Association], October 6, 1955, Series D, RMAR.

54. Frank Godchaux to Allen J. Ellender, June 28, 1954, Godchaux Family Papers.

55. Cyril R. C. Laan to Russell B. Long, October 26, 1954, Series D, RMAR.

56. *Rice Millers Association Newsletter*, No. 1813 (June 24, 1954), Series D, RMAR.

57. *Congressional Record*, August 2, 1955, 12850, 12851–852. See Thomas A. Becnel, "Fulbright of Arkansas v. Ellender of Louisiana: The Politics of Sugar and Rice, 1937–1974," *Arkansas Historical Quarterly* 43 (Winter 1984): 297–98.

58. Allen J. Ellender to John Foster Duller, July 9, 1956, 837.2317/7-956, State Department Central Files: 1955–1959/RG 59.

59. "Text of Radio Address Recorded by Senator Allen J. Ellender of Louisiana," July 14, 1956, Series D, RMAR.

60. Antonio González López, "Negociaciones en Estados Unidos de la cuota deficitaria de arroz," November 12, 1954, and Miguel Angel Campa, Minister of State, to Joaquín Martínez Sáenz, President of the Banco Nacional, January 25, 1955, both in "Expediente que contiene correspondencia relativa entre otros asuntos al informe técnico-económico sobre la expansión de arroz," Fondo Banco Nacional de Cuba, Banco de Fomento Agrícola e Industrial de Cuba, Caja 735, Núm. 8, ANC.

61. Harvey Wellman, "Memorandum of Conversation: Rice and Sugar Problems with Cuba," April 6, 1954, 837.2317/4-654, State Department Central Files: 1950–1954/RG 59.

62. "Memorandum of Conversation: Resumption of Cuban-U.S. Rice Discussions and Possibility of Announcement of Supplementary Low-Duty Quota for 1954-55 Quota Year," April 29, 1955, 837.2317/3-2955, State Department Central Files: 1955–1959/RG 59.

63. John Foster Dulles to Arthur Gardner, April 7, 1954, 837.2317/4-654, State Department Central Files: 1950–1954/RG 59.

64. John Foster Dulles to Arthur Gardner, June 28, 1954, 837.2317/6-2554, State Department Central Files: 1950–1954/RG 59.

65. Harvey Wellman to Robert Woodward, June 28, 1954, 837.2317/6-2854, State Department Central Files: 1950–1954/RG 59. In Havana, economic affairs counselor Clarence Boonstra wrote in September 1955, "The Embassy has discussed this matter frequently with representatives of the Cuban Government in an effort to obtain ... revocation of the restrictive measures." Mention was also made, Boonstra reported, "of the impact on public and congressional opinion in the U.S. of the rice restriction at a time when sugar legislation may soon again be a subject for discussion." See Clarence A. Boonstra to State Department, September 27, 1955, 837.2317/9-2755, State Department Central Files: 1955–1959/RG 59.

66. "Combatirá en el senado americano la adquisición de azúcar cubano," *El Mundo*, November 24, 1954, A-1.

67. "Prepara el Senador Ellender otra ofensiva contra el azúcar cubano," *Diario de la Marina*, November 24, 1954, A-1, B-16. The same article included a report indicating

that the government of the Philippine Islands had supported the United States in reducing the Cuban quota.

68. U.S. Congress, Senate, "Senate Bill 1635: To Amend and Extend the Sugar Act of 1948," 84th Cong., 1st Sess., March 10, 1955; "H.R. Bill 5402: To Amend and Extend the Sugar Act of 1948," U.S. Cong., House of Representatives, 84th Cong., 1st Sess.

69. U.S. Congress, Senate, *Hearings before the Committee on Finance, Sugar Act Extension*, January 16 and 17, 1956, 84th Cong., 2nd Sess. (Washington, D.C., 1956), 243.

70. Asociación Nacional de Hacendados, "Our Rice Production Is Subject to International Limits," *Alerta*, February 9, 1953 (English translation found in Series D, RMAR).

71. "Desea conocer el colonato las medidas de las cuotas de arroz," *Diario de la Marina*, January 16, 1958, 1-A, 14-A.

72. A. Valdés Rodríguez, Executive Director, Asociación Nacional de Proveedores e Importadores de Víveres, to Fulgencio Batista, January 27, 1953, published as "Importadores de arroz recaban urgencia en el abastecimiento," *Diario de la Marina*, January 30, 1953, 2.

73. Alberto León Riva, "Arroz y azúcar: Defensa de cuotas y mercados," *El Mundo*, April 6, 1954, A-10.

74. Alejandro Suero Falla to Joaquín Martínez Sáenz, President, Banco Nacional de Cuba, September 21, 1954, in "Expediente que contiene correspondencia relativa entre otros asuntos al informe técnico-económico sobre la expansión de arroz."

75. John R. Nuber to J. P. Gaines, August 25, 1955, Series D, RMAR.

76. John R. Nuber to J. P. Gaines, September 3, 1955, Series D, RMAR.

77. John Nuber to William M. Reid, February 14, 1953, Series D, RMAR. Emphasis in original.

78. "Report on Rice in Cuba," unpublished manuscript, December 1955, Series D, RMAR.

79. William M. Reid to Fletcher H. Rawls, June 29, 1951, Series D, RMAR.

80. Frank A. Godchaux to Allen J. Ellender, July 5, 1954, Godchaux Family Papers.

81. Gerald P. Doyle to Joseph Dore and Clark Smith, August 27, 1955, Series D, RMAR.

82. "Text of Cuban-U.S. Memorandum on Economic and Trade Relations," Department of Commerce, *Foreign Commerce Weekly* 52 (November 29, 1954): 7–8. A slightly different account of this meeting was reported as "U.S.-Cuban Discussions on Economic Relations," *Department of State Bulletin* 31 (November 29, 1954): 815–16. See also Alberto León Riva, "Arroz amargo en Washington," *El Mundo*, November 24, 1954, A-12.

83. Joaquín Martínez Sáenz, *Por la independencia económica de Cuba: Mi gestión en el Banco Nacional* (Havana, 1959), 55, 142.

84. "Cuba produjo en esta cosecha 2 millones de quintales de arroz," *Diario de la Marina*, January 7, 1951, 3.

85. "Lo que opina el 'Diario,'" *Diario de la Marina*, October 16, 1955, 1-D.

86. Terrance G. Leonhardy, "Memorandum of Conversation: Cuban Political Situation and Other Matters," January 6, 1958, 737.00/1–2058, State Department Central Files: 1955–1959/RG 59.

87. "Núñez Portuondo contesta de modo justo a Ellender," *Diario de la Marina*, July 17, 1956, 1-A, 12-A.

88. "El arroz cubano es igual o superior al norteamericano," *Diario de la Marina*, October 12, 1955, 16-B.

89. "Ellender enemigo público número uno de Cuba," *Bohemia* 46 (November 26, 1954): 65.

90. "Es tildado de colonialista Mr. Ellender," *Diario de la Marina*, July 19, 1956, 20-A. See also "Ellender Raked over the Coal by Angry Cuban Senator," *Havana Post*, July 19, 1956, 1.

91. "Cosecheros de arroz refutan los infundios del senador Ellender," *Diario de la Marina*, July 18, 1956, 3-A.

92. Julián Alienes, Departamento de Investigaciones Económicas, Banco Nacional de Cuba, "Expansión de la producción arrocera," September 8, 1954, in "Expediente que contiene correspondencia relativa entre otros asuntos al informe técnico-económico sobre la expansión de arroz."

93. "Cuba ha sacado 220 milliones de sus reservas para mantener un comercio libre con E.U.—Machado," *Diario de la Marina*, February 10, 1955, 1-A, 8-B.

94. "Principales alimentos importadoes de los EE. UU. de América," *Cuba Económica y Financiera* 33 (May 1958): 15.

95. Leonard H. Price to Department of State, April 17, 1957, 837.00/4–1759, State Department Central Files: 1955–1959/RG 59.

96. *Gaceta Oficial de la República de Cuba*, June 11, 1958, 88765; "Cuota deficitaria de arroz para 1958/59," *Revista del Banco Nacional de Cuba* 4 (August 1958): 182; "Cuota deficitaria de arroz por 500,000 quintales," *Cuba Económica y Financiera* 33 (January 1958): 6; "Cuota deficitaria de arroz," *Cuba Económica y Financiera* 33 (June 1958): 5.

97. Andrés Bianchi, "Agriculture," in *Cuba: The Economic and Social Revolution*, ed. Dudley Seers et al. (Chapel Hill, 1964), 73.

98. John R. Nuber to William M. Reid, June 29, 1958, Series D, RMAR.

99. Raúl Cepero Bonilla, "Actualidad económica," *Carteles* 37 (January 1, 1956): 24.

100. Chester E. Davis to Harold M. Randall, May 27, 1955, 837.2317/9–2055, State Department Central Files: 1955–1959/RG 59.

101. Oscar Pino Santos, "¿Quieren arruinar en Cuba la producción arrocera?," *Carteles* 37 (January 8, 1957): 50.

102. *New York Times*, January 5, 1956, C-78.

103. Pino Santos, "¿Quieren arruinar en Cuba la producción arrocera?," 50.

104. Frank Senior, "¿Cuales son sus puntos de vista sobre la producción arrocera cubana?" *Diario de la Marina*, October 16, 1955, 1-D.

105. Rafael Fanjul to A. García Alvarez, Jefe de Créditos, BANFAIC, n.d., in "Expediente relativo a la solicitud de préstamo formulado al BANFAIC por la Cía. Industrial Arrocera Mayabeque, S.A.," 1953–1955, Fondo Banco Nacional de Cuba, Banco de Fomento Agrícola e Industrial de Cuba, Caja 735, Núm. 13, ANC.

106. "Se arruinará la industria del arroz si no la ayuda el Estado," *Diario de la Marina*, September 30, 1955, 20-B.

107. "Lo que opina el 'Diario,'" 1-D.

108. Antonio Pérez González, "Nacimiento, desarrollo y agonía de la industria arrocera cubana," *Diario de la Marina*, October 19, 1955, 7-B. María Beatriz Masó Fernández reported learning during her field research in Consolación del Sur that in 1954 major rice distributors in Cuba accepted U.S. imports at "dumping" prices that "produced a

fall in the price." See María Beatriz Masó Fernández, "Rice Production in Consolación del Sur, Cuba" (M.A. thesis, Clark University, 1964), 96.

109. Pino Santos, "¿Quieren arruinar en Cuba la producción arrocera?," 92.

110. "Economic Developments in Cuba," U.S. Department of Commerce, World Trade Information Service, *Economic Reports*, No. 58-25, 1958, 5. See also "La industria arrocera mundial," *Cuba Económica y Financiera* 32 (November 2957): 26.

111. Hermanos Alfonso, Cosecheros Industriales de Arroz, to Joaquín Martínez Sáenz, President, Banco Nacional de Cuba, April 23, 1954, in "Expediente que contiene correspondencia relativa entre otros asuntos al informe técnico-económico sobre la expansión de arroz."

112. Oscar Fonts y Acosta, "¿Que medida propone para evitar el colapso del cultivo del arroz?," *Diario de la Marina*, October 16, 1955, 1-D.

113. See A. García Alvarez, Jefe de Créditos, BANFAIC, to Rafael Fanjul to March 29, 1955, in "Expediente relativo a la solicitud de préstamo formulado al BANFAIC por la Cía. Industrial Arrocera Mayabeque, S.A."; and "Solicitud de crédito efectuada al BANFAIC por la Administración del Arroz," 1956–1961, Fondo Banco Nacional de Cuba, Banco de Fomento Agrícola e Industrial de Cuba, Legajo 1037, Núm. 22, ANC.

114. Pino Santos, "¿Quieren arruinar en Cuba la producción arrocera?," 50.

115. See "Expediente relativo al procedimiento judicial seguido contra la compañía arrocera 'San Juan,' S.A., por el Banco de Fomento Agrícola e Industrial de Cuba por deuda refaccionaria," Fondo Banco Nacional de Cuba, Banco de Fomento Agrícola e Industrial de Cuba, Caja 1103, Núm. 2, ANC; and Pino Santos, "¿Quieren arruinar en Cuba la producción arrocera?," 50, 92.

116. Fonts y Acosta, "¿Que medida propone para evitar el colapso del cultivo del arroz?," 1-D; Pino Santos, "¿Quieren arruinar en Cuba la producción arrocera?," 50.

117. Pino Santos, "¿Quieren arruinar en Cuba la producción arrocera?," 92–93.

118. Angel Suárez and Julio Sánchez, "Memorandum al Dr. Gonzalo del Cristo, Vice-Presidente del Banco de Fomento Agrícola e Industrial de Cuba," November 24, 1955, in "Solicitud de credito efectuada al BANFAIC por la Arrocera Majana, S.A.," 1952–1957, Fondo Banco Nacional de Cuba, Banco de Fomento Agrícola e Industrial de Cuba, Caja 1038, Núm. 5, ANC.

119. "Lo que opina el 'Diario,'" 1-D.

120. "Report on Rice in Cuba," unpublished manuscript, December 1955, Series D, RMAR. Copy of the memorandum was obtained by the Rice Millers Association representative in Havana.

121. Chester E. Davis to Harold M. Randall, May 27, 1955, 837.2317/9-2055, State Department Central Files: 1955–1959/RG 59. For an account of failures in Oriente province, see Colonel Alberto del Río Chaviano to Gonzlo del Cristo, Vice-President, Agricultural Division BANFAIC, October 3, 1957, "Expediente que trata otras cosas sobre préstamos y reglamentos de la cooperativa de arroz de la Asociación de Crédito Rural 'La Trocha,'" 1955–1957, Fondo Banco Nacional de Cuba, Banco de Fomento Agrícola e Industrial de Cuba, Legajo 856, Núm. 3, ANC. Colonel Río Chaviano was at the time commander of the Moncada Barracks.

122. *El Mundo*, April 17, 1954, A-8.

123. Fonts y Acosta, "¿Que medida propone para evitar el colapso del cultivo del arroz?," 1-D.

124. "Hay en Cuba bastante arroz para el consumo, hasta el 30 de junio," *Diario de la Marina*, April 4, 1955, 2.

125. Pino Santos, "¿Quieren arruinar en Cuba la producción arrocera?," 46; "La situación del arroz," *Notas Económicas* 1 (November 1956): 5–7.

EPILOGUE

1. U.S. Department of Commerce, *Investment in Cuba: Basic Information for United States Businessmen* (Washington, D.C., 1956), 75.

2. See *Gaceta Oficial de la República de Cuba*, August 14, 1952, 1.

3. J. J. O'Connor to Assistant Secretary of State E. G. Miller, October 17, 1952, 837.319/10–1752, State Department Central Files: 1950–1954/RG 59.

4. Norman Draper to Secretary of State, November 18, 1952, 837.319/11–1852, State Department Central Files: 1950–1954/RG 59; A. W. Gilliam to John Foster Dulles, February 17, 1954, 837.51/2–1754, State Department Central Files: 1950–1954/RG 59.

5. Thomas C. Mann to Willard L. Beaulac, January 1953, 837.319/12–1052, State Department Central Files: 1950–1954/RG 59.

6. See Guillermo Jiménez, *Las empresas de Cuba 1958* (Havana, 2004), 287.

7. W. P. Bomar to Carl D. Corse, September 9, 1949, 837.6584/9–1249, Diplomatic Post Records: 1930–1945/RG 59.

8. E. W. Reed to R. Bolling, February 20, 1950, 837.313/15–1250, State Department Central Files: 1950–1954/RG 59.

9. W. P. Bomar to Dean Acheson, August 20, 1949, 837.313/11–1249, State Department Central Files: 1945–1949/RG 59.

10. E. W. Reed to R. Bolling, February 20, 1950, 837.313/15–1250, State Department Central File: 1950–1954/RG 59.

11. U.S. Congress, Senate, *Hearings before the Committee on Finance: Sugar Act Extension*, 84th Cong., 2nd Sess., January 15 and 17, 1956 (Washington, D.C., 1956), 285. For a brief description of the Burrus mill, see Jiménez, *Las empresas de Cuba 1958*, 454.

12. See U.S. Department of Commerce, *Investment in Cuba*, 78.

13. U.S. Congress, Senate, *Hearings before the Committee on Finance: Sugar Act Extension*, 284.

14. U.S. Congress, Senate, 285, 287.

15. *Congressional Record*, Senate, May 13, 1957, 6798–99. For Cuban reaction to Carlson's threat, see "Nuevos ataques injustos contra Cuba," *Diario de la Marina*, May 15, 1957, 4-A.

16. *Congressional Record*, Senate, May 31, 1957, p. 8143.

17. Philip Bonsal to Department of State, April 15, 1959, in Department of State, *Foreign Relations of the United States, 1958–1960*, 19 vols. (Washington, D.C., 1986–96), 6:466 (hereafter cited as *FRUS: 1958–1960*).

18. "Memorandum of Conversation," February 12, 1959, 737.00/2–1359, Confidential U.S. State Department Central Files, Cuba, 1955–1959, General Records of the Department of State, Record Group 59, National Archives.

19. E. A. Gilmore to Department of State, November 9, 1959, 837.20/11-959, Confidential U.S. State Department Central Files, Cuba, 1955-1959, General Records of the Department of State, Record Group 59, National Archives.
20. Fidel Castro, *Pensamiento de Fidel Castro: Selección temática*, 2 vols. (Havana, 1983), 1:5, 7.
21. Regino G. Boti and Felipe Pazos, "Algunos aspectos del desarrollo económico de Cuba: 'Tesis del Movimiento Revolucionario 26 de Julio,'" *Revista Bimestre Cubana* 75 (2nd Semester 1958): 256-57.
22. Jeffrey J. Safford, "The Nixon-Castro Meeting of 19 April 1959," *Diplomatic History* 4 (Fall 1980): 430.
23. "Discurso pronunciado ante el pueblo congregado en el Palacio Presidencial para reafirmas su apoyo al gobierno revolucionario y como protesta contra la cobarde agresión perpetrada contra el pacífico pueblo de La Habana por aviones procedentes de territorio extranjero," October 26, 1959, Discursos e intervenciones del Comandante en Jefe Fidel Castro Ruz, Presidente del Consejo de Estado de la República de Cuba, http://www.cuba.cu/gobierno/discursos/.
24. "Statement of ... Honorable Thomas C. Mann, Assistant Secretary of State for Economic Affairs," U.S. Congress, Senate, *Executive Sessions of the Senate Foreign Relations Committee*, 86th Cong., 2nd Sess., 1960 (Washington, D.C., 1982), 134.
25. E. A. Gilmore to Department of State, November 9, 1959, 837.20/11-959, Confidential U.S. State Department Central Files, Cuba, 1955-1959, General Records of the Department of State, Record Group 59, National Archives. See also Nivio López Pellón, "Sembrando arroz se han salvado miles de caballerías," *Bohemia* 51 (April 12, 1959): 70-72, 110, 111.
26. "Elevadas importaciones de arroz," *Cuba Económica y Financiera* 34 (October 1959): 24.
27. *Gaceta Oficial de la República de Cuba*, March 5, 1959, 32949; Francisco Pérez Barbosa, "Para su cumplimiento cursa la aduana el decreto No. 647," *Diario de la Marina*, March 17, 1959, 17-A; "Acuerdos del Consejo," *Revolución*, March 4, 1959, 14; "Amparó a los cosecheros de arroz la Revolución 10," *Revolución*, March 11, 1959, 13.
28. *Gaceta Oficial de la República de Cuba*, March 16, 1959, 47532.
29. Rice Millers Association to Senator J. William Fulbright et al., March 18, 1959, Series D, RMAR. The telegram was also sent to Senator Allen J. Ellender and Representatives E. C. Gathings, T. A. Thompson, Harold McSween, and Clark Thompson.
30. William M. Reid to Allen J. Ellender, March 24, 1959, Series D, RMAR.
31. William M. Reid to John Foster Dulles, March 12, 1959, Series D, RMAR.
32. Claude R. Miller, President, Comet Rice Mills, to Committee for Reciprocity Information, Tariff Commission, September 1, 1959, Series D, RMAR.
33. "La importación de productos agrícolas," *Cuba Económica y Financiera* 34 (August 1959): 15. See also Laura J. Enríquez, *The Question of Food Security in Cuban Socialism* (Berkeley, 1994), 12-22.
34. "Elevadas importaciones de arroz," 24.
35. Francisco Dorta-Duque, *Justificando una reforma agraria. Estudio analítico-descriptivo de las estructuras agrarias en Cuba* (Madrid, 1959), 6, 9. The agrarian reform also redistributed the land concentrations that had developed around rice production.

The 10,000-acre Aguilera rice plantation was reorganized into cooperatives. See Antero Regalado, "La cooperativa 'René Almanza,'" *Hoy Domingo*, June 5, 1960, 6–7.

36. Kathryn H. Wylie and Gae Bennett, "What Has Happened to Our Trade with Cuba?," *Foreign Agriculture* 25 (December 1961): 8–10.

37. Thomas C. Mann to Christian A. Herter, October 29, 1960, *FRUS: 1958–1960*, 1091.

38. Roy R. Rubottom Jr. to Christian A. Herter, May 11, 1960, *FRUS: 1958–1960*, 912.

39. Lester D. Mallory to R. Roy Rubottom Jr., April 6, 1960, *FRUS: 1958–1960*, 885. Rice was initially at the center of sanctions. "There was a point where food was needed," recalled Mallory years later, "and they needed rice. I proposed that we stop all shipments of rice to Cuba. The powers that be said no, 'Senator Ellender is from Louisiana, and we can't cross him,' so we didn't stop the rice." See "Interview with Lester Mallory," November 18, 1988, Library of Congress, The Foreign Affairs Oral History Collection of the Association for Diplomatic Studies and Training, http://memory.loc.gov/ammem/collections/diplomacy/.

40. A. J. Goodpaster, "Memorandum of a Conference with the President," January 25, 1960, *FRUS: 1958–1960*, 764.

41. "Nuevas fuentes de abastecimiento de arroz," *Cuba Económica y Financiera* 35 (August–October 1960): 11; *New York Times*, November 16, 1960, 8.

42. Henry C. Dethloff, *A History of the American Rice Industry, 1685–1985* (College Station, Tex., 1988), 180. See also "U.S. Sells More Rice Despite Cuban Decline," *Foreign Agriculture* 24 (November 1961): 23.

43. William R. Reid to John R. Nuber, October 12, 1960, Series D, RMAR.

44. "U.S. Sells More Rice Despite Cuban Decline," 23.

45. "U.S. Rice in World Trade," *Foreign Agriculture* 8 (March 9, 1970): 4.

46. U.S. Congress, House of Representatives, Committee on Agriculture, "Agricultural Trade Development and Assistance Act of 1954," 83rd Cong., 2nd Sess., Report No. 1776 (Washington, D.C., 1954), 11.

47. See U.S. Congress, Senate, *Hearing before the Committee on Foreign Relations, International Food for Peace*, 86th Cong., 1st Sess. (Washington, D.C., 1959).

48. "Interview with Hubert Matos," April 23, 2008, May 1, 2008, and May 7, 2008, Luis J. Botifoll Oral History Project, Cuban Heritage Collection, University of Miami Libraries, https://merrick.library.miami.edu/cdm/compoundobject/collection/chc5212/id/535/rec/44.

49. See Renato Recio de Quesada, "Memorandum: Préstamos arroceras," July 6, 1961, Fondo Banco Nacional de Cuba, Banco de Fomento Agrícola e Industrial de Cuba, Legajo 1040, Núm. 8, ANC; and Salustiano R. Valdivia and José Rodríguez to Nelson Martí, Jefe de Créditos, Oficina Regional de BANFAIC, November 22, 1961, Fondo Banco Nacional de Cuba, Banco de Fomento Agrícola e Industrial de Cuba, Legajo 1040, Núm. 8, ANC.

50. Partido Comunista de Cuba, *Resistir y vencer: Programa alimentario* (Havana, 1991), 29–30.

51. Medea Benjamin et al., *No Free Lunch: Food and Revolution in Cuba Today* (San Francisco, 1984), 136.

52. Fred Ward, "Inside Cuba Today," *National Geographic* 151 (January 1977): 67.

53. John R. Nuber to William R. Reid, October 24, 1960, Series D, RMAR.
54. See Benjamin et al., *No Free Lunch*, 26–39.
55. Nancy Forster and Howard Handelman, "Food Production and Distribution in Cuba: The Impact of the Revolution," in *Food, Politics, and Society in Latin America*, ed. John C. Super and Thomas C. Wright (Lincoln, Neb., 1985), 193; Leon G. Mears, "Cuba's Agriculture: Four Years under the Revolutionary Regime," *Foreign Agriculture* 1 (January 7, 1963): 4–6.
56. Oscar Lewis, Ruth M. Lewis, and Susan Rigdon, *Four Men: Living the Revolution. An Oral History of Contemporary Cuba* (Urbana, 1977), 248.
57. See Linda A. Bernstein, "Cuba's Record Sugar Output—and What It Cost to Attain It," *Foreign Agriculture* 5 (November 23, 1970): 6–8.
58. Benjamin, *No Free Lunch*, 130; Enrique Pérez Marín and Eduardo Muñoz Baños, *Agricultura y alimentación en Cuba* (Havana, 1991); Sergio Roca, *Cuban Economic Policy: The Ten Million Ton Sugar Harvest* (Beverly Hills, 1976); Archibald R. M. Ritter, "Economy: Special Period," in *Cuba*, ed. Alan West Durán et al., 2 vols. (Detroit, 2012), 1:232–241.
59. See Rita De Maeseneer, *Devorando a lo cubano. Una aproximación gastrocrítica a textos relacionados con el siglo XIX y el Período Especial* (Madrid, 2012), 157–239; Comisión Económica para América Latina y el Caribe, *La economía cubana. Reformas estructurales y desempeño en los noventa* (Mexico City, 1997), 212–17.
60. Arturo Rodríguez-Ojea, Santa Jiménez, Antonio Berdasco, and Mercedes Esquivel, "The Nutrition Transition in Cuba in the Nineties: An Overview," *Public Health Nutrition* 5 (2002): 130
61. Comisión Económica para América Latina y el Caribe, *La economía cubana*, 220; Efe Can Gürcan, "Cuban Agriculture and Food Sovereignty," *Latin American Perspectives* 41 (July 2014): 132.
62. José García de Arboleya, *Manual de la Isla de Cuba. Compendio de su historia, geografía, estadística y administración*, 2nd ed. (Havana, 1859), 264.
63. Alex Fleites, "Ajiaco," in *Canta lo sentimental* (Havana, 2012), 43–45.
64. Comisión Económica para América Latina y el Caribe, *La economía cubana*, 223.
65. Larry Luxner, "Rice Exporters See Tremendous Market in Cuba," October 2002, http://www.luxner.com/cgi-bin/view_article.cgi?articleID=1028.
66. See "Crece el arroz en tierras tuneras," *Trabajadores*, August 31, 2009, 9; "Para que más arroz llegue a la mesa," *Trabajadores*, December 13, 2010, 8; "Los arroceros de Granma esperan no cometer los errores del 2010," *Granma*, March 16, 2011, 1; "La urgencia de la cosecha arrocera," *Granma*, September 5, 2011, 8; "Deudas en el arroz," *Trabajadores*, January 23, 2012, 9; "Arroz con incertidumbre," *Granma*, February 24, 2012, 16; "Producción arrocera en el sur del Jíbaro, Sancti-Spíritus," *Granma*, November 30, 2012, 16; "Producción de arroz en Granma: La planificación es esencial," *Granma*, January 25, 2013, 16.
67. See Department of the Treasury, "Trade Sanctions Reform and Export Enhancement Act of 2000 (TSRA) Program," http://www.treasury.gov/services/Pages/tsra.aspx; and U.S. Department of Agriculture, International Agricultural Trade Report, "U.S. Agricultural Exports to Cuba Have Substantial Room for Growth," June 22, 2015, https://www.fas.usda.gov/data/us-agricultural-exports-cuba-have-substantial-room-growth.

68. Department of Agriculture, International Agricultural Trade Report, "U.S. Agricultural Exports to Cuba Have Substantial Room for Growth."

69. "Cuba to Invest $450 Million to Boost Rice Production," *Latin American Herald Tribune*, 2016, http://laht.com/article.asp?ArticleId=504979&CategoryId=14510.

70. See Guillermo Jiménez, "Food: Revolutionary Period," in *Cuba*, ed. Alan West Durán et al., 2 vols. (Detroit, 2012), 1:356.

71. "Food Imports Put Cuban Reforms at Risk," July 28, 2011, UPI, https://www.upi.com/Food-imports-put-Cuban-reforms-at-risk/86631311867969/.

72. "Rice Group Hopeful of Cuba Sales," April 16, 2001, Delta Farm Press, http://deltafarmpress.com/rice-group-hopeful-cuba-sales; Mary Murray, "Who Needs Cuba Now: U.S. Rice Farmers Say Politics Is Hurting Their Business," MSNBC, 2001, http://freerepublic.com/tag/editorial-news/index?more=553426.

73. U.S. Congress, House of Representatives, *Hearing to Review U.S. Agricultural Sales to Cuba*, 111th Cong., 2nd Sess., March 11, 2010 (Washington, D.C., 2010).

74. Randy Haynie, "Embargo Injures American South," 2006, National Summit http://www.nationalsummitoncuba.org/.

75. Dow Brantley, "Bringing US Rice Back to Cuba," 2016, USA Rice, https://www.usarice.com/cuba.

76. "Cuba Formally Accepts 20 Ton Shipment of Missouri Rice in Effort to Reestablish Trade Relationship," Fox 4KC.COM, May 30, 2016, http://fox4kc.com/2016/05/30/cuba-formally-accepts-20-ton-shipment-of-missouri-rice-in-effort-to-re-establish-trade-relationship/.

77. Marc Frank, "Cuba Slashes Imports amid Ongoing Cash Crunch," *CubaVerdad: News and Facts about Cuba*, October 15, 2002, http://groups.yahoo.com/group/CubaVerdad/message/4399?var=0.

78. Cuba Trade Magazine and the U.S. Agricultural Coalition for Cuba, "The Opportunities for U.S. Agricultural Exports to Cuba: A White Paper," *Cuba Trade*, September/October 2017, 37–38.

79. U.S. International Trade Commission, *U.S. Agricultural Sales to Cuba: Certain Economic Effects of U.S. Restrictions* (Washington, D.C., 2007), E-4.

80. See "Trade with Cuba: Growth and Opportunities: Testimony of Ray Stoesser on Behalf of US Rice Producers Association and Texas Rice Council before the Subcommittee on Terrorism, Nonproliferation, and Trade Committee on Foreign Affairs, U.S. House of Representatives," House Foreign Affairs Committee, March 15, 2016, https://foreignaffairs.house.gov/hearing/subcommittee-hearing-trade-with-cuba-growth-and-opportunities/.

81. Mark A. McMinimy, "U.S. Agricultural Trade with Cuba: Current Limitations and Future Prospects," *Congressional Research Service*, September 21, 2016, https://fas.org/sgp/crs/row/R44119.pdf.

Index

Page numbers in italics refer to figures.
Page numbers in italics followed by "t" refer to tables.

Abella Forcada, Ramona, 7, 13, 15–16
Adelina (Martin), 62
advertisements, 44, *128*, *133*, *160*, *171*, *173*, *176*
Africans, enslaved, 8, 36
Agrarian Reform, 175–77, 179, 235–36n35
agricultural extension programs, 25, 94–96, 122–23. *See also* rice: government programs for
agricultural production: background and overview of, 27, 29, 39; for consumption (*see* agriculture for consumption); in 2000s, 181; war for independence destruction of, 61–63; war for independence recovery of, 64–68. *See also* diversification of agriculture production; rice production in Cuba; sugar production in Cuba
Agricultural Trade Development and Assistance Act, 178
Agriculture, Cuban Department of, 78, 83, 95
Agriculture, U.S. Department of, 94, 99, 106, 145, 177, 181
agriculture for consumption: background and overview of, 22–23, 32–33, 43; in late nineteenth century, 48–50, 52–55, 59, 200–201n145; Machado reform and, 90–94; during and post–World War I, 75–76, 77–83; sugar collapse of 1950s and, 116, 117, 119, 127, 130–33, 137
agriculture reform: of 1959, 175–77, 235–36n35; of Batista, 105, 121, 124–25, 130–31, 132; of Machado, 90–94

agua de arroz, 14
Aguilera, Guillermo, 128, 133, 158
Aguilera, Leopoldo, 130
Aguilera rice plantation, 236n36
ajiaco, 3–4, 5, 8, 54, 180, 185n6, 186n16
"Ajiaco" (Fleites), 180
ajiaco, o la boda de Pancha Jutía y Canuto Raspadura, Un (Grangá), 4
a la criolla (term), 11–12
Alberto, Eliseo, 7
Alienes, Julián, 158
almuerzo criollo, 9
Alvarez, Josefina, 14
Alvarez, Marcelo, 3
Alvarez Díaz, José, 74, 90, 225n114
Ambarina (Auber), 13, 30, 33
American Meat Institute, 166–67
Anales de Ciencias, Agricultura, Comercio y Artes, 27, 34, 40, 43
Andérez Velázquez, Manuel de Jesús, 179
Andersen, H. T., 118
Andueza, José María de, 32
animal fats, 166–67
Arango, Rodolfo, 120, 122, 131, 157
Arango y Parreño, Francisco de, 37
Arca, Manuel, 163
Ardura, Ernesto, 115
arroz con leche, 15, 16, 21
arroz con pollo, 13, 15, 16, 18, 21
arroz de la tierra, 15, 47
arroz del Norte, 15, 47–48
Article 280 of Cuban constitution, 118–19
Asian rice imports to Cuba, 68–69, 72, 86, 87, 101–2, 136–37, 207n57

Asociación de Colonos, 116, 153
Asociación de Hacendados, 152–53
Asociación Nacional de Coshecheros de Arroz, 129–30, 134, 158, 163
Asociación Nacional de Industriales Arroceros, 129
Asociación Nacional de Proveedores e Importadores de Víveres, 153
Auber, Virginia Felicia, 13, 30, 33
Ayala García, Carlos, 158
ayuntamientos, 64, 65

Bachiller y Morales, Antonio, 13–14, 41
Baeza, Danilo, 115–16, 122
Ballou, Maturin M., 13
Balmaseda, Francicso Javier, 42, 43, 48
Balzán, Celestino, 83
Banco de Fomento Agrícola e Industrial de Cuba (BANFAIC), 119, 122–23, 124, 125, 150, 160–63
Banco Nacional de Cuba, 110, 114, 118–19
Baralt, Blanche Z. de, 3, 4, 18, 20
Barbour, Thomas, 18
Barnes, Charles, 93
Barrera Lordi, Alberto, 179–80
Batista, Fulgencio: as colonel, 103; military coup of, 120–21; power legitimacy of, 146; rice dispute of 1950s and, 137, 151, 153, 159, 178; rice production growth of 1940s and, 105, 121, 124–25, 130–31, 132
beet sugar, 55–56, 73, 202n158
Belot, Carlos, 188n62
Benjamin, Medea, 180
Benson, Ezra, 148
Berenguer, Fernando, 78–79
Betancourt, José Ramón de, 5, 55, 201n155
Betancourt Cisneros, Gaspar, 32–33, 34
Bier, Charles, 71, 206n50
Blair, George, 139, 141
Blanco, Richard, 16
Bohemia, 109, 158
Bomar, W. P., 168
Bonsal, Philip, 170, 218–19n27
Boonstra, Clarence, 105–6, 230n65

Boti, Regino, 109, 170–71, 174
Bourdieu, Pierre, 3
Brantley, Dow, 182
Breaux, A. Locke, 87
Brinkley, Homer, 104
broken-grain rice, 126, 139–40, 158, 159, 163
Brooke, John, 66
Burrus Mills, 168–69

Cabrera, Raimundo, 6
Cabrera, Ramiro, 78
Cadenas Adam, Emilio, 162–63
café con leche, 13
Calcagno, Francisco, 5–6
Calderón, José, 50
Calvo Peña, Beatriz, 9–11
Camagüey province, 32, 68, 74, 123–24, 125
Cambeyro, José, 101
Camejo, Rafael, 87
campana de la tarde, o vivir muriendo, La (Rosas), 9
Cárdenas, Armando, 81, 113
Carlson, Frank, 169–70
Cartañá, Estanslao, 83
Carteles, 85, 109, 117–18, 220n51
castigo de tres granujas, El (Calderón), 50
Castro, Fidel, 163, 170, 172–73, 177, 178, 179
Casuso, Teresa, 74–75
Cecilia Valdés (Villaverde), 5
Central Highway of Cuba, 92, 92
Cepero Bonilla, Raúl, 111, 160–61
Chamber of Commerce of Santiago de Cuba, 56
"Chichita, A" (Domínguez), 5
children, diet of Cuban, 13, 14
Chinea Díaz, Sergio Eduardo, 7
Chinese, indentured, 8, 36, 49
chocolate, 12–13, 188n62
Cía. Empacadora de Productos Nacionales y Extranjeros, 166–67
Cintas, Oscar, 214n49
Círculo de Hacendados, 28, 57
cocina criolla, la, 1, 3, 6

cocina cubana, la, 1–3, 6–14, 21, 23
cocina tradicional, la, 11–12
cocinero de los enfermos y desganados, El (Langarika), 10
codfish imports, 36
coffee: in Cuban diet, 12–13, 188n67; farms for, 63, 101, 192n3; production of, 22, 33, 55, 91, 192n3, 192n8, 206n36
Coloma y Garcés, Eugenio de, 197n75
colonialism, 20–21, 35, 50
Comallonga, José, 85, 109
comida criolla, la, 1, 3, 4–5
comida diaria, La, 18
Commerce Department, U.S., 78
Commission on Cuban Affairs of the Foreign Policy Association, 100
communism, 143–44, 146, 148
Congress, U.S.: flour dispute and, 168–70; rice dispute of 1950s and, 141–43, 147, 148–49, 150–51, 153–55, 228–29n28; rice disputes of 1930s and 1940s and, 103, 106, 107
Congressional Research Service, 183
Consolación del Sur, 123, 126
contrapunteo cubano, paradigm of, 22
cookbooks, 2, 9–12, *11*, 18
Cooper, William, 91
cooperative rural credit associations, 119, 221n62
Corbin, H. C., 205n28
corn, 32, 39, 51, 57, 67, 78, 93–94, 101
Cornide Hernández, María Teresa, 12
Cortés Cruz, Cecilio Rodolfo, 7
Costales, Manuel, 38
Cotter, Colleen, 10
credit: diversification and, 49, 94, 105, 106, 118–19, 122–23, 125–26, 160–62; favoring sugar, 100–101; for surplus agriculture, 178; war for independence recovery and, 65
credit associations, cooperative rural, 119, 221n62
Cristo, Gonzalo del, 161
Crosby, Laurence, 18, 152
Crowley Rice Milling Company, 71–72

Cruz, Francisco J. de la, 52, 54–55
Cuba: crisis of 1933 of, 97–99; cuisine of, 1–3, 6–14, 21; at end of eighteenth century, 27–29; military coups of, 98–99, 120–21, 146; in 1920s, 88–89; in 1950s, 109–10, 111–15; population growth of, 36, 114, 218–19n27; post-war for independence in, 64–67, 204–5n11, 205n32; revolution in, 170–72, *171*, *176*, 178–80; war for independence in, 62–64
Cuba Económica y Financiera, 175, 225n114
"Cuba for Cubans," 170, 178
Cuban Academy of Medicine, 54
Cuba News, 82
Cuba Review, 73, 77
Cucalmbé, El, 8
cuestion del arroz en Cuba, La, 20
cuisine of Cuba, 1–3, *2*, 6–14, 21, 23; differentiation of, 12–13, 188n62; variety in, 5–6
culture and cuisine, 7, 8–9, 12, 14, 20
cuota deficitaria, 136–37, 151, 159
Customs-Tariff Law, 89–91, 92–93, 94, 98, 99, 100

Davis, Chester, 145, 147, 225–26n119
Decree 647, 174
Decree 695, 174
Decree 1781, 126, 139
Decree 1827, 137
Decree 1865, 159
Delgado, Morúa, 6
Department of Agriculture, Cuban, 78, 83, 95
Department of Agriculture, U.S., 94, 99, 106, 145, 177, 181
Department of Commerce, U.S., 78
Department of State, U.S.: lard dispute and, 166–67; rice dispute of 1950s and, 121, 141–48, 150–51; rice exports of 1930s, 94, 96, 97, 102, 103; sugar dispute of 1950s, 150–51
Depression, the, 92, 94, 95–96
DeRouen, René, 102

242 INDEX

Dethloff, Henry, 177
Diario de Cuba, 76–77
Diario de la Marina: on agriculture for consumption, 23, 53, 77, 82; on diversification, 82, 133–34; on food imports, 39, 51, 52, 59; on hurricanes, 201n145; on National Rice Day, 130; on rice, 41–42, 43–44, 46, 49, 124, 157, 161–62, 163; on sugar, 81, 152, 202n158, 230–31n67; on tobacco, 210n103; on transportation, 76; on war for independence, 62
Diario de Matanzas, 43–44
Diccionario cubano, 47
Diccionario gastronómico cubano (Piña), 3, 11–12, 188n67
Diccionario provincial casi-razonado de vozes cubanas, 47
diet of Cuban children, 13, 14
Dihigo, Juan, 47
diplomatic relations suspension, 175–77
diversification of agriculture production: background and overview of, 24–25, 32, 166, 177; Customs-Tariff Law and, 89–91, 92, 94, 100; Export-Import Bank and, 105, 106, 107; post–Cuban revolution, 171, 172; rice dispute of 1950s and, 145, 146–47, 159, 163; rice expansion of 1950s and, 116–17, 118–19, 122, 124, 130, 131–34
docks, labor at, 39–40
Domengeaux, James R., 108
domestic agriculture. *See* agriculture for consumption
Domínguez, Julio, 63
Domínguez, Luis F., 5
Dore, Gordon E., 135, 138
Dorta-Duque, Francisco, 117, 175
Dos habaneras (Riesgo), 2, 8
Doyle, Gerald, 149, 155
DuBroco, Graciela, 4
Dulles, John Foster, 142, 147, 148, 151, 174
duties. *See* tariffs

Echarte, Pedro Pablo, 161
Economic Commission for Latin America (ECLA), U.N., 111–13, 116, 125, 126, 127
economy of Cuba: background and overview of, 23–25, 27, 165–66; in nineteenth century, 29, 34–37, 40, 50, 53, 59; in early twentieth century, 86, 88; in 1920s and 1930s, 90, 98; in 1940s, 106, 107; in 1950s, 110–14, 116–18, 120, 130, 143–48, 158–59, 163; under Castro, 170–74, 179–80. *See also* export economy
Eisenhower, Dwight, 140, 177
Ellender, Allen, 141–42, 150–51, 152, 158
Ellender Bill, 152
Ellis, Leonard, 145
embargo of 1959, 182–83
emigration to U.S., 114, 219n29
Engle, Margarita, 16
English rice imports to Cuba, 69, 72
Erénchun, Félix, 27, 192n9
Escalada, Miguel, 14, 41, 43, 46
Ewert, Frank, 18
Exiled Memories (Medina), 16
export economy: background and overview of, 24–25; dependency on imports and, 40, 53; post–Cuban revolution, 170–74, 179; post–war of independence revival of, 65, 66–67; railroads and, 46; of 1950s, 110–11, 114; sugar and, 34–38; during World War I, 77–78. *See also* economy of Cuba; sugar exports of Cuba
Export-Import Bank, 105–7
exports, U.S.: in early twentieth century, 72–73, 78, 86–88, 89t, 94, 200n128; of machinery and equipment, 129, 134, 145–46, 225–26n119; in nineteenth century, 45–48, 57–60; in 1930s, 88, 89t, 94, 95, 96, 104; in 1960s, 182–83

Fakler, Herman, 169
Falcón Paz, Bartolomé, 65
familia Unzúazu, La (Delgado), 6
Fanjul, Rafael, 161
farms, small: credit to, 119, 162; in

nineteenth century, 31–32, 33; post–war of independence recovery and, 63, 64, 65, 67, 205n32; rice production and, 43, 45, 88; during World War I, 75–77, 208n82

Faro Industrial de La Habana, El, 201n145
fatalista, El (Pichardo), 5
Ferguson, Erna, 18
feria de la caridad en 183, Una (Betancourt), 5, 55, 201n155
Fernández, Susan, 45
Fernández Concheso, Aurelio, 105
Fernández de Castro, Rafael, 57
Fernández Juncos, Manuel, 39
fertilizer, 123, 129, 145–46, 147, 206n40
Figuera, Fermín, 32
Figueras, Francisco, 198n94
Fleites, Alex, 180
flour, 36, 38, 57, 167–70
Folch, Christine, 12
food as leverage, 176–77. *See also* sugar: as leverage for American rice
Food for Peace, 178
food narratives: of *la comida criolla*, 4–6, 8; nationality and culture and, 3, 10; rice in, 16–17, 21
food preparation, 2–3, 9–12, 15–16, 18
food production, 22, 53–55, 78, 81, 83–84, 180–81. *See also* rice production in Cuba; sugar production in Cuba
foods, historiography of non-rice Cuban, 22–23, 191n130
food shortages, 52–55, 57–60, 82–83, 179–80
foreign exchange. *See* trade
Fornet Piña, Fernando, 12–13, 188n67
Foscue, Edwin, 92
Foster, J. A., 86–87
Foster-Cánovas Reciprocal Trade Agreement, 23, 57, 59
Franck, Harry, 75
free trade, 38
Frías, José de, 195n32
frutos mayores, 23

frutos menores: importance of, 37; production of, 32, 34, 37, 52–53, 55, 79–80, 195n32; small farmers and, 76–77; sugar collapse and, 81, 83; term of, 23, 191n28

Gangá, Creto, 4
García Alvarez, Alejandro, 46
García de Arboleya, José, 8, 14, 41, 47, 180
Gener, Benigno, 49
General Agreement on Tariffs and Trade (GATT), 136–37, 139, 140–41, 145, 153, 159, 174, 227n3
Generales y doctores (Loveira), 6, 8
German production and exports, 56, 69, 72, 73, 94
Glover, David, 85
Godchaux, Frank, 102, 122, 141–43, 149, 155
Gómez Roubaud, Rafael, 29
González de Cuoto, A., 118
González López, Antonio, 150
government subsidies, 25, 79–80, 118–19, 123, 160
Grant Advertising, 114
Greitín, Mario, 133
Guerra y Sánchez, Ramiro, 75–76
Guggenheim, Harry, 94, 96
Guillén Nicolás, 6, 17
Güines, 29, 30
Gutiérrez de la Llana, Ruy, 162

Havana province, 29, 68
Haven, Gilbert, 39
Haynie, Randy, 182
Hazard, Samuel, 17
Higiene, La, 82
hogs, 167
Hood, Amelia, 145, 146
Howe, Julia Ward, 4
Hull, Cordell, 99, 100, 214n49
hulling of rice, 43–45, 47, 95, 129
hunger, 23, 52–55, 82–83, 165, 176–77, 180
hurricanes, 192n3, 200–201n145

Ichijo, Atsuko, 7
identity, Cuban, 4, 7, 12
imports, Cuban: collapse of sugar and, 80; disruptions to, 51–52, 57–60, 131n200; of food, 33, 36, 58t, 93, 181; of machinery and equipment, 129, 134, 225–26n119; post-war of independence, 67; reciprocity agreement of 1934 and, 100; of 1940s and 1950s, 113, 117, 121; during World War I, 78–79, 79t. *See also* rice imports to Cuba
imports, U.S., 23–24, 58t, 59t
indentured Chinese, 8, 36, 49
inmorales, Los (Loveira), 6
International Bank for Reconstruction and Development, 113, 116, 117, 124, 165, 191n128
Island of Cuba, The (von Humboldt), 36, 196n52

Jacobo, Juan, 116
Jacomino, Alfredo, 131–32, 133–34
Jameson, Robert Francis, 30, 42
Jessup, Philip, 97
Jiménez, Guillermo, 181
Jones-Costigan Act, 99
Junta de Fomento, 31, 43, 50

King, John, 182

Laan, Cyril R. C., 149
Labadía, José, 42
Lake Charles (La.) American Press, 107
landownership concentration, 175, 235–36n35
land values, 29–30, 33, 77, 123–24
Lane, Jill, 4
Langarika, Enrique, 10, 15
language and recipes, 10
Larcade, Henry, 107, 108
lard, 51, 93, 166–67
Lavedán, Enrique, 64
Law of Agrarian Reform, 175–77, 179, 235–36n35
Leal Spengler, Eusebio, 16, 188n74

lechón asado, 13, 18
Lee, Fitzhugh, 62
legal paper and public document loss, 63–64
Legrán, José, 10
Lehrer, Marvin, 165
Leonhardy, Terrance, 157
León Riva, Alberto, 116, 153–54
Letamendi, Francisco, 31
Lezama Lima, José, 7, 115
Llanos, Adolfo, 200n128
Lluriá de O'Higgins, Maria Josefa, 15, 17
loans. *See* credit
lobbies, rice: Cuban, 129–30; U.S., 144–45, 148–49, 182
Lobo, Julio, 111
Lonja Mercantil de La Habana, 30
López, Faustino, 44–45
López Matoso, Antonio, 3–4
Loveira, Carlos, 6, 8
Lucha, La, 59–60

Machado, Eduardo, 16
Machado, Gerardo, 89, 90, 97–99, 212n21, 214n49
Machado, Luis, 159
Machado government, 89, 92, 94, 95, 98, 215n51
Madden, Richard, 40
Mallory, Lester, 177, 236n39
Mann, Thomas, 167, 172–73, 176
Manual del cocinero cubano, 10
Marino Perez, Luis, 84
Marmier, Xavier, 40
Marrero, Levi, 7, 14, 36, 114, 117, 118, 130
Martí, Carlos, 74, 77–78, 81
Martin, Mike, 182
Martin, Pedro Pablo, 62
Martínez Fraga, Pedro, 103
Martínez Sáenz, Joaquin, 114, 154, 156
Masó Fernández, Maria Beatriz, 232–33n108
Mastrafa, Francisco, 64
Matanzas province, 29–30, 55, 68, 95, 201n145

Matos family, 178–79
McCleary, James, 62–63, 64
McFaddin, W. P. H., 72
McKinley Tariff, 56–57
Medina, Pablo, 16
Melero, Marcos de J., 54
Menocal, Mario G., 83
menu, sample weekly, *19t*
Mercedes Santa Cruz y Montalvo, María de las, 27, 30, 41
Messersmith, George, 106–7
Meyer, Joaquín, 157
military coups of Cuba, 98–99, 120–21, 146
military occupation, 64–67
Miller, Claude, 174–75
milling: credit and investment in rice, 123, 125, 161, 206n40, 226n124; of Cuban rice, 68, 72, 95, 120, 127, 223n87, 226n126; of flour, 167–69; of sugar, 28–29, 30, 75, 111, *112t*, 192n5, 192–93n9, 217n10; technology and, 43–45, *44*, 47, 129, *132*, 192n5, 194n14, 198n94, 226n119; of U.S. rice, 174–75, 200n128
Minneman, Paul George, 100–101
Mintz, Sidney, 1
Moreno Fraginals, Manuel, 34, 193n12, 195n34
moros y cristianos, 16, 20
Morton, Thruston, 142, 143, 145–46, 147
Morúa Delgado, Martín, 6
MR 26/7 (26th of July Revolutionary Movement), 172, 178
Mundo, El: on railroads, 76; on rice imports, 106, 118, 152; on sugar, 75, 81, 83–84; on U.S., 85; on wars for independence, 61
music, rice in, 21

Nápoles Fajardo, Juan, 8
national cuisine, 1–4, 2, 6–14, 21, 23
national identity, 4, 7, 12
nationalism, Cuban, 88–89, 130–31, 156–58, 166, 170–72, 178, 211n12

nationality and food, 1, 3, 7–13
National Rice Day, 130
Nelson, Lowry, 20, 77, 109
New York Times, 52, 102
nineteenth-century Cuban food, 7–13
Nixon, Richard, 172
Nuber, John, 121, 127, 130, 139–40, 154–55, 159–60, 179
Nuevo manual del cocinero criollo, 18
Nuevo manual del cocinero cubano y español, 10
Nufer, Albert, 104
Núñez, Emilio, 61
Núñez Portuondo, Emilio, 157
nutrition, 18–19, 80, 82

O'Connor, J. J., 166
Ogden, E. B., 103, 140, 227n11
Oriente province, 67, 68, 74–75, 77, 95, 123, 125, 178
Ortega, Josefina, 4
Ortiz, Fernando, 4, 22, 76
Ortiz-Lamadrid, Rubén, 115
oxen, 29, 63, 194n14

paella, 12, 15, 18
Paláez, Ana Sofia, 7
Paponet-Cantat, Christiane, 165
Pardo Jiménez, Angel, 116
Paula Serrano, Francisco de, 47
Pérez, Clemente, 162
Pérez González, Antonio, 128
Pérez-López, Jorge, 90, 100
Pertierra, Ann Cristina, 20
Pezuela, Jacobo de la, 41, 47, 192n9
Pichardo, Esteban, 5
Pierson, Warren, 106
Piña, Anibal, 161
Pinar del Río, 30, 45, 68, 92, 95, 123–25, 201n145
Pino Santos, Oscar, 109, 163
Pitts, Edith, 74
plantations: corporate, 75; rice, 120, 123, 223n87, 236n35; sugar, 28, 32, 56
Pogolotti, Graziella, 4

population growth of Cuba, 36, 114, 218–19n27
ports, 182, 183, 194n21
Pozo Fernández, Alberto, 7, 12–13, 185n6
preparation, food, 2–3, 9–12, 15–16, 18
Price, Leonard H., 159
Prío Socarrás, Carlos, 119–20
private investment in Cuba, 66, 111, 217n10
property rights, 64
public documents loss, 63–64
Pujol y de Camps, Marcelo, 54
purchasing power, 93, 95, 113–14

"Queen of Rice" pageant, 130, *131*
Quesada, Gonzalo de, 14, 191n131
Quintín Suzarte, José, 39, 52
quotas: on rice, 121–22, 136–37, 139–41, 150, 155, 159; on sugar, 99, 103, 110, 148–55, 158–59, 172, 175

railroads, 28, 30, 46, 76, 79, 80
Ramírez León, José, 119
Randall, Harold, 123, 134
Ranta, Ronald, 7
rationing, food, 179–80
Rawls, Fletcher, 144–45, 148–49, 230n52
Real Junta de Fomento, 33
Real Sociedad Económica de La Habana, 24, 38–39
Real Sociedad Patriótica de La Habana, 33, 35, 43, 46, 50
recipes, 9–12, 15, 187n47
reciprocity, 23–24, 56–57, 85, 135, 155, 165–66, 191n131. *See also* Reciprocity Treaty of 1903; Reciprocity Treaty of 1934
Reciprocity Treaty of 1903, 23, 69–71, 88, 206n50
Reciprocity Treaty of 1934, 23, 98–100, 101–2, 103, 214n49, 214n51
Recuerdos de antes de ayer (Calcagno), 5–6
Reed, E. W., 168

regional cuisine, 12
Reid, William M.: on post–Cuban revolution taxes, 174; on loss of Cuban market, 177; reaction to Cuban trade restrictions of, 135, 138–39, 140, 141–44, 229n31, 229n35; reciprocity and, 85, 102–3; on rice competition, 71, 88, 96–97; U.S. reduction in rice supply and, 121
Resolution 98, 126, 139–41, 228n25
Revista de Jurisprudencia y de Administración, 53
Revista de La Habana, 37, 38
Revista Económica, 48, 49
Reynoso, Alvaro, 37–38, 51
Riccardi, Antonio, 113
rice: advertisements about, *44, 128, 133, 173*; broken-grain, 126, 139–40, 158, 159, 163; as "condition," 14; consumption of, 18–20, 22, 45, 114, 179, 180, 181, 190n15; consumption tax on, 95; convention on, 151; cooperatives for, 100, 104, 236n35; cost of, 51, 82, 105, 106, 162, 232–33n108; government programs for, 25, 94, 118–19, 122–23, 161, 178, 221n62; grading of, 126, 139–40; milling of, *44*, 68, 72, 95, 120, 127, 223n87, 226n126; as part of Cuban culture and history, 16–17, 20–21, 25, 165; as part of *la cocina cubana*, 13–14, *19t*, 188n74, 188n77; post–Cuban revolution, 172–75; preference for North American, 47; preparation of, 15–16, 17, 18; religious significance of, 21; surpluses of, 86, 88, 95–97, 137, 161, 178; trade organizations of, 129–30 (*see also specific organizations*); travelers to Cuba and, 17–18; U.S. exports of, to non-Cuban countries, 178; U.S aid for Cuban production of, 105–8; varieties of, 14–15. *See also* rice dispute of 1950s; rice imports to Cuba; rice industry in Cuba; rice industry in U.S.; rice production in Cuba
Rice Belt Journal, 88

rice dispute of 1950s: collaboration of U.S. rice industry and Cuban sugar producers and, 155; Cuban import controls and, 139–41, 157–58; Cuban positions on, 156–58; GATT and, 136–37, 139; outcome of, 158–63; sugar as leverage in, 149–55; U.S. Congress and, 141–43, 147, 148–50, 151, 228–29n28; U.S. rice industry and, 137–44, 148–50, 227n11; U.S. State Department and, 121, 141–48, 150–51

rice imports to Cuba: background and overview of, 22–23, 24–25, 191n127; in 1800s, 38–40, 45–48; in early 1900s to 1920s, 68–72, 70t, 73t, 86–88, 87t, 89t, 94; in 1930s and 1940s, 72–73, 73t, 87t, 89t, 95, 96, 103–4, 105t, 207n57; in 1950s, 126, 138t, 159 (*see also* rice dispute of 1950s); post–Cuban revolution, 175–77, 253–36n35; in 2000s, 181; sugar as leverage for, 102–3, 143, 149–55, 167, 168–70, 175

rice industry in Cuba: 1940s, 106, 107; 1950s, 109, 120, 133, 147, 156, 158, 160–62, 174

rice industry in U.S., 97, 102, 107–8, 137–45, 174–75, 177–78, 181–82

Rice Journal, 61

Rice Millers Association: in early twentieth century, 71; post–Cuban revolution, 174; rice dispute of 1950s and, 126, 127, 137, 138–41, 149–50, 155; in 1920s and 1930s, 86, 96–97, 101–2, 104. *See also* Reid, William M.

Rice Millers Association Newsletter, 141

rice production in Cuba: background and overview of, 22–23, 25; in nineteenth century, 40–46, 44, 50, 197n75, 206n36; in early twentieth century, 68–69, 198n94; in 1930s and 1940s, 95, 101, 105–6, 127t; in 1950s, 124, 127–34, 127t, 136–37, 160–63, 225n114; in 1960s, 179; in 2000s, 181; technology and, 43, 68, 94, 129, 133, *133*, 174, 198n94

rice water, 14
Riesgo, Pascual de, 2, 8
Rivero, Eliana, 16
roads, 30–31, 65, 76, 92, *92*, 161, 212n21
Roberts, Walter Adolphe, 18
Robertson, Samuel, 69–71
Rodriguez, Miguel, 29
Rodriguez Herrea, Estaban, 3, 15
Rodríguez Quintana, Arsenio, 17
Roosevelt, Franklin D., 74, 95–96, 99
Rosas, Julio, 9
Rossiter, Fred, 148–49
Rubottom, Roy R., 177
Rural Credit Association Tranquilino Sandalio de Noda, 126

Sabí, Camilo, 124
Saco, José Antonio, 31, 40
Sagra, Ramón de la, 27, 31–32, 34–35, 52, 193n9
Saint-Domingue, 28
Sala, George Augustus, 188n62
Sánchez, Julio, 163
Santana Guedes, José Luis, 9, 187n47
Santovenia, Emeterio, 122
scarcity of food, 52–54, 83. *See also* hunger
Sedano, Diego José de, 32
seed programs, 119
self-awareness, 1
self-determination, 89, 122, 156–57, 166, 172, 178
self-sufficiency: background and overview of, 22, 25, 32, 177–79; post–Cuban revolution, 172, 175; in 1920s, 90, 91–94; in 1950s, 117, 122, 130–34, 137, 140, 152–53
Senior, Frank, 161
Siglo, El, 42–43, 48–49, 54
Skywriting (Engle), 16
slave labor, 35–36
slavery and Cuban food origins, 8
Sofía (Delgado), 6
sovereignty, national, 7, 156–57, 166, 172

Soviet Union, 180
Spain: beet sugar and, 56, 202n158; Cuban imports from, 39; influence of, on Cuban food, 189n77; lost Cuban public records and, 64; rice consumption in, 20; trade agreements and, 56–57, 202n162
Special Period, 180–81
squatters, 64
Squiers, Herbert, 69
standard of living, Cuban, 92, 113–14, 153, 218–19n27
State Department, U.S. *See* Department of State, U.S.
steam power, 28, 192n5, 194n14
Steele, James, 17, 40, 41
stew, 3–4, 5, 8, 54, 180, 185n6, 186n16
Suárez, Angel, 163
Suárez, Virgil, 17
subsistence agriculture. *See* agriculture for consumption
Suero Falla, Alejandro, 154
sugar: background and overview of, 22–25, 34, 180–81; collapse of, in 1920s, 80–84; consequences of expansion of, 29–34, 35–36, 193nn11–12, 194n30; Cuban culture and, 36–37; Cuban import of, 181; as leverage for American rice, 102–3, 143, 149–55, 167, 168–70, 178; loans for, 100; milling of, 28–29, 30, 75, 111, *112t*, 192n5, 192–93n9, 217n10; North American investment in, 86; post–World War I collapse of, 80, 209n103; quotas on, 99, 103, 110, 148–55, 158–59, 172, 175; trade agreements and, 56–60, 100. *See also* Sugar Act of 1951; sugar collapse of 1950s; sugar exports of Cuba; sugar production in Cuba
Sugar Act of 1951, 110, 146, 148, 151, 154, 159
sugar collapse of 1950s: diversification and, 116–17, 118–19, 122, 130, 135; economy and, 110–14; government programs addressing, 118–19, 122–23, 125–26, 221n62; public mood and, 109, 113–16, 130–31; rice and, 117–18, 119–20, 121–22, 123–25, *124*, 220n51; success of programs addressing, 126–34; U.S. Embassy on, 147–48
sugar exports of Cuba: in nineteenth century, 35–39, 55–60, 202n158; of 1920s and 1930s, 84, 92, *93t*, 99; of 1960s and 1970s, 179. *See also* sugar production in Cuba
Sugar Extension Act, 159
sugar production in Cuba: background and overview of, 27–29; in nineteenth century, 34, 55–56, 66–67, 192nn4–5, 192–93nn8–11; during World War I, 74–75, 208n73; in 1930s, *112t*; in 1950s, 110–11, *112t*, 125, 217n6. *See also* sugar exports of Cuba
surpluses, agriculture: Cuban, 95, 161; U.S., 86, 88, 96–97, 137, 178

Taboadela, José, 80
Tamargo, Agustín, 219n29
tariffs: in 1930s, 95, 96, 99–102, 103–4; on animal fats, 166–67; on corn, 67; Customs-Tariff Law and, 89–91, 92–93, 94, 98, 99, 100; GATT and, 136–37, 139, 140–41, 145, 153, 159, 174, 227n3; in late nineteenth century, 50, 56–60, *59t*, 200n128; on machinery, 174; reciprocity and, 23, 69–72, 100, 149, 165–66, 206n50; on sugar, 56–60, 99, 154–55; on wheat and flour, 168
Taussig, Charles, 92–93, 100
taxonomy of rice, 15
Taylor, John Glanville, 33–34
technology and rice production, 43, 68, 94, 129, 133, *133*, 174, 198n94
Thompson, Theo Ashton, 135
Thrasher, John Sydney, 36, 196n52
tobacco: diversification and, 83, 91; overview of, 22, 27, 63; versus rice, 33, 206n36; sugar take-over of, 29, 192n8; during World War I, 77, 78, 209–10n103
Todd, Frederick, 91–92, 93–94, 95
Torrente, Mariano, 51

trade: Cuban tie to U.S. due to, 56; overview of, 35, 36–40, 113, 165–66; reciprocity of (*see* reciprocity); resumption between U.S. and Cuba, 181–83. *See also* imports, Cuban; imports, U.S.; sugar exports of Cuba; trade agreements
trade agreements, 23, 56–60, 69–71, 165–66, 206n50. *See also specific trade agreements*
trade organizations, 129–30. *See also specific organizations*
transportation: ports and, 182, 183, 194n21; railroads and, 28, 30, 46, 76, 79, 80; rice and, 45, 182; roads and, 30–31, 65, 76, 92, 92, 161, 212n21
Triay, José, 18
26th of July Revolutionary Movement (MR 26/7), 172, 178
"typical" dishes, 2, 13, 17

Uncle Ben's Rice ad, *160*
unemployment/underemployment, 25, 111, 114, 125, 134
Union blockade (U.S. Civil War), 51–52
United Fruit Company, 77
United States: agriculture surpluses of, 86, 88, 96–97, 137, 178; civil war in, 51–52; Cuban crisis of 1933 and, 96–99; Cuban recovery from war for independence and, 64–67, 69–72, 204–5n21, 206n50; Customs-Tariff Law of Cuba and, 92–93; economic sanctions on Cuba by, 175–77; emigration to, 114, 219n29; imports of, 23–24, 56–60, *58t*, *59t*, 85, *93t*; quotas of, 110, 121–22; rice industry of, in 1960s, 177–78; sugar investment in Cuba of, 86. *See also* Congress, U.S.; exports, U.S.; rice industry in U.S.; *specific government departments of*
USA Rice Federation, 181–82
U.S. Public Law 480, 178
U.S. Trade Sanctions Reform and Export Enhancement Act, 181

Valdés Rodríguez, A., 153
Valdés-Roig, Luis, 79–80
variety of Cuban dishes, 5–6
Vega Ceballo, Victor, 17
Vesa Fegueras, Marta, 7, 12
viandas, 32, 54, 195n32
Victoriano Betancourt, Luis, 13
Villapol, Nitza, 16
Villareño, El, 67–68
Vocabulario cubano, 47–48
voluntarios y bomberos, 21
von Humboldt, Alexander, 36, 194n21, 196n52

wages, Cuban, 111, 113–14, 125
Wagner, Mike, 165, 182
Wallace, Henry Christopher, 100
wars for independence, Cuban: destruction of, 61–64; recovery from, 64–68, 204–5n1, 205n32
Welles, Sumner, 97–99, 103, 214n49, 214n51
Wellman, Harvey, 150–51
wharves and piers, labor at, 39–40
wheat, 49, 167–70, 181
Williams, Ramon, 56, 59
Wilson-Gorman Tariff Act, 57
Wisdom, John Minor, 144
Wise, F. W., 126
Wood, Leonard, 64, 66, 69, 204–5n21
World War I, 72–79, 82, 209–10n103, 226n126
World War II, 104–6
Wright, Irene, 74
Wurdemann, John, 39–40
Wurslow, Calvin, 146

yellow rice, 13, 15, 21

Zanetti Lecuona, Oscar, 46
Zapata, Pascual, 80
Zengotita, Juan de, 134

www.ingramcontent.com/pod-product-compliance
Lightning Source LLC
Chambersburg PA
CBHW030536230426

43665CB00010B/917